P9-CDJ-284

WITHDRAWN

CRITICAL ISSUES IN LAW ENFORCE- MENT

WITHDRAWN

CRITICAL ISSUES
IN
LAW ENFORCEMENT

Edited by

HARRY W. MORE, JR., Ph.D.

Chairman

DEPARTMENT OF ADMINISTRATION OF JUSTICE
SAN JOSE STATE UNIVERSITY

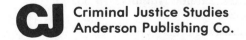
Criminal Justice Studies
Anderson Publishing Co.

CRITICAL ISSUES IN LAW ENFORCEMENT

Copyright © 1972, 1975 by The W.H. Anderson Company
Copyright © 1981 by Anderson Publishing Company

All rights reserved. No part of this book may be used or reproduced by any means without written permission from the publisher.

Library of Congress Catalog Number: 79-55205
ISBN: 0-87084-582-9
Edited by the Publishers Staff

363.23
C 934

Contents

37462

Preface

The police—some 420,000 people working for approximately 24,000 separate agencies that spend more than $2½ billion a year— are the part of the criminal justice system that is in direct daily contact both with crime and with the public. The entire system—courts and corrections as well as the police—is charged with enforcing the law and maintaining order. What is distinctive about the responsibility of the police is that they are charged with performing these functions where all eyes are upon them and where the going is roughest, on the street. Since this is a time of increasing crime, increasing social unrest and increasing public sensitivity to both, it is a time when police work is peculiarly important, complicated, conspicuous, and delicate.

Because the police have the responsibility for dealing with crime hour by hour, where, when and as it occurs, there is a tendency on the part of the public, and often of the police themselves, to think of crime control almost exclusively in terms of police work. One response to the recent increases in the volume of crime has been the charge that the police lack the competence or the will to keep crime within bounds. A far more common one has been the assertion that the police could keep crime within bounds if only the appellate courts, or civilian review boards, or corrupt politicians, or an uncooperative public allowed them to. "Take the handcuffs off our police" is a cry familiar to everyone.

The fact is, of course, that even under the most favorable circumstances the ability of the police to act against crime is limited. The police did not create and cannot resolve the social conditions that stimulate crime. They did not start and cannot stop the convulsive social changes that are taking place in America. They do not enact the laws that they are required to enforce, nor do they dispose of the criminals they arrest. The police are only one part of the criminal justice system; the criminal justice system is only one part of the government; and the government is only one part of society.

The police are confronted with a broad spectrum of critical issues such as the police role in a democracy, the use of deadly force, police unionization, and police professionalization. Other vital areas of concern are stress, organized crime, terrorism, and police discretion.

These topics were selected for inclusion in the text because they represent what might best be defined as potentially perennial problems.

Students of criminal justice must give serious consideration to these problems if law enforcement is to be relevant in today's society.

I wish to express my appreciation to the authors and publishers who so graciously granted permission to reprint their work. In addition, I would like to dedicate this book to my wife, Ginger, for her assistance and encouragement.

HARRY W. MORE, JR.
Santa Cruz, CA.
1981

Contributing Articles

(Reprinted with permission of the author and/or publisher)

Richard M. Ayres, "Police Strikes: Are We Treating the Symptoms Rather Than the Problem?" *The Police Chief*, Vol. XLIV, No. 3, March 1977, pp. 63-67.

Harry E. Bolinger, "Police Officers' Views on Collective Bargaining and Use of Sanctions," *The Police Chief*, Vol. XLI, No. 2, February 1974, pp. 39-42.

Edward M. Davis, "Professional Police Practices," *Federal Probation*, Vol. XXXV, No. 1, March 1971, pp. 29-34.

Lawrence J. Dempsey, "The Knapp Commission and You," *The Police Chief*, Vol. XXXIX, No. 11, November 1972, pp. 20-29.

Peter J. Donnelly, "Investigation of the Use of Deadly Force," *The Police Chief*, Vol. XLV, No. 5, May 1978, pp. 24-26.

Herman Goldstein, "Police Policy Formulation: A Proposal for Improving Police Performance," *Michigan Law Review*, Vol. 65, No. 6, April 1967, pp. 1123-1146.

Herman Goldstein, *Police Corruption: A Perspective on its Nature and Control* (Washington, D.C.: Police Foundation, 1975), pp. 6-8.

Mary Jan Hageman, Robert B. Kennedy, and Norman Price, "Coping With Stress," *The Police Chief*, Vol. XLVI, No. 2, February 1979, pp. 27-28 and 70.

George L. Kelling, "Police Field Services and Crime: The Presumed Effects of a Capacity," *Crime and Delinquency*, Vol. 24, No. 2, April 1978, pp. 173-184.

Kenneth R. McCreedy and James L. Hague, "Administrative and Legal Aspects of a Policy to Limit the Use of Firearms by Police Officers," *The Police Chief*, Vol. XLII, No. 1, January 1975, pp. 48-52.

Richard V. Mecum, "Police Professionalism—A New Look at an Old Topic," *The Police Chief*, Vol. XLVI, No. 8, August 1979.

Catherine H. Milton, Jean W. Halleck, James Lardner and Gary L. Albrecht, *Police Use of Deadly Force* (Washington, D.C.: Police Foundation, 1977), pp. 38-64.

James M. Sands, "Counterterrorism Target Assessment Form," *The Police Chief*, Vol. XLV, No. 12, December 1978, p. 83.

Charles B. Saunders, Jr., *Upgrading the American Police* (Washington, D.C.: The Brookings Institution, 1970), pp. 13-34.

John G. Stratton, "The Terrorist Act of Hostage-Taking: Considerations for Law Enforcement," *Journal of Police Science and Administration*, Vol. 6, No. 2, June 1978, pp. 123-134.

John G. Stratton, "Police Stress: Considerations and Suggestions," *The Police Chief*, Vol. XLV, No. 5, May 1978, pp. 73-76.

Leonard Territo and Robert L. Smith, "The Internal Affairs Unit: The Policeman's Friend or Foe," *The Police Chief*, Vol. XLIII, No. 7, July 1976, pp. 66-69.

John B. Wolf, "Anti-Terrorism: Operations and Controls in a Free Society," *Police Studies*, Vol. 1, No. 3, September 1978, pp. 35-41.

James C. Zurcher and S. Betty Cohen, "Officer Discretion: Limits and Guidelines," *The Police Chief*, Vol. XLIII, No. 6, June 1976, pp. 38-40.

Reports

President's Commission on Law Enforcement and Administration of Justice, *Task Force Report: The Police* (Washington, D.C.: U.S. Government Printing Office, 1967), pp. 30-35.

The Pennsylvania Crime Commission, *Report on Police Corruption and the Quality of Law Enforcement in Philadelphia* (Pennsylvania: Pennsylvania Crime Commission, 1974), pp. 5-26.

Chapter 1
POLICE IN A FREE SOCIETY

Introduction

There are no greater immediate needs in this free society than the control and reduction of crime. The accomplishment of these objectives is of the utmost concern of all Americans. In recent years, the tasks performed by criminal justice agencies have become increasingly complex, especially those of local law enforcement agencies. Evaluating the goals of police departments has never been more important or necessary than it is today. Time has wrought many changes in our society. In the decades ahead, societal transformations will require law enforcement administrators to evaluate their programs and prepare their agencies to meet new challenges.

Law enforcement officials must make a serious and realistic attempt to outline a police role that will be accepted by all segments of society; above all, that role must be made fully understandable to the public. Some authorities feel that the police must not reflect an attitude of moral self-righteousness, an attitude that gives the public the impression that the sole purpose of law enforcement is to "enforce the laws." An analysis of actual police performance, however, clearly shows that enforcing the laws is only one facet of police work.

A review of the literature reveals four strikingly similar definitions of traditional police duties. The customary police role is generally defined by the following objectives:

1. Protection of life and property.
2. Maintenance of the peace and public order.
3. Control and prevention of crime and vice.
4. Traffic control.
5. Regulatory responsibilities.[1]

O.W. Wilson, a leading police administrator, has written that police duties may be classified according to their more immediate objectives:

1. The prevention of the development of criminal and anti-social tendencies in individuals.
2. The repression of criminal activities.
3. The arrest of criminals, the recovery of stolen property, and the preparation of cases for presentation in court.
4. The regulation of people in their non-criminal activities and the performance of non-regulatory services.[2]

---

1. V.A. Leonard and H.W. More, *Police Organization and Management*, 4th ed. (Brooklyn: The Foundation Press, 1974), p. 14.
2. O.W. Wilson and R.C. McLaren, *Police Administration*, 3rd ed. (New York: McGraw-Hill Book Company, Inc., 1972), p. 22.

Another authority, John P. Kenney, has stressed that, "It is well accepted that under our form of government, the general purpose of the police is to protect life and property and to preserve peace. In light of present trends, an additional end may be sighted—rendering special services to the public." The basic police functions, according to Kenney, are:

1. Control of crime.
2. Crime prevention.
3. Control of conduct.
4. Provision of services.[3]

Finally, J. Edgar Hoover defined the basic responsibilities of the police as being:

1. The protection of life and property.
2. The preservation of the peace.
3. The prevention of crime.
4. The detection and arrest of violators of law.
5. The enforcement of laws and ordinances.
6. The safeguarding of individual rights.[4]

The authorities cited above reflect a consensus as to the *fundamental* tasks police are expected to fulfill. And this consensus reflects the general expectations of the public at large: very simply and on the broadest terms, the public expects the police to preserve the peace and protect society from crime through the enforcement of laws.

The American Bar Association, however, in its 1972 study, suggested that local committees should recognize that most police agencies are also given responsibility by design and default. This study provides a list of responsibilities that clearly extends the police task beyond the "basics" as presented in the preceding lists. According to the Bar's study, the police are expected to:

1. Identify criminal offenders and criminal activity and, where appropriate, to apprehend offenders and participate in subsequent court proceedings.
2. Reduce the opportunities for the commission of some crimes through preventative patrol and other measures.
3. Aid individuals who are in danger of physical harm.
4. Protect constitutional guarantees.
5. *Facilitate the movement of people and vehicles.*
6. *Assist those who cannot care for themselves.*
7. *Resolve conflict.*

---

3. John Kenney, *Police Management Planning* (Los Angeles: Jack Kenney, 1956), p. 70.
4. J. Edgar Hoover, *Should You Go Into Law Enforcement* (New York: New York Life Insurance Company, 1961), p. 7.

8. Identify problems that are potentially serious law enforcement or governmental problems.
9. Create and maintain a feeling of security in the community.
10. Promote and preserve civil order.
11. *Provide other services on an emergency basis.*[5] [Emphasis added.]

A careful analysis of this list indicates that the police in our cities are expected to spend a considerable portion of their time involved in activities that are completely unrelated to criminal activities. This list also reveals the fact that the police perform many duties which they have assumed by default of other governmental agencies or by virtue of their being the only primary municipal agency available at all times. Through the years, then, the police have been required to provide such services as animal protection, ambulance attendance, tax collection, and licensing. Police administrators are in general agreement that these duties should be performed by other units of government.

On the other hand, the National Advisory Commission on Civil Disorders believes that police can, and should become involved in community services. It stresses that there will be benefits for law enforcement equal to those for public order. The Commission points out that the police, because of their front-line position in dealing with community problems, are in an excellent position to identify situations that may lead to disorder. Second, they are more capable of handling incidents requiring police intervention, particularly marital disputes that have violence potential. Police effectiveness in handling domestic disturbances affects the incidence of serious crimes, including assaults and homicides. Third, willing performance of such work can gain police the respect and support of the community. Finally, an increase in the number of positive contacts can create an atmosphere that provides the police with intelligent sources of information concerning the communities they serve.

A variety of methods has been devised to improve police services. Typical of these is the New York Police Department's experimental "Family Crisis Intervention" program to develop better police response to marital disputes. There are also neighborhood service centers opening in some cities, usually established in tense, high-crime areas, and in easily accessible locations such as store-fronts or public housing projects. Staffed by a civilian city employee as well as a police officer, these centers provide information and services that direct citizens to the proper agencies for aid or advice. This gives the beat patrolman somewhere to refer a marital dispute; it gives the local resident a clear, simple contact with official ad-

---

5.   Advisory Committee on the Police Function, *The Urban Police Function* (New York: American Bar Association, 1972), p. 53.

vice; in general, it gives the police the opportunity to provide services, not merely to enforce the law.[6]

Whether police services will become the trend in the future is not yet clear, but they certainly establish a mandate for assessing present-day police functions. Law enforcement professionals must make a realistic appraisal of the duties they actually perform. Then possibly the image of "crime busters" will be placed in its proper perspective.[7]

Additional problems are inherent in the present classification of police duties. In terms of actual performance, the police objective of crime prevention defies definition. Is it the same as "the control of crime" or "the repression of criminal activities," or is it something that is unique and distinct? Is it something peculiar to the police function or do other components of the criminal justice system have primary, secondary, or even tertiary responsibility in this area?

Another area of current dispute is the parameters involved in "maintaining the peace." On the one hand, there is an increasing cry for "law and order"; and on the other hand, some still espouse a policy of "absolute permissiveness" in the cause of democratic freedom. The police have always suffered from the tension caused by this dichotomy. It is imperative, then, in setting standards for this aspect of policing that standards also be established that will protect us from anarchy while allowing for reasonable dissent.

*

There are two conflicting approaches that must be resolved before the policeman's role can be clearly defined. It is believed by some that law enforcement must consider societal inequities that place many individuals and groups at a disadvantage and, consequently, in conflict with the law. At the same time, many feel that there should be a structured standard by which all must abide, regardless of their position or station in life.

Reconciliation and convergence of these dissenting views is essential. Experience tells us that double standards cannot be tolerated and that the perpetuation of such divergent beliefs has led and will continue to lead to chaos. A deep discontentment exists because of the perpetuation of a police role that has frequently permitted differential treatment of violators because of race, political pressure, influence, or graft. There is,

---

6. The National Advisory Commission on Civil Disorders, *Report of the National Advisory Commission on Civil Disorders* (Washington: U.S. Government Printing Office, March 1, 1968), p. 167.

7. Police must be sincere in the performance of community services. They must, by initial formulation, presentation, and depth of consideration, prove that their intent to serve the community is genuine. Otherwise, police services will not be taken advantage of by a public that may have learned not to expect the police to honor their commitments.

of course, a genuine need for police discretion in enforcement of the law, but it must be based upon a clear-cut policy reflecting a dynamic and viable police role. But the police, while fully aware of their wide discretionary powers, have never given serious attention to this issue and its relationship to responsible law enforcement. In short, the police must be responsible to both the community and to political leadership in local governmental units, but a mode of control must be established that places police administration above "partisan politics." Law enforcement officers need positive public and political support which will allow them to render services that are both equitable *and* effective.

*

Many factors will influence the analysis and eventual definition of the functions to be performed by the police of tomorrow. These include such constituents as urbanization, the population explosion, technological advancement, a larger youth population, a changing morality, and a more educated populace. Each must be carefully assessed and evaluated in light of the evolving needs of society. For example, the potential influence of these factors is best illustrated by the fact that in a short time this nation will be close to being megalopolized. By 1985 about three-fourths of our population will be living in metropolitan areas, and at that time, 59 percent of the population will be under twenty-five years of age. During the same period of time, the number of people over age sixty-five will increase by 20 percent. This growth and change will certainly create social problems that one can hardly envision; the prediction of human behavior will continue to defy an immediate or simple solution. The role of the police will, then, of necessity, have to be such that it is flexible, and at the same time cognizant of the "cross-functional ripple effect."[8]

The changing morality of this nation presents an additional dilemma. Support for many of the sumptuary laws is no longer evident. In the past, it was far easier to obtain community consensus for the control and regulation of behavior based on moral grounds. If it is clear to the police that a law is not appropriate to the "times," it is imperative that they work toward changing the law. To be effective, a law must be accepted by the majority of the people. The police are the implementors of the law and therefore are in an advantageous position to measure and interpret popular morality.

*

The National Advisory Commission on Criminal Justice Standards and Goals pointed out that if the overall purposes of the police profession in

---

8.   The solution of one problem usually creates or modifies another. For example, censorship will control pornography and at the same time infringe on the freedom of the press.

America were narrowed to a single objective, that objective would be to preserve the peace in a manner consistent with the freedoms secured by the Constitution. Yet the police alone do not bear the responsibility for preserving a peaceful society; that responsibility is shared by each element of society—each person, each institution, and each area of government within that society. However, because crime is an immediate threat to the order of all communities, the police exist foremost to overcome that threat and to reduce the fear of it.

The degree to which society achieves public order through police action depends on the price that its members are willing to pay. That price is measured, literally, in tax levies and the surrender of certain liberties. For example, if the people are willing to live in a totalitarian state where the police had unlimited resources and power, they might find their parks always safe to walk in, but impossible to enjoy. Obviously, a balance must be struck that permits enough freedom to enjoy what is secured by sacrificing unlimited freedom. That balance must be determined by the people if a productive relationship with their police is to be achieved.[9]

Unfortunately, it is clear that there is no single or simple answer to what the role of the police should be in a free society. The studies that follow define some of the problems inherent in defining the police role, examine the factors involved, and present proposals for role definition of a democratic police force.

---

9.   National Advisory Commission on Criminal Justice Standards and Goals, *Police* (Washington: U.S. Government Printing Office, 1973), p. 13.

1. PROFESSIONAL POLICE PRINCIPLES

EDWARD M. DAVIS

Federal Probation, Vol. XXXV, March 1971. Reprinted by permission.

Anyone going into a business is well advised to understand the philosophy of that business. Each business has general principles and philosophies that are essential to a successful enterprise. This observation leads to asking questions of our own law enforcement business. What are the objectives of the police? What are the major functions of law enforcement? The President's Crime Commission stated that the country spends $4 billion a year on policing. For what is the money spent? Why?

Most of the answers can be found in nine principles of law enforcement first enunciated about 1822 by Sir Robert Peel, founder of the British Police system. They are ancient, but principles do not change and all the solutions to crime are here and all the solutions to community relations can be found here.

I have gone through each of these nine principles and have amplified on some of them, but I believe the essence of successful law enforcement can be drawn from these fundamental observations from a century long past.

Prevention of Crime is the Basic Mission of the Police

Principle Number 1. The basic mission for which the police exist is to prevent crime and disorder as an alternative to the repression of crime and disorder by military force and severity of legal punishment.*

The goal of the police establishment still remains the absence of crime and disorder. That is the desired end product. Police engage in three major functions to achieve this primary goal. The function of first priority is prevention. When the police fail in this first function, the second function is activated—that of deterrence, or what the textbooks call repression. The third function is the apprehension of offenders and the gathering of evidence for prosecution.

Now, the police themselves cannot prevent crime. True prevention of crime is to generate in society a desire to do the right thing, to live by ethical standards of conduct. The police cannot take over the parents' job, the minister's job, and the school's job in this respect. However, the police play a major role as the catalytic agent in society to assist the process of "feeding back" to the rest of society information on what is happening in terms of crime and disorder. No one else can perform this function but the police. No one else is in contact with crime and disorder in its totality. No one else has the machinery or perception or access to the basic facts as do the police.

The police cannot prevent the development of criminality in any individual. However, through a feedback process, information on crime can be passed to social institutions which may hopefully generate programs to prevent criminality of individuals in the future.

When there is a failure to prevent crime, the police perform the next function of deterrence—attempting to be as obvious as possible and creating the impression of omnipresence. This is the reason police drive black-and-white cars; this is why police wear distinctive uniforms; this is why police attempt to be overt rather than covert in as many operations as possible.

The police helicopter is predicated largely on this second function of deterrence. Deterrence plucks the conscience strings of the guilt-ridden. The criminal who wants to do something but chickens out because of the omnipresent "chopper" is a good example of this deterrence function.

That is deterrence. That's why police don't wear green blazers with an emblem on the pocket to look like a sport. Police should look like police or they violate the very principle of deterrence.

Now, when police fail to deter, then they must invoke the third function, that of apprehension and gathering of evidence. The police serve as the first entryway into the criminal justice system, followed by the prosecutor, the courts, appellate courts, then institutional commitment, probation, or parole. We know from the rate of recidivism that the effectiveness of rehabilitation in this system is minimal. However, the system has value because it tends to reinforce the societal prohibitions against doing certain things and thus serves to deter prospective offenders. But police activities directed toward apprehension and gathering of evidence are of minimal value in preventing crime—the primary police goal.

The losing game of apprehension absorbs a major share of police resources. The resultant return in preventing crime and disorder is relatively small considering the vast investment. The function of deterrence absorbs a very small share of police resources, yet the return in crime prevention is better, dollar for dollar, than for apprehension. The function of prevention—the function best directed toward achieving the primary police objective—receives even less in the way of resources.

The information now gathered by police is directed wholly toward prosecution of a suspect or future apprehension of that same suspect. Police gather virtually no information for relaying to society, saying, "This is what is happening, and it is happening under these circumstances." This unarticulated but necessary mission for developing better methods of interfacing with society's institutions must be fulfilled. We must provide them with relevant, demographic data on crime that will spur them to actions which will result in an achievement of the primary goal of preventing crime and disorder.

Police Must Have the Full Respect of the Citizenry

Principle Number 2. The ability of the police to perform their duties is dependent upon public approval of police existence, actions, behavior, and the ability of the police to secure and maintain public respect.

Arthur Niederhoffer, a 20-year New York police lieutenant, wrote a book entitled *Behind the Shield.* In it he makes observations which are not very comforting to policemen. He believes that the American police tend to hide behind a self-pity syndrome; they tend to become paranoid and withdrawn. If his thesis is correct, if policemen believe that people don't support them, that they operate in a wholly hostile environment, then there would be little hope.

The police must not allow themselves to be caught up in this "Niederhoffer syndrome." There are only two policemen for every 1,000 people in Los Angeles and five for every 1,000 in New York. The police could not even exist in a totally hostile community.

One of the important roles of police-community relations is to establish and maintain ties with all segments of the community so that the police can develop broad-based support. Associations with such groups will help individual policemen recognize the very real public support for the police which exists in every community regardless of its ethnic makeup.

A Citizen's Respect for Law Develops
His Respect for the Police

Principle Number 3. The police must secure the willing cooperation of the public in voluntary observance of the law to be able to secure and maintain the respect and approval of the public.

One hundred and thirty years ago Abraham Lincoln, then a young legislator, made the following statement:

> I hope I am over-wary; but if I am not, there is now an ill omen amongst us. I mean the increasing disrespect for law which pervades the country. Accounts of outrages committed by mobs from the every-day news of the times.
>
> The question recurs, "How shall we fortify against it?" The answer is simple.
>
> Let every American, every lover of liberty, swear never to violate in the least particular, the laws of the country and never to tolerate their violation by others. Let every man remember

that to violate the law is to tear the character of his own and his children's liberty. Let reverence for the laws be breathed by every American mother to the baby. . .on her lap. Let it be taught in schools, and in colleges. Let it be written in primers and spelling books. Let it be preached from the pulpit, proclaimed in legislative halls and enforced in courts of justice. And in short let reverence for the law become the political religion of the nation.

This truth has not changed over the intervening years.

It is the job of every policeman to seek the willing cooperation of individuals on his beat in helping to attain the police objectives of the absence of crime and disorder. In the same tradition, it is the responsibility of every police officer to seek the voluntary observance of laws in his community. His mission is to "turn on" that community, regardless of ethnic makeup, to get the police job done.

There is a principle of "leverage" in economics. By this principle a small amount of money is manipulated to do the work of a much larger amount. Police must operate by this principle. Through the cooperation of the community, one policeman can be as many in achieving the police mission. If any policeman comes from the Academy thinking that he is going to save the world, he is going to be a total failure. We need a vision of the old-time cop-on-the-beat who never seemed to work hard. But, he had people in the community telling him things about crime and questionable activities. He had the help of his community and he got the job done. That is the only way to get the police mission accomplished.

Cooperation of the Public Decreases as the Use of Force Increases

Principle Number 4. The degree of cooperation of the public that can be secured diminishes proportionately the necessity for the use of physical force and compulsion in achieving police objectives.

The professional, competent, emotionally secure police officer does not approach situations with a "bristle." He actively solicits the cooperation of the individual or group where the public peace is endangered. An officer with the ability to firmly but pleasantly solicit the cooperation of individuals or groups can frequently accomplish, through their cooperation, what it might take scores of officers to accomplish through the use of a "hard" approach to the situation.

In areas where there has been a pattern of using strong physical force to achieve police objectives, a concurrent pattern of resistance develops within the individual or group. The result is resistance and lack of cooperation on the part of the law violator and the subsequent necessity for resorting to force on the part of the police. The use of force is thus self-perpetuating.

Less than a year ago the British, with all their majesty, used their vast military forces to reconquer a tiny island protectorate of Anguilla. They were wise enough to take some "bobbies" along when reinstalling their administrators. During the skirmishing, two bobbies were injured. The citizens dressed their wounds and apologized to them. The reputation of the bobbies had preceded them. The British police have done a pretty good job of recognizing that when cooperation can be secured, the necessity of physical force is proportionately decreased.

Police Must Render Impartial Enforcement of the Law

Principle Number 5. The police seek and preserve public favor, not by catering to public opinion, but by constantly demonstrating absolutely impartial service to the law, in complete independence of policy, and without regard to the justice or injustice of the substance of individual laws; by ready offering of individual service and friendship to all members of society without regard to their race or social standing; by ready exercise of courtesy and friendly good humor; and by ready offering of individual sacrifice in protecting and preserving life.

The policeman's boss is not his sergeant or the chief. The policeman does not work for the white people or the black people; he doesn't represent the "establishment." The policeman is a servant of the law.

Several years ago Thurgood Marshall, then chief counsel for the NAACP and now an Associate Justice of the Supreme Court of the United States, made the following statement during a speech to police officers at Michigan State University: "If there is a bad law on the books that says that a Negro cannot . . . eat at the same store counter you can, you go ahead and enforce that law. If it is a bad law, we will take care of the law; but if you enforce any of your personal prejudices, we will take care of you."

It is not the job of a policeman to determine what the legislators should say constitutes a crime. It is not the mission of the police to judge whether any law is good, bad, too harsh, or too lenient. Laws are made by legislators and are an imperfect reflection of society's mores. Laws are subject to change. However, when the law is established it is the job of the policeman to enforce the law impartially.

In California marijuana is illegal. Whether it is good or bad is a problem for the sociologists and physicians. However, as long as the law stands on the books, police should put people in jail for violating that law. Law enforcement does not have to apologize for enforcing the law, because we do not make the laws. There is an established democratic process for enacting and altering the law, but it is essential that police construe the law as it is.

The fifth principle further states: Public favor is sought by individual service, friendship to all members of society, the ready exercise of courtesy and friendly good humor, and by individual sacrifice. There are many examples of police officers sacrificing even their lives in the line of duty. If a robbery-in-progress call comes through, it may be a crummy liquor store and the police officer who responds to the call may not even like the owner. But, he would go in and give up his life in a gun battle to protect that merchant. Any officer driving down the street at 4 a.m. in the middle of a ghetto area would not hesitate to dash into a burning building to rescue the occupants. Every year the Police Department gives out medals for this type of valor. Yet the same police officer might not be friendly to the citizen he would risk his life for, because that citizen is different in some way.

The police must develop this thing called friendship for all members of society. If you were to call the Department, the man who answered might respond, "Robbery, Smith." You might receive the same stereotyped, staccato response at the "desk." The result is a reputation of cold efficiency. Members of minority groups will believe police personnel are cold to them because of prejudice; others would call it plain discourtesy. It is vitally important to police-community relations that each officer take it upon himself to maintain friendly, good-humored relations with each citizen.

A British bobby was watching the burning of the Union Jack at an English university. It is not a crime over there to burn the flag. Instead of responding with anger, he said, "Blimey, can you imagine it takes a college education to do that?" He approached that situation with friendly good humor. A prime element of any community relations program is friendliness of each officer to each member of society.

Physical Force is Used Only as the Last Resort

Principle Number 6. The police should use physical force to the extent necessary to secure observance of the law or to restore order only when the exercise of persuasion, advice, and warning is found to be insufficient to achieve police objectives; and police should use only the minimum degree of physical force which is necessary on any particular occasion for achieving a police objective.

The police in some areas of the country have been under fire recently because of purported cases of excessive use of force in quelling demonstrations. When this happens, the police end up being the central figure in the disturbance. Above all else, the police must remain neutral in any confrontation. The police represent only the law.

Very recently, there was a demonstration on the campus of a State College. During the course of the demonstration certain laws were violated and it was, therefore, necessary to place about 200 people under arrest. The police officers were trained in weaponless defense. The 200 arrests were made in front of television cameras, and not one flailing baton appeared. The police did their job and there were no resulting charges of over-reaction. The police did not become the central figure.

With calm leadership the police can talk their way around many incidents through advice, warning, persuasion. If police have to use force, that is their job, but only after the alternatives have been tried.

The Police are the Public and the Public are the Police

Principle Number 7. The police at all times should maintain a relationship with the public that gives reality to the historic tradition that the police are the public and that the public are the police; the police are the only members of the public who are paid to give full-time attention to duties which are incumbent on every citizen in the interest of community welfare.

Charles Reith, in his book, *The Blind Eye of History*, delineated his belief that any civilization that depends on using its own military forces to control its people is doomed to failure. History bears out this theory. Britain was in the position of needing some force to repress disorder in the early 1800s. Finally, in 1829, Parliament passed an act establishing the British police system, the first full-time professional police department. However, Parliament was fearful of a police organization because of possible infringement on individual rights. Out of this fear the idea was spawned that it was every citizen's obligation to help police his society, but certain citizens would be set aside to do this work on a full-time basis. They would help all citizens do their job.

In England, if you smack a bobby in the eye trying to make an escape, you might get 10 years. After all, the bobby is helping every citizen do his job. England has given reality to the historic concept of the citizen being the police and vice versa. Here in America, because of a lack of philosophical leadership or because of the prohibition era, or because of the "Niederhoffer complex," the police are separate from the citizenry in many ways. The most technologically advanced, best financed, best staffed police department in the world is never going to solve the problems of crime and disorder. That is because our police have not given reality to the truth that the public are the police. Our police must communicate to the citizens that solving these problems is their job, their obligation. As police, we are merely helping them. Regardless of ethnic or economic background, the estrangement between public and police must be eliminated in favor of a coordinated effort to achieve police objectives.

A police reserve corps is one method of creating closer ties between the public and the police. It is one way of fulfilling the historic tradition that the public are the police. In having a reserve corps we open the Department to any citizen who qualifies. We have nothing to hide. We train the reserves as assistants in doing the police job.

I recently had a man tell me how much better his police organization was than the Los Angeles Police Department in every respect. I was sure he was some ranking officer. He turned out to be a reserve officer who worked as a policeman one day a week. He was a 40-hour-a-week salesman of some kind. He was also a salesman for his police organization, and for police ideals.

A trained corps of reserve officers gives tremendous flexibility to administrators in the event of any unusual occurrence. More than that, they are the public serving as the police. They will help sell the police mission to their friends, neighbors, and co-workers.

Police Represent the Law

Principle Number 8. The police should always direct their actions strictly toward their functions and never appear to usurp the powers of the judiciary by avenging individuals or the state, or authoritatively judging guilt or punishing the guilty.

Police officers do not judge guilt; they do not punish; they do not act as executioners. Policemen represent the law. If the law says a man should go to jail for a certain act, the police arrest the man, gather the evidence, and do not take upon themselves any adjudication or correction.

I have known officers who were mad at every suspect they ever arrested. These officers were actually angry because of what the suspect had done, said, or looked like. This unprofessional, judgmental attitude breeds resistance and hostility, making the police job more difficult, if not impossible.

I have also known detectives who never seem to lose their cool. They know their job in its true light. I can think of one in particular. He always smiled. He offered the suspects a cigarette or a cup of coffee. He talked to them in friendly tones, and he made good arrests. He did not make his job any more difficult than it already was. He kept his cool. He was the epitome of a professional policeman.

The quality we look for here is equanimity. The professional policeman does not demonstrate emotional involvement in his work to the public. He does not demonstrate anger to the offender; he does not go into a rage when verbally abused. He keeps his cool.

The Absence of Crime and Disorder is the
Test of Police Efficiency

Principle Number 9. The test of police efficiency is the absence of crime and disorder, not the visible evidence of police action in dealing with them.

If you approach the typical police officer in a radio car and ask him what he has to do to keep his job, he might tell you: "I should write 'X' number of citations every week; I have to turn in 'X' number of field interview cards; I should make 'X' number of arrests each month." On the other hand, imagine you are the chief of police and are called to City Hall and told you are going to be fired unless you could prove you are doing a good job. Are you going to tell City Hall how many traffic citations have been written and how many arrests have been made during your tenure? No, you are going to tell them that during your tenure, crime was reduced by X-percent and the number of traffic accidents have been reduced.

The higher echelon of police administration know their job is to stop crime; but there is a real danger that the officer on the street may think of his job as a "numbers game," to provide a quantity of tickets or arrests. There is a failure here. The failure is not with the policeman. He is really responding to the kind of pressures that are put on him by police management. It is easier to judge men by the quantity of tickets they write than it is to judge them on their effect on traffic flow. It is easier to judge a man by the number of arrests he makes than it is to judge him on the quality of his work stopping crime. Because the "numbers game" is easier, there is a real temptation to resort to it.

The challenge of police management is to communicate the true nature of the police mission to the man in the radio car on the street. Management has to sell the policeman a piece of geography and say, "This is your district. Your job is to stop crime and disorder here. We don't want burglaries or stickups or street-fights. If you have to arrest someone for violating any law, do it. You have been trained to stop crime. Do it in your area, and get the community to help you."

We in the police field spend a lot of time talking about "numbers" in the crime field. We spend even more time talking about mechanical gadgets and developing programs of one kind or another. I believe one of our major failings is that we have not spent enough time talking about principles.

I believe that if we can agree on the nine principles set forth by Sir Robert Peel, we can all do a better and more professional job in achieving our goal.

---

*   The nine principles presented are a paraphrase of those which have evolved since the time of Sir Robert Peel, originator of the English police system.

2. POLICE FIELD SERVICES AND CRIME: THE PRESUMED EFFECTS OF A CAPACITY

GEORGE L. KELLING

Crime and Delinquency, Vol. 24, April 1978. Reprinted by permission.

During the past fifteen years, policing has been recognized by the public and its leaders as a major social institution—one in need of great political and financial support. While some have perhaps overstated the importance of the police in problems occurring during the last two decades (e.g., Godfrey Hodgson has asserted that the police were largely responsible for most of the riots in the sixties), it is fair to say that the police contribute significantly to both the solution and the exacerbation of social problems.

This period will also be noted in the history of policing as the time when the remarkable insularity of the police ended. The police began to collaborate—at first begrudgingly but finally with enthusiasm—with other major institutions such as universities, foundations, and research institutes.

Other changes occurred as well. Salaries for police increased greatly. The size of police departments doubled and tripled. Major investments were made in technology. Women and minorities were slowly admitted into police service. University programs developed to educate the police, and officers entered these programs on both a preservice and a postservice basis. Entrance requirements were modified in light of this emphasis on education. Many police benevolent associations became powerful unions, forcing police managers to adjust to a new force in police policy making. Finally, the police and police services were probably more thoroughly scrutinized and evaluated than almost any other part of the criminal justice system.

It is not hard for many of us to remember those days when police agencies were almost totally inaccessible to researchers. Police business was considered to be just that—police business. However, during the past fifteen-year period, researchers and police have developed interorganizational and interprofessional strategies and techniques which allow for successful collaboration. The police have learned that they can become successfully involved in research and that research can contribute significantly to the improvement of public service.

The purpose of this paper is to review research related to the changing police role to determine what this suggests about the future of police tactics. On the surface, much of the research seems contradictory and confusing, but I believe that consistent themes do emerge. These themes provide the basis for continued research, development, and innovation.

The Police as a Public Service Agency

The myth of the police as primarily a crime-fighting, deterring, and investigating agency is deeply ingrained in our society. This view is reinforced each day by the media, which portray the police as going from critical event to critical event, constantly dealing with crime, and often resorting to weapons. The effect of this is considerable. Young persons are drawn toward policing as a career because of the excitement of such activities. The police themselves cite crises in their attempt to get public, financial, and moral support. Even today, some police chiefs go beyond the title "law enforcement officers" and describe themselves as "crime fighters enforcing the law."

However, considerable research done since 1950 has shown this image to be inaccurate.[1] The police have been found to spend a relatively low percentage of their time on crime-related matters (less than 20 percent); most of their time is spent in activities related to public service—settling family fights, handling drunks, dealing with teenagers, maintaining order, and so on.

The consequences of this knowledge are not inconsequential. If it is true—and every bit of evidence suggests it is—almost every aspect of present police organization is affected. As Herman Goldstein has pointed out, this awareness of the multiple functions of the police has significant implications for recruitment, training, and organization.[2] Thus, if service activities do dominate over crime-fighting activities, the police will have to recruit different kinds of people than those attracted to the stereotypical crime-fighting functions. Training will have to focus less on legal and crime-related matters and more on conflict management and social relations. Less organizational emphasis need be placed on command, control, and on technological systems to get police to the scenes of crime

1.   W. A. Westley, *Violence and the Police* (Cambridge, Mass.: MIT Press, 1970); E. Cumming, I. Cumming, and L. Edell, "Policeman as Philosopher, Guide and Friend," *Social Problems,* Winter 1965; James Q. Wilson, *Varieties of Police Behavior* (Cambridge, Mass.: Harvard University Press, 1968); A. J. Reiss, Jr., *The Police and the Public* (New Haven, Conn.: Yale University Press, 1971); American Bar Association, *The Urban Police Function* (Chicago: American Bar Association Project on Standards for Criminal Justice, 1971).

2.   Herman Goldstein, *Policing a Free Society* (Cambridge, Mass.: Ballinger, 1977).

quickly. More can be placed on developing quality relations with citizens. Further, people tend to concentrate on performing well in those activities for which they receive rewards—both financial reimbursement and promotions. Unless organizations reward non-crime-related activities, successful performance in these functions will remain less crucial.

But the most important consequence of this mistaken conception of the police function is its impact on patrol. By defining themselves as crime fighters the police have developed crime-prevention strategies that emphasize patrol; allocation for patrol, in turn, is almost entirely based on police functions that relate directly to crime. We are only now beginning to understand that this strategy has been at the expense of other important activities.

Preventive Patrol as the Primary Means of Police Service Delivery[3]

O. W. Wilson has best described—and best justified—the concept of preventive patrol, as we know it today.[4] According to Wilson, the automobile was first used to increase the patrol range of foot beat officers by enabling them to move quickly from one beat to another.[5] While cars could be used to pursue offenders, their primary function was to increase the number of beats officers could handle. The theory of preventive patrol developed only after cars had been used for some time transporting officers between stations and between beats. Wilson theorized that, by moving police vehicles rapidly through beats and unpredictably past likely crime targets, police could create the feeling of police omnipresence. The benefits of this omnipresence were to be decreased crime, increased apprehensions, reduced citizen fear, and increased citizen satisfaction. Coupled with rapid response to calls for service, this police omnipresence would dramatically and effectively reduce crime.

With some variations, this attempt to affect crime through preventive patrol became the dominant mode of delivering police service. Beats were structured to facilitate this proposed impact. As allocation models became more complex, it became apparent that, although the police had multiple functions, patrol came to be organized around the presumed effects of police on crime. Some persons called for "getting rid of" the non-crime-

---

3. For a wider discussion of this and the following section, see George L. Kelling and David Fogel, "The Future of Policing," in *Sage Criminal Justice Annuals*, vol. 9, Alvin W. Cohn, ed. (Beverly Hills, Calif.: Sage Publications, Spring 1978).

4. O. W. Wilson and Roy Clinton McLaren, *Police Administration*, 3d ed. (New York: McGraw-Hill, 1963).

5. Ibid.

related functions;[6] others developed models for "interception patrol,"[7] a form of rapid patrol with the goal of intercepting crimes in action. Still others advocated covert patrol,[8] a form of inconspicuous patrol in which the police force would "blend into" a community.

As practice and theory developed, the use of the car substantially changed. Whether intentional or not, that change in the use of the car brought a substantial skew in the activities of the police. Wilson continued to advocate police-citizen interaction,[9] but the trend was away from this personal contact. Modeling theorists such as J. Elliot and Richard Larson provided a justification for police officers' remaining in their police vehicles rather than using them as a means of getting from place to place.[10] Police came to describe themselves as being "in-service" when they were cruising in their cars—attempting to create the effect of police omnipresence—and "out-of-service" when outside their vehicles actually dealing with citizens. To be patrolling was to be "in the action"—or at least apparently available for "action." The goal of police action was to "bust criminals." Obviously, contact with citizens diminished in importance.

This rationale behind the creation of police omnipresence was logical. In many respects, it made sense. But were the effects as predicted?

The theory of preventive patrol was first challenged in the early 1960s. Albert Reiss found that the time spent in preventive patrol was remarkably unproductive, contradicting the idea that the self-initiated, proactive (interception) activities of the police would increase apprehensions.[11] James Press found mixed effects of markedly increasing manpower.[12] The Institute for Defense Analysis reported that interviews with prison inmates suggested fear of police was not a significant deterrent.[13] Donald Fisk studied the Indianapolis Fleet Car Plan, an effort to simulate

6.   William J. Bayer, "Service-Oriented Functional Management in Patrol," *The Police Chief*, April 1975, pp. 42-45.

7.   J. F. Elliot, *Interception Patrol* (Springfield, Ill.: Charles C. Thomas, 1973).

8.   James D. Bannon, "Foot Patrol: The Litany of Law Enforcement," *The Police Chief*, April 1972, pp. 44-45.

9.   O. W. Wilson, "Put the Cop Back on the Beat," *Public Management*, June 1953.

10. Elliot, *Interception Patrol*; and Richard C. Larson, *Urban Police Patrol Analysis* (Cambridge, Mass.: MIT Press, 1972).

11. Reiss, *The Police and the Public*.

12. J. S. Press, Some Effects of an Increase in Police Manpower in the 20th Precinct of New York City, Report R704-NYC (New York: New York City Rand Institute, October 1971).

13. "Part III: Analysis of Response to Police Deterrence," unpublished study cited with permission (Washington, D.C.: Institute for Defense Analysis, 1966).

police presence by having police officers use their police vehicles off duty, and essentially found no positive effects.[14] In the Kansas City Preventive Patrol Experiment, preventive patrol once again failed to demonstrate its proposed effect.[15]

Other, nonempirical challenges to preventive patrol can be inferred from the report by the President's Commission of 1967 on Law Enforcement and Administration of Justice[16] and from researchers studying the problem of police-citizen alienation.[17] The commission report, while backing preventive patrol because of its assumed crime-preventive effectiveness, conceded that the strategy may create serious community relations problems. Others have suggested that the tactic of preventive patrol has contributed to police officers' image as an alien force that is remote from the community. In minority communities, police vehicles have grown to symbolize the establishment's repression and occupation. The result has been a mutual withdrawal—the police from the citizens, and the citizens from the police. Proposals for community relations programs and public service officers can now be seen as attempts to make up for some of the problems created by preventive patrol. However, since preventive patrol has failed to demonstrate its effectiveness, it becomes clear that such proposals were misplaced attempts to change image rather than improve service.

If police critics are correct, the strategy of preventive patrol has not only failed to demonstrate its effectiveness but has also created the worst possible situation: an ineffectiveness which alienates citizens.

Response Time

As preventive patrol strategy developed it was linked with a second and, in many respects, complementary tactic—rapid response to calls for service. If police could reduce the time between commission of a crime and the arrival of the police on the scene, increased apprehension of offenders, deterrence, increased citizen satisfaction, and decreased fear should result. The goal of most police departments became a response time of three minutes. Evaluators became so convinced that there would be a

---

14. D. Fisk, *The Indianapolis Police Fleet Plan* (Washington, D.C.: Urban Institute, October 1970).

15. George L. Kelling et al., *The Kansas City Preventive Patrol Experiment* (Washington, D.C.: Police Foundation, 1974).

16. President's Commission on Law Enforcement and Administration of Justice, *Task Force Report: The Police* (Washington, D.C.: U.S. Govt. Printing Office, 1967).

17. Irving Piliavin, "Police-Community Alienation: Its Structural Roots and a Proposed Remedy" (Andover, Mass.: Warner Modular Publications, Module 14, 1973), pp. 1-25.

causal link between response time and police effectiveness (apprehensions, deterrence, etc.) that response time itself became an outcome variable, an indicator of police effectiveness.

Two recently published studies measured the effects of response time. Studying data from the Kansas City Police Department, Deborah Bertram and Alexander Vargo found that response time had no effect on apprehensions for the crime of robbery.[18] They also learned that citizens who have experienced serious crimes allow considerable periods of time to elapse before contacting the police. Pate et al. correlated response time with levels of citizen satisfaction and found that response time was not the critical variable in determining citizen satisfaction.[19] What was important was the expectation of how long it would take the police to arrive. If police response time exceeded the citizen's expectation, he tended to be dissatisfied; if, however, response time was shorter than anticipated, the citizen was generally satisfied. The authors suggest that dispatchers could play an important role in controlling citizens' expectations about the police arrival.

As in the case of effects of preventive patrol, it appears logical that police response time should make a difference in effectiveness. But this strategy lacks empirical support. It was assumed that citizens called the police immediately. In fact, citizens called someone else first and considerable time elapsed.

Here we have a police strategy that is expensive to develop and maintain. To reduce response time, multimillion-dollar automatic vehicle locator systems have been developed. Yet evaluations of the strategy have bypassed the question of whether it affected apprehensions, only measuring the extent to which it reduced response time.[20] But it has been a tremendous expense in terms of its effect on police allocation plans, in the way it confines police in their automobiles, and in its impact on police supervision and organization.

Team Policing

One of the most promising developments in the past several decades has been the concept of team policing. There is much about it that seems "right": Team policing encourages close interactions between citizens and police; it emphasizes a decentralized decision making by police officers

---

18.   D. K. Bertram and A. Vargo, "Response Time Analysis Study: Preliminary Finding on Robbery in Kansas City," *The Police Chief*, May 1976, pp. 74-77.

19.   Pate, et al., *Police Response Time: Its Determinants and Effects* (Washington, D.C.: Police Foundation, 1976).

20.   Richard C. Larson, Kent W. Colton, and Gilbert C. Larson, "Evaluating a Police-Implemented AVM System: The St. Louis Experience," Phase I (unpublished paper).

and supervisors actually working in the prescribed area; it acknowledges the multipurpose functions of the police and often provides general and special training for police; and it encourages police officer familiarity with community agencies and other resources.

Yet the implementation of this promising form of policing has been an elusive goal. Team policing has been tried in Detroit, New York, Dallas, Cincinnati, and many other cities, but no large city has been able to implement or maintain it on a city-wide basis.

A recent evaluation of team policing in Cincinnati may best illustrate this point.[21] Team policing was begun on an experimental basis with great enthusiasm. After the first year, citizen satisfaction had increased, crime had decreased, and officers remained enthusiastic about the project. The program appeared to be a truly amazing success. However, at the end of year two, citizen satisfaction had returned to levels comparable with other areas of the city, crime had returned to comparable levels, and officer satisfaction had diminished. Team policing simply expired. Police officers went back to "business as usual," and authority was recentralized.

Two interpretations are possible. The first is that an "innovator effect" was operating during the first year; in other words, programs tend to start with flourish and promise because of factors such as participants' enthusiasm and publicity. This might well explain Cincinnati's initial success.

However, there is a second interpretation which I find more plausible since the Cincinnati experience followed the pattern of almost every other team policing effort. Team policing can start with enthusiasm, commitment, and great promise and then either remain confined to one or two districts or, as in Cincinnati, simply be terminated.

Two factors seem to operate. First, team policing represents a real threat to police departments' formal and informal power distribution. While officers can mobilize considerable enthusiasm for such attempts, organizational decentralization threatens established and entrenched interest groups which have considerable power inside the organization, often control employee organizations, and, in the case of detectives, often have important ties with the press and politicians.[22]

The second factor is that the present police orientation around rapid response to service calls is essentially incompatible not only with team policing but also with almost every other approach which emphasizes planning of "out-of-service" activities. Meetings with citizens' groups and

21.   Alfred I. Schwartz and Sumner N. Clarren, *Evaulation of Team Policing in Cincinnati (after 30 months of Experimentation)* (Washington, D.C.: Police Foundation, 1978).

22.   A forthcoming evaluation of the attempt in Dallas to decentralize operations and develop generalist/specialist police officers will describe this resistance in detailed and stark terms.

with individual citizens involve considerable out-of-service time. Regardless of what a sergeant or team leader may plan for police officers during any tour of duty, as long as the primary goal of the police department revolves around rapid response to calls for service, that will have priority over almost every other activity.

The conflict between supervisory and dispatch goals may well have contributed to the failure of innovations such as team policing. Yet the role of supervision has received little attention. So far as I know, there is not one good study examining the impact of the sergeant on the police force. Jonathan Rubinstein suggests both sergeants and dispatchers may significantly control police activities,[23] but we have little understanding of how this operates.

Information

At least five studies suggest that, to the extent that police can affect crime, availability of information and the management of that information seem to be of critical importance. These findings, though still tentative, run counter to the present police concern with interception of crimes or rapid response to calls for service. The Rochester program, which studied case management to identify factors contributing to the solution of a crime,[24] the Rand study of investigative effectiveness,[25] the Police Foundation's evaluation of the Criminal Information Center in Kansas City,[26] the San Diego program of field interrogations,[27] and the San Diego community profile program[28] are exploratory studies, but they suggest that continued research and program development in the gathering and managing of information may be useful.

These findings lead to the following questions. How can we improve the quality and quantity of police-citizen contacts so that citizens report more crime, give police information—both formally and infor-

---

23. Jonathan Rubinstein, *City Police* (New York: Farrar, Straus and Giroux, 1973), pp. 73-87.

24. Peter B. Bloch and James Bell, *Managing Investigation: The Rochester System* (Washington, D.C.: Police Foundation, 1976).

25. Peter W. Greenwood, et al., *The Criminal Investigation Process*, 3 vols. (Santa Monica, Calif.: Rand Corporation, 1976).

26. Tony Pate, Robert A. Bowers, and Ron Parks, *Three Approaches to Criminal Apprehension in Kansas City: An Evaluation Report* (Washington, D.C.: Police Foundation, 1976).

27. John E. Boydstun, *San Diego Field Interrogation: Final Report* (Washington, D.C.: Police Foundation, 1975).

28. John E. Boydstun and Michael E. Sherry, *San Diego Community Profile: Final Report* (Washington, D.C.: Police Foundation, 1975).

mally—about crime patterns, and discuss their community concerns? How can we improve the ability of the individual police officer and the organization to gather that information, store it, and bring it to bear on appropriate events and issues? How can we improve the police officer's and the police organization's ability to understand their community so that they can better interpret the information they receive? How can we modify the reward structures of police organizations so that sharing, not retaining, information is properly encouraged and rewarded? These questions combine issues of police organization, police strategy, and police technology.

Organizational issues pertinent to effectively obtaining information include supervision, training, and incentives for gathering and sharing useful information. Strategy issues include how to maximize police-citizen contacts so that they can be most productive of relevant information. The technological issue is how to properly arrange for the easy storage and retrieval of information.

Investigations

The myths about investigative work are perhaps best summarized by Goldstein:

> Part of the mystique of detective operations is the impression that a detective has difficult-to-come-by qualifications and skills; that investigating crime is a real science; that a detective does much more important work than other police officers; that all detective work is exciting; and that a good detective can solve any crime. It borders on heresy to point out that, in fact, much of what detectives do consists of very routine and rather elementary chores, including much paper processing; that a good deal of their work is not only not exciting, it is downright boring; that the situations they confront are often less challenging and less demanding than those handled by patrolling police officers; that it is arguable whether special skills and knowledge are required for detective work; that a considerable amount of detective work is actually undertaken on a hit-or-miss basis; and that the capacity of detectives to solve crimes is greatly exaggerated.[29]

Both the Rand study and the Rochester study underline this issue. The Rand study, which has been the subject of much controversy, suggests that the role played by investigators in crime solution has been overrated. The study is exploratory, but the authors' findings and recommendations are highly plausible. The Rochester study demonstrated that one problem in investigations is case management. Thus, investigators found that their

---

29. Goldstein, *Policing A Free Society.*

time could be spent more efficiently if they concentrated on those cases which had a high probability of success. Further, it was found that patrol officers could provide the necessary information for that screening process by identifying "solvability factors."

Clearly, much research is still needed. Only preliminary studies of the relationship between patrol and investigation are available. However, the combined findings of the Rand study and the Rochester study identify significant problems in investigation and suggest means of using patrol officers to improve investigative effectiveness.

Technology

There have always been high hopes that technology would greatly enhance police effectiveness or would at least give officers an "edge" over the criminals. In 1929, when the radio was first installed in police vehicles, some predicted that radios would enable police to eliminate city crime altogether.[30] While we may not be as enthusiastic today, we continue to invest heavily in devices such as helicopters, computers, new weapon systems, and surveillance systems, with the expectation that new technology will significantly improve police functioning.

Certainly, innovations such as the personal radios have great utility for police agencies. Radios—especially personal radios—can be used to both protect the officer and increase his effectiveness. Yet one might argue that they are more important as management devices than as crime-fighting instruments, for there is little evidence that radios have given police any "edge" over criminal offenders. Recent lightweight bullet protection devices are useful and should be available; however, they are warm, uncomfortable, and restrictive. It is unlikely that more than a few officers are willing to wear them routinely.

With these possible exceptions, there is no evidence that any technological devices have significantly improved the effectiveness of police service. Helicopters may have been useful as ambulances, but their effectiveness in patrol remains hypothetical. And the cost of use has not been analyzed.

Computer-aided dispatch and automatic vehicle locator systems have failed to demonstrate that they can reduce response time.[31] Besides, there is no evidence that reduced response time achieves anything. This is not meant to imply that computers and other instruments cannot be used effectively in police departments. I have no doubt that they have great

---

30. Rubinstein, *City Police.*
31. Joseph H. Lewis, "Evaluation of Systems Effectiveness," unpublished paper (Washington, D.C.: Police Foundation, 1964).

potential in efficient management. But their impact on the multiple police services remains to be seen.

Critics of technological innovation generally see new devices as being, at worst, expensive, useless "toys." But this criticism does not go far enough. The "worst" is not the wasting of money but the deterioration in the quality of service. The radio, for example, has been used to decrease police response time. The beneficial effect of rapid response to calls for service was presumed, not proved. Nevertheless, the radio created a priority, spawning other hardware such as computer-aided dispatch and automatic vehicle locator systems. All this came as a result of a capacity to achieve a *presumed effect*.

Technology does not, "at worst," create wasteful expensive toys; technology used in organizations can lead to goal displacement, the dominance of one function over another because of presumed effects, and a substantial change not only in how services are delivered but also in what those services are.

In discussing technology and the military, Joseph Lewis has suggested that when people have money and are facing difficult problems, they are easily diverted to the technology which seems to be related to those problems (capacity for presumed effect).[32] It is much more fun to play with computers (be scientific) than to solve hard problems. You can prove that you are "doing something about the problem" by spending large sums of money in dignified, scientifically respectable, socially acceptable ways.

> The problem can also be stated quite briefly in this way. What we have been saying is that there is not a firm bridge in the area of command and control between scientific and technical capabilities and operational utility. In most areas of application of science and technology, it is easy to see the connection between the scientific or technical ability to do something and the use that can be made of doing that something. That is not true here. There is technology lying around in heaps that we have not the remotest idea how to employ usefully. There is technology lying around in heaps that we know something about employing but have no valid way to establish what it is worth, or how much we should pay for it.[33]

The question in policing is, technology for what purpose? That question simply has not been answered.

Conclusion

The police have developed strategies oriented around just one of their

32. Ibid.
33. Douglas Hay, et al., *Albion's Fatal Tree* (New York: Pantheon, 1975).

many functions. These strategies have not only failed to obtain their desired results but have also led the police to ignore other important functions and have alienated citizens, whose support is vital in effective police performance.

Except for the period between World War I and World War II, our cities and countryside have probably never been safer. Those who respond hysterically to our present crime problems and claim that we are experiencing a complete breakdown in law and order should read about crime in the past.[34] Cities have always been unsafe places. And, not long ago, those leaving the city to travel in the countryside were hardly better off. Unless they hired protection, travelers were lucky to arrive at their destination with their horse (if they had a horse) and their boots. Even with protection, it was essential that they reach their destination—or stop in a city or at an inn—before nightfall. Today, one can travel throughout the countryside with little fear of crime. Campers can sleep outside with little risk of losing their equipment. A person can safely walk in most city neighborhoods during the day with relatively little fear. If one is reasonably prudent, the probability of becoming a victim is really quite low.

I do not mean to suggest that crime is not a serious problem. It is. But our fear far exceeds the danger and is seriously affecting our lives in the cities.

At this time, it appears that the police officer's impact on crime must remain relatively limited. This is not only because of the kind of open society in which we live but also because of the nature of particular kinds of crime. Most assaults and murders are hard to control because they involve friends, neighbors, relatives, or lovers. Subtract these from the total number of murders and assaults and the number of potentially suppressible crimes is greatly reduced. Subtract those crimes committed indoors or in places inaccessible to police, and those committed by professionals, and the number decreases further.

Consider armed robbery, a threatening, potentially violent crime. If the Vera Institute study is correct, fully one-third of all armed robberies are committed by people who are known by their victims.[35] Here too, if one subtracts those robberies committed in inaccessible places and those committed by professionals, the number that actually may be suppressible is reduced to an extremely low level.

---

34. See, for example, Christopher Hibbert, *London: The Biography of a City* (London: Longmans, Green and Co., 1969).

35. Vera Institute, "Felony Arrests: Their Prosecution and Disposition in New York City's Courts," monograph published by Vera Institute of Justice, 1977.

Consider child molestation, most of which occurs in the home. How do the police mobilize to deal with this?

Certainly there are murders, assaults, armed robberies, and child molestations that are potentially suppressible. However, it is likely that a "floor effect" is operating—that the remaining cases are at such a low level that massively mobilizing the police to deal with those problems can have only a very marginal effect and at enormous cost. And that cost probably includes undesirable police-citizen relations.

Acute problems or a threatening series of crimes may demand mobilization, but as a routine policy this seems to have a limited effect and be enforced at enormous financial cost and at the expense of other functions.

What does this mean for the development of future plans, styles of policing, strategies, and research innovation? Briefly, the critical need is to improve the quality and quantity of police-citizen interaction. This must be a central task, not for the purpose of improving the police image but rather to encourage the normal social control exercised by a healthy community. The police must be seen as only an aid to the community, as the community itself deals with social problems. The police certainly are essential, but policing is too important to be left to the police alone.

Police methods must reflect the entire police task. We must examine how information is handled and how officers are rewarded for sharing it. The focus on rapid response time must be modified in part by changing citizens' expectations about police service. Police must see reduction of fear as an important part of their purpose. Citizens must be encouraged to use streets prudently but comfortably. We have never tested the hypothesis that it is the extent to which the police provide the full range of police services—in a civil and helpful way—that determines the degree to which *citizens* fully exploit and mobilize the police to deal with crime. The time has come when we should test that hypothesis. As Lewis has suggested with the military,[36] we should declare a ten-year moratorium on technology and concentrate hard on learning just what it is that the police should—and can—do.

---

36. Joseph H. Lewis, "Evaluation of Systems Effectiveness" (lecture sponsored by the University of California, 1964); shortened version published in *Operational Research and the Social Sciences,* J. K. Lawrence, ed. (London: Tavistock, 1966), p. 46.

3. UPGRADING THE AMERICAN POLICE

CHARLES B. SAUNDERS, JR.

Upgrading the American Police (Washington: The Brookings Institution, 1970). Reprinted by permission.

In a time of rising crime and violence, racial conflict, social unrest, and the politics of protest and confrontation, the police have achieved a new visibility. After decades of public neglect, the vital role of the police in society is demonstrated daily in the nation's press. Concerned citizens, public officials, and national commissions testify to the heavy responsibilities borne by the police and the serious consequences which may result when they are unable to meet those responsibilities.

Public Attitudes Toward the Police

Yet the increasing attention paid the police reflects widespread misunderstanding of their role. Many Americans view them as solely responsible for controlling crime. But as the President's Commission on Law Enforcement stressed, crime cannot be understood as a narrow range of behavior by certain types of people: it pervades all strata of society, and its control cannot be accomplished by the police or by the courts and correctional system by themselves.

Another serious cause of misunderstanding is the failure to recognize that law enforcement is an occupation demanding a high order of skills and intelligence. This failure contributes in myriad ways to the problems of the police. It helps explain why there is so little public support for efforts to upgrade police personnel and why policemen throughout the nation are so often poorly prepared to perform their essential tasks. It explains the stereotype of the "dumb cop."

The stereotype is confirmed in the memory of many adults who recall the days when any able-bodied man with the proper political allegiance could find a place on the force. American society is still only a few decades away from the time when immigrants, denied employment in the skilled trades, found the urban police force one of the few open avenues to cultural assimilation; when policing in rural areas was largely a job of chasing stray animals, and when frontier justice asked only that the lawman handle a gun.

One commentator has observed that "the American is not overly impressed by police authority, considering the police officer as a badly paid job holder, not above being 'fixed' by a bribe."[1] A remarkably similar assessment was delivered decades earlier:

> There is little conception of policing as a profession or a science to be matured and developed. It is a job, held, perhaps, by the grace of some mysterious political influence, and conducted in an atmosphere sordid and unhealthy.... Instead of confidence and trust, the attitude of the public toward the police is far more often than not one of cynicism and suspicion.[2]

The assumption that anyone with a strong back and a weak mind can walk a beat is reflected in the relatively low rating of police compared with other professions in national surveys of occupational prestige. Police rank forty-seventh on a list of ninety occupations—below machinists, undertakers, electricians, welfare workers, agricultural agents, and all of the professions.[3] At the same time, polls show a markedly higher rating for federal law enforcement agents.[4] This difference may reflect the fact that the work of federal agents is almost entirely investigative, which appeals to the public fascination with the science of criminal detection.[5] Television drama and the literature of detective fiction illustrate this ambivalence toward policemen, portraying them either as supersleuths or as mental pygmies, constantly outwitted by daring criminals and dashing private eyes.

Another element in popular attitudes is fear of a strong police force—a fear deeply ingrained in the national psychology and a major influence in the historical development of our fragmented police system. Fear and distrust of governmental authority are reinforced by strong cultural values emphasizing individual freedom. The police are the most evident symbol of the limitations imposed on the individual. Their intimate involvement in the lives and problems of citizens increases the ambivalence felt toward them. Police deal with people when they are:

> most threatening and most vulnerable, when they are angry, when they are frightened, when they are desperate, when they are drunk, when they are violent, or when they are ashamed...

1. Max Lerner, *America as a Civilization* (Simon and Schuster, 1957), p. 433.
2. Raymond B. Fosdick, *American Police Systems* (The Century Co., 1920), p. 380.
3. Robert W. Hodge, Paul M. Siegel, and Peter H. Rossi, "Occupation Prestige in the United States, 1925-1963," *American Journal of Sociology*, vol. 70 (November 1964), pp. 290-92.
4. Louis Harris, *Washington Post*, July 3, 1966.
5. Pointed out by Arthur L. Stinchcombe in "Institutions of Privacy in the Determination of Police Administrative Practice," *American Journal of Sociology*, vol. 69 (September 1962), p. 159.

[It] is inevitable that the public is of two minds about the police: most men both welcome official protection and resent official interference.[6]

These factors must be reckoned with in any effort to improve law enforcement. They help explain why one of the oldest and most important functions of municipal government has undergone so little substantial reform.

The Police Task: A Historical Perspective

The view of police work as undemanding is an anachronism dating from the early development of metropolitan forces in the mid-1800's as a force of political appointees paid to serve as watchmen. An early student of police administration wrote:

It is certainly not necessary and some have even maintained that it is not desirable that police patrolmen be men of large intellectual ability... [It is] extremely unlikely that, for the present at least, any considerable number of men who have enjoyed even a secondary education will turn to the police business.... The most important asset of the ideal policeman is unquestionably his physical constitution and condition.[7]

But this view of the police was obsolete by the time it appeared in print. In the same year, August Vollmer, chief of police in Berkeley, California, was applying new principles of organization and professionalism which made him a pioneer of scientific criminal investigation and police administration.

A decade later, the first scholarly assessment of American police emphasized that:

The heart of police work is the contact of the individual policeman with the citizen.... The action that is first taken by the policeman of lower rank, operating independently, must, in each case, remain the foundation of the department's action ... the quality of a department's work depends on the observation, knowledge, discretion, courage and judgment of the men, acting as individuals.... Only as the training of the policeman is deliberate and thorough, with emphasis on the social implications and human aspects of his task, can real success in police work be achieved.[8]

A concurrent judgment was expressed by Chief Vollmer, then beginning a single-handed campaign within the police profession to raise per-

---

6. U.S. President's Commission on Law Enforcement and Administration of Justice, *The Challenge of Crime in a Free Society* (Government Printing Office, 1967), pp. 91-92.

7. Leonhard Felix Fuld, *Police Administration* (G.P. Putnam's Sons, 1909), pp. 90-91.

8. Fosdick, *American Police Systems*, p. 306.

sonnel standards. In 1916 he founded the first school of criminology at the University of California and advertised in the college newspaper for bright young men to enter law enforcement as a career. Vollmer argued that:

> The police service has been completely revolutionized in the last few years, and an entirely different type of individual is needed. In addition to higher personal qualifications, there must also be added the professional training in order that the service may not be hampered and police candidates may be educationally equipped to perform the duties that are now assignable to policemen.[9]

Informed observers outside the law enforcement field agreed. An early specialist in public administration called attention to the growth of heterogeneous urban populations and the attendant problems which "this country has barely begun to approach ... rationally." The police department, as the direct crime prevention agency, "is concerned with a social problem that is interrelated with all the social and economic conditions in the community.... Obviously, the task of combatting crime calls for superior abilities together with training and education."[10] Since effective law enforcement may require the exercise of more power than is actually conferred by law, the authority of police to use personal discretion "should be increased and the character of personnel improved so that this discretion will be wisely exercised."[11]

The International City Management Association told its membership in 1931 that "because of the enormity of the task of policing a community it is necessary to emphasize the fact that the best human material in the country is none too good for police service."[12] A joint study by the Los Angeles Police Department and the California State Department of Education in the early 1930s found that a competent patrolman should possess knowledge of one hundred fifty-eight different fields.[13]

Bruce Smith, the foremost scholar of police administration, emphasized the human factor in the law enforcement equation in his landmark study which appeared in 1940:

> The policeman's art, then, consists in applying and enforcing a multitude of laws and ordinances in such degree or proportion

---

9. Letter (1932) quoted in Donald E. Clark and Samuel G. Chapman, *A Forward Step; Educational Backgrounds for Police* (Springfield, Ill.: Charles C. Thomas, 1966), p. 22.

10. Lent D. Upson, *Practice of Municipal Administration* (The Century Co., 1926), pp. 324-25.

11. Ibid., p. 321.

12. *City Managers' Yearbook, 1931* (International City Managers' Association, Chicago), p. 143.

13. U.S. Department of the Interior, Office of Education, *Training for the Police Service*, Vocational Division Bulletin No. 197, Trade and Industrial Series No. 56 (1938).

and in such manner that the greatest degree of social protection will be secured. The degree of enforcement and the method of application will vary with each neighborhood and community. There are no set rules, nor even general guides to policy, in this regard. Each policeman must, in a sense, determine the standard which is to be set in the area for which he is responsible. Immediate superiors may be able to impress upon him some of the lessons of experience, but for the most part such experience must be his own.... Thus he is a policy-forming police administrator in miniature, who operates beyond the scope of the usual devices for popular control....

Hence the task of raising the level of police performance does not hinge upon the use of mechanical aids, as so many suppose. It depends upon sound organization and efficient procedures which are applied to—and by—alert and intelligent servants of the police organism. Since the human factor proves the most difficult to control and may actively resist all change, the process of raising the general level of police service sometimes proves to be a lengthy one....[14]

In the last three decades the human factor has assumed ever greater importance as police agencies have had to cope with the tensions and dislocations resulting from population growth, increasing urbanization, developing technology, the civil rights revolution, changing social norms, and a breakdown of traditional values. Such factors have enormously complicated the law enforcement task, making more critical the need for the "truly exceptional men" Vollmer sought in the 1930s.[15]

Today's local patrolman must be aware of these factors and understand their psychological and sociological implications for his community. He must deal with all of its citizens—rich and poor, young and old, of whatever cultural and ethnic backgrounds—in ways which will maintain their support and confidence. He must be able to provide a variety of services while serving as protector of life, property, and personal liberty. He must be a law enforcement generalist with a working knowledge of federal, state, county, and municipal law, traffic law, and criminal procedures.

The Police Patrolman: A Job Description

The complex demands of the patrolman's job and the attributes required

---

14. Smith, *Police Systems in the United States* (New York: Harper & Bros., 1940), pp. 21-22. The continuing validity of this point is indicated by the use of the identical passage two decades later in the second revised edition (Harper & Row, 1960), pp. 19-20.

15. August Vollmer, *The Police and Modern Society* (University of California Press, 1936), p. 223.

for successful performance have recently been analyzed by a university research team whose findings, reported as a list of essential behavioral requirements, serve as scientific validation of the point Vollmer made three decades earlier. On the basis of extensive field observation, the scholars concluded that a patrolman must:

1. endure long periods of monotony in routine patrol yet react quickly (almost instantaneously) and effectively to problem situations observed on the street or to orders issued by the radio dispatcher (in much the same way that a combat pilot must react to interception or a target opportunity).
2. gain knowledge of his patrol area, not only of its physical characteristics but also of its normal routine of events and the usual behavior patterns of its residents.
3. exhibit initiative, problem-solving capacity, effective judgment, and imagination in coping with the numerous complex situations he is called upon to face, e.g., a family disturbance, a potential suicide, a robbery in progress, an accident, or a disaster. Police officers themselves clearly recognize this requirement and refer to it as "showing street sense."
4. make prompt and effective decisions, sometimes in life and death situations, and be able to size up a situation quickly and take appropriate action.
5. demonstrate mature judgment, as in deciding whether an arrest is warranted by the circumstances or a warning is sufficient, or in facing a situation where the use of force may be needed.
6. demonstrate critical awareness in discerning signs of out-of-the-ordinary conditions or circumstances which indicate trouble or a crime in progress.
7. exhibit a number of complex psychomotor skills, such as driving a vehicle in normal and emergency situations, firing a weapon accurately under extremely varied conditions, maintaining agility, endurance, and strength, and showing facility in self-defense and apprehension, as in taking a person into custody with a minimum of force.
8. adequately perform the communication and record-keeping functions of the job, including oral reports, preparation of formal case reports, and completion of departmental and court forms.
9. have the facility to act effectively in extremely divergent interpersonal situations. A police officer constantly confronts persons who are acting in violation of the law, ranging from curfew violators to felons. He is constantly confronted by people who are in trouble or who are victims of crimes. Besides his dealings with criminals, he has contact with para-criminals, informers, and people on the border of

criminal behavior. (He must also be "alley-wise.") At the same time, he must relate to the people on his beat—businessmen, residents, school officials, visitors, etc. His interpersonal relations must range up and down a continuum defined by friendliness and persuasion on one end and by firmness and force at the other.

10. endure verbal and physical abuse from citizens and offenders (as when placing a person under arrest or facing day-in and day-out race prejudice) while using only necessary force in the performance of his function.

11. exhibit a professional, self-assured presence and a self-confident manner in his conduct when dealing with offenders, the public, and the courts.

12. be capable of restoring equilibrium to social groups, e.g., restoring order in a family fight, in a disagreement between neighbors, or in a clash between rival youth groups.

13. be skillful in questioning suspected offenders, victims, and witnesses of crimes.

14. take charge of situations, e.g., a crime or accident scene, yet not unduly alienate participants or bystanders.

15. be flexible enough to work under loose supervision in most of his day-to-day patrol activities (either alone or as part of a two-man team) and also under the direct supervision of superiors in situations where large numbers of officers are required.

16. tolerate stress in a multitude of forms, such as meeting the violent behavior of a mob, arousing people in a burning building, coping with the pressures of a high-speed chase or a weapon being fired at him, or dealing with a woman bearing a child.

17. exhibit personal courage in the face of dangerous situations which may result in serious injury or death.

18. maintain objectivity while dealing with a host of "special interest" groups, ranging from relatives of offenders to members of the press.

19. maintain a balanced perspective in the face of constant exposure to the worst side of human nature.

20. exhibit a high level of personal integrity and ethical conduct, e.g., refrain from accepting bribes or "favors," provide impartial law enforcement, etc.[16]

These behavioral requirements are basic to the job of a patrolman, regardless of the size and nature of the community in which he works. If

---

16. Melany E. Baehr, John E. Furcon, and Ernest C. Froemel, *Psychological Assessment of Patrolman Qualifications in Relation to Field Performance*, Preliminary Report to Office of Law Enforcement Assistance, Department of Justice (processed, 1968), pp. II-3 to II-5. The project was conducted by the Industrial Relations Center of the University of Chicago under a grant to the Chicago Police Department.

competent performance of the law enforcement task is expected, these attributes should characterize every member of the force, from the newest recruit to the oldest veteran. They should be standard equipment for any man in uniform, whether he patrols a sleepy rural street, a congested business district, or a ghetto alley.

Numerous proposals have been made for restructuring the patrolman's job by freeing him from such routine tasks as checking parking meters, directing traffic, delivering summonses, or performing social services. None of these proposals would alter the behavioral requirements outlined above. However his job may be restructured, the patrolman will continue to be the first to respond in any community when citizens call to report a serious traffic accident, a noisy crowd of teenagers on the street, trouble in a bar, a domestic quarrel, a mental patient on the loose, a man unconscious on the sidewalk, prowlers in a building, or a neighbor burning trash. The abilities, skills, and intelligence of the men who answer such calls are of vital concern to every member of the community.

The Peacekeeping Function

One fundamental but generally neglected aspect of the police role is that of peacekeeping. The enforcement function, which occupies only a small part of the policeman's time, is carefully recorded by reporting procedures. The peacekeeping function, which consumes most of the officer's time and includes all occupational routines not directly related to making arrests, is largely unaccounted for. Police departments literally do not know and cannot explain how individual patrolmen spend most of their time. When asked how they discharge the peacekeeping function, officers say they merely use common sense, although they admit that experience is valuable. Police textbooks and manuals give little attention to peacekeeping, except to suggest that it takes personal wisdom, integrity, and altruism. To the public, this phase of the policeman's duties is a constant cause of misunderstanding:

> . . . the citizen will observe that when the patrolman is not handling the citizen's momentary emergency, he is standing on a street corner, walking along the sidewalk, or driving a patrol car—apparently "doing nothing." What he *is* doing, of course, is waiting to be called to cope with someone else's emergency, and if he were not "doing nothing" he would not be immediately available. The citizen, forgetting this, is likely to wonder why he isn't out "looking for the man who stole my car," or whatever.[17]

The importance of the peacekeeping function, and its relevance to the

---

17. James Q. Wilson, *Varieties of Police Behavior: The Management of Law and Order in Eight Communities* (Boston: Harvard University Press, 1968), p. 26.

question of preparation and training, is emphasized in a psychiatrist's recent study dealing with the treatment of skid row derelicts by the police. He concludes that peacekeeping requires very real practical skills but that the police themselves are not aware of it:

> Quite to the contrary, the ability to discharge the duties associated with keeping the peace is viewed as a reflection of an innate talent of "getting along with people." Thus, the same demands are made of barely initiated officers as are made of skilled practitioners. Correspondingly, beginners tend to think that they can do as well as their more knowledgeable peers. . . . The license of discretionary freedom and the expectation of success under conditions of autonomy, without any indication that the work of the successful craftsman is based on an acquired preparedness for the task, is ready-made for failure and malpractice. Moreover, it leads to slipshod practices of patrol that also infect the standards of the careful craftsman.
>
> The uniformed patrol, and especially the foot patrol, has a low preferential value in the division of labor of police work. This is in part, at least, due to the belief that "anyone could do it." In fact, this belief is thoroughly mistaken. At present, however, the recognition that the practice requires preparation, and the process of obtaining the preparation itself, is left entirely to the practitioner.[18]

This conclusion is highly significant for several reasons. It exposes the inadequacies of any view of the police task which undervalues the peacekeeping function. It points up a major aspect of police performance which is seriously neglected in training. It identifies a need for further research to determine with greater precision the requirements for effective police patrol. And it emphasizes that even routine police work requires a high order of abilities and preparation. The general failure to understand this last point (by the police as well as the public) has surely contributed to our society's unwillingness to accord the police status "either in the European sense . . . as representatives of the State or in the more typically American sense of prestige based on a claim of occupational competence."[19]

Still another failure of public understanding is the widely held fiction that a patrolman's job is not discretionary but is simply the enforcement of the law by catching criminals. This combines several mistaken views:

---

18.   Egon Bittner, "The Police on Skid-Row: A Study of Peace Keeping," *American Sociological Review*, vol. 32 (October 1967), p. 715.

19.   David J. Bordua and Albert J. Reiss, Jr., "Environment and Organization: A Perspective on the Police," in *The Police: Six Sociological Essays*, ed. David J. Bordua (New York: John Wiley & Sons, 1967), p. 51.

that the crime problem is solely the concern of the police, that their task is mainly one of law enforcement, and that this function requires so little intelligence or imagination that anyone can do it.

This fiction has long been cherished by some apologists for the police who hold that they are "only doing their duty" as well as by civil libertarian critics who maintain that police do not have the capacity to exercise discretion and therefore should not be allowed to do so. But as the skid row study cited above illustrates, discretion is the better part of peacekeeping, which in turn is the bigger part of policing. To deny officers the use of discretion is to misconceive their basic function. The only realistic recourse is to insist that their qualifications and training be sufficient to assure that they exercise discretion well.

No matter how well or how poorly qualified to exercise discretion, the police are forced to do so for a variety of reasons. Many of the laws under which they operate are highly ambiguous, either by intent to permit greater flexibility in enforcement or by accident as a result of the limitations of language or of failure to foresee the day-to-day operating problems encountered in enforcement. In addition, some statutes were never intended to be enforced to the letter, and others are simply obsolete. Limitations on manpower and other resources, and the pressures of community standards, also force the exercise of discretion.[20] Whatever the reason, the policeman must often determine the forms of conduct which are to be subject to the criminal process.

If the extent to which police must exercise discretion is underestimated, this is partly because police themselves usually prefer to project an image of impartial, full enforcement without fear or favor. To admit that they ignore the laws under certain conditions might contribute to a breakdown of respect for all laws, raise the possibility of corruption, and imply that other criteria for enforcement exist which are difficult to spell out and communicate to members of the force as well as the general public.[21]

No code of conduct could possibly cover all circumstances in which policemen must make instantaneous and irrevocable decisions affecting human life and safety, property rights, and personal liberty. Such awesome responsibility for decision making, indeed, sets the police apart from any other profession—after all, the physician may change his diagnosis, the lawyer his pleading. Decisions affecting human life cannot be made more wisely by reducing them to rote and removing police discretion en-

---

20. See Herman Goldstein, "Police Discretion: The Ideal Versus the Real," *Public Administration Review*, vol. 23 (September 1963), pp. 142-43.

21. Ibid. Goldstein nevertheless argues the desirability of publicly acknowledging the need for exercise of discretion as a means of fostering better understanding of the police task and new thinking about ways to improve the criminal justice system.

tirely. Ironically, some proponents of this course describe it as "taking the handcuffs off the police." But without discretion, the police are handcuffed to the limited role of unthinking enforcers, powerless to perform the peacekeeping function which is the most challenging and time-consuming part of their job.

Development of Research on the Police Role

If popular stereotypes about the police have been slow to die, one contributing factor has been an absence of research. Until the last decade the police service has had little capacity for, or interest in, the compilation of basic data about operations and performance. Within the field, leaders who have sought higher standards and personnel reforms have based their case on personal experience and observation rather than on the systematic collection of supporting evidence. J. Edgar Hoover, acting on his own understanding of the need for high competence and constant training, built the Federal Bureau of Investigation from an agency which ranked as "one of the worst law enforcement organizations in the country"[22] in the 1920s into an investigative force with a worldwide reputation for effectiveness. Vollmer and other pioneers at the local level, however, have not been able to attract the national following and support necessary to bring about the changes they sought in the nation's police forces.

The International Association of Chiefs of Police, founded in 1893 to advance the police service, has only recently developed a strong research component. In its early years the IACP established the first national fingerprint bureau and pioneered a system of uniform crime reporting, functions which were subsequently assumed by the FBI. In 1935 it created a safety division at Northwestern University to provide field services, research, and education in traffic safety. These programs were broadened further in 1959, when they were moved to Washington, D.C., and reorganized under the late Ray Ashworth. Quinn Tamm, a former assistant director of training and inspection for the FBI, was named director of the division in 1961 and enlarged the managerial consulting service for local departments, conducting surveys upon request. Named executive director of the IACP in 1962, Tamm began to build a research base for a vigorous drive to raise standards and promote reform. A research and development division was established to collect statistical data for analysis by a professional staff of researchers and specialists, as well as a professional standards division to produce a variety of training materials which are now used in thousands of local agencies. The Center for Law Enforce-

22. W. R. Kidd, *Police Interrogation* (Basuino, 1940), p. 11.

ment Research and a revamped monthly journal, *The Police Chief*, became vehicles for dissemination of new ideas and research findings to IACP's more than six thousand members and to scholars and others interested in the field.

Another landmark in the development of research on police problems was provided by the President's Commission on Law Enforcement. Its two-year study was concluded by 19 commissioners and 63 staff members, including lawyers, sociologists, psychologists, systems analysts, and a variety of specialists; in addition, there were 175 consultants and hundreds of advisers from the law enforcement and academic communities. Release in 1967 of the commission's report, together with the reports of its task forces, consultants' papers, and surveys, made available an extensive collection of basic data.

Outside of the law enforcement community, the problems of police manpower and organization have been the domain of virtually a single scholar, Bruce Smith, until the last decade. The scanty and usually hostile attention of other scholars served more to confirm than question the stereotypes of the police. A sociology text of 1939 pictured a police system which "generally operates in a lawless manner and breeds lawlessness," full of graft, collusion, and brutality.[23] A 1943 criminology text still widely used in American colleges states without qualification that "the chief criticisms of the American police, all of a serious nature, are: (1) their subservience to political bosses through a system peculiar to American cities; (2) lack of professional training and ignorance of the law and of the duties inherent in their jobs; and (3) their ruthless 'third degree' methods."[24]

Such blanket condemnations of the police are now being reconsidered and revised. One criminologist has recently advocated a strengthening and broadening of governmental police power as the best defense against the fragmentation of the social structure by militant interest groups: "General recognition and appreciation of the integrative function of the police power to maintain a stable society in stress and emergency and, for [that] matter on an everyday basis in a large, urban, complex society is necessary to achieve orderly living."[25] Another study has emphasized that the "police above all link daily life to central authority; moral consensus is extended through the police as an instrument of legitimate coercion. At the same time the police in performing this function often deflect the

---

23. Nathaniel F. Canter, *Crime and Society* (New York: Henry Holt & Co., 1939), p. 72.

24. Harry Elmer Barnes and Negley K. Teeters, *New Horizons in Criminology* (Englewood, N.J.: Prentice-Hall, 1943), p. 258.

25. Vernon Fox, "Sociological and Political Aspects of Police Administration," *Sociology and Social Research*, vol. 51 (October 1966), p. 43.

hostility of the mass from the class targets to the police themselves. . . ."[26]
Elsewhere its authors have written:

> Although the police are formally organized to enforce the law
> and maintain public order, it is apparent that they are involved
> at the same time in enacting justice. It is important to note that
> all three key terms—order, legality and justice—are ambiguous
> terms in any social system. But what philosophers, social scien-
> tists, and lawyers have argued over for centuries, the police must
> do every day.[27]

Scholars are thus beginning to give explicit recognition to the extraordinary variety of demands upon the police and their need for a
sophisticated arsenal of highly developed interpersonal skills as well as intelligence:

> In the heterogeneous milieu of metropolitan areas, the range
> and number of values and norms incorporated into vaguely dif-
> ferentiated subcultures present police officers with a variety of of-
> fenses against a primarily middle-class legal structure conditioned
> by the offenders' memberships in these subcultures. Perhaps
> equally important from the standpoint of police work is that these
> subcultures also condition the manner in which their members
> will respond to variations in police handling of citizens. Thus, a
> police officer whose background is likely to be middle or lower-
> middle class in nature cannot rely on his common sense or past ex-
> periences with the middle-class segments of the community when
> he attempts to gain voluntary compliance from those whose com-
> mon sense is predicated on values and norms at variance with his
> own.[28]

Legal scholars, also, are increasingly accepting the necessity for police to
exercise discretion, whereas before their primary concern had been for
police transgressions of lawful conduct:

> The policeman's lot is indeed a difficult one. He is charged with
> applying or enforcing a multitude of laws and ordinances in a
> degree or proportion and in a manner that maintains a delicate
> balance between the liberty of the individual and a high degree of
> social protection. His task requires a sensitive and wise discretion
> in deciding whether or not to invoke the criminal process. He

26. David J. Bordua and Albert J. Reiss, Jr., "Law Enforcement," in *The Uses of Sociology*,
     eds. Paul F. Lazarsfeld, William H. Sewell, and Harold L. Wilensky (New York: Basic
     Books Inc., 1967), p. 282.

27. Bordua and Reiss, "Environment and Organization: A Perspective on the Police," pp.
     32-33.

28. John H. McNamara, "Uncertainties in Police Work: The Relevance of Police Recruits'
     Backgrounds and Training," in *The Police: Six Sociological Essays*, ed. David J. Bor-
     dua, p. 168.

must not only know whether certain behavior violates the law but also whether there is probable cause to believe that the law has been violated. He must enforce the law, yet he must also determine whether a particular violation should be handled by warning or arrest. . . . He is not expected to arrest every violator. Some laws were never intended by the enactors to be enforced, and others condemn behavior that is not contrary to significant moral values. If he arrested all violators, the courts would find it impossible to do their work, and he would be in court so frequently that he could not perform his other professional duties. Consequently, the policeman must judge and informally settle more cases than he takes to court.[29]

The new and sympathetic interest in the police role has also stimulated research in the improvement of police selection standards and techniques by psychologists and psychiatrists. One study, noting that "the increasing complexity of urban law enforcement has placed a premium upon choice of properly qualified men who, by reason of intelligence, temperament, and training, can adequately meet the challenge of social conditions in our metropolitan cities," suggests that personality characteristics provide an index of effective police performance.[30] Emotional stability is listed as most crucial, since it "implies resilience and good judgment in the face of unpredictable surprises and pressures of urban police work." Other factors include social motivation; freedom from crippling personal pathology such as sadism, paranoia, or other forms of emotional illness; freedom from crippling social pathology such as excessively authoritarian attitudes, racial prejudice, or extremist social views; a high level of energy and self-assertion; effective intelligence under conditions of stress; and a facility for written and spoken expression of an order not necessarily guaranteed by a high school diploma or even college credits.

Another more extensive study has concluded that the most desirable attributes for successful patrolmen "are all related to stability—stability in the parental and personal family situations, stability stemming from personal self-confidence and the control of emotional impulses, stability in the maintenance of cooperative rather than hostile or competitive attitudes, and stability deriving from a realistic rather than a subjective orientation toward life."[31] The authors stress that their results "are in

29. Richard C. Donnelly, "Police Authority and Practices," *Annals of the American Academy of Political and Social Science*, vol. 339 (January 1962), pp. 91-92.

30. Robert B. Mills, Robert J. McDevitt, and Sandra Tonkin, "Selection of Metropolitan Police Officers," paper presented at a convention of the American Psychological Association, Los Angeles, Sept. 6, 1964.

31. Baehr, Furcon, Froemel, "Psychological Assessment of Patrolman Qualifications in Relation to Field Performance," p. IX-9.

direct contradiction to . . . those who maintain that psychopathic or even pathological characteristics are required for patrolmen success, i.e., that you have to 'set a thief to catch a thief.' "

The growing body of scholarship is also beginning to influence personnel specialists, who after decades of using identical qualifications and salary scales to recruit both police and firemen, are now advocating separate pay scales:

> The fact is that the cop on the beat must be better qualified to cope with more different and difficult things in a more independent manner than the entrance level firefighter. This fact has not yet been adequately recognized in the establishment of minimum qualification requirements.[32]

The scholarly reassessment of the police role and its requirements now under way provides a hopeful basis for improved understanding and support of higher selection and training standards in the future. But the problem is not simply one of awakening the public and its elected officials to the need for higher standards for the police. The police themselves must accept a view of professionalism which goes beyond the improvement of technical skills and managerial efficiency to a broader understanding of the role of law enforcement in democratic society.

Concepts to Consider

1. Compare and contrast the police role as proposed by the American Bar Association in relation to traditional police duties.

2. Justify the prevention of crime as the basic mission of law enforcement.

3. Support the position that the test of police efficiency is the absence of crime and disorder.

4. Differentiate between the myth of the police as primarily crime-fighters and the police as a public service agency.

5. Describe the impact of response time on police effectiveness.

6. Identify the key elements of the police peacekeeping function.

7. Describe recent research developments that are having a compelling effect on the police role.

---

32. Carl F. Lutz, *Relating Police and Fire Department Salaries* (Chicago: Public Personnel Association, 1966), p. 10.

Selected Readings

Angel, John E., "Toward An Alternative to the Classic Police Organizational Arrangements: A Democratic Model," *Criminology*, Vol. 9, Nos. 2 and 3, August-November 1971, pp. 185-206.

The democratic model presented by the author is an attempt to develop a flexible, participatory, science-based structure that will accommodate change. It is designed for effectiveness in serving the needs of citizens.

Bittner, Egon, *The Functions of the Police in Modern Society* (Washington, D.C.: National Institute of Mental Health, 1970).

This document analyzes the basic character of police work and relates it to the community with which it is intricately involved. The analysis includes cultural and historical factors that influence police functions.

Brown, A. J., "The Changing Theories, Practices, and Role of the Police," *The Police Chief*, Vol. XLIII, No. 3, March 1976, pp. 20-24.

This article reviews some of the changes in our society and reviews modern methods of fostering social order. Presents guide posts for the future role of the police.

Cullinane, Maurice J., "The Police Patrol Officer: The Backbone of the Law Enforcement Effort," *The Police Chief*, Vol. XL, No. 9, September 1973, pp. 37-39.

A discussion of the patrol officer in terms of who he is, what his responsibilities are, and how he accomplishes the police mission.

Farmer, David J., "The Future of Local Law Enforcement in the United States," The Federal Role, *Police Studies*, Vol. 1, No. 2, June 1978, pp. 31-38.

The author examines the prospective role of the federal (or state) government in the crime control process from a new viewpoint—the future of law enforcement.

Germann, A. C., "What is the Developing Mission and Role of the American Police?" *Journal of California Law Enforcement*, Vol. 4, No. 4, 1970, pp. 184-189.

The author contends that he does not expect much development of the police mission and role unless the police are aware of the social dynamics of the contemporary scene and the need for massive administrative changes.

Meyer, John C., "Policing the Future," *The Police Chief*, Vol. XXXVIII, No. 7, July 1971, pp. 14-17.

This article extends Toffler's thesis of "future shock to the police field." The following four aspects of the thesis considered are acceleration, transience, novelty, and diversity. The police are perceived as being on the cutting edge of society with reference to change.

Murphy, Patrick V., "Social Change and the Police," *Police*, Vol. 16, No. 7, March 1972, pp. 63-66.

The author contends that our society has changed immensely in a relatively short period of time, and will change even more in the foreseeable future. The police must move boldly into the mainstream of the tide of change.

Roberg, Roy R., *The Changing Police Role: New Dimensions and New Issues* (San Jose, California: Justice Systems Development, Inc., 1976).

This volume stresses the total role concept of the police. The functions of policing are analyzed in accord with community standards and goals. Considers personnel and organizational implications of the changing role.

Rosenbluh, Edwards S., William A. Reichart, and C. J. Hyde: "Is the Policeman Obsolete?" *The Police Chief*, Vol. XXXIX, No. 5, May 1972, pp. 68-70.

The authors contrast the "neanderthal" and the professional with a role examination of the police officer in contemporary American society.

Schrag, Clarence, *Crime and Justice American Style* (Washington, D.C.: National Institute of Mental Health, 1971).

The author discusses the police as visible symbols of the establishment in terms of crime control. He points out the proliferation of agencies, the prospects for the consolidation of small agencies, and the contradictory models of law enforcement.

Shah, Saleem A., "Some New Ways of Thinking About the Police Role," *The Police Yearbook—1973* (Gaithersburg, Maryland, 1973), pp. 109-115.

The author cites a number of ways in which social scientists and scholars have contributed in recent years to a new understanding of the police role.

Ward, Richard A., "The Police Role: A Case of Diversity," *Journal of Criminal Law, Criminology and Police Science*, Vol. 61, No. 4, December 1970, pp. 142-151.

The author reviews various perspectives on the police role, pointing out that within a societal myriad the policeman functions with an ill-defined role that is open to broad speculation. He proposes a skeletal model for comparing positions and roles along a number of dimensions.

Webster, John A., *The Realities of Police Work* (Dubuque, Iowa: Kendall/Hunt Publishing Company, 1973).

The author presents an analysis and a statistical accounting of all the events to which policemen of a patrol division were dispatched during a 54 week period. The data indicates that the reality of a policeman's role bears little resemblance to the image projected.

Chapter 2
POLICE DISCRETION

Introduction

Enforcement of the law in a dynamic and complex society poses numerous problems to all elements of the criminal justice system, the focal point being the police, especially the officer on the beat. The behavioral, political, and social implications of individual police actions during an arrest are so broad that they defy clear-cut definition and analysis.

The human dynamics involved in an arrest introduce into the criminal justice process a multitude of variables that directly and indirectly affects the stated objectives or roles of law enforcement agencies. Taking an individual suspected of criminal behavior into custody generally occurs in an emotionally charged atmosphere. Because the psychological set of the suspect, victim, witnesses, relatives, observers, and the police officer interjects such a great number of variables, police administrators have allowed officers to establish their individual enforcement standards based upon experience. And as anyone who is familiar with police bureaucracy knows, there has been and continues to be a substantial margin for interpretation of the law in particular situations. The obvious consequence, in the judgment of some, has been selective justice without established standards.

Some police officials have suggested that the courts, in their attempt to minimize discretionary decision making on the part of the police, have actually "handcuffed" the police. Their general attitude has been that law enforcers need greater discretionary power; this can only be construed as an encouragement for individual officers to enforce the law according to their personal standards. Police administrators who suggest that discretionary decisions made during arrests are indispensable (considering the complicity of the situations) are endorsing the concept of selective justice. This stance affects not only all police line and staff activities, but has a patent effect on individuals suspected of criminal behavior. The person who is in conflict with the law and is aware of the broad discretionary judgments available to police officers is in a more manipulative position than if he were confronted with enforcement standards that provided no leeway in the police response.

It has been suggested that a requisite to begin a reversal of police discretionary justice is the formation of a new ambience requiring a modern rhetoric essentially directed to changing attitudes toward discretion, its application, its control, and its significance to the criminal justice system.

A major reason for the perpetuation of this unresolved issue is that the majority of police administrators has expressed a common ideological response that all laws are enforced.

> Continued adherence to the myth of full enforcement of the law results in the police exercising wide discretion without acknowledging that it occurs and without attempting to explain and re-evaluate systematically the criteria by which the discretion is exercised.[1]

---

1.   Wayne R. LaFave, *Arrest: the Decision to Take a Suspect into Custody* (Boston: Little, Brown and Company, 1965), p. 391.

Until this frame of reference is altered, police administrators will not support studies that result in empirical knowledge about police procedures. This traditional reluctance will continue unless there is considerable pressure from judicial, legislative, or administrative levels of government.[2]

Numerous police chiefs become arbiters of the conflicting tasks of promoting aggressive police action while fulfilling legal requirements. In fact, the police become "actors" of what they perceive as the spirit of the law rather than the letter of the law. The development of definite policies would of course require the administrators to acknowledge that some of the police procedures do not conform to legalistic standards. By adopting a "do-nothing" approach, the chief of police avoids a direct confrontation with the issue and supports existing procedures.[3] It should also be kept in mind that many of the extra-legal sanctions practiced by the police have the support of the public. This is particularly true of enforcement of sumptuary laws, although the continuation of such practices raises many civil rights issues.[4]

The disinclination of police executives to deal explicitly with critical enforcement policies is reflected in the prevalent attitude toward "tolerance limits" in the traffic field. The reluctance to publicize "tolerance limits" can be traced to:

1. "a concern that the administrative action which they reflect would be criticized as a perversion of legislative intent—a concern which gives rise to the basic issue of the propriety of police policymaking;
2. a fear that publication would lead to a public debate as to what constitutes an appropriate tolerance and would lead to arguments between the officer and the offender in a given case—a concern which relates to the willingness of police to be held publicly accountable for the policy decisions which they make;
3. a concern that the existence of such a document might be used as a basis for litigation in those situations in which an officer chooses to

---

2. For extended discussions of this problem see Herman Goldstein, "Police Discretion: The Ideal Versus the Real," *Public Administration Review*, Vol. 23, No. 3, September 1963, pp. 140-148 and Frank J. Remington, "The Role of Police in a Democratic Society," *The Journal of Criminal Law, Criminology and Police Science*, Vol. 56, September 1965, pp. 361-365.

3. The President's Commission on Law Enforcement and Administration of Justice, *Task Force Report: The Police* (Washington: U.S. Government Printing Office, 1967), p. 17.

4. See Paul G. Chevigny, "The Right to Resist an Unlawful Arrest," *The Yale Law Journal*, Vol. 78, No. 7, June 1969, pp. 1128-1150 and Charles A. Reich, "Police Questioning of Law Abiding Citizens," *The Yale Law Journal*, Vol. 75, No. 7, June 1966, pp. 1161-1172.

enforce the law and be free to deviate from their own policy in an individual case without having to justify such deviation;

4. a fear that widespread awareness of the existence of such tolerances would result in drivers adjusting their behavior, utilizing the established tolerances rather than the posted and published laws as their guides."[5]

While there are some areas where discretion is limited (such as the handling of juveniles), the majority of law enforcement functions remains outside the purview of carefully defined policies.

There is an increasing demand for greater conformity in the application of criminal law at the arrest stage. If the police are to maintain their proper position in the criminal justice system they must assume a position of leadership in this administrative, policy-making function. Should the police not assume this position, they will certainly become unequal partners within the system. During the last decade there has been a noticeable extension of judicial review through numerous court decisions such as *Mapp* and *Miranda*.[6] A similar extension in the 1980s will certainly restrict, if not eliminate, the police as potential policy makers.

Kenneth Culp Davis is a proponent of administrative rule-making for the police who expresses the opinion that they are one of the most important policy-making agencies in government. The procedures to be followed would be those advocated by the Federal Administrative Procedures Act, 5 U.S.C. §553. Such a program would be implemented by law enforcement agencies publishing proposed rules and requesting written opinions from interested parties. The agency staff then evaluates the proposals and develops a written policy. In the opinion of Davis, this procedure would help to eliminate unnecessary discretionary power and insure equal justice.[7]

An outstanding example of possible accomplishments in the area of policy-making for the police can be seen in the guidelines regarding the "stop and frisk" law, adopted by the New York State Combined Council of Law Enforcement Officials.

Under the "stop and frisk" law the policy statement listed the following factors to be considered in determining whether or not there is "reasonable suspicion" to stop someone:

---

5. The President's Commission on Law Enforcement and Administration of Justice.

6. For early indications of this trend see Richard C. Donnelly, "Police Authority and Practices," *The Annals*, Vol. 339, January 1962, pp. 90-110 and Sanford H. Kadish, "Legal Norms and Discretion in the Police and Sentencing Process," *Harvard Law Review*, Vol. 75, No. 5, March 1962, pp. 904-931.

7. Kenneth C. Davis, *Discretionary Justice* (Baton Rouge: Louisiana State University Press, 1969), pp. 80-96.

1. The demeanor of the suspect.
2. The gait and manner of the suspect.
3. Any knowledge the officer may have of the suspect's background or character.
4. Whether the suspect is carrying anything, and what he is carrying.
5. The manner in which the suspect is dressed, including bulges in clothing—when considered in light of all of the other factors.
6. The time of the day or night the suspect is observed.
7. Any overheard conversation of the suspect.
8. The particular streets and areas involved.
9. Any information received from third persons, whether they are known or unknown.
10. Whether the suspect is consorting with others whose conduct is "reasonably suspect."

(This listing is not meant to be all inclusive).[8]

Policy statements of this nature serve as guidelines for line officers and clearly limit police discretionary powers, while at the same time they allow the policeman a necessary degree of freedom when enforcing the law.

*

Consistent with the policies of local government, the police chief should develop policy to guide employees. Where the chief is silent, the next lower person in the hierarchy may develop his policy. Where there is no policy established by higher authority, the field policeman may develop his own policy, which may not be consistent with that desired by the governing body or police chief executive.

Many chiefs have intentionally avoided establishing written policy in such sensitive areas as the use of force, particularly the use of weapons, because they fear criticism of the policy and other repercussions that could follow employee actions within the scope of the policy. However, employee actions are less apt to have adverse consequences if employees are guided by sound written policy.

With reference to the establishment of policy, the National Advisory Commission on Criminal Justice Standards and Goals suggested that every chief of police should immediately establish written policies in those areas of operations in which guidance is needed to direct agency employees toward the attainment of agency goals and objectives. The chief should promulgate a policy that provides clear direction without necessarily limiting the employee's exercise of discretion, and special em-

---

8. The President's Commission on Law Enforcement and Administration of Justice, p. 39.

phasis should be given to sensitive areas such as use of force, and the use of lethal and nonlethal weapons.[9]

The establishment of clear-cut policies that are reviewed periodically presents a challenge to law enforcement administrators which must be met if the police are to adequately serve the public, and protect life and property.

The following articles discuss the nature of police discretion, the problems of controlling discretion, and means of implementing guidelines.

---

9. National Advisory Commission on Criminal Justice Standards and Goals: *Police* (Washington: U.S. Government Printing Office, January 23, 1973), pp. 53-55.

4. POLICE POLICY FORMULATION: A PROPOSAL FOR IMPROVING POLICE PERFORMANCE

HERMAN GOLDSTEIN

Michigan Law Review, Vol. 65, April 1967. Reprinted by permission.

The police function in this country is much more varied and much more complex than is generally recognized. This is particularly true today in the congested areas of large urban centers where the demand for police services is especially great and where the police are confronted with an increasing variety of difficult situations, many of which stem from dissatisfaction with the economic and social conditions existing in such areas. As law enforcement has become more difficult, it has, for the same reasons, taken on new importance as a function of local government.

Contributing to the major current concern regarding law enforcement is the growing awareness of the fact that the police are simply not equipped to respond adequately to the increasing demands being made upon them. This should not come as a surprise to anyone. Law enforcement agencies, over the years, have never been provided with the kind of resources, personnel, education, and leadership which their responsibilities have required.[1]

Substantial progress has been made in recent years, especially when compared with the rate of improvement in the past, but such progress has occurred in an uneven manner and its effect has frequently been diminished by backsliding. Within this period, standards and goals have been significantly increased, but they remain modest when related to the magnitude and complexity of existing problems.

Recent improvements have centered upon providing the police with better equipment, more personnel, higher compensation, increased training, and improved management techniques. All of these measures are badly needed and each contributes to raising police efficiency. But it is

---

1. Among the most significant works spanning the past half century that document the absence of adequate resources in law enforcement are: Fosdick, *American Police Systems* (1920); Fuld, *Police Administration* (1910); National Commission on Law Observance and Enforcement, *Report on Police*, No. 14 (1931); Smith, *Police Systems in the United States*, 2d ed. (1960).

becoming increasingly apparent that operating efficiency alone is not enough.

Future progress toward fulfilling the law enforcement function is likely to depend primarily upon the degree to which the police and others effectively respond to the numerous problems involved in employing our legal system to deal with the infinite variety of behavioral situations which confront the police. Many of these situations are obviously beyond the control of the police. Their improvement depends upon the correction of existing social and economic conditions, increased effort on the part of community welfare agencies, and changes in the law, in court procedures, and in the functioning and orientation of correctional agencies. Nevertheless, there remain many problems that are within the capacity of the police themselves to resolve.

The issues that are involved in these aspects of the law enforcement problem with which the police themselves can deal are much more difficult to resolve than those that are raised in the attempt to increase operating efficiency. They relate, for the most part, to the highly sensitive and delicate function of exercising police authority. Their solution, difficult as it may be, is essential if the police are to achieve a system of law enforcement that is not only efficient, but also fair and effective. The degree to which the police succeed in meeting these latter objectives will determine, in the long run, the strength of the law enforcement function in our democratic society.

The Nature of the Police Function

The most acute problems confronting the police do not receive the kind of attention that they deserve from persons outside police agencies because of a common lack of understanding of the true nature of the police task. Police officers are daily engaged in handling a wide variety of complex situations, but the nature of such situations is rarely communicated to those outside the police establishment. If the police were to analyze their workload in a systematic manner and to make public the results of their findings, it is likely that several of the most widespread notions regarding the police function would be dispelled.

One common assumption is that the police are primarily engaged in activities relating to the prevention of serious crime and the apprehension and prosecution of criminals. Actually, only a small percentage of the time which an average police officer spends on duty is directly related to the handling of serious offenses. This is especially true in small jurisdictions where few crimes occur. But it is equally true in the most congested areas of our large cities where high crime rates are experienced; for, even in such areas, a police officer, during a typical tour of duty, is occupied with a variety of tasks that are unrelated to the crime problem: assisting the aged and the mentally ill; locating missing persons; providing emergency medical services; mediating disputes between husbands and wives, landlords and tenants, or merchants and their customers; caring for neglected children; providing information about various governmental services and processes; regulating traffic; investigating accidents; and protecting the rights of individuals to live where they want to live and say what they want to say.[2]

Another popular misconception is that the police are a ministerial agency, having no discretion in the exercise of their authority. While this view is occasionally reinforced by a court decision,[3] there is a growing body of literature that cites the degree to which the police are, in fact, required to exercise discretion—such as in deciding which laws to enforce, in selecting from among available techniques for investigating crime, in deciding whom to arrest, and in determining how to process a criminal offender.[4] Broad and oftentimes ambiguous statutes defining their power and the limited resources made available to them are the major factors among several that require the police to assume such a discretionary role.

A third widespread notion regarding the police function is that the primary authority available to and used by the police is that of invoking the criminal process—that is, arresting a person for the purpose of prosecuting him for having committed a crime. However, for every time that a police officer arrests a person, he also disposes of scores of incidents by employing a lesser form of authority, such as ordering people to "move

---

2. While it is rare for police agencies to articulate this range of functions, it is even rarer for them to respond directly to such functions in a structured manner. For an interesting example of the latter, see Winston-Salem, N.C. Police Department, *A New Approach to Crime Prevention and Community Service* (mimeo., 1966).

3. See, for example, *Bargain City, U.S.A., Inc. v. Dilworth*, 407 Pa. 129, 179 A.2d 439 (1960); *State v. Lombardi*, 8 Wis. 2d 421, 99 N.W.2d 829 (1959).

4. See, for example, Banton, *The Policeman in the Community*, 131-46 (1964); LaFave, *Arrest*, 61-161, 490-527 (1965); Skolnick, *Justice Without Trial*, 71-88 (1966); Abernathy, "Police Discretion and Equal Protection," 14 *S.C.L.O.* 472 (1962); Breitel, "Controls in Criminal Law Enforcement," 27 *U. Chi. L. Rev.* 427 (1960); H. Goldstein, "Police Discretion: The Ideal Versus the Real," 23 *Pub. Admin. Rev.* 140 (1963); J. Goldstein, "Police Discretion Not To Invoke the Criminal Process: Low Visibility Decisions in the Administration of Justice." 69 *Yale L. J.* 543 (1960); Kadish, "Legal Norm and Discretion in the Police and Sentencing Processes," 75 *Harv. L. Rev.* 904 (1962); LaFave, "The Police and Nonenforcement of the Law" (pts. 1-2), 1962 *Wis. L. Rev.* 104, 179; Remington, "The Role of Police in a Democratic Society," 56 *J. Crim. L.C. & P.S.* 361 (1965); Remington & Rosenblum, "The Criminal Law and the Legislative Process," 1960 *U. Ill. L.F.* 481.

on," turning children over to their parents, or separating combatants. Furthermore, when an officer does decide to make an arrest, it is not always with the intention of prosecuting the individual; rather it may be for the much more limited purpose of safeguarding the arrestee or controlling a given type of criminal activity, such as prostitution or gambling.[5]

Finally, it is widely believed that, in the investigation of criminal activity and especially in the identification of offenders, police officers depend primarily upon physical evidence that is subject to scientific analysis. Admittedly, collection and analysis of physical evidence does constitute an important facet of police work; in some cases, it holds the key to identification and is the factor upon which the value of all other evidence depends. But, in the vast majority of cases, the analysis of physical evidence, to the extent that there is any, is merely supportive of evidence acquired through some other means. Despite the major and often fascinating advances that have been made in the scientific detection of crime, primary dependence is still placed upon the work of detectives who, once a crime has been committed, set out in search of motives and bits and pieces of information from victims, witnesses, and various other persons who might have some knowledge that will contribute to the identification of the perpetrator of the crime. It is often a rather tedious and undramatic process that depends, for its success, upon the resourcefulness and perseverance of the investigating officers. Involved in the typical investigative effort are such important practices as the questioning of individuals, the search of private premises, the use of informants, and, in some cases, the employment of a variety of "undercover" techniques to acquire firsthand knowledge of criminal activity.

Absence of Adequate Guidelines

One of the consequences of recognizing the true nature of police activities is that one realizes there are vast areas of the police function which, in the absence of adequate legislative guidelines, are left to the discretion of individual officers. Moreover, even when existing laws are clearly applicable, the police are often required to select from among the various alternative forms of action which exist within the outer limits of the authority prescribed by such laws.

There have been some isolated efforts on the part of the police to fill this gap by providing more detailed guidance for the day-to-day work of their personnel. Such efforts have related primarily to traffic enforcement

5. LaFave, "Arrest," pp. 437-89.

techniques and the handling of juvenile offenders.[6] The overall picture, however, reflects a reluctance on the part of police administrators to establish policies to fill the existing void. This reluctance is in sharp contrast to the strong tradition within police agencies for promulgating a variety of standard operating procedures to govern the internal management of the police force. The difference in attitude appears to be attributable largely to the real doubts possessed by the police as to the propriety of their assuming a policy-making role that so closely parallels the legislative function.[7]

Confronted each day by frequently recurring situations for which no guidance is provided, the individual officer either develops his own informal criteria for disposing of matters which come to his attention—a kind of pattern of improvisation—or employs informal criteria which have, over a period of years, developed within the agency of which he is a part. While such criteria are neither articulated nor officially recognized, they tend to take on some of the characteristics of officially promulgated policies. Functioning in this manner and employing their own imagination and resourcefulness, individual police officers often succeed to an amazing degree in muddling their way through: disputes are resolved; dangerous persons are disarmed; people not in control of their capacities are protected; and many individuals are spared what, under some circumstances, would appear to be the undue harshness of the criminal process. Unfortunately, the results are often less satisfactory, primarily because the criteria that are employed emerge largely in response to a variety of pressures to which the police are exposed and are therefore not carefully developed. For example, the high volume of work which an officer must handle dictates a desire to take shortcuts in the processing of minor incidents. The personal conveniences of an officer—in making a court appearance, completing reports, or working beyond a scheduled tour of duty—become important determinants of how a case is handled. The desire to solve crime becomes a dominant consideration.[8] And such

---

6. In the area of traffic enforcement, a number of jurisdictions have developed "tolerance policies" which establish the point above the speed limit at which officers are to warn a motorist or issue a summons to him. Some also provide criteria for making similar decisions with regard to other types of motor vehicle violations. Such policies are most frequently promulgated by state police organizations, and they demonstrate that a need is felt for providing guidelines for the isolated officer who cannot frequently consult with his supervisor or fellow officers. They also reflect a desire on the part of administrators to achieve uniformity in the overall operations of the agency.

7. For a more detailed discussion of this point, see President's Commission on Law Enforcement and Administration of Justice, *Task Force Report: The Police*, Ch. 2 (1967).

8. This factor is explored in some detail in Skolnick, *Justice Without Trial*, pp. 164-81 (1966).

indefensible criteria as the status or characteristics of the complainant, the victim, or the offender may often be among the most seriously weighed factors, since an officer, left to function on his own, understandably tends to respond to a given situation on the basis of his personal norms regarding individual or group behavior.

Continuation of current practices, which can perhaps best be characterized as a process of "drift," is clearly not in the interest of effective law enforcement. The potential for arbitrariness inherent in an uncontrolled exercise of discretion is clearly inconsistent with the objective of fairness that constitutes so basic an element in the exercise of any form of governmental power. Nor are current practices desirable from the police standpoint; in the absence of guidelines, police officials are continually vulnerable to criticism for the manner in which an officer chooses to exercise his discretion. They are "damned if they do and damned if they don't." Police administrators, moreover, are without an effective means for controlling the behavior of individual officers. Thus, since effective restraints are lacking, incidents tend to arise that prompt legislatures and courts to step in and take actions which often have repercussions—in the form of curtailment of police powers—far beyond the specific situation that initially served to arouse their interests.

There is an obvious need for some procedure by which an individual police officer can be provided with more detailed guidance to help him decide upon the action he ought to take in dealing with the wide range of situations which he confronts and in exercising the broad authority with which he is invested. Viewed in somewhat different terms, the challenge is to devise procedures which will result in police officers employing norms acceptable to society, rather than their personal norms, in their exercise of discretion.

Alternative Solutions

There is no single way in which the existing policy vacuum can be filled, nor is it likely or desirable that it can be filled in its entirety.[9] But the width of the existing gap—especially as one views the functioning of the police in our large urban centers—affords ample opportunity for reducing its size.

The police are accustomed to looking toward the legislature and the courts for their guidance. There has, in recent years, been a special focus upon the latter since the appellate courts have undertaken to establish,

---

9. Banton observes that the only long-term solution to the problem of police discretion is for the police and the public to share the same norms of propriety. Banton, *The Police and the Community*, p. 146 (1966).

with increasing specificity, the rules of constitutional, procedural due process.[10] Such judicial activity, especially that of the Supreme Court, has been viewed by one commentator as an action of "desperation," taken because of default on the part of others to fill the existing vacuum.[11] It has been argued that the Court, in taking on this rule-making function, has assumed an uncomfortable role which it is not equipped to fulfill and which constitutes, at best, an awkward and somewhat ineffective process for hammering out detailed rules of criminal procedure.[12] Among the major liabilities which are cited with respect to this approach are the breadth and especially the rigidity of the Court's holdings. In addition, in evaluating the courts as a source of guidance, it must be recognized that many of the most important and perplexing problems encountered by the police never become the subject of court proceedings.

Traditionally, both federal and state legislatures have restricted themselves to providing the police with a minimum set of broadly stated guidelines covering the major elements in criminal procedure.[13] They are often cited as the logical branch of government to remedy the need for additional guidelines since they have the capacity to explore problems on their own initiative, to gather facts, to elicit public opinion, and to act in a manner which is subject to later adjustment.[14] The recent proposal of the American Law Institute, embodied in its Model Code of Pre-Arraignment Procedure, represented an effort to move in this direction, incorporating, as it did, detailed legislative guidelines for police activity during the period from investigation and arrest to the time the suspect is presentenced in court.[15] In at least one major area covered by the Model Code, however, the opportunity for careful legislative consideration has since been significantly restricted by the Supreme Court's action in *Miranda v. Arizona.*

Even if legislatures become active in spelling out guidelines for the police, it must be recognized that there are now, and presumably always will be, many areas—particularly as one gets closer to the day-to-day

---

10. The most specific rules are found in *Miranda v. Arizona,* 384 U.S. 436 (1966).

11. Packer, "Policing the Police: Nine Men Are Not Enough," *New Republic,* September 4, 1965, p. 19.

12. Ibid., p. 18. See also Friendly, "The Bill of Rights as a Code of Criminal Procedure," 53 *Calif. L. Rev.* 929 (1965); Packer, "Who Can Police the Police?" *The N.Y. Rev. of Books,* September 8, 1966, p. 10.

13. See LaFave, "Improving Police Performance Through the Exclusionary Rule—Part II: Defining the Norms and Training the Police," 30 *Mo. L. Rev.* 566, 568-79 (1965); Remington & Rosenblum, "The Criminal Law and the Legislative Process," 1960 *U. Ill. L.F.* 481.

14. See Packer, "Policing the Police," pp. 20-21.

15. Ali, "A Model Code of Pre-Arraignment Procedure," (Tent. Draft No. 1, 1966).

problems encountered by the police—in which it is neither feasible nor desirable for the legislature to prescribe specific police practices. Variations in the size of police jurisdictions within a state, changing social conditions, and variations in the nature of the police function, among other factors, require that there be room for administrative flexibility. It seems apparent that the infinite variety of complex situations which confront the police today makes it essential that the most detailed and specific policies for handling them be formulated at the level closest to that at which they arise.

In light of the above considerations, it seems reasonable that, within legislative boundaries that may in some areas be more detailed than those which now exist, the police themselves be given the responsibility for formulating policies which will serve as guidelines in their effort to achieve effectiveness and fairness in their day-to-day operations, and that there be an explicit recognition by the legislatures of the necessity and desirability of the police operating as an administrative policy-making agency of government. Obviously, such police-made policies would be subject to challenge if they were not consistent with the general legislative purpose or with such legislative criteria as are provided to guide and control the exercise of administrative discretion. Subject to appropriate review and control, the exercise of administrative discretion in this manner is likely to be more protective of basic rights than the routine, uncritical application by police of laws which are often necessarily vague or overgeneralized in their language.

Police participation in the development of policies to fill the existing vacuum and to cope with rapidly changing social and behavioral conditions would be a valuable contribution to the operation of police agencies, to the professionalization of the police, and to the overall functioning of the criminal justice system. Some of the specific advantages are set forth in detail below.

The Maintenance of Administrative Flexibility

The police have always had a great deal of flexibility in their operations, but this has been primarily as a result of legislative default rather than of deliberate, overt legislative choice. The traditional legislative response with respect to difficult issues like the control of gambling activities or the stopping and questioning of suspects has been either to deal with them by means of an overly generalized statute, as is true with respect to gambling activities, or not to deal with them at all, which has been true, at least until recently, with respect to stopping and questioning suspects. The practical consequence has been to leave police with broad flexibility, but the delegation of responsibility has been implicit at best and police have not taken it as a mandate to develop and articulate proper enforcement policies. The action of appellate courts in setting down increasingly specific rules to govern police conduct is partly a result of this failure. This trend toward judge-made rules is inspired in large part by a prevalent assumption that police are unwilling or unable to develop proper policies and to conform their practices to such policies. The police, by assuming responsibility for the development of appropriate administrative policies, will have the opportunity to reverse the trend and, as a consequence, to preserve the flexibility which they need if they are to meet adequately the wide range of problems which they confront under constantly changing conditions.

A Sound Basis for the Exercise of Discretion

The formulation of administrative policies affords the police an opportunity to establish sound grounds for the exercise of their discretion. Careful analysis of existing practices, which is a necessary step in the formulation of policies, should result in the exposure and rejection of those considerations which, according to standards of fairness and effectiveness, are inappropriate. Development of defensible criteria would, in addition, afford an opportunity to incorporate into police decision-making considerations that are based upon existing knowledge regarding the various forms of behavior with which the police are concerned. In the long run, the exercise of discretion in accordance with defensible criteria would create greater confidence in the police establishment. More immediately, it would lead to a reduction in the number of arbitrary actions taken by individual officers, thereby substantially reducing the tensions which such actions often create—particularly in areas in which minority groups are affected.

Acknowledgment of the "Risk Factor" Involved in Policing

Numerous factors contribute to the defensive posture commonly assumed by the police. Among them is an awareness on their part that members of the public will often question their exercise of discretion in a case in which subsequent developments focus attention upon an officer's decision. For example, a police officer may locate one under-age youth in a group of young people engaged in a drinking party. The fact that the youth is only one month under age may prompt the officer to release him with a warning. However, if the youth subsequently becomes involved in a serious accident, the fact that he was released earlier in the evening will often result in the officer's being castigated by his superior, because the officer has no publicly-acknowledged right to exercise discretion although all agree that it is both necessary and desirable that he do so.

Given the wide range of responsibilities that the police have, they cannot be held to a system of decision-making which involves no risk-taking—any more than could psychiatrists in deciding whether to release a person who has attempted suicide or parole board members in voting upon the release of an inmate. The formulation of policy and its articulation to the public would, over a period of time, begin to educate the public to recognize that the police must not only exercise discretion, but must also assume a risk in doing so. Prior statements of policy which "put the community on notice" with regard to police functioning in various areas would afford some relief from the current dilemma in which, in the absence of such policy formulations, the police are subject to both ridicule for not exercising discretion and condemnation for making discretionary judgments when they do not work out.

A Means for Utilizing Police Expertise

Many actions which the police officer takes are based upon the knowledge and experience he has accumulated in his years of service. In concluding that a crime is being committed, an officer may reach a judgment quite different from that which would be reached by an inexperienced layman or even an experienced trial judge, since the officer may have, for example, the ability to recognize the smell of narcotics or the sound of a press used in printing illegal numbers or policy tickets. There has, however, been little effort made to capitalize upon police experience. In order to do so, the police would necessarily have to attempt to assess its reliability; they would have to distinguish accurate inferences (such as, the sound is that of a gambler's printing press) from inaccurate or improper ones (such as, Negroes are immoral). It would also be necessary for the police to systemize their experience so that it can be effectively communicated to new officers through training programs and to others, like judges, when the propriety of police actions is challenged. To the extent that operating criteria reflect police experience, the police are afforded a vehicle in the policy-making process for articulating their expertise.

More Effective Administrative Control Over Police Behavior

While the actions of an individual officer may appear on the surface to be improper, there is often no basis on which his superior can take disciplinary action against him, since his conduct violates neither the law nor any existing departmental policies. In such a situation, the police administrator is caught in a conflict between his desire to be responsive to a citizen who has reason to complain about a policeman's behavior and his fear concerning the reaction of his force to seemingly arbitrary discipline where there is no clear breach of a pre-announced standard of proper conduct.

The reluctance to characterize an officer's conduct as unwise is increased when the administrator feels that to do so will result in either the officer or the municipality being sued for damages. Consideration of this possibility may force the administrator into the position of defending a given action as legal, and thus seemingly "proper," even though it reflected poor judgment on the part of the officer. To minimize the likelihood of similar situations arising in the future, the administrator may urge his subordinates to use "common sense," but such a request is of little value unless he is prepared to spell out precisely what is meant by "common sense."

The promulgation of policies to which police officers are required by regulation to adhere would provide a basis for disciplining those who violate such policies. But, more important, it would serve in a positive way to inform members of a force what is expected of them. Progress in elevating the quality of law enforcement is much more likely to be realized if one views clear and defensible standards as a basis for eliciting a proper response from police officers, rather than considering such standards primarily as the basis for the taking of disciplinary actions against police officers.

The Improvement of Recruit and In-Service Training Programs

Recruit training in police agencies is frequently inadequate because the instruction bears little relationship to what is expected of the officer when he goes to work in the field. In the absence of guidelines that relate to an analysis of police experience, the instructor usually is left with only the formal definition of police authority to communicate to the trainee, and this is often transmitted to the student merely by reading statutory definitions to him. Students are taught that all laws are to be fully enforced. The exercise of police authority is similarly taught in doctrinaire fashion. With this kind of formal training, the new officer finds, upon his assignment to the field, that he has to acquire from the more experienced officers with whom he is initally assigned a knowledge of all the patterns of accommodations and modifications. As he becomes aware of the impracticality and lack of realism of much of what he learned as a student, he unfortunately begins to question the validity of all aspects of his formal training.

Obviously, there is a need for training more directly related to the important problems which the officer will face in the field—training which will not only instruct him on the limits of his formal authority, but also inform him of the department's judgment as to what is the most desirable administrative practice to follow in exercising his authority. Carefully developed administrative policies would serve this important function.

A Basis for the Professionalization of the Police

It is now commonplace to refer to practically any effort that is aimed at improving law enforcement as a contribution to the professionalization of the police. Thus, improved training, application of the computer to police work, adoption of a code of ethics, and increased salaries have all, at one time or another, been cited as contributing to police professionalization.

Certainly, there is much that police do today that would not, under any definition of the term, be viewed as constituting professional work. Directing traffic at a street intersection or enforcing parking restrictions requires stamina, but little knowledge. In sharp contrast to these functions, however, are the responsibilities of a patrolman assigned to police a congested area in which numerous crimes occur; he is called upon to make highly sophisticated judgments having a major impact upon the lives of the individuals involved. Such judgments are not mechanical in nature, but rather are every bit as complicated and difficult to make as are the decisions made by any of the behavioral scientists, and in many instances they are more difficult because they must be made under the pressure of the immediate circumstances.

Development of criteria for dealing with such complex social and behavioral problems will require extensive research, the systematizing of experience and knowledge, and continual testing of the validity of the assumptions and findings upon which the criteria are based. The formulation of such criteria will also require adherence to values relating to the role of the police and law enforcement in a democratic society that are more basic than those values which are involved in a consideration of technical operating efficiency. The making of judgments based upon criteria that are formulated pursuant to extensive experience, research, and experimentation together with a commitment to values that reflect a sense of responsibility to society constitute important elements in the development of a true profession.

A Method for Involving the Police in the Improvement of the System of which They are a Part

Decisions relating to the enforcement function have traditionally been made for the police by persons outside the police establishment. The police have typically not even been consulted when changes have been contemplated in the substantive or procedural criminal law, despite the fact they clearly have more experience than anyone else in dealing with some of the basic issues. Failure to involve the police in most revision projects is probably due to the fact that police personnel are not considered qualified to deal with the complicated questions involved. But, if it is true that police lack the necessary skill to participate in such efforts, this lack of ability is in large measure attributable to the fact that in the past they have not been involved in the making of important decisions.

There is, today, a strong commitment to the involvement of disadvantaged groups, like the poor and the young, in decisions about their roles in society. This commitment is based on the belief that they will respond most affirmatively if they have a feeling of participation in such decisions. The same need is apparent with respect to the police, for, in this sense at least, they also are a disadvantaged group. Law enforcement personnel are more likely to want to conform and are more likely to develop an ability to conform if they are made a part of the process for making important decisions affecting their function.

Practically every aspect of police functioning gives rise to important and sensitive issues of a kind which can and should be dealt with through the careful and systematic development of policies by a law enforcement agency. The following are merely illustrative of the types of functions that are in need of attention, the difficult issues to which they give rise, and the importance of facing up to them.

The Decision Whether To Invoke the Criminal Process

Whether a criminal prosecution is initiated against an individual depends, in most instances, upon police judgment. Theoretically, this judgment is based upon the statutory definition of the crime, although it is abundantly clear that there are many situations in which a violation has in fact occurred and is known to the police, but in which there is no effort by the police to make an arrest. Among the factors accounting for this discretionary decision not to invoke the criminal process are the volume of violations of a similar nature, the limited resources of the police, the overgeneralization of legislative enactments defining criminal conduct, and the various local pressures reflecting community values and attitudes.

The social gambling situation affords a good example of the dilemma which the police face. In most jurisdictions, all forms of gambling are illegal. Yet it is apparent that legislatures neither intend nor expect that such statutes be fully enforced. The consequence is that local police are left with the responsibility for developing an enforcement policy for their particular community. The policy of a department may, for example, be clear, albeit unwritten, that games of chance at church carnivals will be permitted because of their charitable nature.[16] However, in the same community, the police response to gambling in a private home may vary with the circumstances of the individual case. Whether the police take enforcement action may depend on the answers they obtain to several key questions: is there a complainant and, if so, is he adversely affected by the gambling activity; is the gambling the prime purpose for the group's getting together or is it incidental to some other activity or pastime; is the activity organized; do the participants know each other; were they steered to the location for purposes of engaging in gambling or is the assemblage a get-together of old friends; what is the amount of money involved; and is there a profit separate from winnings being realized by the individual hosting the activity or by any of the individuals present. The existence of any one of these factors will not necessarily result in an arrest, but the police usually will take action when there is an insistent complainant or when a combination of factors suggests that the gambling activity is commercial in nature. The difficulty is that the employment of such criteria by individual officers may lead to disparity in practice and, even where practice is consistent, may involve basic policy questions which are not raised and thus not considered or resolved. Complaints may originate from neighbors who are disturbed by the noise or from wives who are either concerned over the monetary losses of their spouses or resent their absence from home. Should a police agency allow itself to be "used" under such conditions? Does the fact that enforcement takes place only when there is an insistent complainant constitute a desirable pattern of action?

The tests used in practice to determine whether the game is "commercial" rather than "social" also raise important policy questions which have not been resolved. Social gambling in a slum area assumes a different form than does social gambling in a middle-class neighborhood: a number of men commonly get together in a private apartment, placing comparatively small bets on a dice game. Such activity is endemic to such an area. When the police investigate such games they typically find that the participants cannot identify each other. The gambling is therefore viewed as not being "social" and thus is considered properly subject to enforcement. Yet, considering the pattern of life in such an area, is there any reason to characterize this behavior as more reprehensible than that engaged in by a group of men involved in a poker game for some financial stakes at a local country club? Pursuant to present practices, the participants in the dice game will generally be arrested, searched,

---

16. For an interesting case study growing out of an unarticulated policy of nonenforcement against bingo in churches and synagogues, see Logue & Bock, *The Demotion of Deputy Chief Inspector Goldberg* (Inter-University Case Program, No. 78) (1963).

transported to a lock-up, detained overnight, and brought before a judge the following morning. The net effect of such actions for the police seems obvious: relationships with the residents of the area, which typically are already very strained, are further aggravated.

The police action with regard to the dice game in the slum area is often in response to complaints from neighbors who are disturbed by the game. It may also be a response to the general police concern, based on prior experiences, that dice games in such areas frequently end in fights, which in turn sometimes result in homicides. Intervention by the police therefore is viewed as serving a crime prevention function. But neither the attitude of the community nor the relationship of the dice game to more serious crime is studied and evaluated. As a consequence, the current police practice gives the appearance of being the product of improper class or racial discrimination.

The police treatment of aggravated assaults raises issues of a different character. This type of offense comes to police attention more routinely because it frequently occurs in public, the victim or witnesses seek out the police, there is a desire for police intervention before more harm is done, or simply because the victim desires police assistance in acquiring medical aid. Even though the perpetrator is known to the victim in a high percentage of these cases, however, there frequently is no arrest or, if an arrest is made, it may be followed by release without prosecution. This is especially true in the slum areas of large urban centers and is due primarily to an unwillingness on the part of the victim to cooperate in a prosecution.

If the parties involved are related or are close friends, the victim is frequently unwilling to establish the identity of the assailant, attend show-ups, view photographs, or even answer questions truthfully. If the victim does cooperate at the investigation stage, he may still refuse to testify at trial and may even express a desire that the assaulting relative or acquaintance be set free. Due to the frustrations police officers have experienced in handling such cases, they often take less than the expected degree of interest in pursuing a prosecution when there is any early indication of reluctance on the part of the victim to participate in the prosecution. In some jurisdictions, the accumulated police experience results in an early decision not to prosecute and, in some cases, not to arrest.

It would be possible for the police to prosecute more frequently those persons who commit assaults by resorting to the issuance of a subpoena to compel the attendance of the victim at trial, assuming the judge would be willing to compel the victim to testify. This procedure, however, is seldom used. Given the high volume of cases and the competing demands upon a police agency, the path of least resistance is to acquiesce in the desires of the victim. Such acquiescence is often rationalized on the ground that the injured party was the only person harmed and the community as a whole was not affected by the crime. These cases can be written off statistically as clearances—which are viewed as an index of police efficiency—and thus the most immediate administrative pressure is satisfied.

There is some question about the relationship between current police practice in slum assault cases on the one hand, and the amount of crime and the community's attitude toward police on the other. If the criminal justice process has some deterrent value, why would it not deter assaultive behavior in the slum area? To what degree does an awareness of the attitude of the police toward assaultive conduct result in the formulation of negative attitudes on the part of slum residents toward law and order in general? What is the impact upon the residents of such an area when an attack by a slum resident upon a person residing outside the area results in a vigorous prosecution?

Today, these and other basic policy questions which can be raised are not dealt with by the police. Routine practices are not examined in the light of overall enforcement goals and, as a consequence, may very well serve to complicate rather than solve important social problems. Were the police to review their current practices, they might well conclude that, insofar as assaults, for example, are concerned, it is desirable to base police decisions to arrest on such criteria as the nature of the assault, the seriousness of the injury, and the prior record of the assailant, rather than primarily on the degree to which the victim is willing to cooperate.

Selection of Investigative Methods

In the past few years, increasing attention has been given by legislatures and particularly by courts to the propriety of current police detection and investigation methods.[17] Nevertheless, there remain many areas in which the determination as to the investigative technique to be used is left to the police. For example, neither legislatures nor courts have yet reflected much concern with the propriety of police use of "undercover" or "infiltration" techniques, surveillance, or other methods which afford an alleged offender an opportunity to commit a crime in a manner which will make evidence of his offense available to the police. If the present trend toward judicial rule-making continues, it is not at all unlikely that current investigative practices thought by police to be proper and effective will be subject to increasingly specific rules. This has already occurred with respect to in-custody investigation, which is now specifically controlled by the *Miranda* decision. Whether this will occur with respect

---

17. The extent to which legislatures and courts have addressed themselves to three specific areas of police investigation—the conduct of searches, the use of "encouragement," and the stopping and questioning of suspects—is explored in McIntyre, Teffany & Rotenberg, *Detection of Crime*, 1967.

to other police practices will depend in large measure upon whether the police can develop policies which differentiate the proper from the improper use of particular investigative practices and can see to it that improper methods are not used as a matter of informal departmental policy or by individual officers out of either ignorance or excessive zeal.

Field interrogation is illustrative of important police investigative techniques which may or may not survive attack. Police have generally argued that their right to stop and question people is essential, especially with respect to those persons who are observed in an area in which a crime has just been committed. With several exceptions, however, there has been little effort made to provide individual officers with carefully developed guidelines so as to assure that such interrogation is sparingly and carefully employed under conditions that justify its use.

The use of field interrogation as an investigative technique is complicated by the fact that it is a part of the total preventive patrol program—which is a current response by police in large cities to the demand that the "streets be made safe." Preventive patrol often involves stopping persons using the streets in high-crime areas and making searches of both persons and vehicles. The purpose of this technique is not only to talk with individuals who may be suspected of having recently committed crimes but, more broadly, to find and confiscate dangerous weapons and to create an atmosphere of police omnipresence which will dissuade persons from attempting to commit crimes because of the likelihood of their being detected and apprehended.

It is probably true that a program of preventive patrol does reduce the amount of crime on the street, although there has been no careful effort to measure its effectiveness. It is also apparent, however, that some of the practices included in a preventive patrol program contribute to the antagonism toward the police felt by minority groups whose members are subjected to them. A basic issue, never dealt with explicitly by police, is whether, even from a purely law enforcement point of view, the gain in enforcement outweighs the cost of community alienation.

The continuation of field interrogation as a police investigative technique depends upon whether the police are willing to develop policies which carefully distinguish field interrogation from street practices which are clearly illegal and to take administrative steps to demonstrate that a proper field interrogation program can be carried out without it leading also to an indiscriminate stopping and searching of persons.

The Decision Not To Prosecute Individuals Who Have Been Arrested

While in some states it is the practice to take all arrested individuals before a judge, it is standard procedure in others for the police to release some individuals prior to their scheduled court appearance. Drunkards are often given their freedom once they are sober; juveniles are often released after consultation with parents or a social service agency; and in large urban areas, narcotic addicts and small-time peddlers are often released with a grant of immunity in exchange for information leading to the arrest of more serious violators.

Where it is the practice to release some drunkards without charging them, eligibility for release tends to be based upon such factors as appearance, dress, reputation, place of residence, and family ties. The process is generally intended to separate the common drunkard from the intoxicated person who "knows better" but, in the judgment of the police, simply had "one too many." Whether this kind of distinction adequately serves an enforcement or social welfare objective is not entirely clear. Certainly police, who are daily confronted with the problem of the drunkard, ought to give continuing attention to whether defensible criteria are being employed and, perhaps more important, ought to lend support to and participate in an effort to develop ways of dealing with the alcoholic which are more sensible than the current arrest and release programs.

Criteria have been formulated in some communities to assist police in deciding whether a juvenile offender should be released to his parents, referred to a social agency, or brought before the juvenile court.[18] In other communities, however, such decisions continue to be made by the police without an articulated basis and the decisions often reflect the use of such indefensible criteria as the color of the child, his attitude toward the police, or the status of his parents in the community.[19]

The practice of releasing some narcotic addicts and peddlers in exchange for information or cooperation raises other complex issues. Persons involved in narcotics control assume that the investigation of narcotics traffic requires the accumulation of knowledge from those who are involved in the distribution or use of such contraband and that convictions cannot be obtained without the help of informants who cooperate in return for immunity. The potential for abuse in pursuing this practice makes it critically important that the standards for extending an offer for immunity and for measuring cooperation be uniformly and fairly ap-

---

18. See, for example, Chicago Police Department, Youth Division, *Manual of Procedure* (1965).

19. See, for example, Piliavin & Briar, "Police Encounters With Juveniles," 70 *Am. J. Sociology* 206 (1964); Goldman & Nathan, *The Differential Selection of Juvenile Offenders for Court Appearance*, in National Research and Information Center, National Council on Crime and Delinquency (1963). For an overall view of the police function in the juvenile process, see Wheeler & Cottrell, *Juvenile Delinquency: Its Prevention and Control*, 28-31 (1966).

plied. There is, moreover, a need for continual evaluation of the practice to determine whether the gain derived from it really justifies the costs which are involved.

The Issuance of Orders to Individuals Regarding Their Movements, Activities, and Whereabouts

The public, whether as pedestrians or motorists, generally recognizes the authority of the police to direct their movements in traffic. There are many other situations, however, in which police regularly tell people what to do under circumstances where police authority is less clear. For example, police order people to "keep the noise down" or to stop quarreling—usually in response to a complaint from a neighbor; direct a husband to stay away from his wife when they have had a fight; order a young child found on the streets at night to go home; order troublesome "characters" to stay out of a given area; and tell persons congregated on street corners to disperse.

Police generally assume that congregating on a street corner is likely to give rise to disorderly conduct, especially if such assembling takes place outside of a tavern, if those assembled are intoxicated to varying degrees, and if there is heavy pedestrian traffic which is likely to be blocked by the congregating group. The technique ordinarily used by police in such a situation is to order the persons to "move on," thus presumably minimizing the risk of a group disturbance. There is a tendency, however, for this technique to become standard operating procedure as applied to all groups that congregate on sidewalks and street corners, without regard to the varying character of the groups. For example, in some cultural groups, congregating on the streets is the most common form of socializing; and in some congested areas of a city, the corner is used because of the absence of adequate public recreational facilities. For police to respond to these situations in the same manner as they respond to the situation involving an intoxicated group outside a tavern may not serve any real enforcement objective and may instead strain the relationship between the police and the residents of those areas in which the street corner is the place of social and recreational activity.

The practice of ordering people to "move on" is one which has major implications and warrants more careful use. In confronting the question of what should be their proper policy in dealing with congregating groups, the police would have an opportunity to give attention to why groups congregate, to distinguish those congregations which create risk of serious disorder from those which do not, and to relate police work to other community programs designed to create positive social and recreational opportunities for persons who now lack these opportunities.

The Settling of Disputes

A substantial amount of the on-duty time of police officers is devoted to the handling of minor disputes between husbands and wives, neighbors, landlords and tenants, merchants and customers, and taxicab drivers and their riders. Relatively little importance is attached to the handling of such matters by police administrators, particularly those in large urban areas. The patrolman who responds to the report of such a disturbance may inform the parties of their right to initiate a prosecution, may undertake to effect a resolution of the dispute by ordering the parties to leave each other alone (as, for example, by advising an intoxicated husband to go to the movies), or may use some other form of on-the-scene counseling. The approach taken in each case is a matter of choice on the part of the individual officer.

Important policy questions are raised with respect to the way the police handle all disputes and, in particular, to the way they handle domestic disturbances. Yet there has been no systematic effort made to measure the results which may be obtained under the alternative methods which police use, nor has there been an effort made to develop more adequate referral resources (such as social agencies) which might, if they existed, provide a basis for a positive police program for dealing with such disputes. In an effort to develop adequate policies to guide the actions of the individual patrolman, police agencies should compile several relevant facts: how often the same families become involved in disturbances that require police intervention; how often the husband or wife swears out a complaint; the disposition of such cases and the impact that varying dispositions have in preventing future disturbances; the number of serious assaults or homicides which result from domestic disturbances and whether these follow a pattern which might enable a patrolman to identify a potentially dangerous situation; and the kinds of cases which can be referred with positive results to existing community resources for dealing with family problems.[20]

Through the process of careful evaluation of existing practices and experience, the police can acquire a competence which should enable them to develop more adequate follow-up procedures in the domestic disturbance case. This added competence should increase the value and effectiveness of the emergency intervention function of the police and should, in the long run, reduce the heavy burden that is presently placed on the police in dealing with this type of recurring social problem.

---

20. The techniques that are used by police in handling domestic disturbances were the subject of a research project conducted with the cooperation of the Chicago Police Department by Raymond I. Parnas, a graduate student in criminal law at the University of Wisconsin.

The Protection of the Right to Free Expression

None of the functions which the police perform illustrates the sensitive and unique role of the police in a democratic society as well as that which is involved in the safeguarding of the constitutional rights of free speech and assembly. Police frequently are called upon to provide adequate protection for a speaker or demonstrating group that wishes to exercise the right to express one's opinions—opinions that are often unpopular and which are often voiced in the presence of a hostile audience.

Many urban police agencies have not developed and formulated policies to guide police action in such situations. Although the issues involved in recent demonstrations reflect many factors which are beyond police control, it is nonetheless a fact that the manner in which police respond to demonstrations will determine, in large measure, whether violence will break out and, if it does, the degree to which the resulting conflict will escalate and spread.

The problem is a particularly difficult one because police officers may themselves identify more with maintaining order in their community, especially to prevent disorder created by outsiders, than with their basic responsibility to protect the right of free expression of social and political views. For example, the officer in a police district which consists of a white neighborhood may view a Negro march through the neighborhood in favor of open housing as a threat to both public order in his district and the values of the very people in the neighborhood upon whom he depends for support in his day-to-day work. In rural areas or small cities the population may be relatively homogeneous and thus the police officer can be responsive to all of the local citizens without this producing conflict for him. But a very real conflict may develop for the officer in a large urban area, since such areas are typically made up of communities which differ in economic, racial, religious, or other characteristics. The officer who protects the right of free expression of ideas may find himself protecting an attack upon the very segment of the community with which he identifies.

In order for the police to respond adequately and consistently in the highly tense situations which arise from political and social demonstrations, there obviously must be a careful effort on their part to work out, in advance, policies which will govern their actions. This development of policies must be coupled with an effort to communicate them to individual officers in a way which will give each officer a basis for identifying with the protection of freedom of expression as an important enforcement objective. In addition, an effort must be made to articulate such policies to the affected community so that the public will understand the reasoning behind police actions. This, in itself, can serve to lessen the likelihood of major disorders.

Implementation

Since police agencies do not presently have the capacity to fulfill the kind of policy-making role that has been outlined in this article, implementation of this program will require numerous adjustments in their existing procedures, orientation, and staffing. The nature of these requirements is discussed in detail elsewhere,[21] but their general character will be summarized here.

As a prerequisite, it will be necessary for the police to develop a systematic process for the identification and study of those aspects of their operations which are in need of attention. Police administrators must take the initiative in seeking out the problem areas by analyzing complaints, by observing the results of police activities as reflected in the courts, and by the various other procedures available for analyzing the functioning of their respective departments. It is essential that the police develop a research methodology for exploring the kinds of problems that are likely to be identified—a procedure that equips them to clarify issues, to identify alternatives, to obtain relevant facts, and to analyze these facts in a manner that provides a basis for the development of a departmental policy. The end product must include clearly articulated criteria that will serve as guidelines for police officers and that will be open to public view. Flexibility being one of the major values in administrative policy-making, it is important that provision be made for the periodic reconsideration of those policies which are adopted so that adjustments to new developments can be effected and corrections may be made of deficiencies which become apparent after functioning under existing policies.

A police agency which accepts policy-making responsibility must develop more adequate systems of control than now exist to assure compliance of its personnel with the policies adopted by its administrators. The agency must also expect and should welcome responsible outside review of such policies as a protection against arbitrary policy-making.

Numerous changes will be required in existing patterns of leadership, personnel selection, training, and organization in order to equip the police to fulfill adequately their broader responsibilities. It is important, for example, that police leaders be provided with an education that will allow them to grasp fully the unique function of the police in a democratic society and that will enable them to support the overriding values relating to individual liberty which often conflict with their at-

---

21. See President's Commission on Law Enforcement and Administration of Justice, *Task Force Report: The Police*, Ch. 2 (1967). With specific reference to the need for controlling police conduct, see H. Goldstein, "Administrative Problems in Controlling the Exercise of Police Authority," 58 *J. Crim. L.C. & P.S.*, June 1967.

tempt to achieve the goal of maximum efficiency in the arrest and successful prosecution of offenders. It is important also that patrolmen, in their training, be provided with a professional identification that is supportive of the proper role of the police and that aids in developing a willingness on their part to conform with administrative policies.

The progress realized in the law enforcement field in recent years, especially in the area of training and education, contributes significantly to achieving some of these objectives. Such efforts, however, have suffered for lack of an adequate definition of direction and purpose. The potential of current improvement programs would be vastly increased if those programs were related to the need for the police to develop their own capacity to formulate and implement law enforcement policies. Incorporating this requirement as an objective would serve to provide such programs with the kind of focus for which the need has long been apparent.

5. OFFICER DISCRETION: LIMITS AND GUIDELINES

JAMES C. ZURCHER & S. BETTY COHEN

The Police Chief, Vol. XLIII, June 1976. Reprinted by permission.

It has been said of police that they are the most important policy makers of our society, making far more discretionary determinations in individual cases than any other governmental agency.[1] The very nature of the profession requires that officers have the flexibility to make on-the-spot determinations in a limitless variety of situations, yet, at the same time, these determinations must be appropriate and fair and conform to the requirements of the law and the Constitution. Despite this fact, many police departments do not provide any formal policy guidelines to officers in such important areas as the decision to arrest, investigative procedures, routine patrol procedures, and the use of force and deadly force.

In recent years, numerous advisory commissions, including the one cited above, and writers on problems of law enforcement and criminal justice have recommended the adoption of guidelines to govern the exercise of officer discretion.[2] In the absence of administratively determined guidelines, police departments find that policy is fashioned either by courts reacting to the most extreme abuses of the profession, or is infor-

---

1. Kenneth Culp Davis, "Discretionary Justice—A Preliminary Inquiry" University of Illinois Press, 1971 p. 222.

2. Increased use of police rule making has been recommended by the National Crime Commission, the National Advisory Commission on Civil Disorders, the American Bar Association Project on Minimum Standards for Criminal Justice, the California Attorney General's Advisory Commission on Community-Police Relations, and a host of writers on problems on law enforcement and justice. See, e.g., President's Commission on Law Enforcement and Administration of Justice, "Task Force Report: The Police" (1967), pp. 13-41; National Advisory Commission on Civil Disorders, for Criminal Justice, "Standards Relating to the Urban Police Function" (Tentative Draft, March 1972), pp. 121-144; Attorney General's Advisory Commission on Community-Police Relations, Report "The Police in The California Community" (March 31, 1973), pp. 1-12 to 1-13, 8-1 to 8-15; Davis, "Discretionary Justice—A Preliminary Inquiry," pp. 80-96; Caplan, "The Case for Rulemaking by Law Enforcement Agencies," 36 *Law and Contemp. Prob.* 500 (1971); Goldstein, "Police Policy Formulation: A Proposal for Improving Police Performance," 65 *Mich. L. Rev.* 1123 (1967); Ingleburger & Schubert, "Policy Making for the Police," 58 *A.B.A.J.* 307 (1972); McGowan, "Rule Making and the Police," 70 *Mich. L. Rev.* 659 (1972).

mally determined at the lowest echelons by the individual officer on patrol.

Where policy is made by the officer on the street, decisions are often made in a fraction of a second, are based on the officer's own understanding of the law and perception of the police role, and may be influenced by his or her personal biases, values, and prejudices. Where a department's selection, training, and supervisory procedures are adequate, officers usually exercise their discretion in a rational way. The potential for errors and for abuse, however, and the enormous consequences that can follow, point up the need for the formal articulation of policy guidelines to govern discretion and insure uniformity in its exercise.

Since some police departments fail to provide and enforce such guidelines, the courts are reluctantly forced to perform this role. The result is rules which reflect an inadequate understanding of police procedures and necessities, and are inflexibly enforced through the mechanism of the exclusionary rule.

Where departments undertake the responsibility of fashioning and enforcing their own rules, the beneficial impact on the quality of law enforcement, on the internal administration of the department, and on police relations with the community can be considerable.

The quality of law enforcement is enhanced by police-made rules in several ways. Police-made rules strike a better balance between the needs of law enforcement and the protection of individual rights than court-made rules which are inflexible and suffer from the lack of police input and expertise. Moreover, carefully drawn policies which anticipate possible legal problems strengthen the case against the guilty while avoiding the consequences of the exclusionary rule. Finally, the mere articulation of formal policies may have a profound effect on officer decision making. As one writer has explained it,

> . . . the officer who wishes to avoid having his personal prejudices influence his decisions but is unaware of their effect would be able to isolate and deal with the problem. If he must think about why he makes each decision, which he would have to do to assure that it was in accord with departmental rules, he is more likely to become aware of the operation of his own prejudices. The officer who wishes to indulge his prejudices will continue to do so under any system of control because as long as he is a policeman, his discretionary function cannot be eliminated. However, his superiors will be considering his actions, and conscientious review on their part should eventually reveal discriminatory practices. Then the officer not willing to deal with the problem himself can be disciplined and, if necessary, removed.[3]

3. Note: "Administrative Control of Police Discretion," 58 *Iowa L. Rev.* 893, 957 (1973).

Knowing that his or her actions are open to review, the officer must now make the acceptability of his decisions a prime concern. Officers adhering to the policies will exercise their discretion uniformly, consistent with departmental policies, regardless of individual biases and law enforcement philosophies.

Articulated policies can strengthen the internal administration of a department in numerous ways. Formal standards assist administrators in the evaluation of officers for the purposes of awards and promotion. Such defined criteria enable individual officers to know what is expected of them and to respond accordingly. They allow administrators to evaluate the performance of officers fairly, while at the same time insisting upon appropriate standards of behavior. In the same vein, they assist the administrator in disciplinary actions. Where no articulated policies exist, the police administrator sometimes finds himself "caught in a conflict between his desire to be responsive to a citizen who has reason to complain about a policeman's behavior and his fear of the reaction of his force to seemingly arbitrary discipline where there is no clear breach of a pronounced standard of proper conduct."[4] Articulated policies provide officers with the security of knowing what is expected of them and that their actions will not bring censure if they can be rationalized in terms of departmental policies.

There are several ways in which formal standards improve police relations within the community. Clearly articulated policies, equal treatment of citizens, and uniform standards remove the appearance of arbitrariness from law enforcement. Standards also limit the likelihood of accidents of very gross abuse, like accidental shootings, which however exceptional, are both tragic and stir public anger and resentment.

One of the most important areas of police discretion is the decision to arrest. Empirical studies have found that few departments have formal guidelines governing the arrest decision and that instead the decision to arrest or to utilize other alternatives is often guided by the values, role conception, biases, and emotions of individual officers.

> The police officer may discriminate between potential arrestees based upon factors such as race, age, nationality; he may zealously enforce one law and virtually ignore another; he may arrest only those who prove uncooperative, sparing the penitent; he may in fact, make his arrest decisions for the best or the worst possible reasons. What is most conspicuously absent in the case of

---

4. The President's Commission on Law Enforcement and the Administration of Justice Task Force, "Report on the Police," (1967), p. 20.

the patrolman, is any clear definition, statutory or otherwise, of just what constitutes the effective limits of his discretionary power.[5]

This is particularly true of minor offenses where there is likely to be less review of officer discretion by the department, the district attorney, or the courts.

An alternative to physical custody and pretrial detention of persons charged with misdemeanors in California is field citation by the arresting officer.[6] In departments where the procedure is utilized, it results in substantial savings of resources without jeopardizing the prosecution, while at the same time, benefits the arrested person both psychologically and financially.

As with the decision to arrest, the decision to release on citation is one which falls to officer discretion. As with the arrest decision, in the absence of a clearly articulated policy, the procedure is subject to the dangers of nonuniform application on the basis of individual officer biases, values, and role conception.

The Palo Alto Police Department adopted the citation procedure in March of 1970 with a general order which relied on largely unguided officer discretion. A study of the procedure performed three years later revealed that in the absence of clear guidelines, officers provided their own, resulting in a lack of uniformity in criteria and occasional reliance on factors which are irrelevant to the purposes of citation. The result was that citation was the exception rather than the rule and that persons were booked who could well have been cited consistent with the purposes of the policy. Furthermore, there were indications of differential treatment on the basis of race in the use of the citation alternative.

After further study of citation practice, we realize that part, if not all of the problem, lay in the misunderstanding of the officers of the purposes of the policy and of the appropriate factors to consider in the exercise of their discretion. To correct this situation, with the assistance of a third-year student from Stanford Law School who served as a legal resource person to the staff, the department formulated a revised general order with articulated policy and guidelines governing the citation procedure. The training officer developed a program to communicate the standards and policies to supervisors and officers, and supervisors developed a plan for the systematic review of officer discretion.

The potential for abuse has been eliminated since officers now have

---

5. 58 *Iowa L. Rev.*, p. 907.
6. "California Penal Code Section" 853.6.

clear guidelines for making their decisions, and irrelevant individual criteria will not hinder the achievement of uniformity.[7]

In an article urging a more active role of police in the formulation of rules governing their conduct, Judge McGowan of the D.C. Court of Appeals, suggested that:

> Imagination and innovation, soundly conceived in relation to specific problems need not be exclusive stock-in-trade of defense counsel or reform-minded legislatures and courts. The police in particular are entitled to the same kind of creative, probing, wide-ranging legal thinking...[8]

For this purpose, the judge urged the formation of legal positions or legal units in police departments to assist the police, among other things, in drafting rules which reflect not only a thorough familiarity with police operation, but at the same time, are sensitive to the claims of an ordered system of liberty. Numerous commissions and writers on police problems have also stressed the importance of house counsel in police departments to perform the tasks that neither city attorneys nor district attorneys have the time to do.[9]

> It has sometimes seemed to me that if only a fraction of the talent and ingenuity available to the defense through court-appointed counsel could be directed toward advising the police in the first instance, then, given a police leadership of similar breadth, the problems of the administration of criminal justice generally, and of the courts in particular, would be greatly mitigated. It is clear that such legal resources must be forthcoming for the police if they are to be accorded a larger role in the formulation of rules governing their own conduct.[10]

The assistance of a legally trained person has proven invaluable in the drafting of departmental policy guidelines. We feel that we have anticipated the courts in providing standards for the fair exercise of discretion to incarcerate or to release on citation without sacrificing any legitimate law enforcement objectives. In the next several months, we hope to evaluate other general orders to provide policy statements, guidelines, training, and review where they are lacking. In this way, we hope

---

7. Robert A. Bush, James C. Zurcher, "Bridging the Implementation Gap," "The Police Chief," May, 1974.

8. Carl McGowan, "Rule Making and the Police," 70 *Mich. L. Rev.* 659, 666 (1972).

9. See for example, National Advisory Commission on Criminal Justice Standards & Goals, "Police," 280 (1973), A.B.A. Project on Standards for Criminal Justice, Standards Relating to the Urban Police Function, 238 (1973), Jorgenson & Levine, "The Police Legal Advisor," 45 *Fla. B.J.* 66 (1971), Caplan, "The Police Legal Advisor," 58 *J. Crim. Law* 303 (1967).

10. McGowan, 70 *Mich. L. Rev.*, p. 667.

to return policy making to the upper echelons where it belongs and provide officers with a clearer conception of how this department expects them to exercise their discretion.

Concepts to Consider

1. Identify the reasons why police executives are reluctant to publicize traffic "tolerance limits."
2. Justify the desirability of the police operating as an administrative policy-making agency.
3. Support the position that there is a limited "risk factor" in police decision making.
4. Describe the impact of recruit and in-service training programs on police discretion.
5. Differentiate between police control and legislative control of police discretion.

Selected Readings

Arcuri, Alan F., "Criminal Justice: A Police Perspective," *Criminal Justice Review*, Vol. 2, No. 1, Spring 1977, pp. 15-21.

This study reviews police opinion of lawyers, judges, and local justices in an effort to determine if their attitudes affect the enforcement of laws.

Bozza, Charles M., "Motivations Guiding Police in the Arrest Process," *The Journal of Police Science and Administration*, Vol. 1, No. 4, December 1973.

This study focuses upon the arrest process and examines the behavioral attitudes of 24 adult males of the Costa Mesa (California) Police Department. It concludes that policemen operate more efficiently in regard to number of arrests with skills and knowledge obtained in the process of education.

Caplan, Gerald M., *Model Rules for Law Enforcement—Eyewitness*

Identification (Tempe, Arizona: College of Law, Arizona State University, December 1972).

Provides for uniform procedures for identification of suspects by eyewitnesses to a crime. Specific rules are provided for confrontations, use of photographs and other likenesses, lineups, and informal identifications.

Caplan, Gerald M., *Model Rules for Law Enforcement—Release of Arrest and Conviction Records* (Tempe, Arizona: College of Law, Arizona State University, May 1973).

Identifies rules for governing the release of arrest and conviction records. The rules identify the purposes for which records may be released, the procedures by which release is to be made, and the persons to whom records may be released.

Caplan, Gerald M., *Model Rules for Law Enforcement—Searches, Seizures and Inventories of Motor Vehicles* (Tempe, Arizona: College of Law, Arizona State University, December 1972).

Establishes procedures for searches, seizures and inventories of motor vehicles. The procedures maximize police efficiency in controlling crime while at the same time limiting invasions of privacy.

Cox, Michael P., "Discretion—A Twentieth Century Mutation," *Oklahoma Law Review*, Vol. 28, Spring 1975, pp. 311-332.

Maintains that unprecedented discretionary power exists at lower levels of justice administration. Emphasizes that its use by law enforcement officials is being regarded as the primary effective agent of the legal system.

Davis, Kenneth Culp, "An Approach to Legal Control of the Police," *Texas Law Review*, Vol. 52, 1974, pp. 703-725.

Suggests that police discretion should be subjected to judicial review. Policy should be open, not secret, and administrators should determine major policy. Recommends the reduction of illegal policy.

Finckenauer, James O., "Some Factors in Police Discretion and Decision Making," *Journal of Criminal Justice*, Vol. 4, No. 1, Spring 1976, pp. 29-46.

A study of the exercise of police discretion utilizing the responses of police recruits to a series of ambiguous, but common police incidents.

Nejelski, Paul, "Social Policy and the Administration of Justice," *Criminology*, Vol. 8, No. 3, November 1970, pp. 295-300.

This report reviews the sources of social policy and identifies some of the many decision makers in the criminal justice system. Each participant in making social policy is identified as having wide discretionary powers.

Knori, Arthur Jay, "An Examination of Literature Pertaining to Police Discretion and Disposition of Youthful Offenders," *Journal of California Law Enforcement*, Vol. 8, No. 2, October 1973, pp. 85-94.

The author reviews the literature on police discretion and the youthful offender and establishes a case for non-judicial disposition by institutions responsible for controlling and preventing delinquency.

Chapter 3
THE POLICE USE OF DEADLY FORCE

Introduction

Introduction

A serious issue facing our society is the use of deadly force by police officers.[1] According to the Vital Statistics of the United States, police officers have killed an average of one person per day since 1970.[2] Furthermore, the ratio of police killed to police killing has remained approximately 1 to 5.[3]

At the same time, according to Kobler, police are the "only representatives of governmental authority who in the ordinary course of events are legally permitted to use physical force against a citizen." Other agencies of state power rely upon request, persuasion, public opinion, custody, and legal and judicial processes to gain compliance with rules and laws. Only the police can use firearms to compel the citizen to obey. The police are also in a special category in that they are sworn to enforce the law at all times, on or off duty in most jurisdictions, so that their access to firearms is constant and legal. The possibility of excessive use of firearms in the course of police duties and thus the power of life and death over the citizen is facilitated by the unique legal definition of the powers and responsibilities of the police in our society.[4]

Although a sizeable number of killings by police officers may be justifiable and necessary, one report (in which 1500 incidents between 1960 and 1970 were examined) has suggested that one-fifth of the homicides studied were questionable, two-fifths unjustifiable, and two-fifths justifiable. According to sociologist Albert J. Reiss, Jr., the homicide rate by police officers has been rising at a rate that is not commensurate with population growth and furthermore, the persons killed are disproportionally minority persons.[5] Some authorities have also claimed that racism is a major factor in these results inasmuch as the laws which set forth the written standards for acceptable police behavior and conduct as well as the judicial apparatus set up to enforce such standards are established and administered by persons with interests and perspectives representative of white Americans.[6] Consequently, the very structures of

1. National Institute of Law Enforcement and Criminal Justice, "Use of Deadly Force by Police Officers," (1979).
2. Larry Sherman, "Homicide by Police Officers: Social Forces and Public Policy," grant proposal (1977).
3. Arthur L. Kobler, "Police Homicide in a Democracy," *Journal of Social Issues*, Vol. 31, No. 1 (1975), p. 164.
4. Ibid., p. 163.
5. Ibid., p. 165.
6. Louis L. Knowles and Kenneth Prewitt, "Racism in the Administration of Justice," *Race Crime and Justice* (Pacific Palisades: Goodyear Publishing Company, Inc., (1972), p. 13.

the legal system, according to Louis Knowles and Kenneth Prewitt, not only reflect the prejudices and ignorance of white society but tend to operate to the disadvantage of the culturally different.[7] To support this argument, statistics are cited from the National Center of Health Statistics, U.S. Public Health Service, which note that of the 376 civilians killed by law enforcement officers in 1973, 79 percent were black.[8] In addition, another study on police killings of civilians found that the police-caused death rate for blacks from 1958 to 1968 was consistently nine times higher than that for whites.[9] One theory is that the friction between the police and minority communities stems from the overwhelming whiteness of most police departments.[10]

To complicate the situation, studies have also shown that police are more likely to exercise force against members of their own race. According to Reiss, 67 percent of citizens victimized by white policemen in his sample were white and 71 percent of the citizens victimized by black police were black.[11] He further theorizes that "though no precise estimates are possible, the facts just given suggest that white policemen, even though they are prejudiced toward Negroes, do not discriminate against Negroes in the excessive use of force. The use of force by the police is more readily explained by police culture than it is by the policeman's race...."[12] Reiss noted that in all cases, two facts stand out: (1) all victims were offenders; and (2) all were from the lower class.[13]

Reiss' theory is further underscored by Fyfe's study in which he found that not only were Blacks and Hispanics disproportionately represented in police shootings of civilians but that possibly due to their location and assignments, the Black and Hispanic New York police officers were far more likely to have fired their guns on duty as well as off duty than were white officers.[14]

There are also legal aspects of the problem that must be examined. State laws regarding use of deadly force by police officers differ substantially, but basically they fall into three major categories: common law,

---

7. Ibid.

8. Catherine Milton, et al., *Police Use of Deadly Force* (Washington, D.C.: Police Foundation, 1977), p. 4-5.

9. S. Harring, T. Platt, R. Speiglmann, and P. Takagi, "Management of Police Killings," *Crime and Social Justice* (Fall-Winter 1977), pp. 34-43.

10. Ibid., p. 14.

11. Albert J. Reiss, Jr., "Police Brutality," *Crime and Justice: Volume II* eds. Leon Radzinowicz and Marvin E. Wolfgang, p. 304.

12. Ibid.

13. Ibid.

14. Lt. James J. Fyfe, dissertation, *Executive Summary Shots Fired: An Examination of New York City Police Firearms Discharges.* Police Academy, New York Police Dept. (1978), p. 2.

forcible felony rule, and the model penal code approach.[15] Under common law, a police officer may be justified in the use of deadly force under
the following circumstances: self-defense, prevention of the commission
of a crime, recapture of an escapee from an arrest or from a penal institution, stopping a riot, or effecting a felony arrest.[16] Twenty-four states still
adhere to the common law justification for the kinds of felonies for which
deadly force may be used; seven states have adjusted the model penal code
approach which restricts the use of deadly force to violent felonies. And
the remaining twelve states do not have justification statutes limiting an
officer's use of deadly force.[17] Furthermore, the definition of felony dif-
fers from state to state.

Police "killings" and the legal complexities surrounding their use of
deadly force are further compounded by the fact that an increasing
number of police officers are the victims of felonious assault or murder.

The following account illustrates the dimensions of this problem:

In 1977, 93 local, county, state, and Federal law enforcement officers
were feloniously killed in the United States, Puerto Rico, and the U.S.
Virgin Islands. During the 10-year period 1968-1977, 1,094 officers were
slain. The number of law enforcement officers killed in Puerto Rico and
the U.S. Virgin Islands for the period 1971-1977 and the number of
Federal officers killed in the period 1972-1977 have been included in the
tabulations with the local, county, and state officers for the 10-year
period.

During 1977, 47 officers were slain in the Southern States, 19 in the
North Central States, 14 in the Western States, and 11 in the Northeastern
States. One officer was killed in Puerto Rico and one in the U.S. Virgin
Islands. The preceding chart shows the number of law enforcement officers killed by region for each of two 5-year periods, 1968-1972 and
1973-1977. The accompanying table presents information on the officers
feloniously killed in 1977 by geographic division and population group.

Ninety-one of the 93 officers slain during 1977 were from 83 different
local, county, and state law enforcement agencies in 31 states and the
District of Columbia. As indicated above, the remaining two were from
Puerto Rico and the U.S. Virgin Islands.

Among the states, California ranked highest with ten officers killed.
The State of New York followed closely with nine officers slain.

More law enforcement officers were killed responding to disturbance
calls during 1977 than under any other circumstance. Twenty-two officers lost their lives while involved in this activity, which includes

---

15. Gilbert G. Pompa, Director of CPS, DOJ speech entitled, "Police Use of Excessive Force:
    A Community Relations Concern," presented to the National Black Policeman's Associa-
    tion on August 25, 1978 in Chicago, Illinois.

16. Larry Sherman, "Homicide by Police Officers," p. 21.

17. Gilbert G. Pompa, "Police Use of Excessive Force," p. 11.

responses to family quarrels, man-with-gun calls, bar fights, etc. Eleven officers were slain by persons engaged in the commission of a robbery or during the pursuit of robbery suspects. Nine officers were killed at the scene of burglaries or while pursuing burglary suspects, and 19 lost their lives while attempting arrests for crimes other than robbery or burglary.

In 1977, four officers were killed in ambush situations. Three of these officers were victims of unprovoked attacks which did not involve any apparent element of entrapment. The remaining officer was slain in a premeditated attack.

Chart 1—Law Enforcement Officers Killed 1968-1977

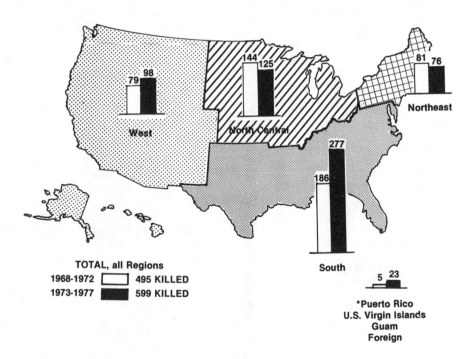

TOTAL, all Regions

| 1968-1972 | 495 KILLED |
| 1973-1977 | 599 KILLED |

*Puerto Rico
U.S. Virgin Islands
Guam
Foreign

*Data not available for years prior to 1971.

Table 1—Situations in Which Law Enforcement Officers Were Killed 1968-1977

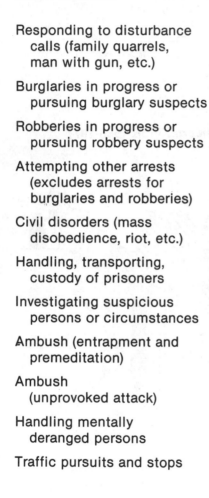
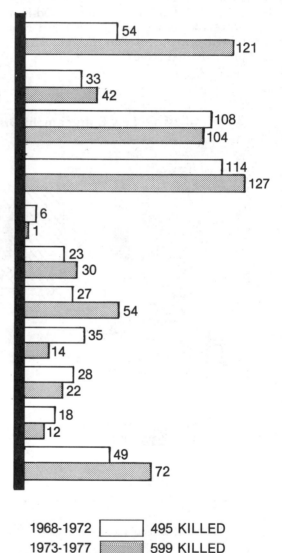

Responding to disturbance calls (family quarrels, man with gun, etc.) — 54 / 121

Burglaries in progress or pursuing burglary suspects — 33 / 42

Robberies in progress or pursuing robbery suspects — 108 / 104

Attempting other arrests (excludes arrests for burglaries and robberies) — 114 / 127

Civil disorders (mass disobedience, riot, etc.) — 6 / 1

Handling, transporting, custody of prisoners — 23 / 30

Investigating suspicious persons or circumstances — 27 / 54

Ambush (entrapment and premeditation) — 35 / 14

Ambush (unprovoked attack) — 28 / 22

Handling mentally deranged persons — 18 / 12

Traffic pursuits and stops — 49 / 72

1968-1972 ☐ 495 KILLED
1973-1977 ▨ 599 KILLED
1968-1977 total: 1,094 KILLED

Twelve officers were killed in 1977 while enforcing traffic laws, nine while investigating suspicious persons or circumstances, and seven while transporting or otherwise engaged in the custody of prisoners.

Patrol duties within law enforcement organizations are the most hazardous types of assignment for officers. During patrol, an officer is frequently in contact with suspicious or dangerous individuals, and each of these situations constitutes a threat to the officer's personal safety. The patrol officer is readily identifiable because of his uniform and/or patrol vehicle. He frequently must determine quickly and accurately if a person is involved in a criminal act. If the suspect constitutes a danger to the officer's personal safety, he must afford himself reasonable protection.

The patrol officer is placed in a variety of dangerous situations and must react to circumstances as they occur without the benefit of detailed information or planning. He often risks attack through frequent encounters with criminal offenders at or near crime scenes.

These perils are substantiated by the fact that officers assigned to patrol duty are the most frequent targets of the police killer. Law enforcement officers assigned in other capacities are confronted with equally tense and dangerous situations while performing their duties, but not with the same frequency.

Sixty-six patrol officers were slain in 1977. Sixty-four of these officers were assigned to patrol vehicles, and two were on foot patrol. Twenty officers were detectives or officers on special assignments. In the highest tradition of the law enforcement profession, seven officers, while in an off-duty status, were taking appropriate police action relative to criminal matters when they were slain. During the period 1968-1977, 66 percent (724) of the 1,094 officers slain were assigned to patrol duties.[18]

---

18. William H. Webster, *Crime in the United States 1977* (Washington, D.C.: F.B.I., 1978), pp. 290-292.

6. ADMINISTRATIVE AND LEGAL ASPECTS OF A POLICY TO LIMIT THE USE OF FIREARMS BY POLICE OFFICERS

KENNETH R. McCREEDY AND JAMES L. HAGUE

The Police Chief, Vol. XLII, January 1975. Reprinted by permission.

All police chiefs face one decision in common: what restrictions should be imposed on the amount and type of force used by their officers. Nearly everyone is aware of instances of police brutality and the flagrant misuse of force by some over-zealous officers. These situations are relatively easy to deal with, because they represent clear violations of departmental rules and criminal law. This discussion does not cover such blatant abuses of force, rather it focuses on those situations where regulations, laws, and circumstances are not so clearly defined.

The first consideration must be the question of what constitutes deadly force. It is generally defined as that amount of force that is likely to produce death or serious bodily injury. While the use of the police baton, fists, or feet sometimes produces the issue of deadly force, incidents in which a suspect is shot by an officer are always considered to have involved deadly force.

The primary legal question is clear: was the use of force reasonable? To be considered "reasonable," the force used must have been no more than was necessary under the circumstances. When a firearm is used, the burden of proof rests with the officer to show that there were no other reasonable alternatives available to him. In addition, reasonable force implies that the crime involved must have been a felony and, at that, a dangerous one—murder, voluntary manslaughter, forcible rape, felonious assault, arson, robbery, or burglary. With the exception of self-defense by the officer, killing or deadly force cannot be used when the crime involved is a misdemeanor.

The high value placed upon a human life in our society and the increasing number of crimes that are considered felonies have caused a gradual circumscription of the power of police officers to use deadly force. Even those jurisdictions which still allow a rather wide use of deadly force in a number of felony crimes require that the element of danger must be clear.

The situations in which an officer is most likely to use a firearm are: (1) while effecting the lawful arrest of a felon, (2) while preventing the escape of a felon, and (3) while preventing the commission or consummation of a felony. In the first situation the officer may use deadly force in defense of his own life, the life of a fellow officer, or of some other person. In the second case deadly force is permitted under certain circumstances. In most jurisdictions, escaping from an institution is usually considered a dangerous felony. However, merely escaping from an officer raises the issue of the dangerousness of the crime as well as the availability of less lethal alternatives. In situation 3, the officer must prove that the commission of a felony was imminent.

There is a discernible trend in law enforcement to limit substantially the use of firearms in cases where a significant danger to bystanders exists.

The above discussion encompasses the legal framework within which the policy decision concerning the use of deadly force must be made. While the variations of circumstances and conditions are endless, any policy must be consistent with legal requirements and prohibitions. Even the absence of a stated policy is a form of policy. In the past when officers were given a few broad guidelines and told to use their good judgment, the controlling factor became norms established by the officers themselves as the result of street experience. These guidelines were simply a knowledge of the consequences of improper action, and considerable emphasis was placed on individual decision making.

Available Alternatives

Before beginning to examine the condition under which a policy decision concerning the use of firearms should be made, we should first explore the available alternatives.

1. *The officers are armed and told to use full discretion.* Little attempt is made by the chief to define the circumstances under which such force should be used. He must rely on the training and competence of the individual officers. Normally, this condition exists because of a lack of any stated policy.

In many respects, this alternative is the most unfair. It requires the officer to bear the responsibility of his decision (which certainly he must ultimately do), but it fails to give him the necessary guidance to make that very important decision.

2. *The officers are armed and given partial discretion.* In this instance, officers are given rather detailed guidelines and considerable training. Such a policy may limit the use of firearms to situations where it is necessary to save the officer's life or the life of some other person. The exercise of discretion would cover circumstances where a reasonable possibility exists for further injury or death involving other persons.

This policy begins to circumscribe the use of force, but still allows the officer to exercise some discretion in unusual circumstances. It also shows the officers that the chief is willing to help them make the decision and to share the responsibility for that decision.

3. *The officers are armed and given no discretion.* When no discretion is given, officers are instructed to use their firearms only in defense of their lives. This means that unless a life is immediately in danger, deadly force should not be used. With this policy, the only decision the officer is required to make is whether or not a life is immediately in danger. Such a condition is fairly easy to identify.

This alternative is beginning to gain some popularity because of the advent of multi-agency communications systems, greater inter-agency cooperation, and the use of helicopters to reduce the possibility of escape. Because of modern technological improvements, much of the necessity for immediate action has been removed.

4. *The officers are unarmed and thus the decision does not become an issue.* This is the system that has long been practiced in England, where the bobbies have traditionally not been armed. This alternative is generally not acceptable in this country because of the frequency with which firearms are involved in calls for police service (not only shootings, but threatening and brandishing of firearms, carrying concealed weapons, etc.); and the frontier mentality dictates that the "law man" is the one who "won the West" with his six-shooter and a lightning fast draw. Many people still view the image of a policeman as incomplete without the gun. Perhaps in the future, when the technology is perfected, the use of nonlethal weapons will become the predominant policy.

From the above alternatives, it can be observed that as the chief's control of the officer's discretion in the use of firearms increases, the officer's discretion decreases.

Participants in Policymaking

There are many participants or actors who play a part in the decision as to what policy should be implemented.

1. *The police chief.* With the chief rests the ultimate decision as to what policy will be instituted. He is influenced by many factors, not the least of which is his own experience as a patrolman. His decision is further influenced by his present role as a decision maker. The chief cannot be guided solely by his own experiences or by his desire to facilitate the interests of his officers. He must also evaluate the opinions, desires, and demands made by each of the other actors.

2. *The police officers.* Each officer will have his own opinion based primarily on three factors. The first is the officer's own experience using firearms while enforcing the law. Secondly, he will be influenced by his

training and perceptions of his own capabilities. The last factor is the norms and opinions of his peer group. Often, these norms are not based on actual conditions but only on what "could" happen. The officers either individually or in concert will have considerable influence because they are the ones to whom this policy will apply.

3. *The city council or other legislative unit under which the police department must operate.* Members are the elected representatives of the people. They express the views of their constituents or, at least, are conscious of their attitudes and feelings. These officials, in most cases, also have the power to remove the chief from office if they feel he is not doing his job properly. For these two reasons, they are very important actors whose opinions must be considered when establishing a policy on the use of firearms.

4. *Courts.* Both local and appellate courts may become involved directly or indirectly in implementing policy. On a case by case basis, the reasonableness of the officer's use of a firearm will be determined by the courts. Whether or not there are legal consequences is also a judicial responsibility. This responsibility includes both civil and criminal liability. The officer's use of his firearm may be criminal if the force is found to be excessive and, therefore, unreasonable under the circumstances. In addition, depending on the status of sovereign immunity in a particular jurisdiction, there may also be civil liability if negligence can be found. There will certainly be liability for state and local officers when, in the federal courts, they are found to have acted unreasonably and thus to have deprived citizens of their federal statutory or constitutional rights. This liability not only applies to the officers involved, but may also include the police administrators who were negligent in the formulation and implementation of policy and training.

All courts, and particularly those at the appellate level, see their role as one of supervision over police activities. Consequently judges make policy for the police by deciding whether police procedures are consistent with the due process and protection of rights of those who are arrested. There is widespread debate about the relative impact of judicial control over police policy making; however, it is difficult to measure accurately this influence.

5. *Interest groups.* These are able to apply pressure to city officials and to the police chief directly by protests and newspaper articles as well as indirectly through legal pressure in the courts. These various interest groups may represent all sides of the same issue simultaneously, so in many respects they may only serve to further complicate the situation.

Interest groups have a quality which sometimes makes their effect more pronounced than it should be. Many interest groups are formed literally overnight, last for a few days, and then dissolve only to be reborn again under a different name. Because of this transience and because of the general secrecy of membership, the exact size of the group represented cannot be determined. The same is true of the rich and politically powerful within the city. The extent to which others share their opinions is also difficult to determine, even though they themselves often exhibit tremendous influence.

6. *Chief's own peer group.* Every chief is involved to some extent with police chiefs from other cities through conventions and professional associations. The opinions and particularly the experiences of the other chiefs will influence other members of the group.

The above list composes the major actors involved in the chief's policy decision. Others may be involved to a greater or lesser degree in other specific situations.

Other Considerations

Political environment. Any consideration of a policy which limits the use of firearms by police officers cannot be extricated from the political environment in which it is made. The nature and strength of local politics will often dictate many of the policy decisions that are made.

Community values are part of this political climate. The degree to which criminality is legitimatized by the members of the community will influence their values and attitudes toward such a policy.

Actual policy versus stated policy. In many police organizations, there is a significant gap between actual policy and stated policy. The actual policy may be a conscious process or it may occur almost accidentally. The classic example of the actual versus stated policy dilemma is the suggestion box. A chief can proudly point to the suggestion box on the wall and exclaim that he actually solicits the opinions of his officers. He may or may not be aware that the first suggestions that were submitted were either ignored or, if enacted, some other ranking member of the department took credit for the idea. In actual practice, then, the suggestion box could be welded shut and no one would notice.

The same is true with regard to a policy covering the use of firearms. The chief may state that he favors the use of discretion by his officers; but when officers are indiscriminately disciplined for what they perceive to be minor violations (called scapegoating), then the actual policy becomes significantly different from the stated policy.

Environment of the policy. The decision to use a firearm is normally implemented in the heat of a conflict. As such, the decision is not the result of a thoughtful or even necessarily a rational process. In the final analysis, the officer will do what his instincts tell him to do in any given situation. The policy will only be enforceable after the fact and by that time irreparable damage may have been done.

Enforcing such a policy seems to include training to make the officers' actions predictable in a given situation. The FBI developed a "Hogan's Alley" to test the agents' reactions and abilities to make life or death decisions. The agents are required to walk down a street, and as they walk targets appear in doors and windows of various buildings. Some of the figures pose no threat to the agents (woman holding a baby), while others are an immediate danger (criminal with a shotgun). The agents are judged on their ability to respond correctly to each given situation. Other experiments have been tried to judge the same accuracy or reaction. The results show that some officers do have better reactions than others. Just how much continued practice will improve faulty reactions is not known, but it appears that short of actual shootings there are few ways to train persons to make these kinds of decisions once the usual "moral and policy" aspects of the use of firearms have been covered.

Predictability of officer contacts with others. Part of the purpose of policy is to introduce a degree of predictability into the behavior of the person to whom the policy applies. A policy which limits the use of firearms by police officers would serve to make their conduct more predictable when interacting with others. As with any other issue, there is more than one point of view.

First is the opinion that if a person had done no wrong, he has nothing to fear from the officer. Community relations studies and experiments have found that this is not always the case. Often, those who have done no wrong still react in fear because of the perceived unpredictability of the officer's conduct. Many people would doubtless find comfort in knowing that the officer's discretion was limited and that he would only use his firearm in certain narrowly described circumstances.

On the other hand, to some this restriction may make the officer's conduct too predictable. If a person who has committed some serious crime believes that the only barrier to escape is a footrace with the officer, he may be willing to chance it. After all, at that price, it would be worth the gamble. If the price is increased to include the possibility of death, that alternative becomes less desirable.

Conclusion

Total use of discretion by police officers is more an indication of failure on the part of the chief than of a sincere belief in the judgment of his officers. This is not an area where no policy can exist. Even in the absence of policy, the norms and experiences of the officers, coupled with judicial decisions, will establish some type of policy albeit informal.

The most appropriate solution, based on the total benefit to the community and the need to provide guidance and support for the officers, is a policy which severely limits the use of discretion but one which also acknowledges that exceptions are possible. Other than for the obvious situations, such as in defense of a human life, the use of firearms by officers is difficult to justify.

Such a policy for officers would give them absolute guidelines to follow and would also assure them of administrative support if they were within that policy. The chief would not have to decide the rightness and wrongness of a particular incident based on some flexible and intangible scale. A guarantee of support for officers should outweigh any disadvantage that such a policy would create.

If the advantage of not making the officer's actions predictable to the criminals is felt to outweigh the reassurance offered to the public, then the policy when established need not be publicized. On the other hand, if a public benefit is desired from the policy, then it could become a valuable public relations tool. The police department would receive the benefit of a reputation for decisiveness, while the public would be more aware of the parameters of police conduct.

A policy which limits the use of firearms to essentially life or death situations also raises several other questions which each administrator must answer before he enacts the policy.

1. *What is in defense of a life or what is a dangerous felony?* How much danger does a felony have to pose, or how much danger does someone have to be in? For example, is the officer's life in danger when he confronts a person who is armed, or when that person actually draws the weapon, or is it necessary to wait until that person fires the weapon?

2. *Does the threat have to be real?* On occasion, perceived threats seem to be real at the time but later are proven to be false.

3. *What will be done in a borderline case?* What action will be taken in cases where the justification was not as strong as it should have been?

4. *Who will review the incident?* Presuming that such incidents will occur, it is necessary to decide who will review the incident and decide whether or not the use of deadly force was justified. Involved in this process is deciding what will be done in instances that are beyond the policy but not violations of law. If no action is taken when violations occur, the effect will be to expand the parameters of the policy.

5. *Methods of determining violations of policy.* When a shooting occurs, it should be investigated immediately. The problem is by whom. Many people feel that to have police officers from the same police department investigate a shooting in which a person was killed by a fellow officer is asking for abuses of the authority. In some cases, this is probably true, especially in smaller police departments where everyone is known to everyone else.

The most advantageous solution is to have the incident investigated by some other nearby investigative agency. For example, if the incident occurred in a city, it might be investigated by the state police or prosecuting attorney's investigative staff. In this way, competence is maintained while the personalities are removed.

When the investigation is completed, the results should be evaluated by some independent agency beyond the control of the police department and representative of the people.

There are several such mechanisms already in existence. The grand jury and, in some states, the coroner's jury are both beyond the control of the police department and are composed of a random cross-section of the community. These juries rotate at regular intervals so there is little chance of co-optation occurring.

A third alternative is a civilian review board, but it is the least desirable of the choices. A CRB too often ends up on one side of the fence or the other. If it decides in favor of the police officer, then the community may lose faith in its judgments. If it decides in favor of the community, then the police officers perceive the board as being hostile to law enforcement. This dilemma can be avoided by using either of the two existing juries.

Summation

Deciding to enact a policy which would limit or restrict the use of firearms by police officers is a necessary but difficult task. It is one that cannot be avoided; some policy will always exist, even if it is only informally. A police chief has an obligation to the members of the department and the community to provide guidance and support. This can best be accomplished by the articulation of a definite and fair policy.

The road to such a decision is not, however, without its crossroads; and at each intersection, the police executive must decide which way to proceed.

Because there are several hundred-thousand police officers in many different police agencies, and daily they interact with millions of persons in various communities, the potential for conflict is great. The more easily that conflict can be resolved, the better the goal of law enforcement will be served.

7. INVESTIGATION OF THE USE OF DEADLY FORCE

PETER J. DONNELLY

The Police Chief, Vol. XLV, May 1978. Reprinted by permission.

You are the chief of police in a small middle-class community which enjoys the luxury of little violent crime.

One of your officers is on routine patrol in a residential area in the early hours of the first watch. He sees a young man furtively leaving the back door of a darkened home, carrying a box. The officer approaches the young man and orders him to freeze. The young man drops his box and runs from the officer.

The officer gives chase, but the young man widens the distance from his pursuer. The officer, fully within the limits of state law, tells the young man to stop or he will shoot. The young man keeps on running.

The officer yells again, and the young man suddenly turns, a "shiny" object in his hand. The officer fires, hitting the man in the chest. The officer calls for an ambulance; upon reaching the nearby hospital the young man is pronounced dead.

He is later identified as a sixteen-year-old community resident with a minor juvenile record. The shiny object recovered at the scene is a chrome flashlight. This incident, in a normally quiet community, is certain to send shock waves, pro and con, throughout the community.

Under the present law of many states, the subject was observed by the officer to be committing the forcible felony of burglary. Under such statutes, the officer was justified in using deadly force, both to protect himself and prevent the subject's escape. Under such statutes, the officer's actions were justified.

Investigation

Each such use of deadly force, however, calls for thorough investigation of the officer's actions. There are several reasons for such investigation. First, public accountability demands an investigation of such police action. Second, from the standpoint of internal control, the officer's actions must be subject to review. Third, and perhaps most important, a thorough investigation protects both the department and the officer involved from unjust criticism.

A deadly force investigation parallels a normal homicide investigation in that the principles of preservation of the crime scene and physical evidence must be adhered to. At the scene, one officer, preferably of command or supervisory rank, should be in charge, assigning duties to those under his command as in the case in an ordinary crime scene investigation.

The first consideration at the scene should be, of course, to secure medical aid for the injured. Even though the victim's death may be readily apparent to a lay observer, he should still be transported to the nearest hospital as quickly as possible. This is done for two reasons: to secure competent medical examination of the victim and to safeguard the department from future criticism. The placement of the body at the scene can be photographed or outlined before removal, and examination of the body may later take place at the hospital, morgue or funeral home. Here, maintaining chain of custody and preservation of the evidence is paramount; and an officer should accompany the body to insure these procedures.

An officer should be assigned to safeguard the scene and control access to it. Photographs should be taken as soon as possible. They should show all aspects of the scene and follow as closely as possible the sequence of events. Particular care should be given to the gathering of physical evidence such as blood, spent bullets, and prints, using a grid search method or other systematic pattern. The officer's weapon should be inventoried for ballistic comparison with any recovered bullets.

An officer or two should be assigned to locate and segregate witnesses to the incident. Written statements should be taken from eye and circumstantial witnesses. Do not rely on third-person summaries of oral witness interviews; written statements preclude changing stories at a later date. The general area of the scene should be canvassed for witnesses. The names of everyone contacted should be recorded and noted whether they saw or heard anything. This again helps prevent "surprise" witnesses appearing with "eyewitness" accounts. The witnesses, in general, should be asked if they were physically in a position to see or hear what happened.

Detailed reports should be received from all involved department personnel as soon as possible, covering their actions in the incident. The involved officer's rights as a public employee do not prevent him from submitting an official report regarding his official actions.

A re-enactment of the incident may be valuable in clarifying points and indicating further avenues of investigation. The re-enactment should duplicate the actual events and setting as closely as possible.

Liaison with other agencies who have an interest in the incident should be quickly established to prevent duplication of effort and conflict of jurisdiction. In many areas, the state's or district attorney is notified of police shooting incidents and immediately begins his own investigation. It is the duty of the police officer in charge of the investigation to cooperate and coordinate with such personnel, such as making witnesses available for on the scene depositions.

The initial offense which led to the shooting should also be thoroughly investigated, just as if the offender were apprehended and facing prosecution. In my hypothetical case, the burglary investigation should not be dropped in favor of the shooting investigation. The burglary investigation should proceed as usual, including processing of the burglary scene and inventory of the missing or recovered property. The burglary case report should then be made part of the shooting investigation file.

Treatment of Officer

There are several special considerations which must be given attention in a deadly force investigation, particularly regarding treatment of the officer involved. Police officers react differently following shootings. Some officers view it as part of the job, something that had to be done. Such an attitude should not be regarded as callous; it may be a product of the officer's past experience and training. Other officers may be upset and in need of immediate counseling by their partner, commanding officer, clergyman, or some other professional. In cases where serious emotional upset is evident, the involved officer's family should be briefed as to what the officer is going through. Relief from normal duties may be necessary in such cases. In many other cases, the officer may be exhilarated, telling and retelling his role in the incident. Such behavior is not boasting, but rather a manifestation of the natural excitement the officer feels.

Unless there is some indication of impropriety, the officer involved should not be suspended or placed on restricted duty pending the outcome of the investigation. If there is no impropriety apparent or emotional disturbance on the part of the involved officer, such action serves no real purpose other than to possibly create a feeling of "guilt." If such action is taken and publicized, undue suspicion regarding the officer's actions can be created in the eyes of the public and the officer's peers. Do not suspend or place an officer on restricted duty unless there is a need to do so. While remaining on duty, however, the involved officer should not take part in the shooting investigation, other than completing his own reports and making a statement.

In a departure from normal investigative procedures, the involved officer is interviewed as soon as possible in the investigation. This is done because the spontaneity of an immediate statement increases recall of details and credibility, and prevents the possibility of a "manufactured" account later on.

In some instances, the involved officer is often viewed as an accused. This is especially true in instances where the officer is required or requested to make a formal statement to a state's or district attorney. Prior to making such a statement, the officer must be advised of his Constitutional rights regarding self-incrimination and right to counsel. In administrative or departmental inquiries, the officer should be advised of the nature of the inquiry and his rights and responsibilities under civil service statutes. In such inquiries, if there is a possibility of criminal prosecution because of misconduct by the officer, the full *Miranda* warnings must be given. If the preliminary investigation discloses a question about the officer's actions in the incident, then the appropriate guidelines regarding the rights of the accused must be followed.

Media Relations

Handling of news media coverage of a shooting incident calls for a sense of timing and an understanding of the media's role regarding the inquiry. Information should not be prematurely disclosed to the news media. Such information should be withheld when it is felt that its release would jeopardize the investigation or expose the department to civil liability. When it is appropriate to release facts, the press release should recount the incident as it occurred. The release may include a brief statement about the legal guidelines regarding the use of deadly force.

In no instance should the release try to "sell" the public on how much of a criminal the victim was. Relating the victim's past record or amplifying the crime involved in the incident serves no purpose and hurts the surviving members of the family. The press release should, of course, be distributed equally to all members of the media; playing favorites here could have a disastrous consequence. The police administrator should not be alarmed, and indeeed should expect, sensational headlines such as "Cop Slays Teen Burglar."

The possibility of a civil suit arising out of a shooting incident should not be overlooked. Each bit of evidence is gathered with the view that it may eventually be presented in court. More simply stated, the investigation should be done properly the first time. As new evidence and witnesses are discovered, even though some time after the original investigation, there should be no hesitation to thoroughly examine the new material and include it in the case file. Information such as major witness discrepancies, which may cast doubt on the justifiability of the shooting, should never be excluded from the case file, just as such information should never be left out of an ordinary criminal investigation. Again, the need for accurately recording witness statements as soon as possible cannot be overemphasized.

Conclusion

In conclusion, consider the importance of preparation. A coherent, flexible standard operating procedure regarding shooting investigations is extremely valuable. Without such an SOP, a police department must "play it by ear" in a sensitive investigation. In the same vein, clearly understood and often repeated firearms use policies are also vital to a police department. What may be legally justifiable may be unacceptable in a practical social context. Therefore, many departments are restricting firearms use to situations involving armed felons, while statutes may allow such force to be used against escaping felons. The police administrator would do well to keep abreast of case law regarding use of deadly force. What may be legally justifiable may also expose a police department to civil liability in the eyes of a jury.

8. POLICE USE OF DEADLY FORCE

CATHERINE H. MILTON, JEAN W. HALLECK,
JAMES LARDNER, AND GARY L. ALBRECHT

Police Use of Deadly Force (Washington, D.C.: Police Foundation, 1977). Reprinted by permission.

The police officer's legal authority to use deadly force is set forth and defined by common law, statute, and case law. Although the principles of common, or uncodified law are essentially the same throughout the 50 states and are for the most part the same as their English antecedents, statutes governing justifiable homicide and police use of deadly force vary widely among jurisdictions. The same is true of case law, the ever-growing body of court decisions in which common law and statutes alike are interpreted and applied to actual situations.

As an adjunct to these elements of law dealing with the question of when a police officer may justifiably take a life, a number of police agencies have promulgated internal rules addressing that subject. Although such rules cannot grant the officer rights broader than those extended by law, they may impose further restrictions on police conduct.[1]

Common Law

The common-law rules governing arrests try to strike a balance between an individual's interest in freedom from government interference and the public's collective interest in the prevention of crime and the apprehension of law-breakers. In reconciling these interests, the common law traditionally has limited the authority to arrest in proportion to the seriousness of the suspected offense. Likewise, the courts have held that the amount of force that may be used to make or maintain an arrest varies

---

1. Promulgation of rules broader than allowed by state law may subject police and other public officials to civil liability. For example, a twelve-year-old youth obtained a $50,000 judgment against both the mayor of Macon, Georgia, and the officer who shot the boy in the leg, pursuant to the mayor's executive order. That order said in part "Those people engaged in lawlessness and anarchy must be stopped. SHOOT TO KILL!" *Palmer v. Hall, et al.*, 360 F.Supp. 120 (M.D. Ga. 1974).

with the severity of the crime. For this purpose, the critical distinction is that between felony and misdemeanor: Under common law, a police officer may, when necessary, use deadly force to apprehend someone reasonably believed to have committed a felony; deadly force is not permitted, however, merely to prevent the escape of a misdemeanant.

The rationale for this simplistic formula is grounded in the fact that until 1800, in both the United States and England, virtually all felonies were punishable by death. A felon was someone who, by his acts, had forfeited the right to life; consequently, when an officer killed a resisting or fleeing felon, the "extirpation was but a premature execution of the inevitable judgment."[2] It should be noted, however, that homicide, rape, arson, mayhem, robbery, burglary, larceny, prison breach, and rescue of a felon were the only common-law felonies; all other offenses were misdemeanors (except treason, a separate category of crime). Today, in most jurisdictions, a felony is an offense punishable by death or a prison term of one year or more.

Recent Developments in the Law

Whatever sense the felony-misdemeanor distinction may have made as a gauge for the use of deadly force has been eroded by two developments: the expansion of the felony category of crime to include a plethora of offenses, many of a nondangerous and relatively minor character; and an increasing reluctance to impose the death penalty as punishment for any but the most aggravated types of serious felony cases.

Although many states still retain the common-law rule or some variant of it, lawmakers increasingly have questioned the felony-misdemeanor rule as a basis for authorizing the use of deadly force and have significantly modified that rule in some jurisdictions. While some have codified the common-law rule of justifiable homicide, which allows the use of deadly force in the apprehension or pursuit of felons; many others have enacted stricter statutes. These statutes vary in terms of the degree of knowledge an officer must have to justify killing a suspected felon. Some require a "felony in fact," some call for "reasonable belief," and some limit the kinds of felonies that will justify the use of deadly force. Others distinguish between an arrestee and an escapee. The modern trend, however, is toward the adoption of statutes that follow the American Law Institute's Model Penal Code.

The impetus for change was generated in 1962, when the American Law Institute announced its view that a substantial reform of the common-law rule was necessary. The Institute drafted a Model Penal

---

2. "Legalized Murder of a Fleeing Felon," 15 *Va. L. Rev.* 582, 583 (1929).

Code authorizing the use of deadly force when the arrest is for a felony and the officer believes:

1. The crime for which the arrest is made involved conduct including the use or threatened use of deadly force, or
2. There is a substantial risk that the person to be arrested will cause death or serious bodily harm if apprehension is delayed.[3]

At least 24 states have codified the common law and provide that deadly force may be used to arrest any felony suspect. Seven states have modified the common-law rule by requiring that felonies for which deadly force may be used in an arrest are limited to "forcible felonies." Another seven states have adopted the Model Penal Code approach.

Modern literature over the past 50 years generally supports a rule which would limit the use of deadly force by police officers to those circumstances in which its use is essential to the protection of human life and bodily security, or in which violence was used in committing the felony. Moreover, the FBI has adopted a policy which provides that agents are not to shoot any persons except when necessary in self-defense—that is, when they reasonably believe that they or others are in danger of death or grievous bodily harm. Deadly force is such force as under normal circumstances poses a high risk of death or serious injury to its human target, regardless of whether or not death, serious injury, or any harm actually results. Shooting at a human target involves the use of deadly force.[4]

Oregon's new criminal code sanctions the use of deadly force "in making an arrest or preventing an escape of a person who the officer reasonably believes attempted or committed a felony involving the use or threatened imminent use of physical force against a person. Such felonies include murder, manslaughter, robbery, rape, and felony assault." The statute goes on to add kidnapping, arson, first-degree burglary, and first-degree escape to the list. Similarly, the proposed new federal criminal code limits the use of deadly force to those situations in which such force is reasonably required to arrest or prevent the escape of a person who "had engaged in, or attempted to engage in, conduct constituting an offense that involved a risk of death, serious bodily injury, rape, or kidnapping"

---

3. Model Penal Code, Sec. 3.07(b), 1962.

4. For a more extensive discussion of statutory changes in the common-law concept of justified use of deadly force in cases of criminal conduct, see DeRoma, "Justifiable Use of Deadly Force by the Police: A Statutory Survey," 12 *William and Mary L. Rev.* 67 (1970); Tsimbinos, "The Justified Use of Deadly Force," Vol. 4, No. 1, *Crim. L. Bull.* 3 (1968); Rummel, "The Right of Law Enforcement Officers to Use Deadly Force to Effect an Arrest," 14 *N.Y. L. Forum* 749 (1968); "Justification for the Use of Force in the Criminal Law," 13 *Stan. L. Rev.* 566 (May, 1961); Comment, "Deadly Force to Arrest: Triggering Constitutional Review," 11 *Harv. Civ. Rights—Civil Lib. L. Rev.* 361 (1976); *Mattis v. Schnarr*, 547 F.2d 1007 (8th Cir., 1976).

or who "was attempting to escape by the use of a weapon...."[5] The
Senate Committee report accompanying this bill comments that while
this provision has roots in common-law principles, it is much more restrictive than the common-law rule because of "the greater respect of our
modern society for human life...."[6]

The Trend in the Courts

Since 1967 there has been a court-imposed moratorium on capital punishment in the United States. Whatever the stated reasons, this refusal to
sanction official execution in all but the most aggravated cases clearly
reflects a judicial conviction that respect for individual human life must
temper the state's response even to the most culpable criminal conduct.[7]

Given this concern for the lives of persons duly tried and convicted of
capital offenses, it is hardly surprising that the courts should challenge the

---

5. *Criminal Justice Reform Act* of 1975, S.1, 94th Cong., 1st sess., Sec. 541. Both the
   Oregon statute and the proposed new federal code also contain broad and somewhat ambiguous language that could conceivably be interpreted as contradicting the narrow
   clauses quoted here. In Oregon's statute there is a passage permitting the use of deadly
   force "in making an arrest or preventing an escape of a person who the officer reasonably
   believes attempted or committed a felony, and under the total circumstances at the time
   and place, the use of such force is necessary." The revised federal code now before Congress ends with a phrase allowing the use of deadly force by a public servant when it is
   "otherwise authorized by law." This language apparently refers to executions; it is
   unclear whether it may turn out to have any other application.

6. *Report of the Committee on the Judiciary,* U.S. Sen., 93rd Cong., 2d sess., to accompany
   the Criminal Justice Codification, Revision, and Reform Act of 1974, vol. II, p. 126.

7. *Furman v. Georgia,* 408 U.S. 238 (1972), decided by the United States Supreme Court,
   held that death penalty statutes were invalid if applied unequally. Since *Furman,* death
   penalty statutes were reenacted in some 35 states. Recently, the Supreme Court decided
   another series of cases challenging the death penalty statutes in five states. Those five
   opinions, announced July 2, 1976, held that the North Carolina and Louisiana statutes
   violated the Eighth Amendment by making the death penalty mandatory in certain
   homicidal offenses. The statutes in Georgia, Florida, and Texas were upheld because
   they required the sentencing court to weigh the circumstances carefully before imposing
   the death penalty, or because they provided in some other way for consideration of ag-
   gravating or mitigating factors, or allowed other safeguards within the procedures used
   to foreclose any automatic imposition of the death penalty.

   Clearly, the Court intended that only in the most serious and aggravated homicides
   should the death penalty be imposed and then only according to well defined criteria for
   application of discretion by courts and juries. The statutes in 18 states were either
   declared unconstitutional or cast into doubt, while 14 others seem to pass muster.
   However, as the possibility of the lifting of the nine-year moratorium on executions draws
   near, a new wave of public protest seems to be emerging to counteract the views of some
   that the death penalty should be imposed in certain selected, aggravated cases. The Court
   recognized that society may be said to accept the death penalty as appropriate sanction,
   but it also pointed out that evolving standards of community values have been reflected in
   the humane feelings of jurors who reserve the irrevocable sanction for a small number of
   extreme cases.

use of deadly force by police merely to apprehend or prevent the escape of a felony suspect. The Supreme Court has observed that officers "who decide to take the law into their own hands and act as a prosecutor, jury, judge and executioner plainly act to deprive a prisoner of the trial which due process of law guarantees him."[8]

Most recently in a civil action against two police officers, brought by the father of a slain 18-year-old, the Eighth Circuit Court of Appeals concluded that the Missouri statute allowing the use of deadly force against any fleeing felon is unconstitutional, as applied to fleeing felons suspected of a nonviolent felony, if the officers do not reasonably believe the felons will use deadly force against the officers or others. (The unarmed deceased was shot while running from a golf-driving range office at 1:20 A.M.)

The Court recognized the fundamental right of an individual to life, a right protected by the Fifth and Fourteenth Amendments to the Constitution. The court concluded that the situations in which the state can take a life, without according a trial to the individual whose life is taken, must be determined by balancing the individual's right to life against the interest of society in insuring public safety.

Finding that the court has the ultimate responsibility to determine whether the balance struck is a constitutional one, the Eighth Circuit said that felonies are of an infinite variety and that a police officer cannot be constitutionally vested with the power and authority to kill any and all escaping felons, including the thief who steals an ear of corn as well as one who kills and ravishes at will. Rather, an officer will be required to use a reasonable and informed professional judgment, constantly aware that death is the weapon of last resort, to be employed only in situations presenting the gravest threat to either the officer or the public at large.[9]

The number of civil suits filed against police departments and individual officers rises each year, and almost 30 percent of these filings contain some claim of excessive use of force.[10] Although many claims are settled, as the number of cases coming before the courts increases, the result may very likely be more decisions refining and extending tort liability for the unjustified use of deadly force.[11]

---

8. *Screws v. United States,* 325 U.S. 91, 106 (1945).

9. *Mattis v. Schnarr and Marek.*

10. Americans for Effective Law Enforcement, Inc., *Survey of Police Misconduct Litigation, 1967-1971* (1974), p. 6.

11. Another aspect of the increased number of civil suits is reflected by the experience of Miami and Dade County, Florida. Insurance premiums covering government protection in cases of police misconduct while on duty rose in one year from $60,000 to $150,000. It should be noted perhaps, that in some instances settlement reflects cost effectiveness (costs of insurance premiums vs. court costs) rather than an admission of fault. Nevertheless, the results are the same: increased insurance premiums for the jurisdiction.

Police departments should carefully note this trend, not only because of the threatening prospect of more and larger recoveries by victims and their families, but also because of the legal philosophy underlying such decisions. In a sense, a collective social judgment is emerging through the resolution of lawsuits that accuse the police of using too much or the wrong kind of force. Citizens are increasingly aware of the existence of judicial remedies to enforce their rights. Judges and juries (in civil cases, at any rate) seem to be placing greater emphasis on the individual's right to life and physical integrity.[12] The correlative result is to place a greater degree of responsibility on departments, as well as officers, in their use of deadly weapons.

Police Rule Making to Limit the Use of Deadly Force

It seems unlikely that judicial supervision over police firearms practices will soon abate. The willingness, or as some would no doubt call it, the eagerness of the judiciary to impose restraints upon police conduct flows from the principle that government agencies must be accountable to the people they serve, a fundamental tenet in our legal heritage. "Accountability" in this context means that official agencies—especially agencies such as police departments, which engage in discretionary decision making—must be subject to public control according to known and uniform rules. The significance to the police of this judicial distaste for broad, unstructured discretion is readily apparent, inasmuch as discretion is a pervasive and often necessary feature of day-to-day police work.

Police departments are organized in a fashion that delegates greater amounts of discretion as one moves *down* the chain of command, and the courts are apt to perceive an absence of rules in this setting as particularly dangerous. Although the judiciary historically has been reluctant to intervene in matters of internal police management, courts are now reaching the conclusion that external controls upon the police, through exclusionary rules and doctrines of tort liability, are often insufficient.

---

12. In Madison, Tennessee, in January 1976, a man shot in the back after he fled from an officer writing a red-light ticket was awarded $35,000 by the court, which the city would have to pay. Additionally, the involved officer, fired from the department, also faced the prospect of criminal charges arising from the shooting.

Settlement payments and jury awards in police brutality cases cost the city of Philadelphia about $400,000 in 1975. More than 70 percent of the damages resulted from deaths of civilians shot by police. One jury award amounted to $116,570; another case was settled for $130,000.

Substantial case law precedent now exists for the proposition that courts may compel police administrators to promulgate internal rules to provide guidelines for the conduct of their officers.[13] It is a reasonably safe prediction that departments soon will have to become actively involved in developing rules or guidelines to govern a wide variety of police behavior, or face the prospect that the courts will insist that such rules be made.

This development should not trouble police administrators. For too long the police have foregone the initiation of policy, content to respond passively to judicial direction. Internal rule-making offers an opportunity to reverse this process. As a former legal advisor to the Washington police department observes, rule-making gives law enforcement agencies the chance to develop policy that is sensible from the police perspective,

---

13. See, for example, *United States v. Bryant*, 439 F.2d 642 (D.C. Cir. 1971) which required the Bureau of Narcotics and Dangerous Drugs (now the Drug Enforcement Administration) to "show that it has promulgated, enforced and attempted in good faith to follow rigorous and systematic procedures designed to preserve *all* discoverable evidence gathered in the course of a criminal investigation." The Court also said: "Although we leave it up to the various investigative agencies to draft rules suited to their own method of operation, all such rules will be subject to review of their adequacy to the assigned task."; *Quad City Community News Service, Inc. v. Jebens*, 334 F.Supp. 8 (S.D. Iowa 1971), enjoining a police department from refusing press passes to an underground newspaper until the department issued available standards for the evaluation of all press pass applications; *Hicks v. Knight*, 10 *Race Rel. L. Rptr.* 1504 (E.D. La. 1965), directing police administrators, under penalty of contempt, to formulate and make public a plan for the handling of demonstrations, ordering them to reduce to writing specific instructions to individual officers and their supervisors for the execution of the plan, and to adopt in writing a disciplinary procedure to be instituted against any officer who failed to follow his assignment under the plan. See also Davis, "An Approach to Legal Control of the Police," 52 *Tex. L. Rev.* 703, 708-12 (1974); McGowan, "Rule-Making and the Police," 70 *Mich. L.Rev.* 659, 684-85 (1972); K. Davis, *Discretionary Justice* (1969); A. Amsterdam, "The Supreme Court and the Rights of Suspects in Criminal Cases," 45 *N.Y.U. L. Rev.* 785 (1970). Professor Davis urges a revival of the non-delegation doctrine in order to place police investigative procedures under strict rule governance. Professor Amsterdam locates a firm constitutional basis for the requirement of rule-making by the police. Recently, however, the Supreme Court has indicated that federal courts can go too far by requiring local police to engage in certain administrative investigations of citizen complaints. In *Rizzo v. Goode*, 96 S. Ct. 598 (1976), a lower federal court order requiring the Philadelphia police department to set up new procedures to deal with citizen complaints against police was reversed by a 5 to 3 decision which held that the lower court order was an unwarranted intrusion by the federal judiciary into matters entrusted to local officials. This decision in no way reverses the powerful modern trend in the law which rejects blind reliance on the unstructured exercise of official discretion in favor of a new judicial willingness to require police and other law enforcement agencies to promulgate and follow rules.

rather than having to react to the often less informed dictates of the judiciary.[14]

Many police chiefs, however, are unwilling to adopt strict internal regulations governing the use of deadly force. In some instances, police union pressures militate against such strict or specific forms of regulations. Hervey Juris and Peter Feuille observe in their book, *Police Unionism:*

> Consistent with their "hard line" on the handling of civil disorders, police unions have pressed for heavy armaments and minimal restrictions on the police right to use force, especially fatal force...[T]he San Francisco union was able to persuade the chief and the police commission to change a proposed set of gun guidelines so that an officer involved in an on-duty homicide is not automatically suspended pending an investigation. In Seattle, the union negotiated a contract clause providing that no officer can be required over his objection to work without a gun....[A] union in a western city pressed unsuccessfully for the right of each officer to carry the weapon of his choice. In an eastern city, the union lobbied the city council for the right to carry shotguns in squad cars, but the chief was able to muster sufficient opposition to have the union voted down.[15]

---

14. Caplan, "The Case for Rulemaking by Law Enforcement Agencies," 1971 *L. & Contemp. Probs.* 500, 505, Duke University School of Law 36 (1971), p. 4. Provides a striking example of how police rule-making can influence subsequent judicial action. The courts had disapproved as unduly suggestive uncounseled one-to-one confrontations between victim and suspect for the purpose of securing identifications; however, the decisions indicated that some identifications obtained in this manner would be acceptable if sufficiently proximate in time and place to the commission of the offense. The courts did not specify how long after an offense such confrontations might be permissible, preferring instead to consider the problem on a case-by-case basis.

In March 1970, the Washington police department issued an order to provide its officers with clear and concise identification procedures. The order adopted a one-hour limit for street confrontations. That is, a suspect apprehended within one hour of the offense in an area reasonably near the site of the crime could be returned to the scene for viewing by the victim. If the arrest occurred after the passage of an hour, the suspect could not be returned.

Although their previous decisions suggested that the courts would have preferred a much shorter interval between arrest and confrontation, the courts accepted the department rule: "We see in this regulation a careful and commendable administrative effort to balance the freshness of such a confrontation against its inherent suggestiveness, and to balance both factors against the need to pick up the trail while fresh if the suspect is not the offender. *We see no need for interposing at this time any more rigid standard by judicial declaration.*" (emphasis added). *United States v. Perry,* 449 F.2d 1026, 1037 (D.C. Cir. 1971). Washington's experience demonstrates that courts will be sympathetic and receptive to department attempts to clarify the law by responsible rule-making.

15. Hervey A. Juris and Peter Feuille, *Police Unionism* (Lexington, Mass.: Lexington Books, 1973). See also, *San Jose Police Officers Ass'n v. City of San Jose, et al.,* Sup. Ct., Santa Clara County, Ca., No. 325818, decided June 20, 1975.

Frequently, police administrators want their officers to exercise restraint, but are reluctant to commit that desire to paper, for fear that a narrow department firearms policy will merely invite more civil suits and judgments in the wake of police shootings. The administrators believe that courts will, in effect, hold departments accountable to their own strict policies despite more lenient or ambiguous state laws.

This is not a groundless fear. The Supreme Court of California, for example, has held that a department's written firearms policy may be introduced into evidence in a wrongful death lawsuit and that a police officer's deviation from that policy is evidence of negligence.[16]

It would be a mistake, however, to assume that an individual officer or department can escape liability by the gambit of not committing a firearms policy to print. First, oral policy directives may be just as admissible in civil litigation as written ones. Second, the very lack of specific guidelines may itself be held to constitute negligence by the department. Liability could be imposed upon a municipality which failed to provide its officers with adequate instructions and training in the use of firearms. Finally, and most important, failure to promulgate written policy for fear of increased exposure to civil liability might result in more shooting incidents.[17] Ultimately, the absence of written policy may lead to an increase rather than a reduction in the number of successful civil suits.

The Range of Department Firearms Policies

Despite concerns about establishing an increased basis for civil liability, the clear trend across the country seems to be toward the adoption of department firearms use policies, generally narrower than either the statutory or decisional state law that is applicable. All of the seven sample departments have formal policies and most of those policies have been adopted within the last few years.

It is not a simple matter, however, to categorize firearms use policies as "restrictive" or "permissive." Oakland, for example, instructs its officers not to shoot at fleeing burglars.[18] Indianapolis imposes no such restriction. But in Indianapolis the officer who fires at a fleeing felon must have *positive knowledge* that the person committed a felony, while in Oakland the officer needs only *reasonable belief*. Thus, on one hand, Oakland has the more restrictive policy, while, on the other Indianapolis has.

Most firearms policies are really the sum of many components, each addressing a particular set of circumstances in which an officer might con-

---

16. *Grudt v. City of Los Angeles*, 2 Cal. 3d 575, 86 Cal. Rptr. 465, 468 P.2d 825 (1970).

17. Hahn, "A Profile of Urban Police," 1971 *L. & Contemp. Probs.* 449, 464.

18. See Table 1. Oakland policy restrictions apply to the felony categories of burglary and auto theft only.

sider firing a weapon. Depending on local attitudes and the pattern of shooting incidents in a particular city,[19] the firearms policy may be unusually restrictive when it treats one type of situation and yet unusually flexible when it treats another. For example, former Oakland Chief C.R. Gain decided to change his department's policy on burglary after examining how the courts were treating persons charged with that offense:

> Considering that only 7.65 percent of all adult burglars arrested and only .28 percent of all juvenile burglars arrested are eventually incarcerated, it is difficult to resist the conclusion that the use of deadly force by peace officers to apprehend burglars cannot conceivably be justified. For adults, the police would have to shoot 100 burglars in order to have captured the eight who would have gone to prison. For juveniles, the police would have to shoot 1,000 burglars in order to have captured the three who would have gone to the Youth Authority.[20]

Although the Oakland department prohibits the shooting of burglars and auto thieves, it says nothing, at least officially, about other nonviolent felonies, such as grand larceny. It is reasonable to assume that if an Oakland police officer did shoot a person who had committed a grand larceny, the department would adopt a rule to prevent such shootings in the future.

Indianapolis is the one city among those we visited with no written firearms policy at all beyond a restatement of state law. Birmingham, however, had no deadly force policy until March 1975. Because Alabama was one of those states without a statute establishing when an officer may use deadly force, the previous guiding principle of the decisional law was a 1915 Alabama case in which the court approved the use of deadly force to apprehend the operator of an illegal whiskey still as he ran from the premises.

Where guidelines have been formulated, the policies vary widely among departments. Some are decidedly narrower than the governing state law; some merely reiterate the law. Portland, for example, has a policy identical to Oregon law except for a single opening paragraph of general philosophy. Some policies are precise and technical; some are laced with statements of morality and strong rhetoric. Some policies amount to only a few paragraphs; some run on for pages. Until 1968, one

---

19. Frequently, written firearms guidelines evolve as a response to public outcry and media coverage surrounding some particular shooting incident. In 1974, a new set of written guidelines in Port Arthur, Texas, followed the killing of a youth after he was stopped for speeding. In 1975, a new set of guidelines in Cleveland, Ohio, following the police killing of a 20-year-old motorcyclist.

20. Charles R. Gain, "Discharge of Firearms Policy: Effecting Justice Through Administrative Regulation," unpublished paper.

southwestern department with more than 100 sworn members had the following policy on the use of a firearm (quoted in its entirety):

> Never take me out in anger; never put me back in disgrace.[21]

A southern department had eight pages of its rules devoted to uniform specifications and allowances, yet had less than one page on the use of firearms:

> Unnecessary and careless handling of firearms may cause accidents, and the drawing, aiming, or snapping of firearms within Police Headquarters, or in other places, is forbidden.

Samuel Chapman, writing for the Task Force Report on the Police, also noted other similar policies:

● Officers shall not intentionally fire their guns except as authorized by law.

● Leave the gun in the holster until you intend to use it.

● Shoot only when absolutely necessary to apprehend a criminal who has committed a major felony.

● Never pull a sidearm as a threat, and if it is drawn, be prepared to use same.

● It is left to the discretion of each individual officer when and how to shoot.

Before June 1975 the policy in Cleveland, Ohio, provided simply that "Officers and members should use only such force as necessary to effect the arrest and detention of persons."

This great variety, Chapman remarks, "reflects, in far too many instances, a failure on the part of police administrators to provide adequate guidance for officers faced with situations where they must decide instantaneously whether or not to use their firearms in discharging their official responsibilities."[22]

A common feature of many firearms policies is that they *appear* to be more restrictive than they really are. The Kansas City Police Department, for example, on the first page of its firearms order, states: "An officer is equipped with a firearm to defend himself or others against deadly force, or the threat of imminent deadly force." Two pages later, the policy authorizes the use of deadly force against certain fleeing felons regardless of immediate danger.

The Los Angeles policy (and, modeled on it, the Birmingham policy)

---

21. Samuel G. Chapman, *Police Firearms Use Policy*, Report to the President's Commission on Law Enforcement and Administration of Justice (Washington, D.C.: U.S. Government Printing Office, 1967).

22. Ibid.

hints that while officers may use their firearms to apprehend fleeing felons, they should exercise discretion. "It is not practical," the Los Angeles Police Department manual states, "to enumerate specific felonies and state with certainty that the escape of the perpetrator must be prevented at all costs, or that there are other felonious crimes where the perpetrator must be allowed to escape rather than to shoot him. Such decisions are based upon sound judgment, not arbitrary checklists."

In Washington, D.C., the written policy holds that an officer may use deadly force to apprehend a suspect in a felony involving "an actual or threatened attack which the officer has reasonable cause to believe could result in death or serious bodily injury." The Washington policy is a restatement of the common-law rule of self-defense, which provides that the law of self-defense is a law of necessity. The necessity must be, in appearance, a reality, and must appear to admit of no other alternative before the taking of life will be excused as justifiable on the ground of self-defense.

The following sections describe a variety of approaches, as articulated in department policies, to specific circumstances in which the use of a weapon might be considered. Certain aspects of weaponry are discussed as well.

Self-Defense and Defense of Others

Every policy gives the officer the right to use deadly force in self-defense or in the defense of others. Some policies say just that; others stipulate that firearms may be used only "when all other available means have failed" (Oakland), require a threat of "serious bodily harm or death" (Detroit), or specify that the danger must be "immediate" (Kansas City).

Fleeing Felons

In all seven cities there was some provision for the use of deadly force to apprehend fleeing felons. There was, however, considerable variation in the felonies covered. Some departments itemize specific felonies justifying deadly force, whereas others list the felonies that do not justify such force. Still others state only that the felony committed must itself have involved the actual or threatened use of force (or deadly force); and some departments authorize deadly force in the apprehension of any felon, without qualification.

Where distinctions are made among particular felonies, one offense likely to be excluded is auto theft, presumably on the rationale that most auto thieves are juvenile joyriders. In large cities, a similarly tolerant attitude, although to a lesser degree, seems to be developing toward burglars (while burglary continues to be viewed in rural areas as an implicitly violent crime, every bit as reprehensible as armed robbery).

In the majority of the sample cities, department policy forbids the use of firearms against fleeing burglars; Birmingham and Indianapolis are the exceptions. A very few police departments have drafted policies that virtually forbid the shooting of fleeing felons, regardless of the felony involved. The proposed new San Jose, California, firearms policy states: "The discharge of firearms is never justifiable solely for the purpose of apprehension....A police officer may use deadly force when all other reasonable means have failed and the officer honestly and reasonably believes that such force is necessary to protect himself or another person from death or great bodily injury." San Jose's policy has not yet been put into effect because of a dispute with the police officers' association there.

San Diego's policy says much the same thing, adding only that an officer may use deadly force "to apprehend a violent person who is known to be armed and dangerous and who cannot be apprehended without risking loss of life or serious injury." It is somewhat difficult to reconcile this clause with another section of the San Diego policy that reads: "Firearms are not to be used...to fire at any person fleeing to evade arrest." Which passage would apply, for example, to a situation in which an armed bank robber was running away from the police and about to make good his escape?

Juveniles

Many departments have different standards for juveniles and adults; typically, officers are instructed not to fire at juveniles except in defense of a life. The problem is that it is not always easy to distinguish juveniles from adults; there are few departments that have gone as far as Kansas City, where the policy states: "The Officer will be required to prove that his judgment in the matter of age was reasonable. If there is any doubt as to the age of the subject, the officer should not shoot."

The Birmingham policy's stricture on shooting at juveniles seems slightly less emphatic. "An officer generally should not shoot at a fleeing felon whom he has reasonable grounds to believe is a juvenile. However, when the escape of such a suspect can reasonably be expected to pose a serious threat to the life of another person, then, under these circumstances, an officer may shoot to prevent the escape of such person...."

In Detroit, most police officers feel that they are not to shoot at fleeing juvenile felons. The policy, in fact, makes no mention of juveniles; the only written reference to juveniles is contained in a training and information bulletin: "[I]t may be well to point out that over seventy percent of UDAA's (car thefts) and larceny from person (purse snatching) is committed by juveniles. Neither of these crimes, in most instances, are of such grave nature as to necessitate the use of an officer's firearm."

Innocent Bystanders

One of the points that more extensive firearms policies tend to cover, and briefer policies do not, is the risk to innocent bystanders. No department is known to demand that its officers refrain from shooting *in self-defense* because of a danger to bystanders. But when the purpose is to make an arrest or prevent an escape, the officer may be instructed not to fire in the direction of uninvolved citizens. The Oakland policy, for example, says that in such situations "firearms shall not be discharged if the member has reason to believe, based upon the attendant circumstances, that the discharge may endanger the lives of passersby or other persons not involved in the crime from which flight is being made or attempted."

Shooting from or at a Moving Vehicle

Shots fired from or at a moving vehicle are widely discouraged for two reasons. First, there is an obvious danger to innocent persons in the area if the driver should lose control of the car. Second, such shots are notoriously ineffective. Rather than imposing an outright ban on shooting in these situations, however, departments dealing with the question generally restrict use of firearms to clear cases of imminent danger or merely stress the need for special caution.

New York City has an unusually strong provision: "Discharging a firearm from or at a moving vehicle is prohibited unless the occupants of the other vehicle are using deadly physical force against the officer or another by means other than the vehicle." Officers frequently justify firing at automobiles by testifying that the occupants have attempted to run them down. The New York policy may reflect a suspicion that such claims are often exaggerated or fabricated; from a practical point of view, an officer actually about to be struck by a car could probably find a more promising method of insuring personal safety than the use of a firearm.

Warning Shots

All seven of the sample cities prohibit the use of warning shots in their firearms policy itself, in a supplemental bulletin, or verbally. In explaining such a prohibition, some police officials talk about the risk that a shot intended as a warning may strike an innocent person; privately they may fear something else—that officers shooting at a suspect and missing will claim they were merely firing a warning shot, and thus avoid answering for their actions. In addition, officials point out, warning shots rarely accomplish their purpose, especially if suspects know officers will not or cannot actually shoot them.

Drawing and Display of Firearms

Most departments, taking the view that there are circumstances when drawing or displaying (pointing) a firearm is reasonable and firing it is not, have omitted the subject from their firearms policies altogether. Only a few policies go into the question of when an officer should draw a weapon. The Indianapolis policy (following the wording of Indiana law) begins: "No officer will draw or discharge a firearm except..." and then lists the conditions which apply equally to either act. The Pasadena, California, policy takes a slightly different approach: "Firearms shall be removed from holsters only when the officer reasonably believes that he will have to discharge the weapon...."

While neither of these provisions is unambiguous, both might prompt objections from many veteran police officers if narrowly interpreted. It is common practice for officers to draw their weapons upon arrival at the scene of a holdup or burglary, or on checking out a possible suspect in a violent crime. Certainly, no officer wants to enter a bank or liquor store where a holdup alarm has sounded without weapon drawn. Similarly, no officer wants to confront a reported armed suspect in any alleged offense, yet to display a weapon in these circumstances would seem to go against the Indianapolis and Pasadena policies.

One proposed model policy suggests "allowing the draw but preventing the display." The author, Paul M. Gilligan, believes that it is caution enough for officers to hold a gun alongside their legs. Pointing or aiming, however, "must not be allowed without an accompanying legal justification for the actual use of deadly force."[23]

It is true that officers who point their guns indiscriminately may, at best, unnecessarily frighten and offend people and, at worst, bring about a violent incident. But the job of a police officer is unpredictable, and some would argue that if having their firearms in a ready position can reduce the risk inherent in certain situations, then police should be given that right, even at the sacrifice of ideal police community relations.

A plausible compromise, for a department wishing to restrain the display of firearms without putting its members in jeopardy, is a provision such as that contained in the Dallas, Texas, policy:

> The policy of this Department permits the drawing and/or displaying of firearms when:
> 1. An officer, in the exercise of sound judgment, has reason to fear for his own personal safety and/or the safety of others (this in-

---

23. Paul M. Gilligan, "Police Policy Formulation on Firearms: Some Considerations," *The Police Chief* (May 1971).

cludes but is not limited to the search of a building for a burglar, a robbery in progress) or

2. The offender is suspected of having a deadly weapon in his possession. (The intent of this provision is to permit the officers to protect themselves and others *and* to avoid the necessity of actually having to use a firearm when the threat of doing so might accomplish the purpose.)

Shotguns

Nearly all big-city police departments use shotguns, but not all departments issue them to partol officers. In some jurisdictions only superior officers or members of special units are equipped with shotguns.

The need for a shotgun arises when police anticipate confronting an armed subject or group of subjects at close range. Whether a department should issue shotguns to all its members or have one in every car is a difficult question. It is expensive to train hundreds of police officers in the use of a shotgun, and dangerous to put one in the hands of an untrained person. In addition, the widespread use of shotguns frequently makes for bad public relations. Finally, because shotguns have to be left inside vehicles during many, indeed most, police calls, there is always the risk of theft.

In one city surveyed, an officer observed a subject breaking into a basement window, chased him, ordered him to halt, and fired at the subject with a shotgun from a distance of more than 200 feet. Although the shot struck its mark and a burglar was thereby apprehended, such an incident raises at least two questions: First, wasn't there a substantial risk to innocent persons from the expanded shot pattern over so great a distance; and second, would the officer, had he not been carrying such a heavy and cumbersome weapon, have been able to apprehend the suspect without the use of any firearm?

Since the time of our site visit, Portland has put shotguns in patrol cars, a step prompted by an alarming increase in armed attacks on officers. This step was taken, however, only after considerable thought and planning, resulting in a set of procedures and policy guidelines that tell officers when and when not to take shotguns with them on assignments. Each patrol car is equipped with a shotgun mount but the weapons are issued only at the discretion of supervisory officers.

Second Guns

In two of the seven sample cities, it is not uncommon for officers on duty and in uniform to carry a second or "back-up" weapon. Detroit expressly permits the practice. Indianapolis, at the time of our visit, tolerated it despite a regulation that could be interpreted to the contrary. In July 1975, a revised general order was put into effect in Indianapolis which specifically stated that "officers wishing to carry a second gun may do so providing it is a departmental approved weapon and remains concealed from public view."

The rationale for a second gun, presumably, is that it will protect officers should they be disarmed, run out of ammunition, or have mechanical difficulties with the primary weapon. But there are many possible pitfalls. First, the practice is likely to make it harder to prevent the improper carrying of "drop guns"—weapons carried for planting on a suspect in order to build a case or justify a police shooting. In a department in which no additional firearms are permitted, the sight of a second gun protruding from an officer's pocket will be cause for immediate investigation by a passing superior. In cities such as Detroit and Indianapolis, where second guns are allowed, the passing superior might reasonably assume that such an extra gun was merely an officer's back-up weapon.

In addition, the practice may cause an officer to be less cautious—perhaps to take unnecessary risks rather than call for assistance. It could also hamper the investigation of an incident by making it harder to trace a bullet to an officer's gun.

Finally, by leaving so important a question as the carrying of a second gun to the discretion of the individual officer, a department risks reinforcing the belief of many rank-and-file officers that desk-bound command officials have no idea what it is like out on the street. If officers are allowed to decide for themselves what weapons they should carry, why not decide for themselves when to use them?

Structure and Language of Firearms Policies

Many police firearms policies seem poorly organized, badly worded, or both. Sometimes, apparent conflicts within a policy may be the result of a department's attempt to say two things at once—one thing to officers for their own information and another thing to the courts for the handling of incidents gone awry.

In some cities, it is difficult even to locate a complete copy of the firearms policy, which may be split among several department orders issued over a period of years. Oakland's provision against shooting fleeing burglars, for example, is contained in an order separate from the main firearms policy. Policies also can be long and confusing. The Kansas City policy, the longest of those studied, was written immediately after the shooting of a 15-year-old prowler, an incident that generated considerable controversy, and may, therefore, be reflecting the trying circumstances in which it was conceived.

Some firearms policies are far too complex or the language too convoluted to be of practical use to police officers. For example, the Dallas policy, composed mostly of excerpts from Texas law, includes among its many sections and subsections the following:

(c) A peace officer is justified in using deadly force against another when and to the degree the peace officer reasonably believes the deadly force is immediately necessary to make an arrest, or to prevent escape after arrest, if the use of force would have been justified under Subsection (a) of this section and:
1. the actor reasonably believes the conduct for which arrest is authorized included the use or attempted use of deadly force; or
2. the actor reasonably believes there is substantial risk that the person to be arrested will cause death or serious bodily injury to the actor or another if the arrest is delayed.

Some policies, or parts of them, are heavily philosophical. A one-page order issued by a former chief of the Indianapolis department in 1974, for example, concludes with the following paragraph:

The Indianapolis Police Department values life so highly that each individual member is sworn to give a substantial portion of his or her own life at great risk to make certain that all other lives are safeguarded. The fabric of civilization and law which makes possible enjoyment of life and property in our community is worthy of careful and certain defense.

Not only is the precise meaning of this passage unclear, but some officers could find its moralistic tone patronizing. As impressive as such discursions may be to outsiders, their impact on the conduct of police officers is questionable.

Conclusion

Our survey of the literature, the law, and recent court decisions, as well as a review of shooting incidents in seven cities has left us with the strong feeling that police departments should adopt written firearms policies. The administrative objective in adopting a formal policy is twofold:

1. Control over police use of firearms and protection of the community. Although no study has yet extensively documented the impact of formal policies on the rate or nature of police shootings of civilians, it stands to reason that the desired result is more likely to come about if the intent of a police administrator is conveyed in a clearly written document that lets officers know what is and what is not permissible behavior. A formal policy also tells the community what standard of conduct it can expect from the police department.

TABLE 1—Comparative Elements in Departmental Policies

	Oakland	Birmingham	Detroit	Kansas City	Indianapolis	Washington, D.C.	Portland
Shooting of fleeing burglars permitted?	No	Yes	Yes	No	Yes[2]	No	No
Auto thieves?	No	Yes	No	No	Yes[2]	No	No
Fleeing juvenile felons?	No	Discouraged	Discouraged[3]	No	Yes[2]	Yes	Yes
Warning shots permitted?	No	No	No	No	Prohibited by unwritten rule	No	No
Must officer have positive knowledge or reasonable belief that suspect has committed a felony?	Belief	Belief	Known "as a virtual certainty"	Belief	Certain knowledge	Belief	Belief
Does policy include caution on firing at or from moving vehicle?	Yes	No	Yes	Yes	No	Yes	No
Carrying an off-duty firearm (in jurisdiction)?	—	—	—	Optional	Mandatory	Mandatory	Optional
Are officers permitted to carry "second guns"?	No	No	Yes	No	Yes	No	No

1. The Portland policy includes a clause not taken into account here, authorizing use of firearms against any fleeing felon if, "under the total circumstances at the time and place, the use of such force is necessary."
2. The policy includes the proviso: "[after] all other reasonable means of capture have been expended."
3. The subject of juveniles is discussed obliquely in supplemental training bulletin.

2. Reduction in the number and degree of adverse results from both criminal and civil litigation arising from shooting incidents. These benefits can be expected to flow not only to individual police officers but to the department and to governing agencies. A clearly stated policy removes much of the uncertainty that can surround many situations confronting both individual officers and department administrators, and will certainly help to resolve subsequent legal issues that may arise after a shooting incident.

It is not enough, however, just to commit a policy to paper. If police officers are to respect the departments which employ them, it is important that rules be (and be perceived as) clear and reasonable. Firearms policies, and policies in general, should be written for use on the street rather than for public relations or for after-the-fact insurance against liability. The best way to accomplish this seems to be to examine other departments' firearms policies and perhaps to borrow elements from "model" or existing policies, adding whatever provisions seem appropriate for the individual department in light of local and state statutes and local community needs.

Concepts to Consider

1. Describe the impact of the use of deadly force by police officers on minorities.

2. Identify the types of situations that are most hazardous for police officers.

3. Justify the inclusion of police patrol officers as participants in the development of policy concerning the use of firearms.

4. Differentiate betweeen "actual" policy and "stated" policy governing the use of firearms.

5. Support the position that there is a need for greater legal control of the use of deadly force by police.

Selected Readings

Chapman, Samuel G., *Police Murders and Effective Countermeasures* (Santa Cruz, Ca.: Davis Publishing, 1976).

This text is a report analyzing the murder of 41 Oklahoma police officers. It discloses what happened to suspects who took the officers' lives. The book also discusses effective countermeasures.

Kania, Richard R.E. and Wade C. Mackey, "Police Violence as a Function of Community Characteristics," *Criminology*, Vol. 15, No. 1, May 1977, pp. 27-48.

The authors find that existing models concerning police violence are not designed to explain variation among the states in the rates of police use of deadly force. It is suggested that the police use of violence is a culturally determined characteristic.

Kobler, Arthur L., "Police Homicide in a Democracy," *Journal of Social Issues*, Vol. 31, No. 1, 1975, pp. 163-184.

The author postulates that many more people are killed by police than the number that kill police. It is suggested that police regulations are more limiting than the law, but there is little indication that departmental rules are stringently enforced.

Kobler, Arthur L., "Figures (and Perhaps Some Facts) on Police Killing of Civilians in the United States," *Journal of Social Issues*, Vol. 31, No. 1, 1975, pp. 185-191.

Presents official data for a 20 year period that shows police killed about five civilians for every officer killed. Includes a study of newspaper reports from 1965 to 1969 which shows that about half of the police and their victims were young male minorities in urban areas.

Lester, David, "A Study of Civilian-Caused Murders of Police Officers," *International Journal of Criminology and Penology*, Vol. 6, No. 4, November 1978, pp. 373-378.

This study has found that civilian-caused murders of police are found in states with a high incidence of all kinds of violence and in southern and politically conservative states.

Moorman, Charles B., "Peace Officers Murdered in California 1973-1977: Awareness and Learning Points Survey," *Journal of California Law Enforcement*, Vol. 13, No. 2, October 1978, pp. 62-69.

An analysis of California peace officer murders during the period 1973-1977 that is utilized to assist other peace officers in performing their duties in a safer manner, based on awareness and related training programs.

Robin, Gerald D., "Justifiable Homicide by Police Officers," *Journal of Criminal Law, Criminology, and Police Science*, Vol. 54, 1963, pp. 225-231.

A study of an eleven year period during which there were 32 cases of police slayings of criminals in Philadelphia. Data comparison is made with nine other cities in terms of race, sex, and offense.

Van Meter, Steve, "Deadly Force," *Journal of California Law Enforcement*, Vol. 12, No. 3, January 1978, pp. 116-122.

This article raises issues and identifies factors police administrators should consider in developing or reformulating department policies dealing with the use of deadly force.

Chapter 4
REVIEW OF POLICE CONDUCT

Introduction

In the eyes of most police administrators, the effectiveness of law enforcement rests on the relative autonomy which society has invested in the police. Therefore, any demands made for public review of police misconduct are typically regarded as intrusions upon that autonomy and as threats to effective law enforcement. Such demands are also reviewed by many administrators as an attempt to politicize the police. This is especially resented because, during the last quarter of a century, police agencies have gained relative freedom from partisan political interference. It is commonly felt among police administrators that when officers become subject to public review for their actions they will become, once again, instruments of pressure group politics. Finally, it is feared that public analysis of police conduct by review boards or other similarly constituted bodies will erode officers' morale by stripping away the self-contained authority to both discipline and control misconduct among the ranks.

There are other objections to public review of police conduct. One of the major contentions is that review boards threaten administrative authority. Management theory in all aspects of public administration repeatedly supports the position that a chief administrative officer is responsible for the conduct of his agency; concomitant with this responsibility is adequate authority. Dispersal of this formal authority will reduce the decisive and dramatic characteristics that are essential aspects of agency leadership.[1]

Compromise and conciliation are essential if this critical problem is to be resolved. The Michigan State study visualized two distinct alternate possibilities for the police:

1. They can refuse to initiate any changes and be prepared to tolerate decreasing public respect and suffer increased violence; or
2. They can admit some fallibility, welcome criticism, compromise a little, and objectively initiate considered changes in an effort to enhance public support and avoid violence.[2]

*

---

1. For detailed discussion of administrative authority, see John M. Pfiffner, *Public Administration* (New York: The Ronald Press Company, 1967), pp. 212-216 and Peter Blau, *The Dynamics of Bureaucracy*, 2nd Ed. (Chicago: University of Chicago Press, 1962).
2. Michigan State University, A report submitted to the President's Commission on Law Enforcement and Administration of Justice, *A National Survey of Police and Community Relations, Field Surveys V* (Washington: U.S. Government Printing Office, 1967), p. 256.

The proposals for review of police conduct can be categorized as follows:

Internal Review.

Civilian Review Boards.

The President's Commission in February of 1967 pointed out that:

...formal machinery within every police department for the investigation of complaints against police activity or employees is an absolute
necessity. It is also important that the complainant be personally informed of the results of the investigation and the disposition of the complaint. Every large department has machinery of some kind for dealing
with charges of misconduct by its members, whether those charges
originate inside or outside the department. It typically consists of a board
of high-ranking officers or, in some cases, nonsworn departmental officials, that investigate the facts of alleged dereliction and make a recommendation to the departmental administrator. He properly has the
authority and responsibility to take disciplinary action. When this kind of
machinery is fully and fairly used it succeeds both in disciplining
misbehaving officers and deterring others from misbehaving.

If the complainant remains dissatisfied with the disposition of the case,
there are other avenues of appeal outside the police agency: the local prosecutor; the courts; elected officials such as councilmen or the mayor; the
state's attorney general; the U.S. Department of Justice; and various civil
rights or human relations commissions. While all of these are traditional
institutions of legal redress they are frequently too formal, awesome, or
geographically far removed for the often bewildered citizen. Some of
them lack the machinery or resources to process grievances. Some can
take action only if a criminal law has been violated. But many of the
grievances that constitute acts of misconduct will not qualify as a basis for
criminal action.

In going beyond the established legal procedures, the Commission finds
it unreasonable to single out the police as the only agency that should be
subject to special scrutiny from the outside. The Commission, therefore,
does not recommend the establishment of civilian review boards in
jurisdictions where they do not exist, solely to review police conduct. The
police are only one of a number of official agencies with whom the public
has contact, and in some cases, because they are the most visible and con-
spicuous representatives of local government, they may be the focus of
more attention than they deserve. Incompetence and mistreatment by
housing, sanitation, health, and welfare officials can be as injurious to
citizens as mistreatment by the police and should be equally subject to
public scrutiny. These officials, like policemen, are public servants. In
view of the increasing involvement of government officials in the lives of
citizens, adequate procedures for the consideration of such individual
grievances as citizens may have against such officials are essential to effective government. So far as possible, it is desirable that such procedures be
established within the governmental agency involved. To the extent that
such procedures are ineffective or fail to inspire general public confidence, including the confidence of those who may have legitimate

grievances, further recourse is essential. The form that such further recourse should take is dependent on local needs and government structure.[3]

The National Advisory Commission on Civil Disorders during 1968 considered the problem of grievance mechanisms and recommended the following:

1. Making a complaint should be easy. It should be possible to file a grievance without excessive formality. If forms are used, they should be easily available and their use explained in widely distributed pamphlets. In large cities, it should not be necessary to go to a central headquarters office to file a complaint, but it should also be possible to file a complaint at neighborhood locations. Police officers on the beat, community service aides or other municipal employees in the community should be empowered to receive complaints.
2. A specialized agency, with adequate funds and staff, should be created separately from other municipal agencies to handle, investigate, and to make recommendations on citizen complaints.
3. The procedure should have a built-in conciliation process to attempt to resolve complaints without the need for full investigation and processing.
4. The complaining party should be able to participate in the investigation and in any hearings, with right of representation by counsel, so that the complaint is fully investigated and findings made on the merits. He should be promptly and fully informed of the outcome. The results of the investigation should be made public.

   Although we advocate an external agency as a means of resolving grievances, we believe that the basic need is to adopt procedures which will gain the respect and confidence of the entire community. This need can, in the end, be met only by sustained direction through the line of command, thorough investigation of complaints, and prompt, visible disciplinary action where justified.[4]
5. Since many citizen complaints concern departmental policies rather than individual conduct, information concerning complaints of this sort should be forwarded to the departmental unit which formulates or reviews policy and procedures. Information concerning all complaints should be forwarded to appropriate training units so that any deficiencies correctable by training can be eliminated.

A study of this problem completed by the National Commission on the Causes and Prevention of Violence emphasized that:

---

3. The President's Commission on Law Enforcement and Administration of Justice, *The Challenge of Crime in a Free Society* (Washington: U.S. Government Printing Office, 1967), p. 103.
4. The National Advisory Commission on Civil Disorders, *Report of the National Advisory Commission on Civil Disorders* (Washington: U.S. Government Printing Office, March 1, 1968), p. 163.

. . .since internal review has been uniformly sluggish, some kind of outside pressure must be brought to bear to induce voluntary correction of illegal and otherwise abusive police conduct. Mandatory injunctions issued by federal district courts are too cumbersome for this purpose and are susceptible to complete disruption of the internal review mechanism. The civilian review boards are doomed to futility since they pit the aggrieved citizen against the police department in a formal adversary proceeding; in short, someone always wins and someone is always resentful. The ombudsman, on the other hand, shifts the focus from dispute resolution to evaluation of the department's grievance response mechanism. Yet, since the primary goals of an effective complaint mechanism are to provide an objective forum and encourage its use, individual grievances must remain in the forefront, and their dispositions must be publicized.

What is needed is a hybrid of the ombudsman and the external review agency, whose operation would have the following attributes:

1. The primary responsibility for police discipline must remain with the police department itself.
2. There must be an easily accessible agency outside the police department, which processes citizen complaints in their inception rather than on appeal from the police.
3. In each case, this agency should:
    (a) make an independent investigation of the complaints;
    (b) publicly exonerate the police if the complaint is groundless;
    (c) in cases of misunderstanding or minor abuse, attempt to resolve the dispute through an informal conciliation meeting;
    (d) if efforts at conciliation should fail or if the police behavior was unacceptable, make recommendations to the Department regarding discipline or ways to relieve tension;
    (e) keep each citizen complainant aware of the disposition of his complaint.
4. On all matters, the agency should keep the public aware of its actions and the Department's response to its recommendations and should publish periodic reports and conclusions.
5. So as not to single out the police for special oversight, the agency should be responsible for processing citizen complaints not only against the police but also against other basic governmental service agencies, such as those responsible for welfare and employment.[5]

The National Advisory Commission on Criminal Justice Standards and Goals in 1973 pointed out that internal discipline in police agencies often is crisis-oriented. Most agencies simply react to employee misconduct. They do a good job of investigating after incidents have occurred, but they do little to prevent them.

---

5. The National Commission on the Causes and Prevention of Violence, *Law and Order Reconsidered* (Washington: U.S. Government Printing Office, 1970), pp. 393-394.

The key question police chief executives should attempt to answer concerning employee misconduct is "Why?" Police supervisors must ask themselves, "What could have prevented the employee from engaging in this particular act of misconduct?" The answer should be made an integral part of the written recommendation for each complaint adjudication. The police chief executive, even though he is ultimately responsible for internal discipline, should not bear this diagnostic responsibility alone. It is the responsibility of all employees to seek ways to maintain a disciplined police agency.

Although preventive measures may not automatically produce disciplined performance, they may provide the impetus for the development of self-discipline. A self-disciplined employee will save a police agency time and money by reducing the necessity for much of the administration of internal discipline.

Preventive programs differ as much as the police agencies that run them; therefore, each agency must analyze its particular problem and innovate. Most of the preventive programs used by the few police agencies active in this field are controversial. The utilization of these programs is not a panacea for police misconduct. Neither are they blueprints for successful programs. Police misconduct is the result of many factors and cannot always be foreseen, discouraged, or circumvented. But a great deal of misconduct can be prevented by police agency programs and policies.

*

Each of the national studies cited in the preceding discussion has proposed a different solution for the difficult problem of police misconduct and its control, but it remains to be seen whether or not these or other recommendations as discussed in the following articles in this section will prove to be acceptable to the police profession and the community.

9. TASK FORCE REPORT: THE POLICE

**PRESIDENT'S COMMISSION ON LAW ENFORCEMENT
AND ADMINISTRATION OF JUSTICE**

Task Force Report: The Police (Washington, D.C.: U.S. Government
Printing Office, 1967).

The operations of the police, like the operations of any other administrative agency that exercises governmental authority, must be subject to effective legislative, executive, and judicial review and control.
This is important when the police are called upon to carry out specific
legislative, executive, or judicial mandates. It is doubly important in
areas in which the police are left with discretion to develop their own
policies within broad legislatively or judicially fixed limits.

Methods of External Control

While there is a very strong formal commitment to local control of law enforcement in this country, the actual means for exerting control has
become quite obscure. To whom is a police agency responsible? By what
means may citizens influence its functioning?

By City Councils and Mayors

Ultimate control, in local government, is normally exerted through the
ballot box. But efforts to protect the police from partisan political influence have, in many jurisdictions, made the police immune from the
local election processes. Early efforts to assure popular control of the
police did include provisions in some cities for the chief of police to be
elected. In others, the police were made responsible to the local legislative
body. It became quickly apparent, however, that such direct control led
to a pattern of incompetence, lax enforcement, and the improper use of
police authority. Elected office holders dictated the appointment and
assignment of personnel, exchanged immunity from enforcement for
political favors, and, in some cities, made use of the police to assist in the
winning of elections.

In more recent times there has been a continuing effort to compromise
the need for popular control with the need for a degree of operating independence in order to avoid the undesirable practices that have general-

ly resulted from direct political control. Election and city council supervision of the police function gradually gave way to the establishment of administrative boards, variously constituted, in an effort to assure both independence and some semblance of civilian control.

These organizational patterns have, in turn, often led to an obscuring of responsibilities, resulting in a swing back to more direct control in the form of a movement for the appointment of a single executive, directly answerable to the elected mayor or, more recently, to a city manager who in turn is responsible to a city council. Variations of each of these arrangements, including some attempts at State control, continue to this day, with periodic shifting from one organizational pattern to another in response to a community's conclusion that its police force has too much or too little independence.

The record of involvement by elected officials in police operations, to the detriment of both the efficiency and effectiveness of the police establishment, has had a lasting and somewhat negative impact on the lines of control between the citizenry and the police. In cities in which the desire to isolate the police from political interference led to the adoption of special organizational patterns, the change in some instances has had the effect of making the police impervious to citizen demands of a legitimate nature. Although the organizational structure provides for direct control, the results have nevertheless been somewhat similar even in those cities in which the police administrator is directly responsible to an elected mayor.

Fear of being accused of political interference and an awareness of the sensitive nature of the police task have often resulted in the mayor abdicating all responsibility for police operations by granting complete autonomy to his police department. Indeed, the mayors of several of the largest cities, considering police department autonomy to be a virtue, have campaigned for reelection on a platform stressing the independence which they have granted to their police agencies. A mayor's apprehensions are created by his knowledge that any action on his part affecting the police, no matter how legitimate, may be characterized as political or partisan interference. The consequence is that we are now in a period of uncertainty as to the best relationship between police and the city government, the issue aggravated by the situation of unrest in large urban areas.

By Prosecutors

The prosecutor, State's attorney, or district attorney is designated as the chief law enforcement officer under the statutes of some States. However, despite this designation he is not generally conceived of in this country as having overall responsibility for the supervision of police. His interest in police operations is usually limited to those cases likely to result in a criminal prosecution, thereby excluding the non-prosecution-oriented activities that constitute so high a percentage of the total police effort.

Practices vary significantly from one jurisdiction to another as to the degree of involvement on the part of the prosecutor in the review of police procedures and actions in those cases in which the police objective is prosecution. While some cases are subject to review prior to the effecting of an arrest, the vast majority of arrests by municipal police officers are made prior to consultation with the prosecutor. Some prosecutors establish procedures for the review of all arrests prior to their presentation in court, while others do not become involved until the initial hearing is begun before a magistrate. Systematic review of all cases prior to their presentation in court tends to result in the adoption of standards that are informally and sometimes formally communicated to the police agency. Police practices may be criticized or changes suggested, but such criticism and suggestions are not generally viewed as a form of control. Rather, they are seen as being primarily motivated by a desire on the part of the prosecutor to facilitate his task in the review and prosecution of cases. Where there is no prior review, the staff of the prosecutor in large cities often routinely presents in court cases in which the practices by the police were clearly illegal, apparently feeling no responsibility for reacting to the police practice, either in the form of a refusal to prosecute or in the form of a communication through appropriate superiors to the administration of the police force.

In general, instructions or guidelines issued by the prosecutor relating to procedures for the prosecution of criminal cases will be accepted and followed by the police, particularly if the prosecutor is viewed by the police as seriously interested in the effective presentation of the case in court. But neither the police nor the prosecutor assume that the prosecutor has the responsibility either to stimulate or to participate in the development of administrative policies to control the wide range of police practices.

By the Judiciary

In many jurisdictions the trial judge has acted as a sort of chief administrative officer of the criminal justice system, using his power to dismiss cases as a method of controlling the use of the criminal process. But except in those cases in which his action relates to the admissibility of evidence, this has been done largely on an informal basis and has tended to be haphazard, often reflecting primarily the personal values of the individual trial judge.

In contrast, the function of the trial judge in excluding evidence which he determines to have been illegally obtained places him very explicitly in the role of controlling police practices. However, trial judges have not viewed this role as making them responsible for developing appropriate police policies. Many trial judges, for example, when asked if they would explain their decision to the police, indicate that they have no more responsibility for explaining decisions to police than they have with regard to private litigants. When asked whether they would suggest to the police proper ways of acquiring evidence in the future, some judges assert that it would be unethical for them to do so unless they also "coached" the defense.

Occasionally a judge will grant a motion to suppress evidence in order to dismiss a case he feels should not be prosecuted because the violation is too minor or for some other reason. Use of a motion to suppress evidence in this manner serves to confuse the standards that are supposed to guide the police, and has a destructive effect upon police morale.

Most often, the process of judicial review is seen as a decision about the propriety of the actions of the individual officer rather than a review of departmental administrative policy. Judges seldom ask for and, as a consequence, are not informed as to whether there is a current administrative policy. And, if there is one, they seldom ask whether the officer's conduct in the particular case conformed to or deviated from the policy. As a result, police are not encouraged to articulate and defend their policy; the decision of the trial judge is not even communicated to the police administrator; and the prevailing police practice often continues unaffected by the decision of the trial judge.

The effectiveness of trial court review is further complicated in courts of more than a single judge by the disparity of their views about the propriety or desirability of given police practices. Ordinarily the prosecution has no opportunity to appeal adverse decisions. And where appeals are allowed, prosecutors seldom view them as a way of resolving conflict between trial judge rulings. As a result police often tend to ignore all of the decisions, rationalizing that it is impossible to conform to conflicting mandates. While increasing attention has been given to minimizing sentencing disparity through such devices as sentencing institutes, designed to minimize disparity, no similar attention has been given to disparity in the supervision of police practices.

Finally, the effectiveness of the exclusionary rule is limited by the fact that it deals only with police practices leading up to prosecution. Many highly sensitive and important practices are confined to the street and are not reflected in prosecuted cases.

Civil Liability of the Police Officer

One much discussed method of controlling police practice is to impose financial liability upon the governmental unit as well as the police officer who exceeds his authority. A somewhat similar approach is provided for under the Federal Civil Rights Act.

The effect of the threat of possible civil liability upon police policy is not very great. In the first place, plaintiffs are seldom able to sustain a successful lawsuit because of the expense and the fact that juries are not likely to have compassion for a guilty, even if abused, plaintiff. Insurance is also now available along with other protective methods that insulate the individual officer from financial loss.

The attitude of the police administrator is to try to protect his man or the municipality from civil liability even though he may privately be critical of the actions of the officer. Usually legal counsel will instruct the police administrator to suspend departmental disciplinary proceedings because they might prejudice the litigation.

Even in the unusual case where an individual is able successfully to gain a money judgment in an action brought against a police officer or governmental unit, this does not cause a reevaluation of departmental policy or practice.

In general, it seems apparent that civil litigation is an awkward method of stimulating proper law enforcement policy. At most, it can furnish relief for the victim of clearly improper practices. To hold the individual officer liable in damages as a way of achieving systematic reevaluation of police practices seems neither realistic nor desirable.

By Citizen Complaint

Complaints alleging police misconduct may relate to an isolated incident involving the actions of a specific officer or may relate to a formal or informal practice generally prevailing throughout a department. However, the citizen complaint process, like the civil action, is typically limited, in its effect, to the specific case which is subjected to review. Experience has shown that most complaints come not from the ghetto areas where there may be most question about police practice, but rather from middle income areas where an articulate citizen becomes irate over the actions of an officer which deviate from prevailing police practice in his neighborhood.

Most attention in recent years has focused upon the means for investigating such complaints, with public discussion concentrated upon the relative merits of internal departmental procedures versus those established by a form of citizen complaint board functioning in whole or in part outside the department. Whatever the method for conducting an investigation, there is no evidence that the complaint procedure has generally served as a significant vehicle for the critical evaluation of existing police practices and the development of more adequate departmental policies.

Proposed Improvements in Methods of External Control

The primary need is for the development of methods of external control which will serve as inducements for police to articulate important law enforcement policies and to be willing to have them known, discussed, and changed if change is desirable. There is obviously no single way of accomplishing this.

The task is complicated by the fact that popular, majority control over police policy cannot be relied upon alone. Often the greatest pressure for the use of improper police practices comes from the majority of articulate citizens who demand that "effective" steps be taken to solve a particular crime, to make the streets safe, or to reverse what is often seen as the trend toward an increase of lawlessness.

Effective response to crime is obviously a proper concern of police. But it is also apparent that police policy must strive to achieve objectives like consistency, fairness, tolerance of minority views, and other values inherent in a democratic society.

The creation of an institutional framework to encourage the development and implementation of law enforcement policies which are effective and also consistent with democratic values is obviously difficult. To achieve this requires a basic rethinking of the relationship between the police and legislatures, courts, prosecutors, local government officials, and the community as a whole.

The Legislature

Adequate external control over police policymaking requires first an explicit recognition of the necessity and desirability of police operating as an administrative policymaking agency of government. One, and perhaps the best, way to accomplish this is through legislative action which will delegate an explicit policymaking responsibility to police in areas not preempted by legislative or judicial action. Often it is neither feasible nor desirable for the legislature to prescribe a specific police practice; there is a need for administrative variation, innovation, and experimentation within limits set by the general legislative purpose and such legislative criteria as are provided to guide and control the exercise of discretion.

Legislative recognition of the propriety of police policymaking should encourage the development of means to develop enforcement policies and their subjection to adequate external control. It should also encourage flexibility and innovation in law enforcement while at the same time providing some guidance to police policymaking through the prescription of appropriate legislative standards or criteria.

Judicial Review of Police Policymaking

Given explicit legislative recognition of police policymaking, it ought to be possible to develop effective methods of judicial review which will not only serve to minimize the risk of improper police practices but will also serve to encourage the development, articulation, defense, and, if necessary, revision of police policies.

If there is legislative acknowledgment of the propriety of police policymaking, it would seem to follow that it would be appropriate for a person, with proper standing, to challenge existing policy, formal or informal, on the ground that it is inconsistent with general legislative policy. Where there is challenge, courts would have an opportunity to require the law enforcement agency to articulate its policy and to defend it, and, if the challenge is successful to change the policy.

It is possible and certainly desirable to modify the current system of judicial control and to make it consistent with and, in fact, supportive of the objective of proper police policymaking. To accomplish this would require some basic changes in judicial practice:

(*a*) When a trial judge is confronted with a motion to suppress, he, and the appellate court which reviews the case, should request a showing of whether the conduct of the officer in the particular case did or did not conform to existing departmental policy. If not, the granting of such a motion would not require a reevaluation of departmental policy. However, it ought to cause the police administrator to ask whether a prosecution should, as a matter of police policy, be brought when the officer violated departmental policy in getting the evidence.

If departmental policy were followed, the judge would be given an opportunity to consider the action of the individual officer in the light of the overall departmental judgment as to what is proper policy. Hopefully, a judge would be reluctant to upset a departmental policy without giving the police administrator an opportunity to defend the reasons for the policy, including, where relevant, any police expertise which might bear upon the reasonableness of the policy. To do this will slow down the proceedings, will take judicial time and effort, but if judicial review of police policy is worthwhile at all, it would seem that it is worth doing properly.

(*b*) Trial judges in multijudge courts should develop appropriate formal or informal means to avoid disparity between individual trial judges in their decisions about the propriety of police policy. The Sentencing Council, created in the Eastern District of Michigan to minimize judicial disparity in sentencing, would seem to be a helpful model. This council uses a panel of judges to consider what is an appropriate sentence rather than leaving the decision entirely to a single judge. The panel serves to balance any substantially different views of individual judges, and results in a more consistent judicial standard. Again, this involves cost in judicial time.

(c) It seems obvious that judicial decisions, whenever possible, ought to be effectively communicated to the police department whose policy was an issue. Yet it is common in current practice for the police administrator to have to rely primarily upon the newspaper as a source of information about judicial decisions, even those involving an officer of his own department. One way of achieving effective communication might be through making the police officer commonly assigned by departments to regular duty in the courtroom responsible for reporting significant decisions to the police administrator. This would require a highly qualified, legally trained, court officer. In addition, trial judges would have to be willing to explain their decisions at least orally, if not in writing.

(d) If the exclusionary rule is to be a principal vehicle for influencing police policy (as distinguished from disciplining an individual officer who acts improperly) then it seems apparent that the appellate process must be accessible to the prosecution as well as the defense so that inconsistent or apparently erroneous trial court decisions can be challenged. It is nonetheless often urged that allowing appeal in a particular case is unfair to the particular defendant. Moreover, where the authority to appeal does exist, prosecutors often limit appeals to cases involving serious crimes rather than systematically appealing all cases in which an important law enforcement policy is affected.

Other Forms of External Control
Over Police Policymaking

Even with carefully drafted legislation and a more adequate system of judicial review, there will still be wide areas of police practice which give rise to very important issues which must be resolved by administrative action without specific legislative or judicial guidance. This is particularly true with regard to the wide range of police contacts with citizens on the street, contacts which usually do no result in criminal prosecution but which do have a major impact upon public order and upon the relationship between police and the community. It is very important that these practices be the subject of careful administrative policymaking and be subject to appropriate methods of external control.

It has been said that one of the major current challenges to our system of governmental control is to devise appropriate methods for safeguarding the exercise of discretionary power by governmental agencies in situations where judicial review is not feasible or not desirable.

Because there is no "best" answer to the question of control over the exercise of discretionary power, it seems obviously desirable to encourage a multifaceted approach, stressing innovation and experimentation, with the hope that, in the process, enough will one day be learned to afford an adequate basis for deciding what methods are best.

The basic need can be stated briefly, though at some risk of over-simplification. It is for giving police policymaking greater visibility, so that the problems and current police solutions are known to the community; to devise methods of involving members of the community in discussion of the propriety of the policies; and to develop in police a willingness to see this process as inherent in a democratic society and as an appropriate way of developing policies which are both effective and supported by the community.

There are some worthwhile alternatives which can be identified:

The Involvement of the Mayor or City Council in Policymaking

It may be helpful, in the long-range interest of law enforcement, to involve local officials in the process of developing enforcement policies, particularly those which have an impact upon a broad segment of the community. If, for example, a police agency is to adopt a policy to govern individual officers in deciding what to do with the down-and-out drunk, it would seem appropriate and helpful to report that policy to the mayor and city council in order to see whether there is opposition from the elected representatives. Where the issue is significant enough, a public hearing may serve to give an indication of the community response to the particular policy being proposed. Although this involvement of city government may give rise to concern over "political influence," the risk of improper influence is minimized by the fact that the involvement is open to view. The vice of political influence of an earlier day was that it tended to be of a personal nature and was secretive.

The Involvement of the Prosecutor and Trial Judiciary

Where a police policy deals with an issue such as investigative practices, which have impact upon the arrest, prosecution, and conviction of offenders, it would seem desirable to involve those other criminal justice agencies which also have policymaking responsibility.

This will require, in practice, a greater interest by the prosecutor who often today conceives of his role as limited to the trial and appeal of criminal cases rather than the development of enforcement policies which anticipate many of the issues before they arise in a litigated case.

The participation of the trial judge on an informal basis in policymaking raises more difficult questions. In theory, the judge is the neutral official not involved until an issue is properly raised in the course of the judicial process. In fact, some trial judges do act as if they are the administrative head of the criminal justice system in a particular community, and do deliberately try to influence policy with regard to when arrests are to be made, who is to be prosecuted, when charges are to be reduced, and other matters which vitally affect law enforcement.

Citizen Involvement in Policymaking

In some areas of governmental activity, there is increasing utilization of citizen advisory committees as a way of involving members of the community in the policymaking process. In some cases, the group may be advisory only, the governmental agency being free to accept or reject its advice. In other instances, the group is official and policies are cleared through the committee as a regular part of the policymaking process. The advantages of both methods are that they serve as an inducement for the police administrator to articulate important policies, to formulate them, and to subject them to discussion in the advisory group. How effective this is depends upon the willingness of the group and the police administrator to confront the basic law enforcement policy issues rather than being preoccupied with the much easier questions of the mechanics of running the department. Where there is a commitment to exploring basic enforcement policy questions, the citizens' advisory group or policymaking board has the advantage of involving the community in the decision-making process, thus giving a broader base than would otherwise exist for the acceptance and support of enforcement policies.

Official or Unofficial Inquiry Into Police Practices

In some other countries of the world there is a greater commitment to continuing inquiry into governmental activity designed to learn and assess what is going on. Thus, in England a royal commission has, on several occasions, been used as a vehicle for helpful inquiry into the state of police practice there. In other countries, especially in Scandinavia, there has been reliance upon the ombudsman, not only as a way of handling complaints, but also as a vehicle for continuing offical inquiry into governmental practice, including the practices of police.

There has been less tradition for systematic, official inquiry into governmental practice in this country. Where there has been inquiry into police practice, it has commonly been precipitated by a crisis, has been directed toward finding incompetence or corruption, and, whatever the specific finding, has failed to give attention to the basic law enforcement issues involved.

It would be helpful to have systematic legislative inquiry into important police practices at the local, state, and federal level. If devoted to an effort to learn what the existing practices are and to give the police an inducement to articulate their policies and a forum for explaining and justifying them, the process of legislative inquiry can have a positive impact upon the long-range development of the police as a responsible policymaking agency. To achieve this objective, the short run price which police would have to pay in criticism and controversy would be well worth it.

Unofficial studies of law enforcement practices can also be helpful. For example, a bar association may make an important contribution by the maintenance of a standing committee which has as its mandate a continuing concern with important law enforcement policies. The police field would, in the long run, be aided by the critical, but at the same time sympathetic, interest of the organized bar.

There is also need for greater involvement of universities and especially social science research into the basic problems which confront police. Continuing university interest is itself a form of inducement to confront some of the basic policy questions; and by reporting and critically evaluating current law enforcement practices research can serve as a method of review and control in the same way that law review comment has served this function with regard to the appellate judicial process. Greater involvement of the university would also serve as a basis for the development of badly needed social science courses which deal adequately with the tasks confronting police and the role which police play in our society. This in turn should increase the number of educated and articulate citizens who are knowledgeable about and interested in the important problems of law enforcement and who thus hopefully will constitute a support for proper police policies.

Establishing Communication With the Inarticulate Segments of the Community

One of the most important ways of asserting appropriate control over police practice is to have an informed and articulate community which will be intolerant of improper police practice. A difficulty in the law enforcement field is that the groups which receive most police attention are largely inarticulate, and no formal system for the expression of views will be utilized by the groups. There is need, therefore, for development within the minority community of the capacity and willingness to communicate views and dissatisfactions to the police.

Fulfillment of this need would not only be in the interests of the community, but is desirable from the police standpoint. If the minority community could better articulate its needs, a more balanced community support for the role that the professional police administrator sees himself as filling in a democratic society would be provided. A stronger minority voice would also serve to offset some of the pressure brought to bear upon the police to adopt policies and engage in practices that are of questionable nature.

Secondly, the police have a very practical reason for wanting to be informed about what is bothering the residents of an area. However narrow a focus a police administrator may assume with regard to the development of the police function, it seems apparent that if he is to take seriously his responsibility for preventing outbreaks of violence in his community, he must undertake programs which will keep him informed of the basis for unrest.

There has been substantial progress toward meeting this need through the establishment of a wide range of police-community relations programs. The success of these is in large measure dependent on the degree to which they serve as a vehicle for enabling the otherwise unorganized citizenry to make themselves heard. It seems apparent that programs which rely primarily upon contact with well established and organized interest groups, while of value in their own right, do not serve to meet the kind of needs that are most critical. Properly developed, police-community programs afford an opportunity for police to take the initiative in soliciting the kind of insight into their own operations and the way they affect a community, which should in turn contribute to the development of more adequate police policies.

Total dependence obviously cannot be placed upon the police to assist the minority community in articulating its needs. Indeed, the lack of sensitivity to the problem on the part of the police in some jurisdictions may place the entire burden on other methods, such as the development of community action programs and neighborhood law offices. Services of this kind, which are becoming increasingly available, are likely to bring demands upon the various governmental agencies, including demands that the police review some of their policies for dealing with problems encountered in the ghetto area. A sensitive police administrator ought to recognize that such groups can contribute to a process of development and continuing evaluation of important law enforcement policies.

10. THE INTERNAL AFFAIRS UNIT: THE POLICEMAN'S FRIEND OR FOE

LEONARD TERRITO AND ROBERT L. SMITH

The Police Chief, Vol. XLIII, July 1976. Reprinted by permission.

The title of this article suggests that there is some question about whether or not the Internal Affairs Unit (IAU) is a friend or foe of the rank and file police officers. Even raising such a question would tend to offend the sensibilities of those police administrators who have worked so diligently to create and staff highly efficient, impartial, and well-organized Internal Affairs Units. The facts are, however, that in too many instances the rank and file members of a police organization are sometimes suspicious and hostile towards their departments' IAU. This suspicion and hostility results in some cases because of certain questionable practices employed by the personnel of the IAU. In other instances, it may occur because a vast majority of an agency's personnel do not really understand the purpose or need for such a unit.

In April 1974, Charles Otero, a 27-year veteran of the Tampa Police Department, was appointed as that agency's chief of police; and he set as one of his top priorities the creation of an Internal Affairs Unit. Among the many administrative considerations in building this unit was the need to create and to maintain a positive image of this unit in the eyes of the community and his officers.

In previous years, the assignment of internal investigations within the department had not been made with any high degree of administrative consistency. No specific unit was designated as being solely responsible for such investigations, the assignment of internal investigations was not systematically made, and there was no systematic method of filing the results of the investigations. In addition, those individuals who were ultimately assigned to conduct such investigations had no written policies or procedures to guide their investigative actions. Thus, in retrospect, it is not surprising that there was a lack of uniformity in the quality of the internal investigations conducted and a lack of uniformity in the methods employed to conduct these investigations. Such administrative shortcomings can have a very serious, deleterious effect upon morale, and can create considerable suspicion and animosity towards both the chief administrator and those individuals responsible for conducting such investigations, regardless of how fair and impartial they try to be.

Prior to the creation of the Tampa Police Department IAU, serious questions had been raised about certain questionable tactics being employed by some individuals assigned to specific internal investigations. In addition, there was concern that some previous investigations may have been politically motivated; thus, a negative stigma tended to be attached to both the individuals and the responsibilities associated with such investigations. Hence, the Tampa Police Department wanted to accomplish a number of things. First, it wanted to create a unit that would be well organized, highly efficient, and scrupulously fair and impartial in its investigations. Second, it wanted this unit to be trusted and respected by department members and community citizens.

In an effort not to waste time and energy in remaking the proverbial wheel, numerous law enforcement agencies of similar size were contacted and requested to provide administrative data about their Internal Affairs Units. The response was overwhelming, and the subsequent administrative data that were provided were invaluable in developing the foundation upon which the Tampa department eventually built its IAU. Interestingly enough, the one bit of information that was not readily available was specific information about the administrative techniques that could be employed to reduce the negative reactions sometimes fostered by rank and file officers towards the IAU and its personnel. No doubt this was given serious consideration by many police departments, but this issue was not raised in the information collected. In an effort to address himself to this important issue, the newly appointed police chief initially distributed a carefully worded general order which provided a broad overview of what the newly created IAU was intended to do and equally important what it was not expected to do.

The second step was to create a policy and procedure that provided both clear-cut and comprehensive guidelines for the members of the IAU and the members of the department. The policy and procedure that was finally developed was not created in an administrative vacuum, and direct employee participation was encouraged and solicited. In the final analysis this participation was significant in formulating the organizational documents which now govern every phase of all internal investigations.

Administrative Overview

The following IAU guidelines which are presently employed by the Tampa Police Department were formulated based upon Florida State Law,[1] recommendations of the National Advisory Commission on

---

1. Policeman's Bill of Rights, enacted by the legislature of the state of Florida, effective October 1, 1974.

Criminal Justice Standards and Goals, and recommendations by key agency personnel.

1. Rights of Law Enforcement Officers While Under Investigation. Whenever a law enforcement officer is under investigation and is subject to interrogation by members of his agency, for any reason which could lead to disciplinary action, demotion, or dismissal, such interrogation shall be conducted under the following conditions:

(*a*) The interrogation shall be conducted at a reasonable hour, preferably at a time when the law enforcement officer is on duty, unless the seriousness of the investigation is of such a degree that an immediate action is required.

(*b*) The interrogation shall take place either at the office of the commander of the investigating officer or at the office of the Internal Affairs Unit or police unit in which the incident allegedly occurred as designated by the investigating officer or agency.

(*c*) The law enforcement officer under investigation shall be informed of the rank, name, and command of the officer in charge of the investigation, the interrogating officer, and all persons present during the interrogation. All questions directed to the officer under interrogation shall be asked by and through one interrogator at any one time.

(*d*) The law enforcement officer under investigation shall be informed of the nature of the investigation prior to any interrogation, and he shall be informed of the name of all complainants.

(*e*) Interrogating sessions shall be for reasonable periods and shall be timed to allow for such personal necessities and rest periods as are reasonably necessary.

(*f*) The law enforcement officer under interrogation shall not be subjected to offensive language or threatened with transfer, dismissal, or disciplinary action. No promise or reward shall be made as an inducement to answering any questions.

(*g*) The formal interrogation of a law enforcement officer, including all recess periods, shall be recorded, and there shall be no unrecorded questions or statements.

(*h*) If the law enforcement officer under interrogation is under arrest, or is likely to be placed under arrest as a result of the interrogation, he shall be completely informed of all his constitutional rights prior to the commencement of the interrogation.

(*i*) At the request of any law enforcement officer under investigation, he shall have the right to be represented by counsel or any other representative of his choice who shall be present at all times during such interrogation whenever the interrogation relates to the officer's continued fitness for law enforcement service.

2. Representation on Complaint Review Boards. In the event a member requests a complaint review board and the circumstances are of a nature to permit the convening of said board, it shall be organized as follows: A complaint review board shall be composed of a five-member board with two members being selected by the administrator, two members being selected by the aggrieved officer, and the fifth member being selected by the other four members. The board members shall be law enforcement officers selected from within the agency.

3. Civil Suits Brought by Law Enforcement Officers. Every law enforcement officer shall have the right to bring civil suit against any person, group of persons, or any organization or corporation or the heads of such organizations or corporations for damages, either pecuniary or otherwise, suffered during the performance of the officer's official duties or for abridgement of the officer's civil rights arising out of the officer's performance of official duties.

4. Notice of Disciplinary Action. No dismissal, demotion, transfer, reassignment, or other personnel action which might result in loss of pay or benefits or which might otherwise be considered a punitive measure shall be taken against any law enforcement officer unless such law enforcement officer is notified of the action and the reason or reasons prior to the effective date of such action.

5. Retaliation for Exercising Rights. No law enforcement officer shall be discharged, disciplined, demoted, or denied promotion, transfer, or reassignment, or otherwise be discriminated against in regard to his employment, or be threatened with any such treatment, by reason of his exercise of his rights.

Selection of Personnel

The selection of personnel is a key factor in the success and acceptance of the IAU. This was a high priority item in the creation of the IAU of the Tampa Police Department, and it was generally agreed that certain factors were absolutely essential in the selection process. These were outlined as follows:

1. All personnel serving in the IAU must be volunteers. (Because of the nature and sensitivity of the work involved in the IAU it was believed that it would be unwise and unfair to assign someone to this unit who did not have a genuine desire to serve in it.)

2. The personnel who serve in this unit must have demonstrated in their previous performance that they possess a high degree of investigative skills. (This was considered an absolute prerequisite since there was little doubt that the members of the unit would be called upon to conduct a wide range of investigation both of a minor and of a serious nature.)

3. The individuals selected to serve in this unit must have excellent reputations both among their peers and supervisors in terms of their integrity and overall performance as police officers. Since the members of the unit would be called upon to investigate their fellow officers it was deemed important that they themselves not have been found guilty of serious official misconduct in the past. A failure to consider such a factor could later result in charges of administrative hypocrisy.

4. All IAU personnel must become totally familiar with those state statutes, department policies, and procedures which are related to internal investigations (mastery of this body of knowledge would assure that there would be no inadvertent legal or administrative errors occurring during the internal investigative process.)

5. Members of the IAU must be proficient in interviewing and interrogation techniques.

6. A knowledge and understanding of the local communities' ethnic minorities is absolutely essential since, for a variety of social, political, and economic reasons, many citizen complaints will initiate from this group of citizens.

Rotating Tours of Duty

The Tampa Police Department takes the position that there are certain positive advantages to be gained by rotating personnel periodically who are assigned to the IAU. (Investigators will serve a maximum of 24 months.) This approach will have a tendency to foster acceptance and respect for the internal discipline system because of its greater employee participation. Second, it will develop a cadre of investigators who can be used in the future if additional manpower is needed. Third, it should minimize the possibility of alienation from peers and supervisors.

The Use of the Polygraph

The polygraph is employed only after a complete and thorough investigation fails to obtain adequately all of the facts needed upon which to make a final decision in a specific case. Thus, for example, if a complaint is filed against a police officer by a citizen and it is apparent that either the complainant or the officer is not being completely truthful about the facts of the case, then both parties are requested to submit to a polygraph examination. Thus far there have been no instances where both the officer and the complainant involved in the same case have refused to take the polygraph. If the police officer refuses to take the polygraph and the charge is serious enough, the officer can be dismissed.[2] One Tampa police

2.   George J. Roux, Jr., Department of Police, City of New Orleans Civil Service Commission, Case No. 440-A, decided September 6, 1968.

officer who was recently dismissed for his unwillingness to submit to a polygraph examination challenged the department's rights to dismiss him for refusing to submit to a polygraph examination. Following his appeal, a decision by the local civil service board upheld the department's action. On the other hand, if a complainant refuses to submit to a polygraph examination, the officer is still requested to submit to one. In 1974, the Tampa Police Department began to utilize the polygraph as a preemployment screening device. Thus, many Tampa Police officers are now quite familiar with the procedures involved in polygraph examination, and it is strongly suspected that this has had a tendency to reduce any unwarranted fears that might have otherwise arisen regarding the use and operation of the polygraph.

Disclosure of Internal Discipline Statistics

The National Advisory Commission on Criminal Justice Standards and Goals has recommended that police agencies should maintain the confidentiality of internal discipline investigations, although complete records should be maintained. However, the disclosure of internal discipline statistics does not violate the confidential nature of the process, and such disclosures are often valuable because they tend to dispel allegations of disciplinary secrecy voiced by some community elements.[3] The Tampa Police Department has wholeheartedly endorsed, accepted, and operationalized this recommendation not only for the reasons cited by the National Advisory Commission on Criminal Justice Standards and Goals but also because it tends to reduce the rumors and misinformation that may occur internally. Hence, although all of the specific details of an investigation are not normally revealed to the general public or to the total police department (except in certain rare and extraordinary circumstances), the Tampa Police Department distributes a monthly summary of activities of the IAU. Thus, the record is available both within the community and within the agency for all to see. Naturally, the availability and distribution of these monthly bulletins will not totally eliminate all suspicion about the IAU operations, but it will do much to minimize a major portion of it.

New Employee Orientation

In addition to providing department-wide distribution of the monthly summary of complaints the commanding officer of the IAU appears before all new police officers attending the police academy. A four-hour

---

3. *National Advisory Commission on Criminal Justice Standards and Goals* (Washington, D.C., U.S. Government Printing Office, 1973), p. 479.

block of time is set aside to advise the new officers of the purpose and responsibilities of this unit. The investigative personnel of the IAU are also introduced, and certain professional background information is provided on each. A comprehensive orientation is given relating to those state laws, civil service rules and regulations, and departmental rules and regulations which pertain to police officers' rights, internal discipline procedures, and so forth. Sufficient time is allowed for a question and answer period. This method of informing new employees about the IAU tends to reduce the types of negative misconceptions that result when little is known about such units.

In-Service Employee Orientation

Since the IAU was a newly created unit in the Tampa Police Department, it was necessary to provide a certain degree of orientation to older employees also. The vehicle employed to provide this orientation was a departmental closed-circuit television. The TV presentation consisted of a series of the most common types of questions that had been raised or could be raised about the administrative duties and responsibilities of the IAU. The questions were presented to and answered by the commanding officer of the IAU. This type of openness and candor can do much to reduce unnecessary fear or concern about a department's IAU.

Conclusion

The Internal Affairs Unit is an administrative tool and the extent to which it is useful and effective will depend upon the skills and integrity of the chief administrator and the personnel responsible for carrying out the duties assigned to the unit. The IAU is a double-edged sword which may be used by the chief administrator to make plain through sanctions his intolerance to employee misconduct, but equally as important it allows the police agency to defend the lawful and proper conduct of employees in the performance of their duties. Caution should be exercised to assure that the first point is not overemphasized by police administrators at the expense of the second.

Concepts to Consider

1. Compare and contrast the review of police conduct as recommended by the Violence Commission and the Standards and Goals Commission.

2. Identify the various means of external control of police conduct.

3. Justify the need for the office of the prosecutor to assume responsibility for supervising the police.

4. Support the position that the police should not be subjected to review by a civilian board.

5. Describe the role of and the functions performed by an internal affairs unit.

Selected Readings

Broadaway, Fred M., "Police Misconduct: Positive Alternatives," *The Journal of Police Science and Administration*, Vol. 2, No. 2, June 1974, pp. 210-218.

This article reviews the general policy requisites for programs dealing with police conduct, analyzes selected programs in reference to the perceived policy requirements, and proposes a program for dealing with misconduct.

Cohen, Bernard, "The Police Internal System of Justice in New York City," *The Journal of Criminal Law, Criminology and Police Science*, Vol. 63, No. 1, March 1972, pp. 54-67.

This research is a summary of police misconduct and the operations of the police justice system from data which were collected for a broader study of selection, assignment, promotion, and reward procedures in the New York City Police Department.

Flynn, Matthew J., "Police Accountability in Wisconsin," *Wisconsin Law Review*, Vol. 1, No. 4, 1974, pp. 1130-1166.

Presents four objectives in the allocation of power over the police in terms of: police responsiveness to legitimate political influence, shielding the police from improper political influence, grievance procedures, and civil service reform.

Goforth, Billy Ralph, "Police Professionalization and Internal Controls," *The Police Chief*, Vol. XL, No. 7, July 1973, pp. 65-67.

The basic thesis of this article is that departmental integrity and personal integrity are insured in a police department through frank and open monitoring of all police services.

Hewitt, William H., "New York City's Civilian Complaint Review Board Struggle: Its History, Analysis and Some Notes," *Police*, May-June 1967, pp. 10-21; July-August 1967, pp. 14-29, and September-October 1967, pp. 20-33.

In this three-part series the author presents in minute detail a resume of the heated dispute that led to a referendum and the defeat of Mayor Lindsay's review board.

Hudson, James R., "Organizational Aspects of Internal and External Review of the Police," *The Journal of Criminal Law, Criminology, and Police Science*, Vol. 63, No. 3, September 1972, pp. 427-433.

The author compares two organizations that had as a major activity the handling of complaints against policemen brought by citizens in a large American city.

Proub, Robert S., "A Classification of Internal Disciplinary Actions by State Police and Highway Patrols," *The Police Chief*, Vol. XL, No. 11, November 1973, pp. 52-53.

This study presents the methodologies incorporated by state police and state highway patrol organizations in processing complaints against their officers. Forty-four agencies are analyzed in this report.

Pudinski, Walter, "Citizen's Complaints," *California Law Enforcement Journal*, Vol. 7, No. 2, October 1972, pp. 45-47.

The author presents a brief outline of a complaint program. Establishes two categories for complaints and suggests that supervisors should be responsible for accepting complaints.

The President's Commission on Law Enforcement and Administration of Justice, *Task Force Report: The Police* (Washington: U.S. Government Printing Office, 1967), pp. 193-205.

This study considers internal investigations, external review, civilian review boards, the ombudsman and local human relations commissions as means of reviewing police conduct.

Chapter 5
POLICE UNIONIZATION

Introduction *

Police unions you say? Do we really have such a thing; are our police organized? The answer is a big bold YES—yes to the point that, as a recent survey has indicated, 73 percent of all police employees are represented in their employment by some form of union or association.[1] Then you may ask—what are these police unions, how strong are they, how were they organized, what is their legal status? This [introduction] will present a brief overview of the historical development of police unions and will provide some generalized answers to these questions.

---

* Joseph D. Smith, "Police Unions: An Historical Perspective of Causes and Organizations," *The Police Chief*, Vol. XLII, No. 11, November 1975. Reprinted by permission.

1. "Labor Management Policies for State and Local Government," *Advisory Commission on Intergovernmental Relations*," (1969).

Before examining these issues very extensively, a firm definition of the word "union" is needed. For our purposes, a union will refer to any organization which represents or seeks to represent employees for the purpose of discussing with management (or employers) matters relevant to wages, hours, work conditions, and other terms of employment. In the area of police organizations, the term "union" by this definition will refer to a vast variety of organization and association structures. These shall be discussed in more detail later.

The History

Many law enforcement educators use the example of the Boston Police Strike (1919) as the first showing of organized labor among police. However, there were organizations and strikes among police prior to this time.

As early as 1889, the Ithaca, New York, police force, consisting of five officers, walked off their jobs because their pay had been reduced from $12 per week to $9 per week. In 1897, a group of "Special Police" in Cleveland, Ohio, petitioned the American Federation of Labor (AFL) for a local charter. Significant in labor history is the fact that at this time the AFL rejected this bid for a charter on the grounds that it was settled with the chief's agreement to trades association to organize the police, anymore than they could organize the military. The Fraternal Order of Police (FOP) formed its first local in 1915, although until the 1930s the FOP was basically a social-benefit type of association. Last, but far from least, both in size and cause, is the 1918 police strike in Cincinnati, Ohio. Here was a situation of four officers being discharged for their attempts to organize a meeting to discuss a salary increase of $300 per year. Four hundred and fifty officers walked off their jobs when these four were discharged as a protest of the chief's denial of their attempt to meet as a collective body and to discuss job conditions. This strike was settled with the chief's agreement to reevaluate his discharge decision.[2]

This brings us up to the disastrous occurrences of 1919. Early in the year, the AFL, now having recognized the vast potential in organizing the police, opened its door to applications for police locals. The AFL was immediately swamped with a total of 65 applications, and by the summer of 1919, there were 37 locals chartered with a total membership of over 4,000 officers.[3]

---

2. "Police Labor Relations," IACP, *Public Safety Labor Reporter* (1973), p. 2; "Police Collective Bargaining, 1900-1960", *Public Employees Relations Library (PERL)*, IPMA, vol. 18, pp. 1-6.

3. "A Union of Policemen?" *American Labor* (Sept. 1969), pp. 53-59.

In the Boston Police Department, wage and work conditions were very poor—there were dirty station houses, officers had to purchase their own uniforms, wages could not support a family man's economic needs, and the workweek ranged from 78 to 90 hours. Since officers were unable to get answers to their grievances, they decided to form their own union. The Boston Social Club was formed and received one of the AFL charters. This action was in violation of city policy, and nineteen of the union leaders were discharged. The other officers were outraged, and on September 19, 1919, a total of 1,117 officers (from a total strength of 1,544) went on strike.

The actions of the strikers brought public outrage, and there were comments such as those of Massachusetts Governor Calvin Coolidge: "There is no right to strike against the public safety by any body, anywhere, any time." President Wilson argued, "A strike of policemen of a great city, leaving that city at the mercy of an army of thugs, is a crime against civilization."

The net result of the strike was that all strikers were fired and replaced by new officers.[4]

Beyond the fact that over eleven hundred men lost their jobs as a result of the Boston Police Strike, the total effect on the community must be considered. Bostonians learned that a police strike is a terrible threat to the public welfare and safety. In September of 1919, losses due to property damage and theft were high, and even more important was the loss of life. The community discovered that it wanted no more such problems; and even though the union had been stopped, citizens did listen to the demands of the officers. The new officers were granted a $300 per year raise, they no longer had to purchase their own uniforms, and a pension plan was established.[5]

Perhaps the most important result of the Boston Police Strike has yet to be discussed—that is, the effect which it had on police organization attempts. The strike created such negative public opinion concerning police unions that the unionizing efforts of the lawmen virtually collapsed. Few officers were willing to challenge the administration and lose their jobs in an effort to bring in a union. Even those locals already chartered by the AFL went by the wayside. For the next twenty years, the great powers of an organized labor force in law enforcement were to lie dormant.[6]

A final point to the Boston Police Strike is the causative elements. There are two areas which should be examined: (1) the reasons for organizing

4. John H. Burpo, *The Police Labor Movement* (Springfield, Ill.: Charles C. Thomas 1971), p. 4.

5. "Police Labor Relations," p. 3.

6. "Police Collective Bargaining, 1900-1960," pp. 1-6.

and (2) the reasons for striking. The causes for organizing were that the officers could not get anyone to listen to their problems on matters of wages and job conditions. The cause of the strike itself is even more basic and can be found in all of American labor's attempts to organize; that is, the question of the right to organize and bargain collectively. There was no strike until the leaders were fired and the officers were told that they could not meet and speak as a collective body. The police unions had problems similar to all labor organization attempts in its early history, with the right of recognition being a major factor.

Even through the 1950s, the advancement of police unions was greatly restricted, although there was some organizational activity starting at the end of the 1930s. In 1939, the American Federation of State, County, and Municipal Employees (AFSCME—an affiliate of the AFL) opened its door to charter applications from police associations, in addition to the other state and local government employees who were invited into the organization. By 1944, AFSCME had chartered only 39 police locals, but this grew to 61 locals by 1951.[7]

The public-employer resistance to police unions remained strong during the 1940s and 1950s. There are several noteworthy examples which should be cited. Among these are two outstanding 1943 court decisions from the state of Michigan: *FOP* v *Harris* (306 Mich 68) and *FOP* v *City of Detroit* (318 Mich 182). Both of these cases questioned the rights of the municipalities to pass down antiunion policy for the police; in both cases the courts found in favor of the municipalities. Following these decisions, in 1944, the Detroit Police Department went so far as to issue a general order against any organizational activity. In 1944 and again in 1957, the International Association of Chiefs of Police (IACP) issued strong statements against officers' attempts to organize their agencies. Even in 1959, public opinion was still negative on the subject, with a poll showing 55 percent of the population against police unions.[8]

Even with this much resistance, the foundation was laid during the 1950s for future activity in organizing the police. While management would not give in to "unions," they were willing to live with social, fraternal, and benevolent police associations.[9] These associations were the beginning; they eventually became involved in informal negotiations, even though in some cases management was a member of the association. The majority of these associations were not affiliated with any national organization. They were, in most cases, only citywide, although some were to grow into statewide organizations. Because these associations

---

7. Ibid.
8. *Police Unions* (Gaithersburg, Md.: IACP, 1958), pp. 57-74.
9. "Police Collective Bargaining, 1900-1960," pp. 1-6.

were local in nature, they tended to be quite powerful politically, especially those which eventually became active in negotiations.

The only national police organization to evolve out of this period was the International Conference of Police Associations (ICPA). This organization had its beginnings in 1953 when it brought together a number of local organizations. The ICPA soon grew to a strength of 150,000 members in approximately 150 local units. A problem exists with the ICPA in that it is only an "association of associations." It is not active in negotiating contracts for its affiliates; the ICPA is basically a service organization.[10]

During 1958-59, there were attempts by the International Brotherhood of Teamsters to charter police locals. The public pressure was so strong against this move that the Teamsters association was not to become active in police unions for another ten years. It is highly noteworthy that about a month after the Teamsters made its effort to organize the New York City Police Department, the commissioner announced recognition of the New York City Police Benevolent Association as bargaining agent for the officers.[11]

The Future

The 1960s and 1970s represent a time of greatly expanded activity both in organizing efforts and collective bargaining. What are the police organizations of this period and why do the officers feel the need to continue this activity?

Why does the new crop of modern police officers want to organize the police labor force? According to John Cassese, former president of the New York PBA, it is for better wages; these men "want it and want it now."[12] The following increases have been noted over a period from 1939 to 1950:[13] police officers salary, up 52 percent; federal employees salary, up 83 percent; and consumer's price index, up 69 percent. But beyond the wage factor, there are a multitude of needs and complaints for which today's officers are now demanding answers.

First, there are the changes in work conditions; increased danger, increased pressure from politicians for law and order, and ever-increasing liberal attitudes of the court systems. The race riots and general public apathy have also placed added pressures upon the police officer. Not only is he asking for more pay for working with such conditions, he is also try-

---

10. "Labor Relations in the Public Safety Services," p. 27.
11. "Who Will Represent the Police?" *PERL.* vol. 18, pp. 12-13.
12. "A Union of Policemen?" p. 55.
13. "Why Policemen Are Joining Unions," *PERL.* vol. 18, p. 7.

ing to bring these matters to the attention of the public (hoping they will react favorably and offer a solution).

Another problem is the loss of social status for the police officer. In many areas of large cities, he is the "man"—the immediate representative of the legal system—and must bring the law to bear on people. Officers argue that by organizing they will become more professional and draw attention to their situation, and at the same time, show just how important an element in society they are. Professionalization and unionization—will these concepts serve as working partners in bringing social status to the police?

A final point is consistent with the cry for professionalization. In recent years, the police have encountered a fast-changing legal climate; officers must be trained and retrained to do their jobs effectively. A number of states now have mandatory training acts which prescribe a specific amount of training for an officer (anywhere from 120 to 440 hours) before he can be sworn in and assigned to duty. Furthermore, an increasing number of agencies are requiring two years and even four years of college as a selection standard for the police officer job. Officers, by way of their unions, are demanding recognition, respect, and wages commensurate with the level of job difficulty, training, and education.[14]

Many of these causative factors are the same as those observed affecting unskilled laborers as they made their organizational bids in the 1930s. We know that the actions of the 1930s led to such organizations as the Congress of Industrial Organizations (CIO), the United Auto Workers (UAW), and the United Mine Workers (UMW); what are the organizations of today's police officers?

First, there are the numerous local organizations; these are not affiliated with any other association. These organizations present a variety of names, such as: Police Benevolent Association, Police Officers Association, Deputies Association, and others. No matter what the name, by our definition, the vast majority of these local independents are "unions." There are two basic factors which normally determine if a local will remain unaffiliated: (1) that the cost-benefit element of organizing and aiding a small local would be too low for any national organization and (2) as noted before, many local independents have found themselves to be politically powerful within their jurisdiction and are therefore very capable of caring for their own needs.[15]

Next, we should look at the statewide organizations. Examples of such organizations include: Police Conference of New York, New Jersey State

---

14. Ibid.
15. Hervey Juris and Peter Feuille, *Police Unionism* (Lexington, Mass., D.C. Heath & Co.), p. 27.

Patrolmen's Benevolent Association, Police Officers Association of Michigan, California Alliance of Police Associations, and Massachusetts Police Association. Some of these organizations have national affiliation, particularly with the ICPA, but many have remained independent statewide associations. In most cases, these state organizations are service organizations; very few of them become involved in collective bargaining for the affiliated locals.[16]

There remains yet the national organizations. Perhaps the largest of the nationals, by sheer number of members, is the International Conference of Police Associations. The ICPA is only an "association of associations"; while many of the affiliated (but independent) locals participate in collective bargaining, the national appears to be but a service organization. The other extremely large and popular national which is also basically a service organization is the Fraternal Order of Police. The FOP presently claims a membership of approximately 100,000 in over 900 locals.[17]

There are several nationals which are true unions in that they do become involved in collective bargaining and grievances. The most prominent of these is the American Federation of State County and Municipal Employees (AFSCME). The AFSCME is an AFL-CIO affiliate and presently claims a membership of over 10,000 officers in addition to the other government employee members.[18] Since the police see their jobs as a specialty and AFSCME tends to organize an entire employer, their organization efforts have been somewhat weak in the police field. The other outstanding national union for the police is, of course, the Teamsters. In many cases, the Teamsters' well-publicized and widely proclaimed ability of gaining excellent contracts is very attractive to the officers.

One last national union must be presented because of both its potential and its history. This is the National Union of Police Officers (NUPO), which was formed in 1969 by John Cassese, former president of NYPBA. The NUPO made a bid for the AFL-CIO's standing offer of a charter for a national police union, but its bid was denied because it was declared to be not a true national union, with a membership of only 8,000 officers. But, the NUPO has not disappeared from the scene, rather it is now an affiliate with the Service Employees International Union and maintains its commitment of organizing policemen on a nationwide basis.[19]

A brief comment must be made of the legal status of police unions. The facts are plain and simple: Six states have an expressed right to organize

16. Ibid., p. 30.
17. "Labor Relations in Public Safety Services."
18. *The Police Labor Movement*, p. 25.
19. "Police Labor Relations."

for police officers, five states have an expressed right with "conditions," and twenty-four states have an implied right by virtue of a public employees labor-relation act. Also, there are twenty-two states which now have mandatory collective bargaining for police organizations.[20]

When discussing the legal status of police unions, one should note that, like most other unions, the police unions are the weakest in the southern states of the nation. In fact, the ICPA is the only national which is well known to the South.

One might want to believe that the police unions are in good shape, but they presently have a problem. They are not "together." We find that some police unions are affiliates of larger organizations which have busied themselves with the labor problems of a number of occupations. Furthermore, in many agencies we see several organizations—one for patrolmen, one for sergeants and lieutenants, and one for the top managers. Finally, there are those police officers who maintain dual memberships; one with an organization which is social or fraternal and one with an organization which is active in collective bargaining.[21]

There are over 370,000 municipal officers and 44,000 state officers in the United States. Many of these officers are well trained and highly educated.[22] These officers have the potential to become a very powerful labor force, but again, time will be the final factor.

A notable prediction for the future is the growth of minority police unions. Of particular import are the black unions, such as the National Council of Police Societies which claims a membership of over 5,000 black officers.[23] Some of the black leaders are urging militancy in their concern to improve relations between black officers, the agencies, the public, and other officers. Also notable among minority police are women.

To close this section on the future for police unions, perhaps we can best look to the 1972 comments of former Detroit Police Commissioner John Nichols as he quoted the comments of two leaders of the police labor movement: "Chiefs, superintendents, and commissioners are temporal. They'll change. The union is the only permanency in the department.[24] It is us (the union) with whom you will deal; we will make the policy!"

---

20. "Labor Relations in the Public Safety Services," *PERL* and University of Wisconsin, Industrial Relations Research Institute, "The Legal Status of Municipal Police Employee Organizations," *Industrial and Labor Relations Review* (April 1970), p. 360.

21. "Labor Relations in the Public Safety Services," p. 28 and "Who Will Represent the Police?" p. 14.

22. U.S. Department of Labor, Bureau of Labor Statistics, *Occupational Outlook Handbook.*

23. *"Negro Police Ask for Equal Voice,"* New York Times (June 13, 1969).

24. *Police Unionism*, pp. 1-2.

11. POLICE OFFICERS' VIEWS ON COLLECTIVE BARGAINING AND USE OF SANCTIONS

HARRY E. BOLINGER

The Police Chief, Vol. XLI, February 1974. Reprinted by permission.

During the past decade, collective bargaining by police has become a central issue in the area of municipal labor-management relations. However, both municipal administrators and scholars have focused their interest primarily on providing justification for their respective opinions concerning approval or denial of an employee organization, rather than seeking to identify the employees' reasons for alliance with the organization.

Administrators should not permit matters, pertaining to salaries, equipment, and other conditions of employment to deteriorate to a point where reasoning and mutual agreement fail. Also, if executives of the law enforcement agency were to lead the way in obtaining equitable treatment and resolution of legitimate complaints for their employees, labor-management conflicts would be sharply curtailed.

This inattention to employee desires is unfortunate because police are becoming more reluctant to accept the unilateral decisions of city management pertaining to police salaries and conditions of employment. When traditional lines of communication fail and employees have not been provided with an orderly procedure for adjusting grievances, conflicts develop.

Contrary to beliefs held by many administrators, unions do not initiate movements to unionize a police department—they merely respond to the police officers' request for assistance in gaining benefits that have been otherwise unobtainable. The responsibility for attempts to organize the police rests with negligent and autocratic authorities who fail as municipal administrators to identify the problem areas and arrive at mutually satisfactory solutions.

When an attempt, however, is made to unionize the police, many administrators perceive the move as an intrusion by outside agitators and express surprise that the officers would even consider such action. But government officials would do well to seriously consider this statement made at the 1967 Conference of Mayors by Jerry Wurf, president of the American Federation of State, County, and Municipal Employees:

You [the Mayors] represent our best organizers, our most persuasive reason for existence, our defense against membership apathy and indifference, our perpetual prod of militancy, and our assurance of continued growth.... Unions would be unable to sign up a single employee if he were satisfied, if his dignity were not offended, if he were treated with justice....

In the absence of legislation, resolution of a conflict falls back on the mayor, city manager, city council, police chief, or city attorney. Rarely are any of these persons prepared by education, training, or experience to cope with labor disputes. Frequently, the city will make a major effort to resist recognition of the employee organization and may even suffer a work stoppage as a result of ill-advised decisions by management. In this sense, the public sector still experiences strikes over an issue which has long been resolved in the private sector—union recognition.

A concept frequently encountered at the municipal level is that of "right vs. privilege." The Labor-Management Relations Act of 1947, better known as the Taft-Hartley Law, provides the legal means for private sector employees to determine their representative organization and imposes an obligation upon the employer to recognize and bargain with the employee organization. But this law specifically exempts public employees at all levels, and conveniently fits in with the widely held belief that rights which are secured to all other citizens can be withheld from public employees.

In the public sector, federal employees have since been given this right by virtue of President Richard Nixon's Executive Order 11491, but the order does not apply to state or municipal employees. However, the "Report of the Task Force on State and Local Government Labor Relations," issued in 1967 by the Executive Committee of the National Governors' Conference, states in part:

To petition the government is one thing. It is quite another to demand a share in decision making in the domain of wages and employment, or to insist that decisions must have the consent of employee organizations. Some states have enacted laws that give bargaining rights to employee organizations. This action, however, can be interpreted as a *privilege conferred* by the Legislature on employee organizations, and as such it *can conceivably be revoked.* [Emphasis added.]

When police employees encounter municipal administrators who consider their organizational and collective bargaining activities "a privilege" that can "be revoked," they may feel that they are being accorded "second-class citizen" status and look to stronger, more established unions for representation.

The First Amendment to the Constitution of the United States guarantees to all the right to assemble peaceably and to petition the government for redress of grievances. Although the legal right of workers to organize has been well-founded in Constitutional principle, the organization of police unions continues to meet with resistance from many administrators. Whether or not those administrators are successful in defeating the attempt by the police officers to win recognition of a bargaining agent, is of little consequence. Regardless of the outcome, the employees' original problems remain unsolved.

City management may place great emphasis on concepts such as "bargaining is a privilege," but it is vitally necessary that administrators recognize that the benevolent paternalistic attitude of the past is no longer acceptable, and that they should attempt to determine the police needs and desires before a conflict develops. To help make this determination, this author undertook to uncover what police officers deemed to be important in the area of collective bargaining. The research included a survey of nearly four hundred Illinois municipal police and sheriff's officers and in-depth studies of some Illinois municipalities that have experienced labor-management disputes. This information should assist local government administrators to understand the police employees' request and to assess the relative importance to police of their demands.

The Concept of Collective Bargaining

The term "collective bargaining" may be defined as the process in which representatives of the employees and representatives of the employer meet, confer, and negotiate to determine to their mutual satisfaction the terms and conditions of employment. Although there has been general agreement that the municipality could voluntarily enter into collective negotiations, the more militant police officers are beginning to want legislation that will force the city to negotiate. The respondents were asked if police should be permitted to engage in collective bargaining activities with the local governing body; and if so, should the activity be voluntary or mandatory for the governing body.

The concept of collective bargaining was readily endorsed by all of the officers. Overall, 97.7 percent of the respondents indicated that police should be permitted to engage in collective bargaining activities with the municipality. Additionally, of those officers favoring the concept of bargaining, the vast majority felt that the city should be required by law to participate, rather than have the leeway of voluntary participation. While 26.5 percent preferred that the governmental unit enter into negotiations voluntarily, 73.5 percent favored legislation that makes participation mandatory.

Bargainable Issues

One of the most nebulous aspects of collective bargaining is determination of which issues will be bargainable and which will not. In the absence of employment relations legislation, bargainable issues are the franchise of the municipal administrators. Should the city decide to grant police a voice in determining the conditions of their employment, a decision must be made as to which issues will be bargainable and which will remain the prerogative of the city.

One method would be to classify the issues into categories such as found in the public employment relations legislation of other states.[1] Such legislation usually provides for bargaining on the basis of the functional involvement of the employee and generally refers to the issues as:

(1) *Mandatory*—issues which are clearly a matter for employee concern.

(2) *Prohibited*—issues which are clearly part of the management function.

(3) *Permissive*—issues that fall into the grey area and are not clearly either mandatory or prohibited.

Regardless of the method used to classify the issues, the municipality would do well to reflect upon what police considered to be bargainable.

The respondents to the survey were queried in these four general areas: compensation, manpower allocation, disciplinary matters, and promotional procedures. The general areas were further defined to be:

(1) *Compensation*—including salaries, overtime pay, night-shift differentials, court appearance pay, and longevity pay.

(2) *Manpower allocation*—including the hours worked weekly, hours per shift, shift assignment, number of men per car, and work assignments.

(3) *Disciplinary matters*—including any actions of a disciplinary nature.

(4) *Promotional procedures*—including formulation of rules and requirements relating to promotion within the department.

Total response indicates that police officers were primarily concerned about compensation, with 96.5 percent of all officers denoting this as a bargainable issue. The next most important issue was manpower allocation, although the consensus was only 79.2 percent. Promotional procedures followed more closely with 72.4 percent favoring this area; and disciplinary matters were of least interest as a bargainable issue, at 69.9 percent.

---

1. Of the many states that now have an employment relations act, Wisconsin, Michigan, Pennsylvania, Vermont, and Hawaii are cited as exemplary.

Representative Organization

The more militant police organizations are those which have incorporated into their charters, the avowed intent to bargain collectively with city officials on behalf of the organization's members. Some of these police groups remain independent or unite with other police unions, while still others affiliate with labor unions. Although labor unions have traditionally used the threat of a strike as their ultimate sanction, the police charters usually contain a "no strike" clause. Also, membership in the local is restricted to police officers to maintain commonality of interest. Examples of labor-affiliated police unions are found throughout the state of Illinois, most of which are affiliated with the American Federation of State, County, and Municipal Employees, AFL-CIO.

The respondents were asked to select the best type of organization to act as the officers' representative in collective negotiations and were given four alternatives: no organization, an ad hoc committee, a police union affiliated with other police organizations, or a police union affiliated with labor. Over three-fourths of the officers indicated a preference for a union, rather than an ad hoc committee or no organization. Of the 76.4 percent favoring a union, 86.4 percent preferred one affiliated with police while 13.6 percent chose a labor affiliation.

Use of Sanctions

Police employees face a variety of problems in attempting to win collective bargaining rights. One of the most difficult is that of resolving disputes in the face of prohibitions on the right to strike.

Private sector employees usually resolve their serious problems with management in one of two ways—by a strike or arbitration. The strike is generally used if the dispute is over terms of the contract, while arbitration is more likely if the disagreement involves interpretation of the terms. Since law enforcement officers in the state of Illinois have no legal right to strike, there is no pressure to cause municipal administrators to give serious consideration to police demands.

In those states that have employment relations legislation, the acts usually provide that nothing in the bargaining agreement may conflict with the civil service regulations or other statutes. Even in the Illinois communities which have an ordinance providing for negotiation of wages and other economic issues, agreement reached at the bargaining table or by arbitration might not be approved when it reaches the city council.

In the absence of well-defined procedure to settle disputes, police must either accept the terms and conditions as offered by the city administration or continue negotiations and attempt to persuade the legislative body to reconsider the situation. As previously mentioned, officers have resorted to various types of sanctions in an effort to win concessions not otherwise obtainable. As a result of the adverse legal ramifications of striking, police labor groups have developed more sophisticated forms of work stoppage. The sick call or "blue flu" was conceived by the Pontiac (Michigan) Police Officers Association during its 1966 work stoppage in protest of wage scales. Many other police organizations have employed "blue flu" since then. . . .

To gain information concerning the proposition that police officers may resort to the use of sanctions, the respondents were questioned about the use of five types of sanctions—each to be considered individually and not in conjunction with any of the others. The selected sanctions were not intended as a tabulation of the whole spectrum of sanctions available to police but only as examples of a range from mild through severe.

The first sanction, informational picketing, was the least severe. The second, an aggressive action likely to antagonize the administration, was a work slowdown during which time the officers would stop all enforcement activities that result in revenue for the city, e.g., traffic and parking tickets.

The third sanction was a work speed-up in which arrests are made for every infraction observed, however slight. This action has the "advantage" of drawing the general public into the arena, thereby putting pressure on the administration to settle the dispute.

The fourth job action was "blue flu," which is a work stoppage resulting from a massive sick call. All officers feign illness and call in just before they are to report for duty.

The final sanction considered was the strike. Although a strike by police has been held to be illegal—in the absence of legislation to the contrary—officers do occasionally resort to this tactic. Illinois police officers, not having any other particular power to employ and no employment relations legislation to admit them as participants into the bargaining process, are participating in work stoppages with increasing regularity.

Over three-fourths (76.1 percent) of the officers surveyed indicated that police should plan to use sanctions if necessary to enforce demands, and over half (55 percent) favored picketing, the mildest of the examples. However, none of the examples provided enjoyed a consensus such as received by the job action concept itself.

The first three choices—picketing, a work slowdown, and a work speedup—are more or less "legal" in the sense that no legislation specifically prohibits them. The last two examples, "blue flu" and strike, are work stoppages and, therefore, illegal in the state of Illinois. However, many police officers conceive a difference between "blue flu" and a strike—to them, one is illegal and the other is difficult for municipal administrators to disprove.

Cooperation in Work Stoppages

Behavioral decisions are influenced by many factors other than the legality of the proposed activity and personal preference. One of the recognized determinants is the sociological aspect of peer group pressure.

Police officers are engaged in an occupation which sets them apart from other workers in both the public and private sectors. The code of behavior for police, like that for medical doctors and lawyers, is much more stringent than for other citizens. A natural resentment to having one's social transgressions censured by another, not governed by the same code, causes law enforcement officers to seek social acceptance primarily within the police community. Therefore, the individual officer's behavior is determined to a significant degree by the behavior of his fellow officers.

The ramifications of peer group pressure have been reflected countless times in labor disputes in the public section as well as the private. Workers may split in the vote on whether or not to take action, but the decision of the majority is usually accepted by the body.

The respondents were queried as to the nature of their response if their fellow officers chose to engage in a work stoppage by going out with "blue flu" or calling a strike. Would they (1) approve of the sanction and go out, (2) oppose this kind of sanction and remain on the job, or (3) oppose this kind of sanction, but go anyway? The following discusses the extent of their indicated cooperation.

It should be added at this point that the responses were made without benefit of a stress situation such as accompanies a labor dispute and imposition of sanctions. The author believes then that most of the distributions merely reflect the lower limit of those who would actually engage in the job action when called. During an actual work stoppage, when peer pressure is brought to bear, individual values may change or, at least, be seen in a new perspective.

Collectively, 65 percent of the officers replied that they would be out during a work stoppage. Of this group 36 percent favored the action while 29 percent opposed it but would go anyway. Although slightly over 23 percent of the officers under 30 years of age favored use of the strike as a sanction, over 70 percent indicated that they would go out if a work stoppage was called. The officers over 35 years of age appear to be the least militant, but only 52 percent of this older group stated that they would remain on the job.

Also there appears to be a direct relationship between the degree of cooperation and length of service. Over three-fourths (76.6 percent) of the officers with less than one year of service would go out, while only 43.8 percent of the officers with more than ten years responded affirmatively. As the age groups increased chronologically, and the length of service increased in time, so did the percentage of respondents preferring to remain on the job.

When the responses were tabulated according to rank, patrolmen were clearly the most militant as 73.3 percent of them would either approve or support a sick call or strike. Not to be overlooked is the response by officers in the supervision and management ranks. Only 13.3 percent of these officers favored use of a strike in a labor dispute; however, if the officers decided to walk off the job, 45.1 percent of the supervisors and managers would approve of the tactic, and another 16.1 percent would walk out even though opposed to this form of sanction.

When viewed in terms of current union membership, almost three-fourths (73.3 percent) of the officers who belonged to a union and a little more than one-half (59.3 percent) of the non-union police were willing to participate in a work stoppage. Among the union members, 76.4 percent of those affiliated with other police indicated cooperation in a work stoppage. However, only 68.6 percent of the officers affiliated with a labor organization gave an affirmative response. This would seem to contradict the position assumed by municipal administrators who feel that they are better off dealing with a police union.

Conclusion

Because of the scope of the subject matter, it would be a mistake to attempt to reach fixed and firm conclusions based on the results of this survey. However, the body of evidence is sufficient to give direction to identifying the steps necessary to rectify the problems being encountered in police-management relations.

The first step appears to be establishment of effective two-way communications between municipal administrators and police, including the men in the lowest ranks. Collective negotiations need not be a legislated procedure so long as the employees feel that management is concerned and attentive to their needs. However, the concern must be genuine and demonstrated, not merely lip service. Many police labor disputes begin with the city council permitting a police spokesman to state the terms and conditions being sought, then rejoining with terms arbitrarily decided by the council. This is the kind of non-participatory relationship that is being rejected by police more and more each year.

Recently, the City of Waukegan paid an incalculable price as the lamentable result of such frustration. Police felt a need to strengthen their bargaining position with the municipal administration and voted to join the Cook County Police Association.[2] Waukegan Mayor Robert Sabonjian

---

2. The Cook County Police Association has since been renamed the Combined Counties Police Association.

refused to recognize this representative organization; and as a result of the ensuing battle, during which 63 of 78 police officers went out with "blue flu," 80 percent of the police were dismissed. The incident, which ended with the dismissal of the police officers, was precipitated by the thwarted efforts of police to participate in deciding the terms and conditions of their work.

The almost unanimous approval given to the concept of collective bargaining by the survey respondents is attributable, probably to a large extent, to the traditional response of municipal governments to efforts by police employees to participate in the decision-making process. Notably, the consensus of agreement was high throughout the range of personal, institutional, and environmental variables by which interest was measured.

The survey results also imply that police will become even more demanding in the future than they have been in the past. A vast majority of all respondents felt that they should have a voice in the determination of their compensation. Also a large majority felt that the other issues were bargainable as well. Generally speaking, more issues were considered to be bargainable by respondents who are currently members of a police union. Those affiliated with other police were more inclined toward bargaining collectively on the several issues than were the officers affiliated with labor.

More important, perhaps, is the fact that the vast majority of officers agreed that a union affiliated with police is the best organization to represent them in bargaining activities with the governing body. This attitude may be an indication of the tenor that will prevail in future police-management relations.

Police employee relations historically have been on a take-it-or-leave-it basis, because the municipal administrators have not been obligated to confer with police representatives, much less negotiate with them. Concomitant with the denial of a right to participate in determination of conditions of employment, administrators and police were cognizant of legal and social limitations imposed upon the police.

Whenever police have attempted to impose sanctions in an effort to further their bargaining position, opponents denounce the action as being inconsistent with "good police conduct." Also, they say that it is detrimental to the efforts of the entire police service becoming professionals. Overshadowing these limitations is the knowledge that police do not have a legal right to strike. However, events over the past decade have demonstrated that police can and do engage in work stoppages even though they have no legal right to do so.

Most communities find it easier to concede to police demands than to resist past the point of reconciliation and then be forced to replace a majority of their police officers. Even as the Waukegan police officers were engaged in a dispute which resulted in their dismissal, police in the neighboring community of Skokie went out with "blue flu" over a salary disagreement to which the Skokie City Council finally yielded.

Since amnesty for everyone involved in a work stoppage has become part of the settlement, legal sanctions do not pose a serious threat to dissident officers.

Three-fourths of the respondents favored the use of sanctions in collective bargaining when necessary to enforce demands. Further, 65 percent of all the officers, which included the supervision and management ranks, indicated that they would be willing to participate in a work stoppage if necessary to further their goals. As mentioned earlier, however, the author believes this percentage is lower than the number of officers who would participate.

The author also believes that the results of this survey indicate that job actions in the police service including work stoppages are going to become more frequent unless municipal administrators take steps to establish and maintain meaningful relationships with their police. More work stoppages have occurred in the police service during the past ten years than had been experienced throughout the history of police prior to that time.

The findings of this survey make it reasonable to assume that as long as local government administrators attempt to maintain the traditional one-sided power relationship, police dissatisfaction and militancy will continue to increase. The older men, the dissatisfied leaders of today, will be replaced by the younger, more aggressive officers who already indicate a willingness to participate in a work stoppage if necessary to win a voice in the decision-making process.

If municipal administrators are to reverse the trend in police labor relations, they must recognize the police officer's need to be heard, then make a legitimate effort to resolve the issues.

12. POLICE STRIKES: ARE WE TREATING THE SYMPTOMS RATHER THAN THE PROBLEM?

RICHARD M. AYRES

The Police Chief, Vol. XLIV, March 1977. Reprinted by permission.

Although strikes are forbidden in almost all states, in city ordinances and in police department regulations, police unions have not been deterred from participating in them, and they are one of the basic concerns of every administrator whose department is unionized.

It is important at the outset to realize that strikes don't materialize overnight. They build like a volcano, starting with small grumblings that grow into deep employee dissatisfaction. The dissatisfaction develops as a result of poor communication and management's lack of concern and appreciation for employees and for the work they do, to the point where all that is needed is an emotional issue to act as the spark for a strike to erupt.

During the Boston police strike of 1919, Massachusetts Governor Calvin Coolidge exclaimed: "There is no right to strike against the public safety by anybody, anywhere, anytime."

"Anybody" was once again the police, "anytime" became 1975, and "anywhere" became Albuquerque, New Mexico; Oklahoma City, Oklahoma; and San Francisco, California. These were the scenes of the major police strikes of 1975.

These strikes caused police unions to come under heavy criticism by the public, press, and politicians. When strikes occur, one can rest assured that the old adages from the Boston police strike will be resurrected. The sage words of Calvin Coolidge and Woodrow Wilson in 1919 will reappear in the newspapers of every city undergoing a strike by its police. President Woodrow Wilson will be quoted as saying: "A strike of policemen of a great city, leaving that city at the mercy of an army of thugs, is a crime against civilization."

A strike by police today is no less a crime against civilization than it was in 1919, if violence, rioting, and loss of life and property occur. Fortunately, the police strikes of 1975 did not have these elements of violence attached to them. However, this may not always be the case in the future. With cities throughout the country facing financial crises and, as a result, taking a harder line with municipal employees, it is not unlikely that more strikes may occur. As with any police strike, the potential for violence always exists. It is therefore imperative that we take a closer look at our approach and previous responses to these strikes.

A tougher position at the municipal bargaining table by cities may well be applauded and long overdue. But is the "hard line" approach the answer to labor disputes? Have we been attempting to treat the symptom, rather than dealing with the problem itself?

While police officers should be prohibited from striking, it is most disconcerting to note that when they do walk out, many police and city administrators, politicians, editorial writers, and news commentators seem to be concerned exclusively with ways of crushing the strike and have little or no interest in determining the underlying causes of it.

While it may well be necessary to administer harsh penalties for striking employees and to enact strong no-strike legislation, it is now recognized that these are not sufficient measures in themselves to insure labor peace in the public sector. I believe it is therefore important that we stop trying to treat the symptom, the strike, and begin directing our attention to the problem itself—the employee dissatisfaction which caused the strike in the first place.

If police administrators are able to identify the causes of police strikes, they will be better equipped to predict, avoid, and deal with such labor disputes in the future.

Interestingly enough, a careful analysis of the police strikes that have recently occurred reflects that there are some common variables that can be identified in each case. To illustrate, let us focus our attention on the Albuquerque and Oklahoma City strikes of July and October, 1975. I was fortunate to be able to visit these cities and prepare case studies of the strikes by interviewing the major participants—the mayor, members of city council, police and city administrators, labor leaders, and striking officers. Here are some of the findings that evolved from these case studies as to what caused the strikes, along with general guidelines and recommendations for preventing future ones.

Factors Causing Police Strikes

One of the first allegations heard when examining the causes of strikes is bad faith bargaining. This term, of course, can mean many things to many people, depending upon one's perception of the situation. In Albuquerque, cries of bad faith bargaining were heard back in 1973, two years before the strike actually occurred. Following tradition, the police were the first city employees to bargain with the administration. At this time, they accepted a salary increase less than that which they had requested, on the basis that there was no more money in the city budget. The police then watched the firemen and the blue-collar workers go on strike and receive what they perceived to be better benefits than those which they themselves had been given. Comments such as, "Look what the firemen received for going out on strike," and "Look what a good organization can do for its members," were soon heard around the police department.

By 1975, the police were anxious to cash in on the alleged promises by the city that they would be given priority treatment for having been the "good guys" during the last negotiations. Now, when the city refused to meet their demands, the police believed that they were not getting what they deserved, and that the city administration was obviously not bargaining in good faith.

In Oklahoma City, bad faith bargaining allegedly began when the city agreed to a Fraternal Order of Police (FOP) request to call for advisory arbitration to settle the wage-benefits dispute. Hearings were held and the arbitrators returned a decision almost totally in favor of the FOP stance, recommending a 10 percent across-the-board wage increase for the police.

Shortly thereafter, the city council voted 9 to 0 to reject the recommendation of the arbitration board in favor of a smaller pay hike of 7½ percent.

Although the officers admitted that the arbitration ruling was only advisory in nature, they were clearly upset and frustrated with the city's decision. The FOP had led its members to believe that the city had agreed to go to arbitration and would accept the findings. The police viewed the city's rejection as bad faith bargaining. As one officer stated, "The city had asked for arbitration and now they won't let us have it after the award was favorable to the men."

Another commonly heard explanation for police strikes is a breakdown in communications. A large number of grievances that come up to management are traceable to its failure to listen and to get the facts as to why the employee had the grievance.

Complaints often heard by patrolmen in the studies conducted were that they had no voice in management and that no one would listen to them. As the president of one of the unions stated, "The typical feeling among patrolmen is 'Isn't anyone listening to me—I am the one doing the work.' "

However, failure of police management to communicate with its employees is only one segment in the chain of events leading to the total breakdown in communications which precedes a strike. Examining the total labor relations process, we must also cite the failure of the city administration to communicate to the police as well as a lack of proper communication between the union and its membership.

The lack of experience and expertise of the union bargaining team is also cited as being a factor in causing strikes. In both Albuquerque and

Oklahoma City, city administrators contended that the inexperience of the union's bargaining team, due to its rapid turnover of personnel and its inability to bargain professionally, helped to promote the strike situation.

A close corollary to this situation was the lack of experience and inability of the union's leadership in general. It was contended in both cities that the unions should have had better control over their members, and that they were irresponsible in presenting proposals that were impossible to deliver. This type of rhetoric on the part of the union leaders allegedly caused great frustration in the rank and file of the police department, particularly when the union failed to deliver at the bargaining table.

Another factor present in each of these strikes was that the city and union had failed to reach an agreement before the existing contract expired. This exerted even greater pressure on the respective representatives to reach some type of settlement.

A hotly contested election to determine the exclusive bargaining agent will also contribute to a strike atmosphere. In Albuquerque, the Police Officer's Association (APOA) was challenged by the International Brotherhood of Police Officers (IBPO); and in Oklahoma City, the FOP was faced with the Teamsters. In both of these situations, the incumbent organization was victorious, but it placed tremendous pressure on both the APOA and the FOP to come up with a good contract. They had to produce or else. It's like one of the officers put on his ballot in Oklahoma City, "The FOP. We'll give them one more year."

A form of employee dissatisfaction which always seems to be present prior to a strike is that which is caused by poor supervisory practices. This discontent is usually expressed by officers complaining about the lack of concern for employees by their supervisors and their unwillingness to communicate with them relative to the elements affecting their job.

Tied closely to poor supervisory practices is lack of administrative leadership. Many police officers view management as being too autocratic in its implementation of policy regarding transfers, promotion, and discipline. Being expected to blindly obey orders issued by autocratic administrators will cause tremendous employee dissatisfaction. This, coupled with what historically has been a laxity on the part of police and city administrators to recognize and pursue the economic and job needs of the workers, raises the level of employee frustration.

The lack of education and understanding on the part of the legislative body, including the city council, has also been cited as a catalyst for strikes. As one official stated, "Politics plays hell with the process, and creates misunderstanding and fears on the part of both parties which prevent close relationships between the city and union."

The media also plays an important role in the circumstances leading to a strike. It often over-emphasizes and allows an undue amount of unprofessional material to be printed. All of this leads to misrepresentation of the facts thus developing distorted public opinion and preventing the parties involved in negotiations from reaching an amiable solution.

As indicated, there are many causes for police strikes. It is important to note, however, that once these causes are present, and as the employee dissatisfaction grows and the frustration level increases, all that is then needed is an emotional issue to act as a triggering device to set off the strike. In both Albuquerque and Oklahoma City, the triggering device was identical—a rumor, unfounded, regarding the suspension of one of the union members. This rumor was an emotional issue which in light of all the other factors present led the men into taking that unthinkable step—a strike.

The police strikes in Albuquerque and Oklahoma City are not unique; many of the factors present in them are common in most strike situations. Hopefully, we can learn from these experiences and be able to formulate some guidelines based on the variables identified that will help city and police administrators prevent such labor disputes in the future.

Guidelines to Prevent Police Strikes

1. Police and city administrators must work towards developing an atmosphere of trust and cooperation that is conducive to good faith bargaining.

It seems to me that the fundamental difficulty with the usual collective bargaining is that both management and labor approach it as a win-or-lose proposition; consequently, each girds itself to do battle with the other. Both parties come to the bargaining table ready to reject as unreasonable the other's demands. By expecting these things and preparing for them, each sets a tone for a relationship which tends to bring about the conduct expected. As a result, an atmosphere of distrust is created in which good faith bargaining is practically impossible. We must learn to approach negotiations as a "cooperative enterprise," a win-win proposition, where both parties come away with some needs satisfied. This attitude, if adopted, would help create a climate more conducive to good faith bargaining.

2. Police administrators must get politically involved in areas that affect the efficient operation of their agencies.

In all too many cities, the police department has stayed aloof from or uninvolved in important political decisions having an impact on effective police service. The police executive today must begin to articulate department problems to the public and actively pursue the economic and job condition needs of his employees. If police administrators fail to get involved, the union will fill the void created by this leadership vacuum.

3. A more effective internal communications system must be developed in police agencies.

As the size of police departments increases, their executives tend to drift further and further out of touch with their employees. Police administrators must begin to give high priority to establishing fast, easy, up-and-down communications so that no one feels left out and ignored. The answer to eliminating job alienation lies in effective and sincere manager/worker communication in a climate of high trust and credibility.

4. Better communications and relations must be established between the police administrator and the city administration, including elected officials.

Police administrators must try to establish a closely coordinated relationship with the personnel director, city manager, mayor, and other officials responsible for carrying out employee relations policies. Labor relations policy meetings between these top level managers are advisable and essential if empathy and understanding for each other's problems is to be achieved. Moreover, there should be a constant interchange of information and ideas so that the city management team develops a coordinated approach when responding to the police union.

5. Better communications and relations must exist between the police administrator and his union leaders.

Recently, a police chief related that he never dealt directly with his union president. If they wanted to get a message to each other, they did so through a third party. This type of antagonistic approach can only complement conflict. A more preferable approach is to deal with the union in a spirit of cooperation. In this environment, labor issues can often be resolved with a minimum of conflict by utilizing the union and its president as a vehicle for communication.

It is also recommended, depending on the size of the agency and its manpower needs, that the union president be removed from all police duties, making his sole responsibility the operation of the union.

6. Efforts must be made to enhance more effective communications and relations between the union and the city.

In many cities throughout the country, the only time the city administration meets with its labor leaders is at bargaining time. Depending on the duration of the contract, a long period of time may elapse without any contact between the parties. It is, therefore, recommended that regularly scheduled meetings between the police union and the city be held to provide an opportunity to discuss matters of mutual interest and to open the lines of communication. These meetings would be neither a substitute for nor an alternative to collective bargaining, but would act to complement the collective bargaining process.

7. Police administrators must insist on representation of police management at the bargaining table.

The transactions that take place at the bargaining table constitute one of the most important personnel events of the police department, because they have impact on all phases of the management activity. It is essential that a police executive be represented during the entire process to protect management interests and to obtain important feedback on the progress of negotiations.

It is recommended that deputy chiefs or potential chiefs of police be appointed to represent the department in order that they may obtain valuable experience in and understanding of the labor relations process to aid them when they later become the top executive.

8. Efforts must be made to remove all supervisory personnel from the same collective bargaining unit as patrolmen.

At a recent meeting of the California Organization of Police and Sheriffs (COPS), a San Francisco labor attorney advised those present of the necessity for police officers to "consider the strike and reserve the right to strike." This, of course, he stated, assumes that the police bargaining unit is adequately organized and unified to effect such influence when necessary. "So, don't overlook any facet of the police department," he warned. "Remember, the fewer members in your bargaining unit, the more officers there are available to do your work if you should choose to strike."

For this very reason, it is recommended, that where possible, supervisors should not belong to the same bargaining unit as patrolmen. There is a strong bond that naturally develops between employees in the same bargaining unit due to the common issues that will arise. If there is a strike or job action, you want your supervisory personnel remaining loyal to management.

9. Training must be provided for police union leaders in the area of improving their negotiating expertise, leadership, and organizational abilities.

Ken McFeeley, former president of New York City's Police Benevolent Association, remarked at a seminar, shortly after being elected president, that it was a shock to be riding a patrol car one day and to find yourself the next day having breakfast with the Governor of the State of New York. We provide our labor leaders with little or no labor relations training, yet we complain vociferously about their ineptness and inexperience. It is recommended that we provide our union leaders with training to improve their negotiating ability. When management and labor can come to the bargaining table with equal expertise, the negotiations are going to operate more smoothly and productively. Furthermore, we often fail to recognize that the union president, as the head of his organization, is in a management position. It is necessary, therefore, that he obtain training in the area of management, leadership, and organization to help him to operate the union more efficiently. The better the union president can manage the union, the less conflict there is going to be within the department.

10. Training must be provided for police management supervisory personnel.

Training programs must be developed to foster a "management consciousness" among supervisors and to provide them with the expertise necessary to deal with problems of employee discipline, performance evaluation, motivation, and grievance resolution. This is one of the most important steps a police administrator can take to dissipate labor unrest. Supervisory personnel must be trained to become attuned to the needs of employees and see that they receive proper recognition and appreciation for the work that they do.

11. Mixed training programs should be provided for police and city administrators and labor leaders.

Recently, at a seminar on labor relations and collective bargaining in one of the major cities, the city council, heads of municipal agencies, and their labor counterparts all attended. The objective of this seminar was not to teach the attendees the principles of labor relations, but to open lines of communication and develop empathy. More seminars of this type should be conducted, where a cross-fertilization of ideas may take place, and representatives of the various segments of the public sector can get together and discuss matters of mutual interest outside of the bargaining process.

12. "Eleventh hour" bargaining and negotiation in the press must be avoided.

Someone once said that eleventh hour bargaining makes good headlines but poor contracts. Every effort should be made to avoid eleventh hour bargaining. There should be an early exchange of contract proposals and every attempt made to settle the contract before the existing one expires.

Unfortunately, the public news media seldom explores or explains the benefits of a negotiated contract to the community, but spotlights misunderstandings and mismanagement of both participants in the bargaining. The news media must be utilized in a more positive fashion by emphasizing the matters that the negotiating parties have agreed upon and by not dwelling on points of difference.

13. It is necessary to develop and update an effective strike contingency plan.

A strike contingency plan is a valuable tool to a police administrator. A well-publicized contingency plan may be a key factor toward deterring strikes and other related job actions. More importantly, it is essential, if the community is to be afforded interim protection during the strike, absence from violence, rioting, and increased crime. It also allows the administrator to free himself from making hurried decisions in a time of crisis so he can devote his entire effort to the impartial ending of the strike.

Conclusion

In any strike, there are many factors and variables that are peculiar to a given situation. You will have to analyze your own particular setting. However, let me leave you with what is admittedly an oversimplified remedy for preventing police strikes and reducing labor/management conflict. It is this:

Find out what is the cause of employee dissatisfaction in your department and then work toward achieving equitable solutions conducted in an atmosphere of trust and cooperation.

Concepts to Consider

1. Describe the development of unions in the police field.
2. Describe the impact of police unionization on police professionalism.
3. Identify issues that are "bargainable" and not exclusively the prerogative of a governmental unit.
4. Support the position that police officers should not have the right to engage in work stoppages.
5. Justify the need for police officers to have the right to strike.
6. Identify the major factors that have led to police strikes.
7. Describe the guidelines that can be used to prevent police strikes.

Selected Readings

Anderson, Robert U., Ted Bartell, Frieda L. Gehlen, and L. Thomas Winfree, "Support Your Local Police—On Strike?" *Police Science and Administration*, Vol. 4, No. 1, March 1976, pp. 1-8.

A case study of the strike of the Albuquerque, New Mexico police department in mid-July of 1975, concludes that the citizens identified with the police and suggests that the future will bring increased politicization of the police.

Ayres, Richard M., "Police Unions: A Step Toward Professionalism?" *Journal of Police Science and Administration*, Vol. 3, No. 4, December 1975, pp. 400-404.

Discusses the issues related to the suggested incompatibility of police unions and the professionalization of law enforcement. Concludes that unions can contribute to police professionalization.

Brostron, Curtis, "Police Employee Organizations," *The Police Chief*, December 1969, pp. 6-8.

A discussion of police-employee organizations with an emphasis on the development of such groups in the St. Louis Police Department.

Gifford, James P., "Professionalizing Police Labor Relations: The New York City Police Department's Response to Unionization," *Journal of Police Science and Administration*, Vol. 2, No. 1, March 1974, pp. 94-106.

This article describes in detail the regularization and modernization of police labor relations in the New York City Police Department. Part of the response involved the reorganization of personnel and labor relations units.

Igleburger, Robert M. and John E. Angell, "Dealing with Police Unions," *The Police Chief*, Vol. 38, No. 5, May 1971, pp. 50-55.

The authors stress that with the growth of employee groups the classical arguments against police unionization should give way to dealing realistically with unions and other employee organizations.

Meyer, John C., Jr., "Both Sides Now," *The Police Chief*, Vol. 39, No. 4, April 1972, pp. 68-75.

This article summarizes the results of two surveys regarding the attitudes of both police administrators and line officers toward the national police union.

Neel, Steven M., "Collective Bargaining: A Problem for the Civil Service System," *The Police Chief*, Vol. 28, No. 4, April 1971, pp. 72-77.

This article analyzes what a city should do when it decides to retain merit principles and what steps are needed to minimize the conflict between bargaining arrangements and existing merit systems.

Nichols, John F., "Management and Legal Aspects of Police Strikes," *The Police Chief*, Vol. 39, No. 12, December 1972, pp. 38-43.

The author describes the experience of the Detroit Police Department with the "Blue Flu" and other aspects of labor relations in law enforcement.

O'Block, Robert, "The Movement for Police Unionization," *The Police Chief*, Vol. XLV, No. 6, June 1978, pp. 56-57.

Police unions may indeed actually be formed in the near future unless police administrators become aggressively concerned with the needs of officers. The dissatisfied officer will have no alternate course to follow other than to join a large and powerful group in order to register complaints and be assured that action will be taken.

Olmos, Ralph A., "A New Approach to Collective Bargaining for Police Unions," *The Police Chief*, Vol. XLI, No. 2, February 1974, pp. 28-30.

This paper argues that the key to future gains for police unions should be based on an emphasis on professionalization, not on societal concern for law and order.

Chapter 6
POLICE CORRUPTION

Introduction

The fact that official corruption does exist is amply supported by current evidence—but it cannot be allowed to exist. One of the most important needs in a democracy is integrity in government. Programs must be developed for the reduction of criminal opportunities in the public realm.

The National Advisory Commission on Criminal Justice Standards and Goals postulated that:

(1) the corruption of public officials at all levels of government— federal, state, and local—is perceived as widespread by the American public;

(2) such corruption results in a staggering cost to the American taxpayer;

(3) the existence of corruption breeds further crime by providing for the citizen a model of official lawlessness that undermines an acceptable rule of law.[1]

Corruption is not limited to its most egregious and sensational form—cash purchase of official favor. Corruption includes all of the circumstances in which the public officeholder or government employee sacrifices or sells all or part of his judgment on matters within his official purview in return for personal gain. Corruption thus defined includes a direct bargain—cash (or securities, a share in a business venture, or the promise of a future job on the outside)—in exchange for official action or inaction.

Corruption also includes more subtle arrangements in which the bargain is only implied. Such arrangements—frequently described as conflicts of interest—include any and all circumstances in which the officeholder or government employee is or may become the beneficiary of favor from persons with business that comes before him in his official capacity. Such conflicts of interest often involve the officeholder whose business or professional pursuits (e.g., insurance firm or law practice) service or represent those who may benefit from his official conduct.

Finally, corruption, as defined here, may flow from the electoral process itself. The payment, or promised payment, of campaign contributions in return for official conduct constitutes a bribe. Moreover, dependence on a source of campaign funding probably represents the most pervasive and constant monetary shackle on the judgment and action of the elected official.

It is impossible to measure precisely the extent of corruption in America today. But the presence of one especially virulent species—the influence of organized crime syndicates on public officials—has been better documented than most. As long ago as 1931, the National Commission on Law Observance and Enforcement (Wickersham Commission) observed that, "Nearly all the large cities suffer from an alliance between politicians and criminals." The link has been condemned by successive Attorneys General from Wickersham to Saxbe.

---

1. National Advisory Commission on Criminal Justice Standards and Goals, *Community Crime Prevention* (Washington, D.C.: U.S. Government Printing Office, 1973).

In 1967, the President's Commission on Law Enforcement and Administration of Justice noted that:

> The millions of dollars . . . (organized crime) can spend on corrupting public officials may give it power to maim or murder people inside or outside the organization with impunity; to extort money from businessmen; to conduct businesses in such fields as liquor, meat, or drugs without regard to administrative regulations; to avoid payment of income taxes or to secure public works contracts without competitive bidding.[2]

The Commission went on to conclude that:

> Today's corruption is less visible, more subtle, and therefore more difficult to detect and assess than the corruption of the prohibition era. All available data indicate that organized crime flourishes only where it has corrupted local officials. As the scope and variety of organized crime's activities have expanded, its need to involve public officials at every level of local government has grown. And as government regulation expands into more and more areas of private and business activity, the power to corrupt likewise affords the corrupter more control over matters affecting the everyday life of each citizen.[3]

No wonder, then, that a 1971 Harris poll revealed that 80 percent of the American people believe that "organized crime has corrupted and controls many politicians in the country."[4]

Charges of corruption, some of which already have led to convictions, have been brought against many officials throughout the United States. Since 1969, in one large eastern state at least 57 elected or appointed officials have been indicted or convicted on federal or state charges based on federal investigations. These officials include ten mayors, two judges, three state legislators, various local officials, and several state officials including two secretaries of state. Not all officials were charged while still in office. In another, smaller state, similar charges have been brought against at least 24 officials, including a former Governor, two state senators, a state attorney general, and several other state and local officers or employees.

Lincoln Steffens' mordant observation of over half a century ago—"The spirit of graft and of lawlessness is the American spirit"—is far from outdated in these post-Watergate days. But the American public's

---

2. President's Commission on Law Enforcement and Administration of Justice, *The Challenge of Crime in a Free Society* (1967), pp. 187-188.

3. *Ibid.*, p. 191.

4. "Feelings of Alienation up Sharply in Past Year" (The Harris Survey, June 19, 1972); see also, "Public's Trust in Elected Officials has Diminished" (The Harris Survey, November 25, 1971).

confidence in governmental "purity" was far from strong even before the disastrous disillusionment caused by Watergate. A study conducted in 1970 by the Center for Political Studies at the University of Michigan revealed that almost 30 percent of white Americans and almost 50 percent of black Americans believe that "quite a few of the people running the government are a little crooked."[5]

The direct costs of corruption are incalculable, but they are believed to be astronomical enough to support the wry observation of one high U.S. Department of Justice career official who stated that "when we finally stop payoffs to public officials at all levels in this country, we will have found the cure to inflation."

There is no dollar figure that can represent adequately the debilitating effect on human life of such activities as narcotics operations, extortion rackets, prostitution rings, and gambling syndicates that are permitted to flourish because of compliant and corrupt law enforcement.[6]

Consider Herman Goldstein's "Police Corruption: A Perspective on Its Nature and Control":[7]

> Until recently, it has been almost impossible to generate open discussion of corruption by police themselves. If corruption was discussed at all, it was done privately, among officers who knew and trusted each other. Corruption was seldom referred to in police administration and law enforcement texts. It was rarely covered in any depth in police training programs or discussed formally at meetings of police administrators. Most strikingly, administrators of some of the most corrupt police agencies have publicly denied the existence of a problem. When confronted with evidence of wrongdoing, they have de-emphasized the problem by dealing with the wrongdoers and claiming that they, like a few rotten apples, were exceptions in an otherwise clean barrel.
>
> Today there is a greater willingness to discuss the problem. The session on police corruption at the 1973 meeting of the International Association of Chiefs of Police was among the most heavily attended of the entire conference. Articles on the subject are appearing in police journals. Several conferences have recently been held for the specific purpose of encouraging more open concern. But even at meetings called to discuss the problem, some participants try to divert attention from police corruption by insisting that it should be seen as only a part of the problem of corruption in the criminal justice system and society.

5.   Center for Political Studies, University of Michigan, "Election Time Series Analysis of Attitudes of Trust in Government" (Fall 1971).

6.   National Advisory Commission on Criminal Justice Standards and Goals, *Community Crime Prevention*, pp. 205-207 and 267-269.

7.   The Police Foundation, 1975. Reprinted by permission.

Why is open discussion so difficult?

Cynics argue that those who are corrupt or potentially corrupt obviously have an interest in diverting attention from their own improprieties. Honest police administrators who have failed to control corruption have no desire to call attention to their failure. But these explanations do not account for the silence of police leaders strongly committed to rooting out corruptions or the silence of rank-and-file police personnel who themselves are honest.

One major reason for this unwillingness to discuss the problem is that it is difficult to do so without impugning the integrity of honest police personnel and contributing toward an already prevalent stereotype that labels all police corrupt. Many police officials feel that public discussion also undermines public confidence in the police in a manner disproportionate to the prevalence and seriousness of the corrupt acts.

There is little doubt that disclosure of a single instance of corruption in a large police agency adversely affects the reputation of the entire agency and makes all officers suspect in the eyes of a substantial segment of the community. This tends to be true even when an agency ferrets out its own corruption and when the disclosure reflects the agency's intense desire to rid itself of corrupt practices. Likewise, any effort by a newspaper, the mayor, a group of citizens, or even the police administrator to stimulate a public discussion of police corruption tends to besmirch the reputation of all police personnel. The effect sometimes extends beyond the agency involved. The most isolated instance of corruption may impugn the integrity of police personnel in agencies far removed from the area where the corruption is exposed. As a result, the low status accorded police is reinforced, the respect upon which their effectiveness depends is further diminished, and their own self-image suffers. Given the far-reaching and rather indiscriminate effects any ventilation of corruption has on the reputation of police and their morale, police inclination to suppress open discussion is understandable.

Apart from these considerations, there is a strong feeling among police that they have been made scapegoats, that because they are responsible for policing the conduct of others, some segments of the community delight in alleging police corruption. Some personnel even argue that certain elements of the community, by seizing every opportunity to paint the police as corrupt, hope to convince themselves that their own corruption is less serious.

A police officer learns a great deal about the corruption of citizens. He learns how individuals exploit each other and of the existence of a multitude of corrupt schemes in a community. He may witness overt corruption in the prosecutor's office, in the courts, and in the relationships between lawyers and clients. It understandably angers him to know that institutions and professions which enjoy more prestige and status than his are as corrupt, if not more corrupt, but that police are most commonly singled out for attention. What we now know in this Watergate era about corruption in government lends substantial support to these feelings.

Yet, understandable as the reluctance may be, it is impossible to deal in an innovative manner with corruption and to develop community support for confronting it unless the problem is fully discussed. Not addressing it openly will have an even more devastating effect than will the negative consequences of open discussion.

At the same time, it should be apparent that the police administrator who addresses the problem must, in order to maintain his credibility with his personnel, constantly acknowledge the extent to which corruption constitutes a problem elsewhere in society. He must argue convincingly that corruption elsewhere is no reason for tolerating it among police.

He also must guard against becoming a fanatic. The problem can arouse an emotional involvement that can be dysfunctional. Important as it is to address corruption, concern with it must be related to the magnitude of the problem in the given community and be balanced by concern with other problems.

Articles in this chapter have been selected in order to review the problems of corruption in two cities and programs that can contribute to overall police integrity.

13. REPORT ON POLICE CORRUPTION AND THE QUALITY OF LAW ENFORCEMENT IN PHILADELPHIA

THE PENNSYLVANIA CRIME COMMISSION, 1974.

The Commission found that police corruption in Philadelphia is ongoing, widespread, systematic, and occurring at all levels of the Police Department. Corrupt practices were uncovered during the investigation in every police district and involved police officers ranging in rank from policeman to inspector. Specific acts of corruption involving improper cash payments to the police by gamblers, racketeers, bar owners, businessmen, nightclub owners, after-hours club owners, prostitutes, and others are detailed in the Report; more than 400 individual police officers are identified by first name, last initial, and badge or payroll number as receiving improper payments in terms of cash, merchandise, sexual services, or meals.

Corruption and political influence in the Police Department are problems which have plagued the force since its inception. In the 20th century alone, there have been three previous special grand jury investigations, each of which found widespread corruption within the Department. Difficult problems of integrity, political influence, and professionalism still continue, as the following summary of the Commission's factual findings indicates.

Liquor

The time, location, and means of selling alcoholic beverages in Pennsylvania are all subject to strict regulation under the Liquor Code. Many establishments operate in violation of the liquor laws to maximize profits, either by staying open past required closing times or having women solicit drinks from customers. Little social pressure exists in favor of the laws, but the Police Department has had to assume responsibility for enforcing those laws. In many instances, rather than enforce the Liquor Code, the police receive payments to overlook violations. More than 20 officers are identified as having received illegal cash payments from bars and approximately 50 from after-hours clubs. Additionally, more than 25 officers are identified as having been in after-hours clubs after the proper closing time. The Commission found widespread shakedowns of licensed liquor operators on the "Locust Street Strip" by members of the Philadelphia Police Department. The Commission discovered evidence that payments to the police were directly responsible for several illegal and open "bust-out" operations.

Eventually, one bust-out bar owner cooperated with the Commission's effort. He worked with the Commission for over a year and made tape recordings of conversations involving payoffs to police officers. During that time, he or his employees made direct payments to twelve police officers on a periodic basis. The tape recorded conversations which occurred during direct payoffs implicated another five officers. He testified concerning payoffs to two other identified police officers—one when he operated another bar and one when he had been arrested and was attempting to obtain expedited treatment at the Police Administration Building. He paid the police in a highly organized fashion, and his experience is a good example of the payoff system as it presently exists in Philadelphia.

To protect his bust-out operation, the bar owner paid an aggregate of $800 per month to policemen in every unit which had vice enforcement functions in his area. He paid each of the four uniformed squads when they worked the midnight to 8 a.m. shift; three of the squads received $35 and the fourth received $40. The "captain's men," who did plainclothes vice work for the captain of the 6th Police District where the bar was located, were paid $80 apiece each month. The plainclothes officers who did vice work for the inspector of the Central Police Division, the "inspector's men," also received $80 apiece each month. Their lieutenant received $100 per month, which was paid by the bar owner's manager. The manager also paid the inspector and his "bagman" each month—the bagman received $50 and took $100 to the inspector. Two members of the City-wide vice squad, the Chief Inspector's Squad, received $50 per month.

The Commission also uncovered circumstantial evidence of payoffs to police by three other bust-out bars. An officer who was picking up money from the cooperative bar owner commented, in tape recorded conversations, that the bar was only one of a series of stops. Also, other conversations occurred concerning payments being made by the other bars. A police witness for the Commission also confirmed that he had received payments from other operations on the Strip. Because of this evidence and because the bust-out activity continues in such a blatant manner with few arrests being made by the police, a reasonable conclusion is that the owners of those establishments are also paying for protection.

In addition to the Locust Street Strip, the Commission found that certain after-hours clubs routinely and systematically paid police in order to operate past prescribed closing times. After-hours clubs are private clubs licensed to sell drinks until 3 a.m., one hour past the normal closing time for bars.

A pattern of police activity occurred at the clubs which operated illegally after 3 a.m. Officers would enter the club at approximately 3:15 a.m., but make no effort to close it. They would then leave and subsequently return a few minutes before 4 a.m. and close the club. On occasion, an officer would remain at a club during the extra hour, and the bartender would continue to serve drinks in his presence.

This pattern of police activity occurred in all of the clubs for which the Commission has evidence of payments by the club to members of the Police Department. The cooperative bar owner tape recorded conversations with the managers and employees of several clubs in which the employees detailed payments to various police officers including the inspector of the Central Division.

The owner-operator of a Kensington club identified over 40 police officers that he had paid during the period from January, 1970, to September, 1972, including uniformed men up to the rank of lieutenant, two captains, two captain's men, two inspectors, and two inspector's men. The Kensington bar owner's identifications were corroborated by direct observation of payoffs by Commission agents, examination of a ledger the owner maintained in which he recorded police payments, and an examination of police assignment sheets. Incredibly, even after a widespread transfer of men in the 26th District and the East Division, the police did not miss a payment installment; the only result was a slight reduction in payment amounts. Thus, the uniformed squads received $170 each month until January, 1972, and then the new squads received $160. The captain and his men received a total of $110 per month prior to the transfer and $75 afterwards. The inspector and his men received a total of $80 per month prior to the transfer and $50 afterwards.

Illegal liquor sales outlets, "speakeasies," also operate in Philadelphia with both the knowledge and protection of the police. The Commission found two kinds of speakeasy operations: one operates on Sunday when state liquor stores are closed, and the other is similar to an after-hours club and is in operation seven nights a week.

The Commission discovered a typical Sunday operation in Germantown. Agents made numerous purchases from the speakeasy. One former police officer testified he had received steady payments from that speakeasy. The Commission also uncovered a bar which permitted lewd shows under the protection of a policeman moonlighting as a bartender, and a tavern owner who testified under oath that prior to selling his bar he paid the police between $300 and $400 each month.

The Commission thus found evidence of widespread payoffs to police officers from Locust Street Strip establishments, after-hours clubs, and speakeasies in order to conduct operations in violation of the liquor laws. Even legitimate taverns were at times forced to pay to forestall being charged with having violated one or more of the numerous technical provisions of the Liquor Code. Clearly, segments of the Police Department, confronted with enforcing laws about which society cares little, selectively enforce the law for personal gain.

Gambling

The gambling laws prohibit conduct in which large numbers of people engage. The prohibition of gambling is unpopular and is certainly not of as great public concern as the enforcement of laws against such serious acts as burglary, robbery, rape, and murder.

The most prevalent forms of illegal gambling are numbers, horse bets, and sports bets. Commission agents made direct bets or observed bets at more than 200 illegal gambling locations. This does not include the numerous locations where agents saw all the indications of a gambling operation but did not observe or place a bet. An example would be a variety store where very few goods could be found on the shelves, and large numbers of people would enter the store for short periods of time during peak betting hours but rarely buy anything.

The Commission found direct evidence of ongoing illegal gambling in every police division of the City. Gambling operations were found in such places as candy stores, variety stores, restaurants, and bars. Police witnesses identified other locations which were systematically paying for police protection. The Commission documented payoffs to more than 25 police officers from gamblers. As a result of the work of the Commission's police witnesses and other investigations, there is evidence warranting more than 200 gambling raids and the arrests and indictments of more than 50 gamblers on bribery charges.

One of the Commission's more successful ventures was the infiltration of a medium size gambling network in West Philadelphia. The agents also became familiar with a nearby horse betting system on North 64th Street, as well as other gambling operations in the area. Because of their acceptance by these groups, Commission agents also placed bets with the largest operation in West Philadelphia which conducts business from a club on North 66th Street.

Because of the regularity, size, and openness of the business, widespread illegal gambling cannot exist over a period of time without the knowledge of the Police Department. Gambling has historically been tied to police corruption, and the Commission found the same ties exist today.

Each time police raid an operation, the disruption costs the gambler hundreds, and possibly thousands of dollars; consequently, a gambler is willing to pay to prevent the disruption. Confronted by an apathetic public, by gamblers who can evade arrest through the use of rice paper and the telephone, and by courts in many cases unwilling to impose a sentence of more than a small fine or probation, the police have become justifiably cynical about their ability to control a "crime" which few wish to control. However, Department policy demands vice arrests, and many times police officers turn the situation to their own benefit.

The Commission found that police officers throughout the City accept protection money from gamblers. The commission received sworn testimony from its principal police witnesses concerning many gambling locations giving protection payments to police. The Commission's investigation disclosed that the basic pattern of gambling payoffs involved a sum of money paid by a numbers banker to a policeman who acted as the bagman for his unit. The bagman then distributed the money to all the members of his unit who were aware of the illegal activity and who wanted the note. Uniformed squads were paid when they worked the 8:00 a.m. to 4:00 p.m. (day work) shift, every 24 days, with generally about $5 going to a policeman, $10 to the sergeant, and $15 to the lieutenant. Payments to plainclothes units may range from $15 to $50 per man paid through a bagman once each month, usually on the 1st or 15th. Plainclothes officers normally have a number of such regular notes.

The method for handling the payoffs can be well planned and hidden. For example, in West Philadelphia, a middle level gambler pays the uniformed squads $65 a month when they are on day work; he also delivers money for two smaller bankers, each of which pays $50. He also pays a total of $450 to one bagman for the captain's men and inspector's men.

The Commission uncovered other payoff patterns. Some gamblers pay by locations, with office men and writers making their own payments when necessary. Two principal Commission police witnesses gave sworn testimony concerning $5 and $10 notes they had received from many gamblers, usually through a bagman. One banker from South Philadelphia began working with the Commission and taped a payoff with a sergeant. The payoff occurred in a police car, and the police radio can be heard in the background. Other bankers pay their "edge off" houses a fee for police protection.

The Commission also discovered a substantial number of illegal gambling machines in the City. The machines were declared illegal in the late 1950's by the Pennsylvania Supreme Court. Distributors would not place them in the outlying counties but had no hesitation about installing them in Philadelphia. However, the Commission was unable to determine whether the existence of the machines was due to police laxity, ignorance, or payoffs.

A combined program of gambling law revision, adequate police training, and leadership on the corruption issue, as well as the deterrent of an ongoing, institutionalized investigative unit outside the Police Department specializing in integrity are necessary to fight corruption arising from gambling activities.

Prostitution

The Crime Commission investigation into prostitution and its relationship to police corruption concentrated in the Central and North Central Police Divisions. During the course of its investigation, the Commission located various centers of wide-open prostitution operations. Approximately seven police officers were identified as receiving cash payments to permit prostitution; eight others were alleged to have received or demanded sexual services from prostitutes in lieu of arrest. The Commission found that in certain selected localities within those areas, streetwalker and bar prostitute operations flourished due to police protection.

Commission agents received 62 separate solicitations in two limited geographic areas. In the North Central Division, streetwalkers, primarily black, frequent a two-block stretch of North Broad Street. They become known to both the police and the general public and obtain most of their clients from being in a place where prostitutes are "known" to be.

In the Central Division, Commission agents discovered wide-open and fast-moving prostitution rings at two bars at 10th and Race Streets, both within two blocks of the Police Administration Building. In addition, agents received solicitations at other bars in the area.

The Commission interviewed several of the bar prostitutes from the 10th and Race Streets area to determine whether they paid the police in order to operate so openly. Three of the women gave sworn statements that they were required either to solicit four drinks from their clients before they adjourned from the bar to a nearby hotel or to pay the equivalent of four drinks to the bar from the money they earned. It was their understanding that the money was used by the bar to pay police for protection. The witnesses had both observed and been involved in instances which corroborated their understanding. For example, when a prostitute was about to leave the bar with a client and saw a police car outside, she told the bartender. He went outside and the car left. Additionally, a procurer (pimp) who frequents one of the bars testified that he had observed the owner pass currency to a police officer inside the bar. As soon as the Police Department learned of the Commission's activity in the 10th and Race Streets area, the prostitution operations were closed down for a short period, according to one of the police witnesses who testified before the Commission.

A cooperative bar owner tape recorded a conversation with two officers in which they told him bar owners still pay the police for protection of their prostitutes. The same bar owner and his employees told the Commission that police protection involved not only payments of money but also free sexual services. The bar owner identified five police officers who received these services. One prostitute who worked at a Center City restaurant testified that she had sexual relations with police officers several times a week. She also told the Commission of an incident in which two police officers extorted $300 from her, part of which was used to pay for their dinners and a hotel room where they engaged in sexual relations with her. The prostitutes from the 10th and Race Streets area also testified that they were propositioned by police officers. When they did get arrested, an officer would offer to drop the charges if the female would engage in sexual relations with him.

The laws against prostitution, like those regulating gambling and the distribution of alcoholic beverages, are concerned with victimless crimes. The Commission found corruption usually attended the regulation of the conduct by the police.

Narcotics

In terms of patterns and regularities, narcotics related police corruption shares little with the other vice areas. The Commission discovered corruption in narcotics enforcement to be more of an individual than squad-wide activity. While the financial temptation is greater because of the extensive profits involved in narcotics traffic, the long standing law enforcement view of narcotics graft as the "dirtiest" type of corruption and the very nature of the narcotics transaction itself mitigate against systematic corruption. Nevertheless, the Commission received sworn testimony concerning police officers who allegedly have accepted, and in some cases, extorted money and narcotics from drug offenders interested in avoiding arrest. Approximately eight officers have been identified as being involved in narcotics related corruption, although an additional estimated fifteen unidentified officers were said to be involved. This does not include the incidents detailed by the special investigating grand jury.

The most common type of corruption appears to be the "shakedown" where an officer receives money, drugs, or other payment in lieu of arresting a suspected drug offender. An officer who makes a practice of narcotics shakedowns may patrol known drug use areas in search of a "score." When he sees an addict or a pusher, the corrupt police officer stops him as if to make an arrest. At the suggestion of the suspect or on his own impulse, the officer may come to some sort of understanding with the individual. The street addict, pusher, and addict-prostitute make particularly easy targets for the corrupt officer.

A former police officer testifying before the Commission estimated that in 65-70% of narcotics arrests, part of the drugs seized were not turned in as evidence but were kept for farming, paying addicted informants, sales, or personal use. Farming—the planting of evidence—is used to make or strengthen the case against a suspect. This conduct is often rationalized as a means of removing the trafficker from the street.

The Commission assembled evidence about the occurrence of shake-downs and farming in the 16th, 17th, and 18th Police Districts. In some cases, female addicts were allegedly threatened with arrest, beaten, or forced into performing sexual acts with the officers who had stopped them, while males were threatened, beaten, released, and told to "keep their noses clean."

One addicted drug dealer told of four incidents during the last two years when he was detained by police officers and lost more than $2,400. Another told of being detained during a drug raid in North Philadelphia and having all of his cash stolen. A third pusher, a woman, described various instances when officers allegedly obtained sexual services to forestall an arrest, mentioning three detectives and a lieutenant by name. The Commission has received allegations concerning fourteen other instances of Philadelphia police officers taking money, drugs, information, goods, or sex from suspects.

The Commission's findings in this area are supported by the investigating grand jury which unearthed similar examples of narcotics corruption. However, the Commission did not uncover the same widespread, systematic corrupt activity as in other areas of vice enforcement.

Business Notes

The Crime Commission found a broad spectrum of businesses, large and small, making illegal direct cash payments to the police; they included banks, insurance companies, automobile dealers, restaurants, supermarkets, jewelers, construction companies, vendors, country clubs, and moving companies. Businesses were found paying police officers in every one of the twenty-two police districts.

Most of the payments can be categorized as follows: (a) payments made in return for clearly improper acts by policemen, including providing on-duty policemen as private guards and providing confidential criminal records and intelligence information; (b) payments for proper police services rendered during the course of duty, including extra protection, police escort service, and quick response to calls; (c) gifts or payments made to incur "goodwill" on the part of the policemen; and (d) payments by businesses in response to extortionate demands by policemen or as bribes to overlook traffic, building codes, or other violations.

Although only a limited investigation of this matter was undertaken, the Commission uncovered identifying data on more than 200 police officers receiving cash payments from businesses. The names and badge numbers of 129 police officers who have received illegal cash payments were obtained, including one inspector, one captain, seventeen lieutenants, twenty-four sergeants, one corporal, and eighty-five policemen. Hundreds more such identifications would be obtainable through careful examination and correlation of police records with testimony of Commission witnesses. An estimated 700 policemen have received cash from just the businesses named in this Report in 1972-73. In addition, approximately 167 police officers were specifically identified as having received one or more free meals. An estimated 2,000 policemen have received free meals from just one restaurant chain in the above period.

The cash payments uncovered by the Commission are specifically punishable by dismissal and up to 90 days in jail under the Philadelphia City Charter and are potentially punishable as bribery under the criminal laws. The Police Department takes a strong official position opposing such payments, yet the Department never investigates them or punishes officers who receive them. Policemen thus generally refer to business payoffs as "safe notes" or "clean notes."

Police officers high in the chain of command are well aware of and participate in clean notes. Guard service at one company was arranged with at least the knowledge of the commanders of ten police districts. One instance was found in which an inspector in command of a police division was required to share Christmas notes by taking a case of liquor to a downtown staff meeting.

The amounts of money paid to the police for extra services provided to businesses range from $2 for an escort to the bank to $125 paid weekly for a full-time police guard stationed on business premises. Although the amounts of individual payments to police are often small, they can amount to a substantial investment of money. One business paid nearly $60,000 in cash and dispensed $70,000 worth of free meals to policemen in 1972. Another business paid cash to police officers at an annual rate in excess of $23,000.

The clean note presents a serious corruption hazard to any police department, despite the fact that often no criminal activity is being protected. Where police act as regular guards for specific businesses their services are effectively denied to the rest of the public. The Commission found that in the case of one fast-food chain, the services of the equivalent of 22 full-time on-duty police officers were devoted to protecting various business locations. These on-duty policemen were used in place of private guards at a substantial savings in cost to the company. However, the Philadelphia taxpayers lost the services of men who received a combined salary of about $264,000.

In addition to taking police services away from the public, this use of police as private guards was completely inefficient as a means of reducing crime. Close examination of crimes at protected and unprotected restaurant locations shows that the regular presence of on-duty police guards prevented, on the average, less than $13,000 in crime losses due to thefts per year, while the police protecting the stores were paid a combined public salary of about $264,000. At the four major supermarket chains in Philadelphia, extra police services also had no measurable effect on the crime losses of individual businesses.

Failure to enforce restrictions on clean notes thus has led to policemen being given assignments which afforded inefficient and ineffective protection to the public and has resulted in a distorted allocation of police resources.

An even more serious consequence of the clean note is that decisions on where to allocate police personnel are influenced by who is willing to pay extra for them, rather than where they are most needed. In effect, police services are open for bidding with the money going to individual police officers.

The receipt of clean notes also has an impact on the integrity of the individual police officer. The wide acceptance of illegal gifts causes everyone to be compromised to some extent. Some honest officers find them personally degrading and resent the assumption that they can easily be bought. Clean notes are also one means by which officers are tested by other officers who want to see if they will go along with the system. Even an officer who will not personally take a clean note learns that he must look the other way when his colleagues take them, or risk being an outcast.

In some cases where police officers receive a modest but steady clean note, they can become dependent on the extra income, causing them to look for other sources of notes if transferred. The note becomes an expected way of life, and officers may use the wide discretion at their disposal to bring non-paying individuals into line. For example, the Commission discovered that in certain sections of the City, vendors are systematically "shaken down" by the police. One fruit vendor testified before the Commission that he had been operating a fruit truck for the past twenty years and during that period he had to make regular payments to members of the Philadelphia Police Department in order to operate. During the five years that he operated an unlicensed stand at 20th and Johnson Streets, he paid at least $60 a month and at times as much as $75 a month to the police. Each of the shifts was paid $15—$5 for the sergeant and $10 for the sector car. He also usually had to pay $10 a month to an emergency patrol wagon. The vendor believed that everybody in the fruit business has had to pay the police at one time or another. The vendor finally stopped payments to the police in October,

1972, and several months later, his truck was confiscated by the police and shredded.

Police officers become so accustomed to receiving income from vendors they have actually been known to argue over the location of vendors. For example, a former police officer testified about a dispute between officers in the 22nd and 23rd Districts over the side of the street on which a vendor would illegally park. Each wanted access to the free food and cash that would be forthcoming.

Even occasional Christmas notes, free meals, or other presents given to create goodwill have an adverse effect. Although at first the effect of a gift to policemen or other public employees may be to create good feeling and marginally better service, in the long run the recipients grow to expect the presents as their just due. When they are not forthcoming, hostility is often created, and solicitation, or even harassment may take place and service deteriorates.

Car Stops

Police officers often receive cash from motorists who have been stopped for an alleged traffic or other violation. Small cash payments are made in return for failure to issue a ticket; larger amounts change hands when a driver is caught with a stolen car, numbers, drugs, or bootleg whiskey.

According to police witnesses, an expectation prevails among both policemen and motorists that the cash will be offered and accepted. Car stops are one of the first ways a rookie will be tested by his peers to see if he is "trustworthy" in terms of accepting notes. Many officers, according to Commission witnesses, do not solicit such payments but rarely refuse them if offered. Others, if they are aggressive, can make significant amounts of money through car stops.

Unprotected Property

Another common variety of police corruption, and one which offers no clear-cut remedy, is the taking of money or valuables from premises or individuals when the valuables are unprotected. This type of violation occurs when a building is open and unoccupied, presumably because a burglary has been committed. Similar to this practice is the confiscation of money or goods during a search, arrest, or detention of an incapacitated person.

The Crime Commission has received sworn testimony from a Philadelphia police officer concerning several incidents of police burglary that he personally witnessed. His accounts of these incidents indicate that such a practice is pervasive. Further evidence of irregularities which occur during arrests has been provided by a Philadelphia police officer and by individuals who have been arrested and have allegedly had money stolen from them while in the custody of the police. Although the Department promulgates regulations to prevent such occurrences, it is apparent that there is a substantial problem in the area of enforcement and detection.

Stolen Cars

The handling of stolen cars by the Philadelphia Police Department provides a further opportunity for corruption and misconduct. During the course of its investigation, the Commission found evidence of three types of police activity related to the handling of stolen cars. First, the Police Department occasionally uses for its own purposes private automobiles and automobile registrations which have been impounded. Second, there is a general lack of security in the handling of impounded cars which has resulted in an inordinate amount of stripping of impounded automobiles. Third, there are indications that as a result of the stripping of cars at the Police Automobile Pound, insurance companies may have a practice of paying a "reward" to police officers for recovering cars and holding them at the district headquarters instead of sending them to the Pound.

The Crime Commission undertook an investigation of the Pound when a regional claims manager of an insurance company informed the Commission that a system of payments existed between one of its district claims managers and officers of the Philadelphia Police Department in order to secure the retention of recovered stolen vehicles at the district station and prevent the vehicles from being taken to the Automobile Pound. It was the company's experience that once a car went to the Pound it would be completely stripped of tires, wheels, radio, battery, engine, chrome, and grill.

On the basis of these allegations the Commission began a surveillance of the Pound and also subpoenaed representatives from five major insurance companies to see if the company's experience was unique or typical. However, at private hearings, officials of the complaining insurance company denied the payments to the Philadelphia Police Department had ever occurred. Representatives of other companies testified concerning poor security at the Pound and confirmed that on many occasions when they went to the Pound, they would see men surreptitiously working on cars.

Commission investigations also disclosed situations where tires were stolen from inside a locked trunk of a car that was in the sole possession of the Police Department, a car was totally stripped while in the Police Department's possession; and a car was stolen, recovered, but stolen again from the police before the owner could get to the station to claim the car.

Perjury

A Philadelphia police officer's conduct often leads to perjury and offering intentionally false statements in reports and in court. Perjury and intentionally false statements occur in the following contexts: officers swearing to false probable cause sections of search warrants for purposes of conducting a raid; officers falsifying the "evidence found" section of returned search warrants to hide evidence retained by the officers; officers planting vice evidence on suspects or searching them illegally and later lying under oath about the arrest situation; and officers providing false statements to protect themselves or another officer under suspicion of corruption.

Although no perjury is defensible, much police perjury is actually created and almost compelled by the Department's system of vice enforcement, which, despite officially stated policy, is in fact based upon arrest quotas.

The Commission has received sworn testimony concerning the above types of police perjury and false statements. A former Philadelphia policeman testified in detail about the course of events and conditions that brought him to a choice of perjury or testifying against a fellow officer.

Substantial evidence uncovered by the Commission indicates that a number of Philadelphia police officers committed perjury during sworn testimony before the Commission concerning their involvement in the illegal receipt of money from established businesses.

The Corruption Environment

The Commission's investigation has shown that systematic corruption exists in the Philadelphia Police Department. This condition results from the interaction of many factors, including the Police Department's attitude toward the corruption problem, the vice enforcement policy of the Department, various societal pressures on the individual police officers, and the reaction to corruption of other parts of the criminal justice system and the public.

A rookie policeman is assigned to patrol city neighborhoods with complex human problems that society has been unable to resolve. He is placed in difficult situations with almost unlimited discretion to exercise, virtually no guidelines for action, and little or no supervision. There are strong corrupting influences "in the street." His position exposes him to far more temptations than in other occupations. Public apathy to the enforcement of vice laws helps break down resistance to accepting gifts or bribes or ignoring violations of the law. Also, many practices such as tipping and doing favors that are accepted in the business community are not compatible with the police role. Thus, the police are subjected to conflicting pressures.

The attitudes within the Department to the corruption problem do not assist the individual police officer facing temptations and pressures from his peers. The Department takes the official position that corruption exists only in isolated cases and is a matter of individual conscience. This theory, known as the rotten apple theory, is an obstacle to any meaningful attempt to deal with systematic police corruption. It is impossible to fight successfully a problem that the leadership will not acknowledge exists.

To the individual policeman, the action of the Department leadership speaks louder than pious statements on corruption. Department spokesmen assert, for example, that taking clean notes is against departmental policy; yet, despite its prevalence and openness in the Department, there have been no investigations of the clean note problem by the Internal Affairs Bureau. With this type of official response, the burden of the corruption hazard is placed on the individual policeman without the Department leadership doing its part to assist the individual officer face difficult temptations.

Another indicator of this attitude has been the failure of Department leadership to provide adequate training at the Police Academy to educate young officers about the corruption hazard. Many Crime Commission witnesses testified that the Academy failed to prepare young officers for the temptations that would arise once they are assigned to a district.

The Department's vice policy also contributes to the corruption problem. This policy is ineffective as a means of suppressing vice activity. According to Directive 8, the Department's official statement of its vice policy, all units are required to enforce the vice laws and to file various reports about vice activity. These reports are useless as a law enforcement tool. There is little or no correlation among the number of vice figures arrested, the identities of those arrested, and those listed on the vice reports. The Commission's investigation revealed that most vice reports are essentially recopied from year to year.

In addition to this reporting system, the Department has established vice arrest quotas, which emphasize the quantity and not the quality of the arrest. There is much pressure created at every level of the Department for vice arrests. The number of vice arrests made by a police officer is one factor used to evaluate his ability and performance. Yet the Department does not provide sufficient financial support and equipment to enforce vice laws in any effective way. These pressures for vice arrests and lack of support result in illegal conduct to meet the quota requirements.

The current vice policy of the Department, therefore, is not effective as a law enforcement tool but appears to exist as a shield for the Department leadership. Without the pressure for vice activity, very few arrests would be made. Corrupt officers would be content merely to collect their money from vice centers. Such conduct would become obvious to the public.

With current policy, corruption is somewhat hidden from the public by the large number of vice arrests. These vice arrests are not effective against vice centers because the emphasis is only on arrest and not conviction thereby resulting in bad arrests and arrangements between corrupt police and illegal operators to satisfy the quota.

Not only Department policy but pressures created by a "policeman's lot" have an impact on an officer's resistance to corruption. As a young man puts on the police uniform, he becomes a different person in the eyes of many people. His presence creates uneasiness in many people. The paramilitary police organization places further pressures on him and his family. His working schedule isolates him from many prior friends. As a result, he turns inward to the police community. He thereby becomes more susceptible to peer pressures. There will be many pressures on the new policeman to be trusted and accepted by his fellow officers. When a man arrives at a new assignment, he will be tested by the older men to see his reaction to minor indiscretions. He will be told about places he can get the police price on food, clothing, and other merchandise. He will be assigned work which will produce the safe or clean note from a businessman. His reactions and attitudes to police problems and borderline conduct will determine the trust the older men have in him. Once the new man is accepted by the older men, he may be given a permanent sector assignment. When he patrols a permanent sector assignment, he will notice open illegal activity; he must begin to question what is happening. Such inquiry will usually determine whether he will become part of the system. As one officer testified, if he does not go along, he will be "walking the third rail" on subway duty.

For many reasons, there is great hesitancy on the part of police to turn in other police officers. Warnings from supervisors about internal security operations in the district clearly tell the policeman that he should not make any disturbance about activities of fellow officers. If one is caught, he should remain silent.

Systematic corruption of policemen does not occur in a vacuum. Officers succumb to pressures within the Department. Illegal conduct of fellow officers, and especially by superior officers, has a destructive impact on an individual policeman. In Philadelphia, police officers have seen the Police Commissioner held in contempt of court for "blatant disregard" of a court order. They have witnessed the Department leadership fail to take action against open and widespread violations of Department policy such as in the area of safe or clean notes. They see other public officers act in ways suggesting improper influence or corrupt behavior. They perceive the courts treating policemen as a special category of offenders. Very few police cases get to trial and fewer still are sentenced to jail. The general public seems complacent about corruption problems. Even though large segments of the population are victims of it, people generally do not come forward to protest about police corruption.

All of these various factors contribute to the corruption environment in which a police officer in Philadelphia must work. The Department leadership must acknowledge that corruption is a problem that must be dealt with openly and frankly before there will be any meaningful progress made towards eradication of systematic corruption. The attitudes of members throughout the Department must change to deal effectively with the corruption problem. At the Police Academy, the recruit should be educated about the corruption hazard. Commanders must be held responsible for the conduct of their men. There should be changes in the criminal laws to remove the police from attempting to enforce the unenforceable vice laws. The Commission's investigation established that vice laws cannot be effectively enforced without enormous commitment of resources in terms of support and supervision. Departmental policies toward the vice area should be modified to reflect realistically the conditions which exist in an urban community.

Control of the Police

The control of corruption and misconduct by police officers in Philadelphia lies for the most part in the hands of the Police Department itself. The District Attorney's office has shown itself to be ineffective at investigating the police and in fact is forced to rely upon the Police Department to assist in its investigations. The federal authorities also often refer allegations of corruption or misconduct by police officers to the Department, since there is not always a violation of federal law. Although some federal laws do prohibit police officers from taking bribes, the Commission is aware of very few police corruption prosecutions by the federal government in Philadelphia.

The internal control mechanisms within the Police Department are vague, fractionalized, and almost totally ineffective. The Department's attempts at controlling corruption are crippled at the outset by the attitude that there is no widespread or systematic corruption in the Department. Thus, there is little or no serious, active effort made to seek out evidence of corruption in the absence of complaints. Surveillance and exit interviews are conducted but produce few results. There has been no attempt to "turn" a police officer who has been caught and to have him work undercover to help improve the system in exchange for lenient treatment. There has been no attempt made to acknowledge the problem of corruption openly and to create an atmosphere within the Department which would allow honest officers to bring forward evidence of corruption without fear of retribution by their colleagues or their commanders.

The responsibility of investigating allegations of both corruption and police "brutality" (a catchword for improper and excessive uses of physical force on citizens) is shared by the commanding officers of the police officers involved and by the Internal Affairs Bureau. There are no written guidelines on who shall investigate particular matters and no special forms for recording allegations of police misconduct. Which unit investigates a complaint appears to depend on a number of various circumstances such as the source of the information, where it was received, the nature of the matter, and the amount of public attention it receives. According to the testimony of Chief Inspector Frank A. Scafidi, most investigations of corruption and brutality in the Police Department are carried out by the Internal Affairs Bureau, while investigations of lesser offenses are carried out by line commanders. Although complaints against police officers are required by police directive to be recorded, the forms used are the same as those for any matter which requires police action, and there are strong indications that the forms are not always filled out.

As the arm of the Police Department with primary responsibility for investigating corruption, the Internal Affairs Bureau is very weak. Under existing procedures it might never even learn of evidence or an allegation of corruption which turns up at the police district level since it might be covered up. Assuming the matter is duly recorded, the incident report would flow up the chain of command rather than be sent directly to the Bureau. Only if the matter is at some point determined to be sufficiently "serious" might a decision be made to bring in Internal Affairs investigators.

Assuming the Internal Affairs Bureau handles an investigation, there is little assurance the Bureau will conduct it vigorously and thoroughly. The officers assigned to the Bureau do not receive any special training in investigating corruption or in the use of undercover techniques. As previously stated, the Bureau has not attempted to exact cooperation from officers who are caught. The Department does not require police officers to submit to polygraph examinations during the course of internal investigations, although it makes frequent use of polygraphs in non-police investigations. Although the present policy is that a member assigned to the Bureau may remain as long as he wishes, Internal Affairs is not in fact a permanent assignment; and as a practical matter, an officer is subject to being transferred out if he displeases his superiors or an influential commander who may be the subject of an investigation. There is also no assurance that Internal Affairs investigators will not later be required to serve under or alongside officers they have investigated. Finally, the members of the Bureau receive no special rank, status, or pay to go along with the significantly different duties of their assignment.

During the course of its investigation, the Commission came across two incidents which illustrate the manner in which the Internal Affairs Bureau investigates evidence of corruption. In one case, a memorandum was sent from the District Attorney's office to Internal Affairs stating that a Locust Street bar owner had made tape recordings of payoffs to twelve police officers. One of the officers mentioned in the memorandum later testified before the Commission that his immediate commander was notified of the allegation by Internal Affairs and that the officer and his partner were questioned by the commander. At the end of that interview, the two officers were told to go to Internal Affairs the next morning. In the meantime, the two officers had an opportunity to discuss the matter and to make their stories consistent. They decided to deny the allegations. To assist them and to get advice, they also contacted a former policeman. The following day during the Internal Affairs interrogation of the two officers, the former policeman called a staff inspector in Internal Affairs and got a full outline of the evidence against the two officers. Later that day a representative of the Fraternal Order of Police called Chief Inspector Frank Scafidi, head of the Bureau, and was told the two officers need not be concerned since the charges would probably die a natural death. These messages were immediately transmitted to the officers alleged to be involved, which fortified their resolve to deny the whole incident.

In another case, the Commission turned over to the Police Department massive evidence of police officers illegally receiving cash payments from businesses. Seventy-seven officers were identified by name and badge number and one hundred and six were identified by assignment, initials, or signatures as being apparently involved. The evidence consisted of documents and testimony. Thorough examination of relevant police records, together with interviews of all witnesses, could have resulted in criminal or disciplinary actions against several hundred police officers. However, the only action taken was that thirty files were "opened." One officer who was apparently deeply involved had been permitted to resign without charges placed against him. No effort was made to contact the business witnesses who testified or to interview additional witnesses. Furthermore, many police patrol logs which would have contained essential corroboration apparently were not examined and were routinely destroyed.

The weakness of the Internal Affairs Bureau is also illustrated by its lack of concentration on internal police matters. Several of its members were assigned during 1973, to conduct an ostensible investigation of corruption in other City agencies.

There is no question that given existing guidelines, attitudes, personnel, and organization the Police Department cannot effectively police itself. Efforts at internal control should not be abandoned; rather, they should be greatly strengthened and vigorously pursued.

14. THE KNAPP COMMISSION AND YOU

LAWRENCE J. DEMPSEY

The Police Chief, Vol. XXXIX, November 1972. Reprinted by permission.

The eight major recommendations were put forth by the Knapp Commission with the intent to assist in providing a means to curtail corrupt activities by:

1. Eliminating the many situations which expose officers to corruption, such as the changing of the laws;

2. Subjecting the officers to a significant risk of detection, apprehension, conviction, and penalties if they engage in corrupt activities, i.e., the establishment of a special unit within the department for corruption investigations;

3. Providing a means, through increased incentives, for meritorious police performance in fighting police corruption, and to change the total police force's attitude toward corrupt practices on the part of fellow officers by providing various recognitions and compensations within the departmental structure for honesty;

4. Providing to the public a means of redress and avenues for communication with the police department so that the citizen may be able to report alleged police corruption and have action taken in regard to the allegation (investigation by a special force), and be given a certain amount of anonymity by not having to report complaints to the normal line units.

Recommendation No. 1. "That the Governor (Rockefeller), acting with the Attorney General (New York) pursuant to Section 63 of the Executive Law appoint a Special Deputy Attorney General with jurisdiction in all five counties of the City, with authority to investigate and prosecute all crimes involving corruption in the criminal process."

This recommendation has become the most controversial of all the recommendations made in the Knapp report. In fact, the attention paid to this particular recommendation has far overshadowed the remaining recommendations of the report, and has generated the larger amount of news media coverage, and interjected into the total meaningfulness of the report a broad political controversy.

The Knapp Commission report noted that "a basic weakness in the present approach to the problem of (investigating) police corruption is that all agencies regularly involved with the problem rely primarily on policemen to do their investigative work." It went on to add, "In the case of District Attorneys, there is the additional problem that they work so closely with policemen that the public tends to look upon them—and indeed they seem to look upon themselves—as allies of the Department."

The Knapp Commission explained that the recommendation took into consideration the following factors:

1. In recent months there had been numerous accusations of corruption among prosecutors, lawyers, and judges.

2. Any newly created office must have jurisdiction going beyond the police department.

3. An office is needed where everyone—including the policeman—can go with a corruption complaint against anyone involved in the criminal justice process.

4. Any new office must also have authority to prosecute corruption cases in order to insure its independence of the agencies which may come under its scrutiny.

5. There should be independent access to grand juries and the right to issue subpoenas and grant immunity on a city-wide basis.

6. There is a need for an office that can be established immediately, without the delays that would be inevitable should implementing legislation be required.

In comment, the Commission noted that a deputy attorney general should have grand jury power, could employ the investigative techniques required, make suggestions for grand jury presentations, make public any grand jury reports, channel the reception of complaints, use his resources for identification and elimination of patterns of corruption, and keep the public advised of conditions requiring administrative or legislative action.

Recommendation No. 2. Laws against gambling, prostitution, and the conduct of certain business activities on the Sabbath all contribute to the prevalence of police corruption and obviously in different degrees of seriousness; these laws are difficult to enforce; and because the victims of these crimes are usually *willing* participants and seldom complain to the police, the maintaining of the laws on the books provide an invitation to corruption.

In reference to gambling, the Commission recommends that the laws against gambling should be repealed, and the policy should be that even if these laws are not repealed, the police should be relieved from the responsibility for the enforcement of these laws. With regard to Sabbath laws (Blue laws), similar laws have already been repealed in a number of other states and should be repealed in New York; further, enforcement of such laws not repealed should not be a police function. In reference to the laws regarding prostitution, the Knapp Commission did not find that these laws were as corrupting a hazard as first might be assumed, although the Commission did not wish to take a position on the legalization of prostitution. The Commission was not in a position to offer a recommendation on an alternate agency to enforce the prostitution laws.

The Commission noted that the police must continue to assume responsibility for enforcement of laws forbidding the sale and possession of narcotics as long as society deems it necessary to invoke criminal sanctions in this area. The laws regarding marijuana are particularly controversial because of their growing unenforceability and the conviction of many people that such laws are undesirable. The Commission was unable to find evidence that the marijuana laws are a distinct factor in police corruption.

A particular area of noted corruption in New York has been in the construction industry. The police department has been charged with the enforcement of various ordinances and regulations in regard to the construction industry and the carrying on of construction in the city. It has been reported by *The New York Times* that there are millions of dollars in bribes paid by the construction industry every year to public servants, including police. The Commission recommends that the function of regulation in the construction industry should be taken over by another jurisdictional agency and that the police should be relieved of the responsibility of the enforcement of these regulations and code requirements.

Traditionally, bars and other places that have liquor licenses have been subject to regulation and inspection by police officers. These bars and establishments selling liquor have always been a source of corrupt practices in the enforcement of regulations. It was felt by the Knapp Commission that the regulation of these premises dealing in alcohol and having liquor licenses should be taken over by another agency.

The Knapp Commission felt that by eliminating the opportunity for petty graft the department can change the current attitude that such graft is an accepted part of the police job. The Commission stated that it believes the police should be removed from inspections of bars and restaurants as well as from building sites and returned to their principal job of protecting life and property.

Recommendation No. 3. The Commission recommended that within the police department there be established a unit whose sole responsibility would be to arrest policemen who solicit and accept bribes as well as those members of the public sector who try to bribe them. It suggested that the Inspectional Services Bureau (I.S.B.), which includes the anticorruption units in the police department as now constituted, be reorganized along the lines of the Inspections Office of the Internal Revenue Service, so that the new unit would have as its sole responsibility the ferreting out of evidence of corruption by police officers and assisting in the prosecution of officers and civilians who become involved in corrupt activities. It was noted that agents who are assigned to the Inspections Office of the Internal Revenue Service normally spend their complete careers within that office, and it was suggested that if a similar type of unit were established in the police department, the officers might serve their complete police careers in that unit. The Commission stated that the establishment of such a unit, which would report directly to the police commissioner, would place full responsibility upon the commissioner and at the same time provide him with an anticorruption arm that would be unhindered in the execution of its anticorruption functions.

Recommendation No. 4. The Knapp Commission recommended that the police department place special emphasis on the arrest of bribers, especially businessmen and lawyers. It noted that there was apparently almost complete immunity from arrest enjoyed by the givers of bribes as opposed to the takers of bribes. It was proposed that attention be focused also upon the persons who are the bribers, and every possible legal means be taken to make prosecutable cases against them. It was felt that when it became known to members of the community that if they offered a bribe to a police officer, they would place themselves in jeopardy of being arrested, and the practice of offering bribes would soon be discontinued.

Recommendation No. 5. The Commission further recommended that the police department change certain of its personnel practices so that investigation of police corruption would be facilitated. It advocated that certain records which are now maintained at various locations within the department be centralized; e.g., personnel records concerning a single police officer which may presently be spread out over twelve different locations should be centrally filed where the proposed anticorruption unit might have ready access to them.

The Commission also recommended that photographs of police officers be updated as required by regulations in the police department every five years, and that the quality and accessibility of these photographs be improved to assist investigators in their task of identification of corrupt officers.

It was suggested in the conducting of lineups, where police officers are the target of the investigation, that the lineup identification procedures be changed from present practices so that witnesses are not seen by other members of the force and that the witnesses' identities be kept anonymous.

It was also noted that a procedure for handling a complaint from a civilian or a police officer should be established whereby the complaint is immediately recorded wherever in the department it is received, and that the public as well as police officers be encouraged to make complaints and be advised where they may do so. It was also suggested that necessary procedures be instituted to insure adequate complaint follow-up.

Another area that the Commission touched on is that if the department determines to "turn around" an officer (to use a formerly corrupt officer as an undercover agent in a given investigation), the department should be prepared to keep this officer on full pay during his undercover assignment and during period of time after his exposure to the public. It will also be necessary for such officer to be available for court testimony or administrative hearings in order to effectively carry out the prosecution of the investigation. It was suggested that an officer, formerly corrupt, who is now used to the department's advantage, be permitted to resign from the police department in good standing.

Recommendation No. 6. Another recommendation was that the police commissioner be granted increased power and that there be changes made in the present civil service laws of New York providing for a wider range of penalties available in administrative hearings against derelict members of the force. At present, the highest fine penalty that may be imposed by the police commissioner is the loss of thirty days' pay, and only in the ranks above that of captain (who are not civil service) and designated grades (detectives) can the police commissioner presently utilize demotion as a form of penalty. It was recommended by the Commission that the police commissioner be given the power to reduce by one civil service grade the members of the force of the rank of captain, lieutenant, and sergeant who have been found guilty of serious departmental charges.

It was noted by the Knapp Commission that there were certain rules and regulations already on the books of the police department that if effectively utilized could be used as a tool for assisting in the maintenance of integrity and honesty on the part of members of the force. An example of such an existing regulation is that a member of the force is prohibited from associating with gamblers, criminals, or persons engaged in unlawful activities (except in the discharge of official duties or with the permission of the police commissioner), and the rules require that an officer meeting or having conversation with a person so described must make certain entries in his memorandum book and complete certain reports. It was noted that this type of regulation, if enforced, could be used as an effective tool in regard to taking administrative action against police personnel who associate with criminals.

It was also recommended by the Commission that the New York City Council approve a pending bill that would provide for additional hearing officers in police department administrative trials, and this would alleviate backlogs created by the present requirement that only deputy commissioners may preside over these administrative trials.

An additional recommendation by the Commission calls attention to what is indicated to be a serious defect in the police department disciplinary options—the present law requiring that any officer dismissed from the police department automatically forfeits his pension regardless of the nature of events bringing about his discharge. Such factors as the number of years of service, his exemplary record, his rank, or other factors that should possibly be considerations in amelioration of his penalty are not now considered if he is dismissed from the department as regards his pension rights. Although dismissal of a corrupt officer by the police commissioner after a departmental trial may be warranted, the resultant loss of his total pension upon dismissal is a harsh punishment for an officer found guilty of violating departmental regulations. In recent instances in cases brought on appeal by officers who have lost pension rights after dismissal from the police department, the court directed the police commissioner to reinstate the officers because it was determined the punishments were too severe. It was noted that if the police commissioner found it warranted to dismiss an officer from the force, there should be a wholly separate proceeding conducted by the city's attorney, the corporation counsel, to determine whether the offender should be deprived of his accumulated pension rights.

It was noted by the Knapp Commission in its recommendations for changing certain personnel practices that the police commissioner is severely hindered by the present law that permits an officer suspected of misconduct to file necessary papers for his retirement and to retire in thirty days unless he has been administratively tried and a decision rendered within the limited time. It has been suggested that the 30-day limitation be extended to 90 days, and that steps be taken to enact a law providing that there be no arbitrary period of time limit placed on the city for the completion of a proceeding against a police officer even if he has submitted retirement papers.

Recommendation No. 7. The Commission stated that certain police department procedures should be modified in order to eliminate practices that might encourage corrupt activities by police officers. In reference to the practices that should be looked into, they cited:

1. The payment of expense money to personnel entitled to utilization of such funds is inadequate and too slow, and this condition should be corrected.

2. Expense funds allowed to officers should not be arbitrarily limited to $100 per month per officer, but should be flexible to facilitate the officer's function, and that when money is laid out by an officer it should be reimbursed promptly.

3. The existence of informal arrest quotas should be eliminated. The practice of establishing a required "quota" number of arrests or a particular type of arrest has led to a practice of "flaking," "the planting of narcotics upon a suspected individual," or in other incidents the sup-

plementing of the amount of narcotic evidence found on an individual in order to raise the charge to a higher penal law degree.

4. The method of registering and dealing with informants by the police department is too loose, and procedures should be adopted to provide a stricter control of the informer and the registration of an informant to an individual police officer; the informer should not be used by several police officers.

5. The present policy of the New York City Police Department is not to utilize paid informants. It has been found by the Knapp Commission that certain corrupt officers use narcotics or other contraband in order to reward informants for information; the department should make available, in some instances, funds to pay informants.

6. Although there is a regulation in the rules and procedures of the police department to the effect that receiving "any valuable gift" is a violation of departmental rules, the Knapp Commission reports that the rule has not been enforced with any regularity. The receiving of a free cup of coffee, meal, alcoholic beverage, or of any other valuable gift should be clearly stated to be a violation of the department's policies and such policies should be enforced. It was noted that *if* the police department decided to permit policemen to accept free meals or goods, then necessary steps should be taken to require the filing of reports and these reports should be reviewed by superior officers to insure against abuse of such privileges.

7. Since there are occasions during which police officers must remain away from their homes overnight (e.g., court appearances after a late arrest, required appearance on the day shift at administrative hearings, or continued duty for an emergency situation), it is recommended that the department arrange for the provision of sleeping accommodations and to make appropriate reimbursements to the hotels that provide such facilities.

Recommendation No. 8. The Knapp Commission noted that the opportunities and temptations for corruptions are a continuing problem and recommended that certain administrative practices be revised and changes made in order to tighten supervisory control of the police.

The Commission observed that certain steps had been undertaken by the department to increase individual "accountability" and pointed out that one additional way of increasing the accountability is in changing the memorandum book record procedure. The present practice is for each officer to carry a memorandum book, a diary, in which an officer records the entries of all police activities of his tour of duty. The officer keeps the book in his possession, and the Commission considers this a uniformly useless document because many of the diaries contain falsifications and blank spaces.

It was recommended that an improved record document be instituted and noted that the police department was experimenting with a Daily Field Activity Report, which is a triplicate report that is inspected daily by a supervisor and copies retained.

It was also recommended that an arrest reporting form presently used in the police department be revised in order to make more specific the reporting format in reference to describing certain facts. It was stated that the description of an alleged offense is often done by the police officer in such ambiguous terms that he can later testify in a manner exculpating the defendant.

A recommendation that was immediately attacked by the Patrolman's Benevolent Association was that uniformed officers be required to wear name tags on the outside of their uniforms because the present badge number identification is not easily read and because the nameless officer is further isolated from the community.

The Knapp Commission felt there were two general approaches to reducing the susceptibility to corruption among police officers: The first was to improve the screening and selection methods and standards for police recruits, and the second was to change the attitudes of the police. In the area of screening, it was recommended that the practice whereby officers are assigned field work prior to the completion of their complete background investigation be discontinued.

The civil service regulations should be changed to allow lateral entry, permitting individuals of outstanding qualifications from other law enforcement agencies coming into the department to assume supervisory ranks.

It was suggested that as a long-range reform there be established a National Police Academy of college level. The Commission felt that the function of this academy should be that of providing a federally funded, free, four-year education for recruits instead of merely training officers already on the job. This academy would resemble the national military academies. Enrollees should come from police departments, after they had served one year following initial recruit training; then complete a four-year degree program which would include on-the-job training; and then be returned to their original department in the rank of sergeant. In return, the officer then would have a four-year obligation to that department.

The Commission recommended that the department develop a new approach for the first field assignment of a new recruit: a recruit should be assigned to work with a senior "training" patrolman as a partner. Specially selected and carefully screened patrolmen with considerable experience, both in the department and in the particular precinct or unit, would be selected for this role. Also, it recommended that a local or precinct training syllabus be provided for training recruits in all the phases of police work within the precinct in which he will be assigned. Along the same vein, the Commission felt that a new designation be established in the patrolman's rank—that of "master patrolman." The patrolmen would be promoted from the ranks of veteran patrolmen and would be given responsibilities for training new recruits.

The Knapp Commission indicated the second general approach for reducing corruption to be the encouragement of concerned citizens to bring reports of corruption to the attention of the police department and by promptly informing them of the final disposition of their complaints. In this manner, it would give the aggrieved citizen who feels that inadequate action was taken an opportunity to seek a remedy from other agencies.

Concepts to Consider

1. Identify the reasons why it is essential to have open discussion of police corruption.

2. Describe the means by which police corruption can be reduced when they are investigating gambling activities.

3. Support the position that the police should not enforce victimless crime laws.

4. Describe the internal control mechanisms utilized by the Philadelphia police department.

5. Identify the major recommendations made by the Knapp Commission.

Selected Readings

American Bar Association, *The Urban Police Function* (New York: American Bar Association, March 1972).

> Presents minimum standards for urban law enforcement agencies, part of which are directed toward control over police authority. Reviews accountability, sanctions, procedures and municipal tort liability.

Anderson, Ralph E., "Police Integrity: Accent on the Positive," *The Police Chief*, Vol. XL, No. 12, December 1973, pp. 38-42.

Provides a list of programs, policies, and procedures that are effective in maintaining police integrity.

Bracey, Dorothy Heid, *A Functional Approach to Police Corruption* (New York: John Jay Press, 1976), p. 31.

Reviews the persistence of corruption and identifies corruption as a promoter of solidarity, a training device, and a rite of passage. Includes an analysis of corruption as that which fulfills needs not satisfied by the legitimate system.

De Garmo, James W., Jr., "Corruption and Law Enforcement," *The Police Chief*, Vol. XLV, No. 4, 1978, pp. 55-57.

Provides a definition of corruption and discusses the boundaries thereof, utilizing the concept of entropy. Suggests controlling corruption by selective recruitment, personnel development, and accountability.

Dempsey, Lawrence J., "The Knapp Commission and You," *The Police Chief*, Vol. XXXIX, No. 11, November 1972, pp. 20-29.

This article presents a summary of the Knapp Commission findings of police corruption in New York City. Commentary is offered on each of the Commission recommendations with a view toward their applicability in other police departments.

Dempsey, Lawrence J., "The Knapp Commission and You," *The Police Chief*, Vol. XL, No. 1, January 1973, pp. 22-36.

Presents the responses, programs, and governmental actions taken as a result of the Knapp Commission findings. The events are analyzed in terms of their meaningfulness to other law enforcement agencies.

di Grazia, Robert J., "Trends in Police Service, Standards and Ethical Practice," *Journal of California Law Enforcement*, Vol. 6, No. 3, January 1972, pp. 134-136.

Reviews the opening remarks by the author at the first national symposium on police ethical practice. Focuses on the inter-relationship of ethical service and professionalism.

Doyle, Edward and George D. Olivet, "An Invitation to Understanding —Law Enforcement Integrity," *The Police Chief*, Vol. XXXIX, No. 5, May 1972, pp. 34-44.

The authors summarize the ten sessions of an anti-corruption workshop conducted by the New York City Police Department. The format utilized was the small group technique and twelve representatives of the patrol division participated.

Meyer, John C., Jr., "A Descriptive Study of Police Corruption," *The Police Chief*, Vol. XL, No. 8, August 1973, pp. 38-41.

A synthesis of data secured through an empirical study of police corruption for the year 1972 in a northeastern law enforcement agency.

Meyer, John C., Jr., "Definitional and Etiological Issues in Police Corruption: Assessment and Synthesis of Competing Perspectives," *Journal of Police Science and Administration*, Vol. 4, No. 1, 1976, pp. 46-55.

Examines the dual issue of defining and explaining police corruption as a social phenomenon. Discusses police crime, deviance, and corruption.

Murphy, Patrick V., "Police Corruption," *The Police Chief*, Vol. XL, No. 12, December 1973, pp. 36-37.

The author identifies six ways of dealing with the problem of corruption in a police department. The recommendations range from taking an unequivocal stance against corruption to improving legitimate rewards for police work.

"Official Corruption—A Position Statement," *Crime and Delinquency*, Vol. 20, No. 1, January 1974, pp. 15-19.

The Law Enforcement Council of the National Council on Crime and Delinquency presents five specific recommendations for action that represent realistic steps toward the eradication of corruption in the justice system.

Parsons, James C., "A Candid Analysis of Police Corruption," *The Police Chief*, Vol. XL, No. 3, March 1973, pp. 20-22.

A detailed analysis of police corruption. The author presents a planned program for improvement based on strong and uncompromised leadership.

"Police Integrity," *The Police Yearbook—1974* (Gaithersburg, Maryland: International Association of Chiefs of Police, 1974), pp. 74-84.

Summary of a workship on police integrity. Reviews the nature and extent of corruption. Positive programs are analyzed and an analysis is also provided of the police payoff system in Seattle, Washington.

Smith, William H.T., "Deceit in Uniform," *The Police Chief*, Vol. XL, No. 9, September 1973, pp. 20-21.

This article is a forthright discussion of police corruption and the policeman's "code of silence" which leads to perversion of personal and professional ethics.

Chapter 7
TERRORISM

Introduction *

Contemporary terrorism has migrated to industrialized societies in the seventies and now poses a real threat to several nations. Police and law enforcement agencies have become vulnerable to terrorism's twin characteristics—uniqueness and unpredictability—as they have responded to counter, neutralize, and suppress this criminal menace. Officials in West Germany, Italy, and France have been hit particularly hard this year, and "The Troubles" have continued in Northern Ireland. Japan has suffered several defeats abroad because of her concern over foreigners in skyjacking, as evidenced in the September, 1977, skyjacking by the Japanese Red Army. And several Latin American countries have already passed through a solid decade of terrorism. Not all terrorists, however, have been successful. Important defeats have been dished out by the Dutch and West Germans. More will be forthcoming as governments tailor their responses to counter terrorism.

It is widely recognized that a proper response by police and law enforcement officials is critical in winning the struggle. Unfortunately less attention has been directed towards how this response should capitalize on terrorism's weaknesses. Too often police have had to react after a terrorist attack rather than being able to initiate their response beforehand. Understanding this phenomenon is essential in structuring a successful response to defeat terrorism and destroy its mystique of invincibility. This article discusses terrorist strategy and tactics, using a recent European example with the aim of contributing to that understanding, and advances some tentative conclusions to guide the response of threatened governments.

Police and law enforcement officials are the most frequently targeted representatives of threatened governments. Terrorist propaganda begins usually with verbal attacks on the police, using the now familiar epithets, and may move through a phase during which uniformed police officers bear the full brunt of terrorist attacks on society. *"Las Violencia"* and the "Kill a Cop a Day" activities in Latin America are direct examples of how verbal abuse transitioned to murder. Yet, it takes a statement like that of Carlos' accomplice at the OPEC raid in December 1975 that she had just killed a "pig" to place this problem in true personal perspective. In this case, the Austrian policeman, Tichler, was summarily killed when he announced that he was a police officer in answer to her question.

Murder of police is a favorite tactic of terrorists in their attempt to create what Robert Moss terms a "climate of suspicion" in his book, *The War for the Cities*. Such murders are designed to erode the citizen's trust

---

* John D. Elliot, "Contemporary Terrorism and the Police Response," *The Police Chief*, Vol. XLV, No. 2, February 1978. Reprinted by permission.

in his government to protect him. These tactics support a two-phase strategy. In phase one, terrorists strive to achieve a step-by-step increase of abusive power by police and law enforcement agencies until a right wing, authoritarian overreaction takes place among a bewildered public, frightened by its loss of liberty. In phase two, a public which has lost its liberties to a "police state" begins to fall into a "climate of collapse." Then, the urban terrorists expect to become cadre for the new political system.

Great revolutions of past history have relied on slowly winning a favorable degree of mass support for their success. Cuba's revolution was no real exception to this even though questions are still being asked about whether or not a "majority" supported it. That debate does not impact on this discussion simply because the active supporters were where they were needed most, regardless of their total numbers. This is brought out here because urban guerrilla warfare, as theorized and practiced by Che Guevara and Regis Debraz, attempted to alter the classical revolutionary role of mass popular support. They argued that conditions could be created by a small dedicated group to start the revolution, and thereby awaken the masses who would then lend their support. Not everyone has agreed with their *foco* theory, but it is a key element in terrorist thinking and action today.

Contemporary terrorists in industrialized societies believe that small groups can bring the state to a "crisis of collapse" by applying the *foco* theory in an urban setting. This is particularly true for democracies where the freedoms of the individual citizen can be turned on the state by the terrorist with considerable effectiveness. These terrorists are organized for the long-term accomplishment of their objectives, even though the life span of many of them has proven to be relatively short. Terrorism becomes a way of life for them and takes on a parental sheen. Struggle is their only brother.

Contemporary terrorists operate even more clandestinely in urban areas than the classical rural guerrilla. Their surroundings have changed but their utmost concern remains the same: security. To ensure this, they even execute "backsliders" and have been observed to give their wounded comrades the *coup de grace*, as Carlos did in Paris. Their whole purpose in being is to strive for gains by their "political movement." No sacrifice is too great for its success.

Terrorists commit their illegal acts of violence for perceived political purposes and utilize a variety of tactics. Many of these have not changed since the invention of gun powder, but have been modified by the Latin American experience with urban guerrilla warfare. They include kidnapping, bombing, and assassination. Some of the newer modifications include skyjacking and holding diplomats hostage. It need not be pointed out that all of these are criminal acts and their frequency of occurrence has risen steadily over the past decade. By all indications, this trend will continue, particularly bombings, incendiary attacks, ambushes, and assassinations. Moreover, the seriousness of the threat will become worse as terrorists obtain more sophisticated weaponry and stronger international support from radical governments. These conditions combine to make the response of police and law enforcement officials much more difficult.

Contemporary terrorism does not present a new problem to police authorities because terrorist acts are essentially criminal acts employing criminal techniques. It does present a unique problem, however, because of its political ramifications, particularly in democratic societies. Laws in some countries have already been changed to increase their effectiveness against politically motivated violence. When this is done it is essential that the public knows and understands the rationale behind the changes. Such adaptive changes alone will not suffice in a politically charged atmosphere. It is far more important to gain the willing support of an active citizenry for the police and law enforcement agencies. People can become a police multiplier in a democratic society also, as long as the government's response is built firmly on the rule of law.

Specific police tactics in direct response to the terrorist threat have proven just as innovative as terrorist tactics. A major limitation is the use of clandestine techniques by the police. Every democratic constitution serves as a basis for such restrictions, and some nations provide effective means for securing their existence by permitting techniques like electronic surveillance when properly authorized. In those cases, it seems to be the rule that when the police and internal security forces begin to operate like the terrorists and infringe on their own laws, they accelerate the move towards an overreaction desired by the terrorists. Terrorism may be a cyclical phenomenon, as some argue; however, the rule of law must be applied after terrorism passes or is defeated. By this is meant that the police and law enforcement agencies must rigidly adhere to the laws they are sworn to enforce. Obviously, this does not rule out the promulgation of stronger legislation to cope with terrorism. Several threatened nations have already done this.

Contemporary terrorism's organizational features present some additional unique problems that impact on the police response. Most important among these is the fact that many terrorist groups are organized in supporting networks. These are functionally oriented and include a command and control network and four others dealing with intelligence, communications, operations, and logistics. Essentially their role is to protect the terrorist before and after the crime. For example, when a cell is activated by command and control, the individual terrorists know little more than their own mission. Intelligence provides them with what they need to know about the target; logistics provides the essential equipment with which to carry out the mission. Afterwards the terrorists can rely on organized supporters and sympathizers to hide them and assist their escape. Ordinary criminals lack such organization, particularly in the post-operation phase of their crimes. This situation is made even more difficult for police in countries where a complete underground has been developed. Terrorists vanish to be "activated" on call. Many even hold ordinary jobs and live routine lives.

Very sophisticated computer technology is being employed now in several countries in checking for suspects and building authorized intelligence dossiers. Routine improvements have been made as well as in weaponry and communications equipment. Most importantly, significant progress has been accomplished on psychological bargaining techniques and anti-terror combat training. Several successful police encounters with terrorists are directly attributable to these efforts. But most direct success has been the result of long hours of detailed police investigation supported by helpful citizens.

But even when apprehended the unique features of contemporary terrorists continue to confront police and law enforcement agencies. Terrorists are politically motivated and are not affected seriously by fear of severe punishment for their crimes. Many even seem to welcome lengthy prison sentences so they can provide media representation for their cause. Placing terrorists behind bars is only the first step in the struggle, and experience has shown it to be a small step forward in some instances. It is now a common terrorist tactic to demand the release of captive cohorts simply by threatening destructive action. This occurs frequently on an international level with participation by a collection of multi-national terrorist groups. It is not always successful, nor does it always fail.

We also know that, once imprisoned, the terrorists will use every legal means at their disposal to frustrate legal proceedings. Frequently, laws designed to protect citizens within democracies are subverted to accomplish this objective. Terrorists may be assisted in these efforts by defense lawyers, intellectuals with benchmark reputations, and a variety of supporters and sympathizers among the general public.

Government response to counter these unique features of terrorism have proceeded along procedural and substantive plateaus of effort. On the procedural plateau, police and internal security forces are being trained, equipped, and motivated to protect both the apparatus of government and the citizens of the threatened society. Where appropriate, laws are being changed to preclude their subversion by terrorists, and legal procedures are being modified to halt their abuse. On the substantive plateau, massive efforts are in progress to communicate the extent of terrorism's actual threat to the society being attacked. In addition to describing various aspects of the terrorists and their activities, all changes to the process of law are fully explained to the public. Generally, these government efforts have met with success and resulted in a better informed public which supports actively the ongoing work of police and law enforcement agencies.

Today, West Germany provides the best example of how one industrialized nation has combatted terrorism. The struggle between Bonn and the terrorists of the Rote Armee Faktion (RAF) has been going on since the late sixties. The Red Army Faction is an extension of the original Baader-Meinhof Gang; and since the capture of the Gang's guiding elite in 1972, the RAF has ambushed the West German government in the cities using special action Kommandos for each operation. An overview of terrorism in West Germany with emphasis on current events is presented in the following section to provide some concrete examples on how one nation has structured its response.

Contemporary terrorists launched their 1977 offensive in West Germany by assassinating Siegfried Buback, the Federal Chief Prosecutor (equivalent to the U.S. Attorney General) in April. Police response was immediate and better coordinated than previously because of legal adaptations permitting closer investigative and executive relationships between Bonn's federal criminal agency *(Bundeskriminalamt)*, its office for the Protection of the Constitution *(Amt fuer Verfassungschutz)*, and the police forces of the various states *(Laender)*. Police powers are a *Laender* responsibility as West Germany does not have a federal counterpart such as the FBI in the United States.

The pressures of terrorism in the seventies has forced these separate police and law enforcement agencies to collaborate under increasing federal direction. Other specific adaptations have resulted in several changes to West German laws and the activation of special antiterror units. These cumulative changes have played a dynamic role in defeating the 1977 terrorist offensive thus far.

Two of Buback's murderers were apprehended in May with the help of an observant member of German society. This was the first of several defeats the RAF was to suffer during 1977. During the course of the search for Buback's murderers, the remaining "big three" of the Baader-Meinhof Gang—Andreas Baader, Jan-Carl Raspe, and Gudrun Ensslin—had been convicted of their crimes and sentenced to life imprisonment by the Stammheim court. (Ulrike Meinhof had committed suicide by hanging herself in her cell in May 1976). This sentencing was a most important defeat for the RAF. It further demonstrated that a democracy could respond to the terrorist threat and reinforce that response within the rule of law. Terrorist reaction was expected and not long in coming.

Terrorists responded to these setbacks in July 1977, by killing one of the most influential members of West Germany's financial establishment, Juergen Ponto. This signaled a new dimension to the struggle and served notice on all influential members of German society. This precedent was soon to have tragic consequences.

West Germany continued its efforts during the summer to round up the terrorists. Terrorist efforts were highlighted by an unsuccessful attempt to launch a rocket attack against the federal prosecutor's office in Karlsruhe and another hunger strike by the imprisoned terrorists. While police and law enforcement agencies amassed thousands of hours of overtime in their search, they also continued their coordination and training efforts. Parliamentarians debated new legal measures to defeat terrorism. This tension of expectation was rampant in early September when the terrorists suddenly stopped their hunger strike without explanation.

This charged atmosphere exploded when terrorists kidnapped Haans-Martin Schleyer, president of the West German Employers and Industry Federations, on September 5th. Negotiations were begun afterwards with the Siegfried Hausner Kommando of the RAF which demanded release of eleven imprisoned members of the Gang. This demand was expected, as was Bonn's response—stalling for time without concessions. While Bonn imposed a total news blackout, it coordinated searches in West Germany and with neighboring countries under the direction of a cabinet level crisis staff, capable of 24-hour-a-day response.

Bonn stuck to its hard line response, and the terrorists upped the ante on October 13th when "supporting" international terrorists skyjacked a Lufthansa aircraft with 87 passengers aboard in Mallorca. Demands of the four Palestinian terrorists also included release of the Gang. Bonn did not change its tactics in response to the terrorist's escalation of violence. In fact, after a six-day torturous odyssey through the Middle East, policemen of *Grenzschutz Gruppe 9* (GS G9 or Border Protection Group 9) stormed aboard the parked aircraft in Mogadishu, Somalia. Results of the rescue are well known and have met with worldwide approval. Particularly noteworthy for our purposes is the fact that the antiterror unit is composed of police officials. It is an excellent demonstration of how Bonn has structured its response to the uniqueness of the terrorist threat. An important factor is that employment of West German armed forces (the *Bundeswehr*) is reserved for special situations only, similar to those required for use of military forces in the United States and other industrialized societies.

Bonn's success was tempered by the subsequent suicide of three terrorists in Stammheim prison and the murder of Schleyer. Both events have given rise to several important questions that will impact on Bonn's response to terrorism as well as that of other industrialized societies. Parliamentarians in Bonn are debating fiercely over the need for additional antiterror legislation that would speed up terrorist legal proceedings and strengthen the ability of police and law enforcement agencies to combat terrorism. Activities also continue on the international level to produce specific antiterrorist measures at the United Nations and better means to coordinate police efforts across national borders. These efforts had not been as successful as desired in the search for Schleyer and later resulted in a round of mutual allegations. In spite of this, however, there was extensive cooperation among several European and Middle Eastern governments in the hostage rescue. Greater international cooperation is likely to be the future model.

Contemporary terrorists have responded to these activities by declaring war on West Germany. Immediately after the event in mid-October, attacks against "everything German" were launched in several European countries. Radical activities were particularly destructive in Italy and France, underscoring the support for the RAF by radical elements in these countries. Renewed terrorist efforts in West Germany itself are also expected in the near future. For the moment, propaganda activities are of primary concern as terrorists wager they can convert the radical fringe of communist party organizations, frustrated participants of citizen interest groups *(Buergerinitiativen)*, and sympathizers among the general public. It is obvious that the terrorist *foco* hopes to use the suicides of the "Stammheim Trio" as a rallying point for conversion of many new supporters to their cause. In this fashion more than an arithmetic increase in numbers is expected.

Terrorists hope to actually increase their threat potential and operational capability exponentially by fielding more terrorists, supported by more clandestine networks, than the government structure can successfully counter. With these tactics, they hope to achieve their strategy of forcing the government to overreact and precipitate a "crisis of collapse" during which they can take over.

Much of this is wishful thinking on the part of contemporary terrorists. They will experience some tactical success as they continue their offensive, but their strategy is doomed to failure unless Bonn departs from its thus far rigid adherence to the rule of law. West Germany's citizenry is alert to the terrorist threat and well informed concerning Bonn's response. Moreover, the majority not only supports the existing measures, but many are clamoring for harsher measures. Sustained terrorist success in such an environment is not possible. Terrorist attempts to win the general public to their side have failed miserably and will continue to fail as the police response becomes increasingly efficient. One may even advance the hope that many of those who now sympathize with the terrorists will emerge wiser from this experience and more actively support their government.

Contemporary terrorism has many weaknesses that are not effectively attacked by police and law enforcement agencies. Foremost among these is the terrorist myth of invincibility. Far too many societies have accepted this myth at face value when they should be organizing specific responses to combat the predictable characteristics of the terrorist threat. We have seen police success in countering specific acts of hostage taking, skyjacking, and bombings. These efforts have proceeded with a degree of success on the international level also, as is evidenced by the West German success at Mogadishu.

We need to now attack the general aspects of terrorism. Admittedly this is complicated by the oft-quoted thought that "one man's terrorist is another man's freedom fighter," but that must be recognized as merely part of the larger political problem. It can be resolved. Politics is terrorism's weak link in the chain of events used to lash out against industrialized societies. It is here that terrorism must be attacked first and hardest. Societies must illustrate the frailties of terrorism's political arguments for the general public and not tolerate criminal actions. This must be continued using all available media until everyone understands the terrorist threat and the police response. Terrorists are criminals, and this linkage must be strongly established in the mind's eye of every citizen. As long as this is not done, terrorists will continue to garner the advantages of their mystique and win converts.

Terrorists are criminals and must be punished for their crimes. Although every nation will not agree with a London newspaper's solution "to hang them, and hang them high," most will agree that they be imprisoned for criminal offenses. Politically motivated offenses are no less criminal. West Germany's recent experience demonstrates that no special privileges should be accorded these terrorists when being tried or imprisoned. Terrorists must serve their jail terms, and some assurances must be established that they will not return to terrorism when released.

Contemporary terrorists are certain to continue their attacks against established societies. Attacks against police and law enforcement officials will remain a prominent feature of their offensives. In the first ten months of 1977, returning to the West German example, six police officers (five German and one Dutch) were killed by German terrorists, as well as the chief prosecutor and several other persons. The fact that these officials are on the front line is underscored by the difficulties experienced by Bonn in appointing Buback's successor. Yet, responsible men like Dr. Kurt Rebmann will always be found in free societies. It is obvious that there are more available believers in democracy then those responding to terrorism's anarchic appeals to destroy the state.

Contemporary terrorism is destined for the same failure experienced by its classical precedents. Certainly, in the process of defeat we can expect terrorism to continue its rampages and escalate violence perhaps even to the level of nuclear blackmail. Terrorism's defeat will be complicated by the transitions that have placed it in a position to diversify its attack against any nation, while receiving international support from radical governments and possible assistance from communist intelligence agencies. We may take heart that the response is becoming equally diversified with increasingly stronger support from free citizens.

As the struggle continues, the recent advice of the *Economist* is particularly apt for all governments: "The coming struggle should be ruthless in the field, liberal in the courts and much stricter in prison than it has hitherto been. It should be seen to be all three, and to be conducted in defense of a liberal and just society" *(The Economist,* September 17, 1977, p. 14). Actions such as these, when combined with and reinforced by the rule of law, offer the best chance for eliminating the terrorist threat.

15. ANTI-TERRORISM: OPERATIONS AND CONTROLS IN A FREE SOCIETY

JOHN B. WOLF

Police Studies, Vol. 1, No. 3, September 1978. Reprinted by permission.

An act of terrorism or a terroristlike incident may occur almost anywhere. Obviously, it is impossible for law enforcement agencies to plan for every eventuality. As in other areas of operational planning, we have to think in terms of probabilities.

One important task that needs to be accomplished in the early stages of tactical planning is that of priority target identification. If we were planning for a war, we would identify certain high priority enemy targets and make tactical plans to carry out attacks on these selected targets. Counterterrorism target assessment is a reverse process whereby we identify those targets "at home" which have a high probability of being selected by terrorists or those who commit terroristlike acts. By identifying potentially attractive targets ahead of time, we are able to anticipate many of the major incident management problems which are unique to a particular target. Thus, we are able to determine in advance many of the response alternatives we will have if the attack takes place.

The Counterterrorism Target Assessment Form provides a means to systematically identify those potential targets which assign it a numerical rating based upon its value, potential for target selection, and vulnerability to attack. The target can be an individual, a category of individuals in a particular area, a building or other structure or facility, motor vehicles, aircraft, or anything else that may be targeted.

The completed assessment forms are beneficial for further in-depth security and tactical planning as well as for the training of field commanders and special response forces.

The format can be very simple. Ours is typewritten on a legal size sheet of paper and reproduced. The information to be recorded is presented in condensed form at the right.

Rating. The rating is arrived at by adding the target value, potential for target selection, and target vulnerability figures together (highest possible rating is 30). Thus, targets with the highest ratings receive priority for security and tactical planning.

Target Value. To determine target value, consider intangibles as well as tangibles. Historical, cultural, symbolic, political, economic, military and psychological factors, as well as the value of human life, must be considered along with monetary value of the potential target.

Target Assessment. It is desirable that the target assessment be a composite resulting from a group effort. This provides an opportunity for brainstorming with valuable input by the group members who identify potential problems and develop appropriate responses in advance.

Today, in a world largely at peace, the terrorist, covered and concealed by a clandestine organization, is coercing people everywhere by perpetrating criminal acts on a regular basis in places specifically chosen for their vulnerability: an exclusive club situated on San Francisco's Nob Hill, the suburban Belfast home of a prominent financier, a limousine hesitating at a stoplight in Karlsruhe, a commuter train halted near a suburban station on the outskirts of Buenos Aires.[1]

Furthermore, a few of the world's most notorious terrorist groups are associated in a loose coalition which has slashed a trail of violence around the earth, and among their crimes are listed random murder, assassination, bombing of innocents, kidnapping, and hostage siege situations involving the elderly and young children. Among the operations, specifically staged by the terrorist for the singular purpose of obtaining maximum shock action and designed thereby to attract widespread exposure by the media, was the October 1977 joint operation conducted by West Germany's Red Army Faction (also known as the Baader-Meinhof Gang) and a splinter of the Popular Front for the Liberation of Palestine (PFLP) called the "Special Operations Group" who commandeered a jetliner belonging to Lufthansa Airlines.[2]

International Terrorist Coalition and Special Police Operations

For the release of their hostages, the Arab hijackers demanded, among other things, the freedom of the Baader-Meinhof leaders who were being held in maximum security prison cells in Stuttgart. However, ninety minutes before a threatened massacre deadline, a West German police unit, trained in commando tactics and known as Border Protection Group

---

1. "Radicals Bomb Swank Frisco Club," *The Star Ledger* (Newark, New Jersey), September 3, 1977, p. 3; "Financier's Home Bombed By The I.R.A. in Belfast," *The New York Times*, February 14, 1977, p. 6; "Motorcycle Gunmen Kill Bonn Official," *San Francisco Chronicle*, April 8, 1977, p. 1; and "Peronist Guerrillas Burn Train Near Buenos Aires," *The New York Times*, January 14, 1976, p. 4.

2. "Hijacking of Jet With 91 to Dubai Linked With German Kidnapping," *The New York Times*, October 15, 1977, p. 1.

9, stormed the hijacked airliner on an airport runway in Mogadishu, Somalia and ended a five-day, 6,000 mile terrorist episode by slaying four members of the "Special Operations Group" and freeing all 86 hostages unharmed.[3] Similarly, in July 1976, Israel's General Intelligence and Reconnaissance Unit 269 staged a lightning raid on the Entebbe, Uganda airfield and freed 61 Israelis and 43 French nationals held hostage by terrorists associated with the PFLP and the Red Army Faction and linked to "Carlos" an internationally sought terrorist.[4] The group headed by "Carlos the Jackal," a Venezuelan by birth, is a classic example of international terrorist cooperation as it includes Germans, Dutchmen, Latin Americans, and Arabs, and it has been involved in criminal activities in Vienna (the seizure of the oil ministers), the Netherlands, the United Kingdom, and France.[5]

Anti-Terrorist Military and Police Units

The people of free societies have long demanded that military forces be wedded to the concept of minimum force in dealing with urban warfare and regard the commitment of federal military forces as a drastic last resort to be used only after the police and National Guard have used all of their own available force and are thereby unable to further cope with the emergency. However, international terrorism has caused democratic states to organize, train, and utilize specially skilled units of both their police and armed forces to suppress terrorist actions which are in progress.

Last October, following West Germany's rescue of the hostages at Mogadishu Airport, American officials revealed the existence of a United States Army strike force designed for use abroad and consisting of two battalions of Rangers. Constantly on alert, this strike force is geared for an instant response if the United States should be confronted with a crisis situation resembling the Entebbe or Mogadishu affairs.[6]

To deal with terrorist hijackers in the United States, the Federal Bureau of Investigation has created Special Weapons and Tactics (SWAT) Teams and almost all of its field offices have a specially organized group of five agents who train together once a month to meet emergency situations.[7] Additionally, in June 1976, the New Jersey State Police established a

3. "Terror and Triumph at Mogadishu," *Time*, October 31, 1977, pp. 42-44.

4. Terence Smith, "Israelis Staged Raid Rehearsal," *The New York Times*, July 9, 1976, p. 1.

5. Colin Smith, *Carlos: Portrait of a Terrorist* (New York: Holt, Rinehart and Winston, 1976), pp. 99-267.

6. Michael McGovern, "Ranger Force Poised For A Hijack," *The Daily News*, October 30, 1977, p. 2.

7. "F.B.I. To SWAT 'Em Here," *The Daily News*, October 30, 1977, p. 96.

Helicopter Emergency Rappel Team (H.E.R.T.) to handle State Police tactical anti-terrorism, hostage, and civil disorder operations and to efficiently respond to requests for aid in remote or isolated areas.[8] Other State Police organizations now are developing units with a similar capability.

Although some Americans regard SWAT units as a "cure-all" for violent crime, others denounce the units as "shock troops" or "execution squads." The reasons behind the lack of complete public support for SWAT teams may be their military posture and the fact that their training closely parallels that of a military unit. However, the alternative to the police SWAT teams is specially trained military units whose use is difficult to reconcile with a democratic society's demand that minimum force be used to quell domestic violence.

Terrorism: A Worldwide Threat

However, some terrorist groups (i.e., Red Army Faction, California's New World Liberation Front, Fuerzas Armadas de Liberacion Nacional—F.A.L.N.) realize that their choice of a given strategy or tactic and its implementation require a strategic assessment. Uruguay's Tupamaro Insurgents referred to this evaluation process as the "coyuntura," a diagnosis of the political, economic, military, and organizational conditions of both the terrorist movement and the society in which it is enveloped. For the Tupamaros, therefore, the choice of every strategy and tactic was the result of a careful, rational analysis of the present and potential strength of their organization as well as of the general conditions and political climate of Uruguayan society.[9]

Imitating Tupamaro strategic thinking, members of the Red Army Faction hope that their violence will bring about an emotionally charged, indiscriminate, uncontrolled reaction so that they can denounce West Germany as a fascist dictatorship.[10] According to a Puerto Rican spokesman in New York City, F.A.L.N. strategists have decided that at the very least their bombings have reduced tourism to Puerto Rico and are dissuading American corporations from further investments on the island. According to Che Guevara and others, a stalled economy is the best condition for revolution.[11] Attempting also to foster an economic decline and attract sympathizers among the underprivileged, the New World Liberation

---

8. New Jersey State Police Training Center, *Helicopter Emergency Rappel Teams* (Sea Girt, New Jersey: New Jersey State Police, 1977), p. 3.

9. Arturo C. Porzecanski, *Uruguay's Tupamaros: The Urban Guerrilla*, (New York: Praeger Publishers, 1973), pp. 11-12.

10. Craig R. Whitney, "Schmidt Warns Germany to Avoid An Excessive Reaction To Slaying," *The New York Times*, April 14, 1977, p. 43.

11. Michael Kramer, "Will Puerto Rican Terrorism Work Here," *New York Magazine*, January, 1976, pp. 5-6.

Front [in September 1977] set off an explosive device at a swank San Francisco Golf Club and threatened to unleash a terror campaign against the city's tourist industry unless its demands for "decent housing for all" are met.[12]

Use of the "Coyuntura" by Police and Security Forces

In 1976, the Irish Republican Army (IRA), failing to ignite Catholics over the British government's abolition of political prisoner status for terrorists in prison, began to realize that its "coyuntura" no longer favored a sustained campaign of assassination, explosions, and car-bombings in Northern Ireland. Additionally, their "coyuntura" appears to have been usurped by the security forces as reflected in the growing number of suspects being arraigned before the Northern Irish criminal courts as well as a sharp rise in the number of convictions being obtained.[13]

Also, a substantial number of Catholic members of the Northern Ireland peace movement, particularly from the ghettos, which are the traditional havens of the I.R.A., have "turned informer" and are providing the security forces with reliable and accurate information over the confidential police telephones. Aware that the people of Northern Ireland had become weary of more than eight years of terrorism, the British security forces have apparently seized the initiative from the terrorists and consequently, the I.R.A., which once could mobilize up to 700 armed men in Belfast alone, at the time of writing has difficulty in mustering 200 gunmen in all of Northern Ireland.[14]

Democratic States and Terrorism

The initial decisions and reactions of government to an urban terrorist threat are critical as they usually define the issues at stake, the presumed character of the anti-terrorist campaign, and the legitimate basis for any eventual termination of the struggle. But inherent within the framework of the liberal democratic state are factors which impede the collection of intelligence required by decision makers to shape the governmental response to a terrorist threat in its incipient stage. Officials of the Federal Bureau of Investigation, for example, complain that their agency has been too severely restricted in intelligence investigations following the 1976 public disclosures of allegations that F.B.I. agents burglarized the

---

12. "Radicals Bomb Swank Frisco Club," *The Star Ledger* (Newark, New Jersey), September 3, 1977, p. 3.

13. Sean Duignan, "The 'Troubles' In Ulster May, Just May Be Easing A Bit," *The New York Times*, October 16, 1977, p. 3E.

14. "I.R.A. Losing Catholic Support, British Say," *The Chicago Tribune*, October 27, 1977, p. 16.

homes of militant political figures, leftist suspects, and anti-war radicals during the early 1970s.[15]

Controlling the Weather Underground Organization

The Weather Underground Organization (W.U.O.) was the primary target of Squad 47, a unit of the Internal Security Division of the F.B.I.'s New York City field office. Between 1970 and 1973, this squad, consisting of between 20 and 30 agents, conducted operations which were specifically tailored to uncover clues to the whereabouts of some of the better-known members of the W.U.O. These fugitives had accepted limited aid from Cuban espionage agents operating in the United States and Canada and some technical assistance from North Vietnam. After the W.U.O. went "underground" in 1970 and many of them were being sought by the F.B.I. on criminal charges, a group of Cuban intelligence officers from the General Directorate of Intelligence (known by its initials in Spanish as the D.G.I., Cuba's equivalent of the Central Intelligence Agency), assigned to the staffs of the Cuban Mission to the United Nations in New York and the Cuban Embassy in Canada, maintained contacts with them. Additionally a few members of the W.U.O. had received training in practical weaponry, explosives handling, and guerrilla warfare in Cuba by Cuban military officers through the so-called "Venceremos Brigades." Consequently, Castro's Cuba has been the primary training ground and principal foreign supporter of W.U.O. terrorists who raised great havoc in the United States in the late 1960s and early 1970s. Thus, there was serious reason for the F.B.I. to be interested in the activities of any young American who had spent time in Cuba as a member of the "Venceremos Brigade," particularly those who were also active members of the W.U.O. Approximately 1,500 Americans, mostly college students, participated in Venceremos Brigades' activities in Cuba when travel to the Caribbean island was prohibited for United States citizens.[16]

Among the investigative techniques used by agents assigned to Squad 47 in their search for clues to the whereabouts of W.U.O. fugitives, such as Mark Rudd, Bernardine Dohrn, Kathie Boudine, and Cathy Wilkerson were mail openings and surreptitious entries. Mail openings took place as agents used keys to remove mail from apartment mail boxes and then took it back to the F.B.I. field office in New York City, where it was steamed open, copied and then returned.[17] Surreptitious entries were made to

---

15. Joy McIntyre, "F.B.I. Keeping Eye On N.J. Groups," *The Daily News*, March 24, 1977, p. 16.

16. John M. Crewdson, "F.B.I. Asserts Cuba Aided Weathermen," *The New York Times*, October 9, 1977, p. 1.

17. John M. Crewdson, "F.B.I. Reportedly Stole Mail in its Drive on War Foes," *The New York Times*, August 22, 1976, p. 26.

photograph and search records and to place electronic listening devices. Undertaken by specially trained teams of F.B.I. agents, a surreptitious entry involved agents as lookouts, radio watchmen, and in various other stand-by roles as well as the person or persons who entered the premises.[18]

In August 1976, regardless of the linkage between the W.U.O. and hostile foreign governments which was established during the course of investigations conducted by American law enforcement agencies of radical and terrorist organizations, the F.B.I. removed from its intelligence division the responsibility for investigation of domestic extremist groups. Instead, responsibility for this matter was given to its investigative branch where they were treated "like all other criminal cases in that division." This change in organizational responsibility was necessitated primarily as a consequence of the sharp criticism of the "Bureau" by United States Congressmen and others who objected to its use of mail opening, surreptitious entries, and other covert tactics to combat terrorism.[19]

Royal Canadian Mounted Police Operations against the F.L.Q.

Similarly, Royal Canadian Mounted Police (R.C.M.P.) antiterrorist operations have been impaired by the trend to restrict law enforcement usage of covert intelligence collection methods and related police activities. During the 1960s and early 1970s, the security unit of the R.C.M.P. tried to combat the Front de Liberation du Quebec (F.L.Q.), which was involved in successive waves of bombings and bank robberies, efforts to establish guerrilla camps in the Laurentian mountains, kidnappings, and the assassination of Pierre Laporte, the Quebec minister of labor.[20]

Consequently, the security unit became the critical component of at least three distinct R.C.M.P. clandestine operations designed to furnish the Canadian government with accurate information for law enforcement purposes relative to the activities of the F.L.Q. and other organizations which shared its strategic objective of independence for largely French speaking Quebec and also carried F.L.Q. members or their associates on their membership lists. These antiterrorist operations were code named Cathedral, the copying of personal mail; Featherbed, the building of dossiers on selected individuals; and 300, a program of war-

---

18. John M. Crewdson, "F.B.I. Burglaries Said to Be Focus Of Major Inquiry," *The New York Times*, June 24, 1976, p. 1.

19. John M. Crewdson, "F.B.I. Chief Curbs Intelligence Arm In Command Shift," *The New York Times*, August 12, 1976, p. 1.

20. Robert Moss, *The War For The Cities* (New York: Coward, McCann and Geoghegan, Inc., 1972), pp. 112-113.

rantless entries.[21] Thus, in 1972 members of the security unit surreptitiously entered the premises occupied by the Agence de Presse Libre, a leftist news agency, and in 1973 they used similar methods to gain access to the Montreal offices of the Parti Quebecois for the purpose of seizing and copying its records.[22]

Apparently some Canadians, presently complaining about R.C.M.P. intelligence activities, have forgotten that the F.L.Q. succeeded in one of its tactical goals: "to bring the army into the streets and place in doubt the norms of democratic society." On October 16, 1970, Prime Minister Pierre Trudeau introduced the War Measures Act and Canada, for the first time in its history, was placed on a wartime footing to face an internal emergency. Current restrictions placed on R.C.M.P. public security activities portend the future use in Canada of war measures.[23]

Information Gathering: Police Patrol Practices

During the past decade there have been many innovations designed to alter traditional American police organizational arrangements. One of these alterations, known as Team Policing, is designed to make the police officer a part and an accepted member of the community he serves and to encourage the people of a neighborhood to become important contributors to the social order. A team policing unit consists of an integrated group of patrol officers, detectives, and community relations specialists whose task is to acquire the help of the neighborhood in accomplishing the police mission.[24]

Additionally, police-sponsored crime prevention programs (Block Watchers, Neighborhood Watch, etc.) are also intended to encourage people to become alert to suspicious criminal activity and to report it to the police, facilitating thereby a police department's effort to control crime generally, and terrorism specifically, in all areas of a city.

However, the main problem confronting the police of a free society engaged in antiterrorist operations is the development of politically acceptable and legally permissible methods to gain reliable information

21. "Canada Mail Was Opened By Mounties," *The Star Ledger*, November 10, 1977, p. 50; Robert Trumbull, "Trudeau Faces Cover-Up Charges In Case Involving Illegal Break-In," *The New York Times*, June 3, 1977, p. 16; and "Quebec Liberals Say Police Raided Office," *The New York Times*, December 2, 1977, p. 12.

22. Robert Trumbull, "Quebec Party Data Stolen By Mounties," *The New York Times*, October 29, 1977, p. 7 and Robert Trumbull, "Questionable Acts of Mounted Police Reported in Canada," *The New York Times*, January 10, 1978, p. 10.

23. Robert Moss, *The War For The Cities* (New York: Coward, McCann and Geoghegan, Inc., 1972), pp. 112-113.

24. Donald T. Shanahan, *Patrol Administration: Management By Objectives* (Boston: Holbrook Press, 1975), pp. 441-460.

about terrorists for immediate tactical use. Consequently, increased emphasis could be placed on the further development and cost reduction of computer-based police tactical information systems. These systems greatly enhance police patrol as they accomplish in minutes a series of record checks that once required as much as an hour or more to complete. Computerized police patrol operations, including routine and regular checks of all motor vehicles, would also seriously impede terrorist operations and thereby force the terrorists to place increased reliance upon the people of particular neighborhoods for services and support; a practice which could prove to be disastrous for them once team policing units have established a city-wide informant system. Last October, the West German Police, attempting to track down the kidnappers of the Red Army Faction, applied many of the above-mentioned techniques.[25]

Thus, in a free society a terrorist organization is best controlled by the systematic application of routine police patrol, investigative and crime prevention techniques, provided that the police themselves are aware of the effective antiterrorist capability of a democratic policing service.

Information Gathering: Covert Police Methods

At a May 1976 meeting, the National Advisory Committee on Criminal Justice Standards and Goals published a report that outlined a variety of legislation intended to authorize anti-terrorist measures designed to help American society defend itself against terrorists. One of the recommended measures is the use of police tactics designed to cause havoc and chaos within a terrorist organization by infiltrating police officers into these groups, not merely to gather information, but to inhibit or provoke hostile activity among individual terrorists or cells.[26]

The F.B.I. has for years been engaged in special programs of disruptive techniques and surreptitious entries against racist organizations, the Ku Klux Klan particularly, and leftist political groups. According to F.B.I. officials, these activities are needed to combat subversive activities of a clandestine nature aimed directly at undermining and destroying the United States.[27] The F.B.I., however, is currently being studied by the Senate Select Committee on Intelligence Operations and many of its counter-subversive activities have, as a consequence, been curtailed.

Wiretapping and other forms of electronic eavesdropping are viewed with mixed emotions by many Americans who apparently see them as the

---

25. Paul Hoffman, "West Germans Hunt 16 Terror Suspects," *The New York Times*, October 21, 1977, p. 1.

26. Daniel Hays, "Terror And The Law," *The Star Ledger*, May 3, 1976, p. 1.

27. "F.B.I. Burglarized Leftist Offices Here 92 Times In 1960-66, Official Files Show," *The New York Times*, March 29, 1976, p. 1.

epitome of an unjustified and nondirective invasion of privacy. Yet, court-authorized electronic surveillance fulfills a vital investigative purpose, especially in cases involving terrorism where evidence from other sources is often simply not available. . . .

Police Intelligence Systems

In a free society, a public security intelligence unit must be particularly responsive to the legal principles and public policies that develop with respect to the collection, storage, and dissemination of domestic intelligence as their assessments are used by law enforcement agencies to make the informed judgments and preparations required to police adequately the disorders, meetings, rallies, parades, and strikes that take place in their jurisdiction. Therefore, to ensure that this vital task is completed without violation of civil rights, certain measures must be carried out.

All police working in intelligence units, including undercover agents, must be given intensive instruction in relevant constitutional principles. It is urgent, also, that intelligence units draft, adopt, and enforce guidelines and procedures for the recording and storage of information in public security files and for the intra- and extra-departmental dissemination of these data. Perhaps the most critical of the guidelines are those having to do with the use of informants. The steps to be followed in the processing, registering, and payment of informants must be clearly spelled out. It is important, too, that a Criminal Source Control Office be created to legitimize and ensure the most efficient use of intelligence obtained from informants.

In order to control terrorism, police intelligence units must have strategic and tactical analytical capabilities, as well as traditional field-information collection units and sources. These requirements can be met by establishing public security intelligence modules which are comprised of a team of field investigators and a desk analyst who work together as a unit and concentrate on a specific area of concern, such as right-wing or left-wing extremist groups.[28]

National Intelligence Services

Intelligence is a vital prerequisite for anti-terrorist operations. Therefore, it is essential for nations to cooperate with each other in a systematic effort to pool information about terrorist organization and tactics. MI-5, a British counter-espionage agency, for example, needs information which could be supplied by the American C.I.A. regarding clandestine

---

28. John B. Wolf, *The Police Intelligence System* (New York: John Jay Press, 1978), p. 1-4.

shipments of Armalite AR-15 rifles to the I.R.A. and the Ulster Defense Forces (U.D.F.), MI-5 most certainly has information which the Spanish could use regarding alleged connections between the I.R.A. and Basque terrorist groups (E.T.A.), and the French Territorial Surveillance Bureau might also profit from MI-5's information on Breton separatist groups. The C.I.A. undoubtedly could use any information supplied by foreign intelligence services which links domestic American extremist groups to foreign terrorist organizations. The West German Bundesnachrichten-dent (BND), the equivalent of the American C.I.A., also might want to exchange information on terrorist groups as it is the central depository for information gathered by the special West German Police Kommando Unit which tracked down and captured the leaders of the Red Army Faction, who had connections with terrorist groups comprised of nationals from other countries.[29]

After the 1972 Munich tragedy, which illustrated that international terrorism had reached the point where innocent people anywhere could be victimized, the United States established a Cabinet Committee Working Group. The working group's function is (1) to ensure collaboration among U.S. agencies and departments with domestic and foreign responsibilities and (2) to recommend countermeasures that can close gaps in the security screen around Americans at home and abroad, as well as foreigners in the United States, whom the agencies represented in the working group help to protect. With respect to the task of protection, the working group relies heavily on the customary local and federal agencies. Thus, it is kept informed by the F.B.I. of the international potentialities or implications of domestic terrorist groups and uses the C.I.A. as an important tool in foreign incidents.[30]

The Antiterrorist Assessment and Response Group

Although the American public is largely against surveillance, data banks, dossiers, or any other facet of a long-term intelligence operation, intelligence is the only way we can learn about terrorist plans and predict terrorist acts. Consequently, there is a definite need for legislation to establish an Assessment and Response Group at a high level of the national government. The activities of this group would supplement the work of the Cabinet Committee Working Group and serve as an immediate information resource for other authorized agencies. It would not duplicate the work of the C.I.A., which is restricted by law from per-

29. John B. Wolf, "A Global-Terrorist Coalition—Its Incipient Stages," *The Police Journal*, October-December 1977), pp. 337-338.

30. U.S. House Committee on Internal Security, *Terrorism Hearings*, 93rd Congress, 2nd Session, May 8, 14, 22, 29-30, June 13, 1974, Part 2, pp. 3080-3190.

forming internal security functions. Nor would it supplant the F.B.I., which does not collect intelligence abroad or employ analysts with sufficient expertise in international politics to function in a strategic public security capacity. This new group would be staffed with people who know how to gather and analyze public security information from both domestic and foreign sources for regular dissemination to law enforcement agencies on a "need-to-know" basis.

The antiterrorist Assessment and Response Group should contain three primary units: an assessment unit, a teaching unit, and a response unit. The assessment unit would receive information on terrorists from members of the Cabinet Committee Working Group, municipal law enforcement agencies, and the response unit. It would then process this information for its own use and for dissemination in strategic reports to other agencies. The teaching unit would provide training for local law enforcement agencies in subjects relating to terrorism that are not currently taught by the F.B.I.

The response unit, composed of experts in such disciplines as management, law enforcement, psychology, and public relations, would travel to the site of a terrorist act whenever an American citizen or corporation is involved. Although fully respectful of the sovereignty and sensitivities of other nations, the jurisdictions of other agencies and, of course, the wishes of the victim, the response team would urge other governments to accept all the American resources that could be put at their disposal, including intelligence and communications. Additionally, the response unit would collect specific field information for the assessment team on foreign terrorist groups with the capability to infiltrate highly trained teams into the United States.[31]

Antiterrorism and the Police

Confronted with proliferating and increasingly sophisticated terrorist groups at home and abroad on the one hand, and the necessity to maintain the basic constitutional freedoms and safeguards that are the hallmark of a democracy on the other, the United States must develop programs and policies to combat terrorism. In America today, by virtue of a process of governmental debate and freedom of the press, it is fortunately almost impossible to undertake a program of pure repression. If we examine the political culture within which Americans function, it is evident that there exist well-defined convictions about what the government may or may not legitimately do and a broad consensus on the fundamental rights of man. Our democratic system is thus both a necessary

---

31. John B. Wolf, "Controlling Political Terrorism In A Free Society," *ORBIS, A Journal of World Affairs*, Winter 1976, pp. 1301-1302.

and a sufficient limitation on the use of repressive force. Moreover, any illegal action by a democratic state is undertaken with peril since it can be manipulated by the terrorist to serve his own purposes. But Americans' desire to maximize individual freedom also blinds them to the dangers presented by terrorism and at times prevents them from seeing the necessity for deterrent action.

However, during the past five years the American police have gained increased sophistication in the areas of communication, mobility, and information gathering and consequently they have caused domestic terrorist groups to carefully regulate and restrict their membership. Some law enforcement officials believe that the F.A.L.N., for example, might contain as few as twelve members. Consequently, the primary organizational requirement for urban terrorist groups now operating in the United States is to develop a structure that is impervious to penetration by the police yet sufficiently flexible to enable them to exploit opportunities for surprise. It is anticipated, therefore, that terrorism, providing the current state of socio-economic conditions in the United States remains relatively stable, will continue to be perpetrated inside this country by small groups knowledgeable in the techniques of terrorist organization and management, although police pressure will force them to adopt a more clandestine method of operation. Terrorist attacks, however, are apt to be conducted with increased efficiency and marked by a higher degree of technological sophistication designed to balance the increased effectiveness of the American police in the area of antiterrorist operations.

16. THE TERRORIST ACT OF HOSTAGE-TAKING: CONSIDERATIONS FOR LAW ENFORCEMENT

JOHN G. STRATTON

Journal of Police Science and Administration, Vol. 6, June 1978. Reprinted by permission.

Hostage-taking is a worldwide activity, not limited to a particular country, nationality, race, sex, or cause; and, as a result, successful solutions to such occurrences have been sought by most law enforcement agencies. Like other situations that have no simple answer, the suggested ideas for handling hostage-takers range from meeting no demands to giving the hostage-takers whatever they request at any cost. The show and use of force also is approached from various theoretical positions, ranging from using extreme and drastic force, as exhibited at Entebbe, to almost complete pacifism. Two major occurrences, which spotlighted international concern and were the impetus for law enforcement's examination of its handling of hostage situations, were the Munich Olympics and the Attica prison takeover. Before applying any judgments, it must be noted that examining a situation after the fact does not have the hazards of being present; and all too often critical incidents or turning points are not available for scrutiny.

For a relatively clear understanding of both Attica and the Munich Olympics, or any other such situation, it is most important to review the reports of everyone, official and otherwise, as well as what is portrayed by the media. An in-depth study of the behind-the-scenes activity involving dangerous and delicate decisions is most enlightening and can give one a very different perspective of what has occurred. A review of an address by Dr. Manfried Schreiber, president of the Munich Police, gives one a more detailed insight into law enforcement's concerns and decisions about the Munich incident than those highlighted by the media.[1]

A common method of improving one's approach and techniques in numerous fields of endeavor is to examine the situation after its conclusion to see what was effective or ineffective in arriving at approaches to be used in the handling of similar situations when they occur again.

---

1. Manfried Schreiber, address to International Assn. of Chiefs of Police, San Antonio, Texas (October 1973).

Especially after the tragedies of Munich, law enforcement worldwide began examining the hostage-taking phenomenon and, through ongoing experience, has developed some general guidelines and procedures to effectively handle these delicate situations.

However, it is important for law enforcement personnel to keep in mind that working with people who take hostages involves *negotiations*. Negotiations involve some type of equality where two equal or at least powerful parties work out a compromise. Negotiations by law enforcement officials, even with criminals, involve communication, understanding, and compromise. It is not simply giving orders, ultimatims, or threats. Rather, it is a recognition of equality of power as the terrorist who has hostages has more control over their lives than do the law enforcement officials he may be negotiating with. Any consideration of guidelines concerning hostage negotiations must keep this in mind.

The guidelines to be explored are exactly that—guidelines—not hard-and-fast rules which must never be broken. Each hostage occurrence is unique, dependent in part upon the hostage-taker, hostages, location, law enforcement and its response. The specifics of the particular situation are of utmost importance for successful resolution of the problem; however, the guidelines which will be discussed have worked effectively for law enforcement. Each one of the guidelines mentioned has been broken or eliminated because of the specific hostage situation without effecting favorable solutions to the problem.

Guidelines

The guidelines which follow have been developed as a result of the author's interviews and discussions with leading law enforcement negotiators in the United States and Europe. Although there may be some international disagreement about the following guidelines, it is believed they are representative of the majority of experts in the field, especially in Europe and the United States.

Time

Initially time is the most important commodity of all. Developing the communication and relationship needed between the law enforcement official and the perpetrators in order to negotiate takes time. This is also true of the relationship between the hostages and hostage-takers. The first few minutes appear to be the most critical as the emotional state of everyone involved, especially the hostage-takers and the hostages, is extremely fragile. With emotions at this extremely high level, people can often act inappropriately; but, as time is drawn out, the results seem to be a lowering of the initially high emotional pitch. This can be conceptualized by a teeter-totter where initially emotion is high, reason is low; and, as time passes, these two dynamics can move toward a more equal level (see Figure 1).

Figure 1

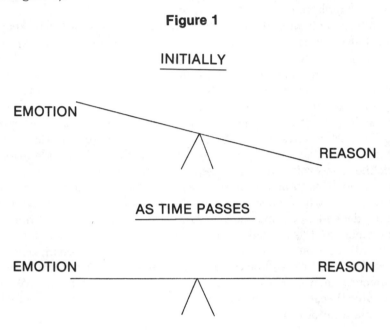

To accomplish this lowering of emotion, law enforcement must refrain from performing acts which would elevate the hostage-taker's emotional state. The establishment of communication and rapport between the hostage-taker and negotiator is of utmost importance and develops only by careful nurturance. Law enforcement's initial mission is to secure and contain the location, as well as the outer perimeter, but to do nothing that indicates an assault on, or a threat to the hostage-taker.

Another aspect when considering time guidelines concerns procedures after the emotionally high pitch has decreased and leveled off to a point where the hostage-taker appears somewhat comfortable about believing law enforcement is not going to attack. One school of thought believes at this point the law enforcement negotiators should alternately raise and lower the hostage-taker's emotional levels so that he can experience numerous changes in feeling tone in a short period of time and subsequently tire and surrender. The other school of thought believes once the emotional leveling off has occurred, it is best to do nothing to aggravate the hostage-taker, but attempt to keep things calm and wait for his surrender (see Figure 2).

Figure 2

DIAGRAM OF FIRST APPROACH

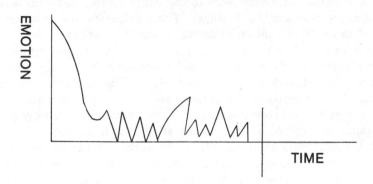

DIAGRAM OF SECOND APPROACH

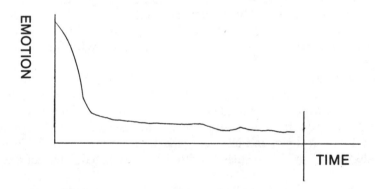

Both of these approaches have brought about favorable resolution in the past. It is the author's belief that utilizing the second approach of containment and waiting will bring about additional saving of lives. The raising and lowering of the hostage-taker's anxiety appears to have some potentially dangerous aspects, as it is extremely uncertain how an individual in a particular situation will react to various kinds of pressure.

The Hostages

Initially the hostages are viewed by their captors as a commodity in the marketplace of their demands. They are viewed as a means to an end with no more intrinsic worth than a valuable means of exchange. They are not seen as individuals with personalities, wants, and needs, but in terms of what they may be able to bring in return for their lives.

An interesting phenomenon has occurred in a number of hostage situations worldwide, which concerns the relationship that develops between the hostage-taker and his hostages. Their existence and subsistence is dependent on the whim and interest of the hostage-taker. As a result, whether hostages live or die, eat, or starve, are comfortable or miserable, is dependent on how they identify and relate with the hostage-taker who has the ultimate control over their lives. The hostages are highly motivated to understand, cooperate, and even love their momentary demagogues to avoid destruction. This phenomenon of survivor identification has occurred too often to be attributed to chance.

These occurrences are often referred to as the "Stockholm Syndrome," which resulted from four hostages being held in a bank vault in Sweden over a period of several days. As a result of their captivity, the hostages in a very short period of time attempted negotiating with law enforcement officials, as they became concerned about what would happen to the hostage-takers. When the decision to surrender was made, the hostages insisted on walking in front of their abductors so that the law enforcement officers on the scene would bring no harm to them. In addition to the fact they refused to testify against their abductors, one of the hostages divorced her husband and married one of the men who had taken her hostage.[2]

There are also several airline stewardesses, having been victims in air hijackings, who continue to pay weekly visits to their abductors in prison, with at least two of the couples currently engaged to be married.

Statements from both male and female hostages, such as "I hope there is a day I can sit down and leisurely talk politics with them," "They are dedicated men," or "Their sincerity should be respected," are not uncommon.[3]

With the passage of time, the hostages can become more and more comfortable with their abductors and even fearful of those trying to rescue them, namely law enforcement. They trust the person allowing them to live and whom they have developed a relationship with, even more than they trust the uniformed officials outside. The hostages fear law enforcement may ultimately assault them to capture the hostage-takers, which potentially could cause injury or death to themselves. As a result, law enforcement must be careful in its communications and dealings with the hostages as any information concerning strategies or tactics may be quickly communicated to the hostage-taker and prolong the negotiating pro-

2. F.J. Hacker, *Crusaders, Criminals, Crazies* (1976).

3. B.M. Jenkins, *Hostages and Their Captors-Friends and Lovers* (Santa Monica: Rand Corporation, October 1975), p. 5519.

cess. Although difficult to acknowledge, it is probably best that law enforcement recognize the tremendous pressures the hostages are under, and not rely on information from them, nor give them information about their law enforcement procedures.

In recognizing this and being concerned for the safety of the hostages, it would be appropriate for law enforcement to foster this transference between hostage and hostage-taker and even encourage it by creating activities which may allow them to work together through such things as the preparation of food (e.g., instead of sending in ready-made sandwiches, send in loaves of bread, butter, lettuce, and a variety of ingredients allowing the people inside to get involved in the preparation).

Hostage-takers, especially highly organized terrorist groups, are aware of this phenomenon. Recently some of them have used tactics to keep the hostages isolated from their abductors, allowing the hostages to have only one spokesman, and not allowing the terrorists to talk, or intermingle with their captives. There has even been talk of terrorist plans to put hoods over their hostages' heads and to keep them totally contained and isolated so the transference that has occurred in other instances will not interfere with their mission.

The Negotiator

Selection of the negotiator is of critical importance as he will become the link between law enforcement and the hostage-taker. Criteria for selection will be discussed at a later point; however, there are several guidelines which apply to the negotiator role in these delicate situations.

Primarily, the negotiator must establish a favorable and supportive relationship with the hostage-taker. The psychological concept of transference, which was discussed in dealing with the hostage and hostage-taker relationship, is also important between the hostage-taker and negotiator. As many terrorists experience difficulties with authority, it is suggested that the negotiator develop his relationship with the perpetrator as a friend—a neutral agent—and not as the authority or decision maker. The negotiator attempts to understand and reach some form of identification with the hostage-taker so that he can relay the perpetrator's case to the decision makers. This procedure demands more time, but allows for a decrease in the emotional level, and allows the relationship between the negotiator and the hostage-taker to develop more fully.

Similar types of reactions, although less dramatic than the relationships that develop between hostage and hostage-taker in survivor identification, can also occur between the negotiator and the hostage-taker. Relationships of such understanding and trust have been developed where the hostage-taker will only make agreements or keep commitments made to the negotiator and no one else. This trust can transfer positively to the effective release of hostages and the surrender of the perpetrator.

Occasionally there have been instances when accord was developing well between the perpetrator and negotiator; but when a higher ranking official decided to take over, it resulted in a less effective solution. The negotiator, in general, should not be a high-ranking official, friend, relative, lawyer, or anyone who is not fully cognizant of the intricate and detailed procedures of the law enforcement operation. At times psychologists and psychiatrists have been used, and again this should generally only occur when there is a good and thoroughly defined relationship with clearly set roles, so that the behavioral scientist and the law enforcement organization can work effectively together.[4]

The use of relatives or other parties who are important to the hostage-taker should be done only after careful scrutiny and consideration. Extremely difficult decisions have to be made by law enforcement in determining how or if to use relatives and friends who have appeared voluntarily or by request. They are frantic, want to help, and generally each believes that they would be the most successful in "reaching" the hostage-taker. However, law enforcement must determine who will be the most appropriate communicator. This can be accomplished by interviewing all interested persons about the hostage-taker and employing psychologists and other highly trained personnel to develop quick psychological profiles, which will hopefully identify the best approach to accomplish the life-saving mission.

All too often the individual most insistent on being the negotiator is viewed by the immediate family and friends as inappropriate and may actually have been the precipitator of the hostage situation. Frequently a close relative, e.g., father or wife, who had had a serious split with the hostage-taker, decides that now is the time to reconcile their differences. Other family members are fearful that any communication with that person may trigger the hostage-taker into carrying out his threats. In fact, hostage-takers may ask to see a particular person because they may be angry at that individual and may attempt to injure or kill him if they could. Stratton has outlined numerous other behind-the-scenes activities which normally occur in hostage situations.[5]

The optimum choice for a negotiator would appear to be a trained member of law enforcement, who is not a high-ranking official, but who has access to consultation and advice from a behavioral scientist who understands law enforcement operations and parameters.

---

4. John G. Stratton, "The Department Psychologist: Is There Any Value?" *The Police Chief*, vol. XLIV, no.5 (1977).

5. John G. Stratton, "Hostage Situations: Behind the Scenes," accepted for publication by the *San Francisco Examiner* (1977).

Truthfulness Versus Dishonesty

The issue of honesty is a difficult one in the area of hostage negotiations and communication with hostage-takers. Honesty is a moral issue, and on the surface no one questions its merit. However, in life-and-death hostage situations, a higher value of human life clouds the moral decision. There are basically two schools of thought (both of which have been successful so far) concerning lying or deception on the part of law enforcement.

Truthfulness. The honest approach believes that if you lie to save one or more lives, the next occurrence of a hostage situation will have placed the terrorist on notice to distrust or not believe the law enforcement negotiators. Their concern involves a continuum of decisions, with the long-range focus on how their deception will be remembered by those who may have future dealings with law enforcement officials who make promises. They are committed to the saving of lives and believe that an honest approach by law enforcement officials throughout the world will save more lives than a deceptive approach to save one or more hostages in the current situation. This approach was most evident in the Hanafi seige in Washington, D.C., where the leader, Hamaas Abdul Khaalis, was released on his own recognizance for the safety of the hostages he and his associates held. Another example is the President of the United States talking to a hostage-taker as a result of his releasing his hostages.

Dishonesty. The second approach is also committed to the worth and dignity of human life and appears to place an individual life over the value of honesty or reputation. Their deceptions are limited to a specific situation where they feel a deception or lie will save a fellow human being. Truthfulness is important to them, but life more important; and they do not see law enforcement's reputation being hindered by an individual case. Examples of this approach are the Indianapolis incident involving Anthony Kiritsis, where he was promised immunity from prosecution for his releasing of Hall and his subsequent surrender. After the agreement was made that effectuated Hall's release and Kiritsis' surrender, he was imprisoned. Likewise in Maryland, a police officer impersonated a man's son to effectuate the release of the hostages and the man's surrender. In both incidents the human lives in question were of utmost importance, and the effect on future law enforcement negotiations was seen as minimal.

This is truly a difficult dilemma, and the theme throughout these articles emphasizes the response and approach being based on the specifics of each individual occurrence. There are no clear-cut decisions in hostage situations; however, it would appear the more publicity and notoriety a case receives, the more likely the approach used by law enforcement will be generalized by the terrorist to other agencies and locales throughout the country.

Suggestions

There are authorities who believe that negotiators should never make suggestions to the perpetrators as it could possibly give them ideas that they had not considered previously. This position is supported where a terrorist requests something law enforcement is against such as a submachine gun. It would not be advisable to suggest a .44 magnum as an alternative.

On the other hand, with the terrorist's anxiety level and his thinking clouded, suggestions to the hostage-taker which may ease some of his stress and be of benefit to police goals may be acceptable. A perpetrator who does not want to be seen by television cameras or reporters and therefore does not want to come out the front door of the location may be receptive to a suggestion about coming out the back door, which would help him save face and at the same time meet law enforcement's desired goal.

Suggestions, then, should only be made if they are in keeping with the stated objectives of law enforcement and should never be made when they implant ideas to help the perpetrators accomplish their aim.

Hostage-Taker Requests

An often-stated principle in negotiations is never give something to the hostage-taker unless you receive something in return. This principle has been utilized many times enabling hostages to be released for such things as a cheeseburger or a pack of cigarettes.

However, there are others who believe, at least initially, while establishing the relationship and in the initial discussions with the hostage-taker, that meeting his demands or requests for food or smoking material will demonstrate the negotiator's "good faith." It is also felt this will behaviorally communicate law enforcement's interest in cooperation with the hostage-taker to effectuate the release of the hostages.

There are certain demands which are almost universally seen as not acceptable and therefore not granted. Demands for weapons, hostage exchanges, drugs, or alcohol are almost never granted. Transportation is also seen as not acceptable; however, several agencies have contingency plans in case a particular situation arises where the moving of hostages may be permissible.

Killed Hostages

The general rule concerning procedures to be used when hostages have been killed has been to use offensive tactics as soon as possible. The reasoning behind this approach is based on the belief that once a person has taken another's life, he is capable of taking more lives and recognizes that the crime he has committed is so serious that there is no way out for him and further negotiations would be fruitless. Continued negotiations should remain in progress to allow law enforcement time to prepare its offensive measures.

Again, with each situation being unique, it is important for officials to remember that most hostage or spectator killings or injuries usually occur at the onset of the seige and that several cases have been resolved with the release of hostages and the surrender of the hostage-takers even though they have murdered people at an earlier stage in the incident.

Conversational Cues

The most important consideration in conversations with any hostage-taker is dependent upon their idiosyncrasies, personalities, and psychological makeup. However, there are certain topics which appear important for negotiators to avoid if at all possible. If deadlines or ultimatums issued by the perpetrator can be glossed over by engaging the person in conversation about other issues, in an attempt to allow the time limit to pass while he is still talking, the police are in an advantageous position as the hostage-taker has now let a deadline that he made pass by without incident.

It would also appear advantageous for law enforcement concerns not to talk about the crime at hand, especially if lives have already been taken. It would probably be best to be optimistic in tone, especially concerning the criminal activity committed; and any exploration should deal with leniency of the courts as opposed to length of prison sentences. If at all possible, deal with current needs and concerns, as opposed to the crime committed and sentences to be imposed.

Numerous issues concerning procedures in hostage situations have been discussed. As has been mentioned frequently, there are no clear-cut, either/or situations with rules that apply for every occurrence. Every rule, every guideline, may be altered or changed as a result of the particular situation; however, the alternatives and reasoning presented should be an important consideration in any decision-making process.

Selection of Hostage Negotiators

Several agencies in the United States and throughout the world have developed hostage negotiators. Having personnel as negotiators requires procedures and determinations as to whom the negotiators should be. Should they be administrators? Patrol officers? SWAT officers? Personal friends? Or other volunteers? Due to the nature of the assignment, additional stresses, and possible conflicting role patterns, it is suggested that special consideration be given to all personnel assigned to this interesting but very demanding assignment.

Several agencies have developed various methods for selection of negotiators. Generally, criteria consists of the selection of officers who have been on the department for a number of years, who are adept at maintaining conversations, who are emotionally mature, physically fit, flexible in their decision-making process, and volunteers. Methods of selecting the personnel who most nearly meet these requirements can be accomplished by examination of their performance records, i.e., the nature of commendations and complaints and driving and shooting records. Information concerning the individual's background in the behavioral sciences gained through college instruction and evaluations by current commanders and peers would also be valuable. Some agencies have used psychological tests and interviews to help in determining the applicant's concern for people, ability in interviewing techniques, and whether they have homicidal or suicidal tendencies.

Large agencies, such as the Los Angeles County Sheriff's Department, New York City Police Department, and San Francisco Police Department, have formed three- to five-man teams to handle their hostage cases. Smaller agencies generally have selected one to three persons in their agency to be trained so that they could assist the department in the event of a hostage situation.

As more and more departments utilize trained personnel for hostage situations, they must carefully examine their selection procedures for negotiators and the training they should receive.

The Training Curriculum

Once a department has decided to adopt a plan for hostage negotiators and has selected effective volunteers, attention to the training curriculum must be addressed next. Negotiators must be able to step out of what has been their normal role—a take-charge person who carries a considerable amount of authority. The negotiators need to be mature and sophisticated enough to maintain control under all circumstances, to be able to control their desire to take charge, to make demands, and to be able to refrain from denigrating the hostage-taker's position. Explaining the negotiator's duties and inclusion of material designed to help the officer adjust to this new role and behavior are necessary aspects of the training program.

Negotiation is also communication; therefore, prospective negotiators must learn effective communication techniques including methods of imparting such things as empathy, genuineness, self-disclosure, respect, as well as the importance of listening effectively.

Extremely critical communication times for negotiators, such as starting conversations, keeping conversations going, the first "NO" (the first time negotiators must inform the captor his stated demands will not be met), and ending conversations successfully are important and anxiety-producing moments for negotiators. How effectively the negotiator handles each one of these critical points can affect the whole future course of the communication. At each one of these steps, negotiator relationship, wording, and timing are extremely important.

Hostage negotiations also involve communicating with people who may be in a crisis state. Crisis intervention theory, techniques, and application, plus other psychological dimensions, such as the psychological makeup of hostage-takers, defense mechanisms, and theories of frustration are all important.

Other topics of importance would include law enforcement's role in hostage situations, legal parameters and responsibilities, stress and stress management, understanding of aggression, frustration, violence and terrorism, and physical fitness. A major emphasis must also be placed on teamwork as relating to the function and role of negotiators to other units on the scene. These interrelationships must be clearly established and understood. For those departments with a team concept, how the individual negotiators must work together as a team and be totally aware of the role each must play would need to be emphasized.

Training to be really effective should include role-playing situations involving conversational techniques, reenactments of actual situations, and teamwork procedures defining role responsibility. A truly effective training program for hostage negotiators includes a wide range of topics and areas of instruction. Negotiating is first of all a form of communication, so a major emphasis in time and effort throughout the training program should deal with communication exercises and experiences. Figure 3 shows the training format for a comprehensive 64-hour hostage negotiation training program used by the Los Angeles County Sheriff's Department.

Figure 3—Los Angeles County Sheriff's Department 64-Hour Hostage Negotiating Training Format

DAY 1

1 HR. HISTORY AND THEORY OF HOSTAGE NEGOTIATIONS:
An overview of contemporary development of hostage negotiating programs and theories concerning selection and establishment of teams.

2 HRS. ROLE OF THE NEGOTIATOR:
The position and responsibility of the negotiator.

2 HRS. PROCEDURES FOR HOSTAGE & BARRICADED SUSPECT SITUATIONS:
Tactical methods for dealing with hostage incidents.

2 HRS.   PHYSIOLOGICAL EVALUATION:
A class designed to test cardiovascular condition, physical limitations, and to stress the need for fitness.

1 HR.   ROLE PLAYING & PROBLEM SOLVING:
The role playing process as a learning method for effective communication.

DAY 2

1 HR.   ROLE PLAYING & PROBLEM SOLVING: (Communication exercises continued.)

1 HR.   OVERVIEW OF VIOLENCE AND AGGRESSION:
Causes and effects of violent and aggressive behavior.

2 HRS.   PSYCHOLOGICAL ASPECTS OF PERPETRATORS:
Basic types of hostage-takers and methods of communicating with them.

2 HRS.   STRATEGIES FOR DEALING WITH HOSTAGE-TAKER:
Basic guidelines for hostage situations.

2 HRS.   DISARMING TECHNIQUES:
Basic disarming methods with emphasis placed on individual limitations.

DAY 3

2 HRS.   CRISIS INTERVENTION:
An examination of techniques used in crisis intervention and how they may be applied to hostage situations.

2 HRS.   TECHNIQUES OF NEGOTIATION:
Methods and concepts of negotiating.

2 HRS.   CASE HISTORIES:
Review and critique of hostage and barricaded suspect incidents handled nationally and locally.

2 HRS.   STRESS MANAGEMENT:
Introduction to stress effects and prevention methods.

DAY 4

8 HRS.   ROLE PLAYING & PROBLEM SOLVING:
Enactment of scenarios depicting hostage incidents.

DAY 5

2 HRS.   CASE HISTORIES: (Continued.)

1 HR.   LEGAL ASPECTS OF NEGOTIATION:
Determining criminal status of perpetrator; civil liabilities.

1 HR.   SURVIVAL IDENTIFICATION:
Understanding the hostage.

2 HRS.   SPECIAL WEAPONS TEAM METHODS:
Tactics used by Special Weapons Teams.

2 HRS.   STRESS MANAGEMENT: (Continued.)

DAY 6

2 HRS.   FIREARMS:
Instruction in the use of highly concealable weapons.

2 HRS.   ELECTRONIC EQUIPMENT:
Instruction in use of bull horn, transmitter, tape recorder
and other electronic equipment.

4 HRS.   TEAMWORK:
Hostage negotiating team interaction as a unit and relationship with other personnel.

DAY 7

8 HRS.   ROLE PLAYING.

DAY 8

2 HRS.   CASE HISTORIES: (Continued.)

2 HRS.   PHYSIOLOGICAL EVALUATION.

2 HRS.   COMMUNICATION EXERCISES.

2 HRS.   EXAMINATION & CRITIQUE.

Suggestions for the Law Enforcement Community

As the law enforcement community and individual agencies become more
sophisticated in hostage negotiations, they have developed methods of
handling most eventualities. The terroristic act of taking hostages does not
seem to have any immediate total deterrent as it is virtually impossible to
effectively screen citizens who have weapons and who are potentially
dangerous.

Hostage situations require special handling to help disengage the
human time bomb—the hostage-taker. Specialized roles and skills require
unique training for those selected as negotiators. In addition to the initial
training, periodic followup training involving discussion of cases, techniques, and keeping up on relevant literature is also encouraged.

Agencies who decide to utilize negotiators and provide them with training should also be sure to implement appropriate call-out procedures,
team roles, and assure that proper equipment is available for their personnel when an incident occurs. There are numerous instances where considerable time, money, and personnel are devoted to training employees,
with implementation not being considered until a situation occurs. Implementation procedures should be developed which would include role

definitions, duties, procedures to be utilized and other units, such as special weapons teams, to fully realize the training.

Law enforcement administrators should continually examine their security procedures and even provide specialized training to those employees who come within categories which would expose them to the possibility of being taken hostage, such as security and custody personnel. Constant vigilance on subversive and terrorists groups can aid in deterring or perhaps halting a tragic hostage situation before it can be finalized.

Lastly, everyone in law enforcement must cooperate to the fullest extent in the sharing of information and the exchange of ideas. Sometimes there appears to be competition rather than cooperation with individuals or agencies trying to be the first and the best. This attitude can impede the free flow of information and be detrimental to the public. Competition in law enforcement no doubt has brought about beneficial changes, but it is important to share the results. The advances in hostage-negotiating techniques and procedures through experience, exchange of ideas, and methods can only add to the entire law enforcement effort of saving hostages, their captors, and law enforcement personnel as well.

17. COUNTERTERRORISM TARGET ASSESSMENT FORM

JAMES M. SANDS

The Police Chief, Vol. XLV, December 1978. Reprinted by permission.

COUNTERTERRORISM TARGET ASSESSMENT

Target Name: .... Rating: ....
Location: ....
Type of Jurisdiction: ....

Category of Attack

Kidnapping   ☐   Armed attack   ☐
Barricade-hostage   ☐   Hijacking   ☐
Incendiary bombing   ☐   Assassination   ☐
Explosive bombing   ☐   Sniping   ☐
Letter bombing   ☐   Theft, break-in   ☐

Other action, specify. (Includes occupation of facilities without hostage seizure, shootouts with police, and sabotage):
....
Probable purpose of attack..................................
Probable method of attack...................................
Probable weapon(s) used.....................................

Probable Category of Attacker(s)

Politically motivated-transnational ☐ Politically motivated-domestic ☐ Criminal deviant ☐ Mentally unbalanced ☐
Other, specify: ....

Probable Consequences of Successful Attack

Potential number of casualties..............................
Potential extent of property damage.........................
Estimate of economic consequences...........................
Estimate of political consequences..........................
Other...

Prevention and Response

Existing attack prevention problems.........................
....

Anticipated incident management problems....................
....
Anticipated special equipment requirements...................
....
Primary and alternate locations for field command post...........
....
Primary and alternate assembly points for response force.........
....

Target Priority

Target value (Circle one):

1	2	3	4	5	6	7	8	9	10

Low   High

Potential for target selection (Circle one):

1	2	3	4	5	6	7	8	9	10

Low   High

Target vulnerability (Circle one):

1	2	3	4	5	6	7	8	9	10

Low   High

Remarks (Continue on reverse) ....
....
Assessment completed by: Date: ....
....
        Signature

Concepts to Consider

1. Describe the unique problems presented by contemporary terrorism.

2. Identify the key features of a counterterrorism target assessment form.

3. Compare and contrast the United States and Canadian response to terrorism.

4. Describe the intelligence systems utilized by the police to combat terrorism.

5. Identify the guidelines that can be utilized in hostage negotiations.

Selected Readings

Crelinsten, Ronald D., Danielle Laberge, Altmejd and Denis Szabo, *Terrorism and Criminal Justice* (Lexington, Mass: Lexington Books, 1978).

A comparative approach to political terrorism that emphasizes its challenge to the democratic tradition. Focuses on the components of the criminal justice system and how each is affected by terrorism.

Crosby, Andrew and Leslie Gibson, "Protecting Airports Against Terrorism," *The Police Chief*, Vol. XLV, No. 2, February 1978, pp. 38-39.

Reviews a security program designed to be readily implemented by any airport administrator. Considers such factors as security awareness, training and management planning.

Epstein, David G., "Terror and Response," *The Police Chief*, Vol. XLV, No. 11, November 1978, pp. 34 and 82-83.

Describes the need for responding to terroristic actions. Calls for a prolific intelligence service and the utilization of the military as a reactionary force.

Horan, James J., "Processing Letters from Terrorists and Other Criminals," *Journal of Police Science and Administration*, Vol. 5, No. 2, June 1977, pp. 145-147.

Muirhead, J. C., "Some Comments on the Hostage Situation," *The Police Chief*, Vol. XLV, No. 2, February 1978, pp. 46-47 and 81.

Describes a series of experiments using blindness, distraction, and increased distance as variables in order to determine their effect on police officers shooting at a hostage holder.

National Advisory Committee on Criminal Justice Standards and Goals, *Disorders and Terrorism* (Washington, D.C.: U.S. Government Printing Office, 1976).

Identifies standards and goals that deal with virtually every facet of disorders and terrorism. Places a heavy emphasis upon social programs as a means of reducing community tensions.

Sloan, Stephen and Richard Kearney, "An Analysis of a Simulated Terrorist Incident," *The Police Chief*, Vol. XLIV, No. 6, June 1977, pp. 57-59.

Describes a simulated terrorist attack at an airport as a training device. A detailed analysis was made of the incident by utilizing videotape and log books to record the sequence of events.

Stratton, John G., "The Terrorist Act of Hostage-Taking: A View of Violence and the Perpetrators," *Journal of Police Science and Administration*, Vol. 6, No. 1, March 1978, pp. 1-9.

Deals with the terrorist act of hostage-taking, including a view of the perpetrators, their motives, commitments and values, and law enforcement considerations in negotiating with these individuals.

Wolf, John B., "Urban Terrorist Operations," *The Police Journal*, Vol. XLIX, No. 4, October 1976, pp. 277-284.

It is the author's contention that the urban environment presents the best opportunity for launching an insurrection. This action is very different from a rural guerrilla struggle, and the differences are discussed.

Chapter 8
STRESS

Introduction *

Stress, its implications and wide-reaching effects, has become a major concern of the American public and the people who are responsible for their mental and physical health. Research has shown that law enforcement personnel are at the upper end of the spectrum when stressful jobs are measured (Kroes & Hurrell, 1975).

For years both the public and law enforcement viewed officers as superior to experiencing emotional or physical distress. Traditionally, there was a tendency to view officers as people who were equipped to handle any situation and move from one emotionally wrought scene directly to another while remaining solid detached supermen. However, today both administrators and the line officers are becoming more aware of the implications and dangers that a law enforcement career can create for an individual.

---

* John G. Stratton, "Police Stress: An Overview," *The Police Chief*, Vol. XLV, No. 4, April 1978. Reprinted by permission.

This recognition has led to awards from both courts and workmen's compensation boards to law enforcement officers suffering from heart disease and nervous disorders as a result of stress (Stratton, 1975).

Enlightened and forward-looking officials such as Peter J. Pitchess, sheriff of Los Angeles County, are recognizing the difficulties and have provided special services for their employees. In Los Angeles these include various psychological services available to all staff such as confidential counseling, special training programs for spouses to reduce stress in law enforcement marriages, and special courses offered to law enforcement personnel on stress and coping mechanisms (Stratton, 1976, 1977).

Just the word "stress" has acquired negative connotations. A working definition of stress is the "demand placed on a system." However, stress is necessary to effective functioning and should not be considered harmful. It is mismanaged stress or an overabundance of stress which creates havoc for the system.

Stress, if inappropriately handled, can cause loss of health, loss of families, jobs, and possibly loss of life. Some stress victims become alcoholics, emotional cripples, and physiologically old well before their time in chronological years. People under stress make mistakes. Law enforcement officers under stress may make mistakes at extremely critical moments, because stress has pushed the officer into making bad judgments. Thus, mismanaged stress can be extremely destructive and even lead to death.

Recently a 32-year-old law enforcement officer, who was thought to be extremely competent and always in good control on the job, died because he internalized his stress. He literally allowed his system to destroy itself; his stomach was eaten away with ulcers, and consequently he hemorrhaged to death.

Research has also indicated that law enforcement personnel commit suicide 2 to 6 times more often than the norm for other occupations (Guralnick, 1950). Most of the time, these people appear to be coping well; but when the pressure becomes overwhelming, they choose this maladaptive way of handling their stress.

Earlier, stress was defined as the demand on a system. There are some analogies which quickly lend themselves to illustrating the concept of stress. Every system, human or mechanical, operates on a formula of laws, demands, pressures, and tensions.

Electrical sockets are designed to put out a limited amount of power; and when more energy is demanded than can be released by the system, the circuit is broken or a fuse is blown. The United States phone system normally operates better than any other; but in attempting to place a call on Mother's Day or Christmas, chances are a recording will announce that "all circuits are busy; please hang up and try again." Even with our advanced computer systems, when too much information is fed in, the machine will report back that the information does not compute.

Human systems resemble machines in that they all have their breaking point. Individual differences vary just as individual differences in body temperatures vary. Normal for most people is 98.6. However, as temperatures deviate either higher or lower, the operational level varies, with some individuals being able to function higher or lower than the norm. People who operate with a fever, ignoring their internal control system, will perform less effectively; and if their temperature rises too high, their life could be in jeopardy.

Unfortunately, human stress doesn't have such a convenient measuring tool. In law enforcement, facing a life-disturbing situation demands adrenalin from the system. When this occurs, the officer experiences an autonomic nervous system response which increases heart rate, blood pressure, and muscle tone. The normal response is a fight or flight reaction which would enable the individual to strike out at the stress agent or remove oneself from the scene (Selye, 1956). Unfortunately, officers can't do either; the job simply does not allow for fighting or running away from the stress-producing agent.

Hans Selye (1974) describes three stages in adapting to stress. The first stage is *alarm:* a situation where the human organism is totally aroused and all resources are focused on the stress agent. The second phase is *resistance* where reactions become specialized in an attempt to bring the effects of the stress agent within tolerable levels. If successful in containment, stress is overcome and the human organism returns to the usual level of adjustment. Once the resistance level stops functioning, the third stage of *exhaustion* sets in; the defenses against stress give way and the effects of stress become dominant. The ultimate results at this level are severe: on a physiological level it can be death; on a psychological level it can be functional psychoses.

The coping process, according to Selye, can lead to "diseases of adaption," which include: coronary heart disease, ulcers, high blood pressure, headaches, gastric disorders, rheumatic or allergic reactions, kidney disease, and emotional problems.

Many medical authorities believe that stress is one of the leading causes of physical disorders, with some feeling that stress is the number one cause of physical ailments. Some physicians have attributed as much as 90 percent of all physical illness to stress.

Stressors can be defined as anything which produces an autonomic nervous system response in an individual. In law enforcement, stressors have been identified in various ways. Authors such as Kroes (1976), Eisenberg (1975), and Reiser (1976) and leading authorities such as Roberts (1975) have tried to categorize the various stressors impinging on law enforcement.

A summary of these law enforcement experts' identification of stressors can be broken down into four parts: (1) stressors external to the law enforcement organization, (2) stressors internal to the organization, (3) stressors in police work itself, and (4) the stressors confronting the individual police officer.

External stressors include such things as frustration with the criminal justice system, i.e., the court's leniency with offenders, decisions which restrict methods of criminal suppression, the endless waiting and often inconsiderate scheduling of judicial proceedings, negative or distorted media presentations, unfavorable attitudes of some minority communities, attitudes of administrative bodies who have the power to restrict law enforcement and funding, too few and generally lacking community resources, and the ineffectiveness of the rehabilitation programs offered through the criminal justice system and its subsidiaries.

Internal stressors found within the agencies themselves include such things as poor training, supervision, equipment, and pay; inadequate career development opportunities; poor reward or reinforcement systems for work well done; policies within the department which are viewed as offensive; excessive paperwork; failure of administration and the citizenry to appreciate the police officer's effort and performance; and the political implications which often enter into everyday decisions.

The stressors found in police work itself are many: shift work, especially rotating shifts; court time and holdover time; role conflict between enforcement and providing service to the community; the ongoing interplay between fear and danger; the fragmented nature of the job where rarely one person follows a case all the way to conclusion; constant exposure to other human beings in distress; boredom alternated with the need to become totally alert in order to handle a suddenly developing situation; responsibility for other people's safety; work overloads; and the need to present the "superman" image in all situations.

The stressors confronting individual police officers include such things as: worries about one's competency; being fear-ridden; the necessity to conform; being a member of a minority; being a female in the law enforcement community; problems arising out of the job including social status in the community, involving the attitudinal changes that develop toward an individual simply because he is an officer; marital and family difficulties; and the necessity of taking a second job or continuing education to aid in professional advancement.

There are some major stressors which exist as a result of the above categorizations:

1. The large number of situations in which the officer's body is called upon to be in an alert state (autonomic nervous system response) whether acted on or not.

2. The various situations in which an officer is responsible for an in-

dividual's life and sometimes for large numbers of people in the community as a result of his assignment.

3. The shift changes which are a necessary part of any law enforcement organization which can bring about tremendous havoc on the individual's body, and the biological changes it must experience including the adjustment in one's circadian rhythm (Kroes, 1976).

4. These shifts not only play havoc with the individual officer and his personal biological and social adjustment, but also infringe inevitably and often-times in drastic ways on the significant others in his life, i.e., spouse and children.

Concern is widespread about police stress and what is expected of the officer as evidenced by such comments as found in the report of the President's Commission on Law Enforcement and the Administration of Justice (1967) which states: "In practically every department, the caseloads carried by detectives are too heavy to allow them to follow through thoroughly on more than a small percentage of the cases assigned to them."

Also often addressed is the problem of lack of proper equipment and materials which is a stressor shared with other professions. For many officers, support services are in short supply or even lacking; and as a result, officers fail to get the needed backup. Many officers must act, in addition to all their other responsibilities, as a secretary and painstakingly fill out form after form, when the officer and many other people see it as more important to be out on the street suppressing crime.

French and Caplan (1972) found that when officers had to change partners, patrol areas, duties, supervisors, or otherwise cross the organizational boundaries, it was a source of stress and posed a threat to the officer's health. It should also be noted that daytime sleep in controlled laboratory testing has been found to be qualitatively different from nighttime sleep and less satisfying (Kroes, 1976). A Police Federation study (1963) determined that 30 percent of officers interviewed upon leaving the force, left because of domestic problems.

With the wide variety of stressors confronting law enforcement, it is not surprising that policing is considered one of the most stressful occupations in the country. Because of the stress, some officers unfortunately feel they have to choose between family or job, with the final result that they leave the family for the job or the department to be with the family. Many officers who ultimately leave the department because of family problems, leave a job that they personally find rewarding and fulfilling. Conversely, the officer who leaves his family because he can no longer perform an effective job, leaves a relationship and investment he had personally found rewarding. Marriage or work doesn't have to be all inclusive; there are ways to adjust which can resolve these difficulties successfully for the individual officer, his family, and the department.

An important ingredient for effective policing is the ability to use emotional control. Society, the law enforcement organization, and law enforcement personnel all expect the individual to shut off or suppress emotional responses to the multitude of situations he encounters. Unfortunately, human beings cannot turn their emotions on and off as easily as putting on a uniform or getting into a black and white car—but that is what is expected of law enforcement officers.

To meet these demands, the officer may keep too tight a rein on his emotions, and over a period of time isolate his feelings and become uncomfortable in expressing them. This can be analogized to a pressure cooker that has its top spout tightened down so that the steam which builds up can't escape. Eventually with the constant buildup of steam the pressure cooker will explode.

Similarly, if one were to drive a car without ever releasing the emergency brake, the car would eventually break down. The emotions need to be released too or the individual may break down.

A quick way to demonstrate the debilitating effects of tension would be to clench your fist as tightly as possible while reading this article. Very rapidly it would become noticable that the body cannot maintain that kind of pressure at the same level for any period of time. The fist will begin to shake, its strength breaks down, and the hand's ability to function will steadily lessen.

As a result of the concern about stress and how it is dealt with, several studies have been conducted concerning its effects on the police officer.

Kroes, Margolis and Hurrell (1974) found that all 100 police officers interviewed in their study stated that the job adversely affected their family life. Digestive disorders were reported by 32 percent and 24 percent reported headaches as compared with 14 percent of the civilian population.

Richard and Fell's (1975) study examined hospital medical records and revealed that the suicide ratio for police was very high. There was an extremely high number of "premature deaths" in the officer population, and admission to hospitals were significant in the areas of circulatory problems and digestive tract problems. No significant difference was found in the frequency of use by officers of mental health facilities. This study examined criteria similar to Guralnick (1950), whose findings indicated many similar factors of concern.

Grencik (1973) found that the onset of strain occurs early in an officer's career. Medical findings determined that 15 percent of the officers had levels of cholesterol which rendered them twice as prone to coronary heart disease; triglycerides were elevated in 27 percent of the officers. Some 56 percent of the officers were from six to twenty pounds overweight, while 28 percent were more than 21 pounds overweight. The heart index risk categories found 11 percent with low risk, 61.9 percent with average risk, 24.7 percent with medium high risk, and 2.4 percent with a high risk of coronary heart disease. Some 86 percent of the officers performed little or no exercise.

Jacobi (1975), in studying workmen's compensation cases, reported that police officers submit claims six times the rate of other employees. Approximately 30 percent of their claims are concerned with lower back pain with about one-third of those involving psychological problems. Some 50 percent of all claims involved high blood pressure, an early indicator of coronary heart disease.

In addition to these studies concerning police officers, there are several other studies regarding stress which have implications for law enforcement because of their relationships to bodily functions.

Adrenal glands play an important role in law enforcement work. However, it has been found that overworking of these glands, caused by physical danger, emotional crisis, or continuing emotional or mental tension, can cause bodily disorders characterized by tiring easily, needing more sleep than normal, and marked mental lethargy involving lack of concentration and inability to think clearly. The adrenal glands release cholesterol into the bloodstream during periods of stress. Many doctors now believe that such diseases as arteriosclerosis, coronary thrombosis, and cerebral hemorrhage may be the result of constant overstimulation of the adrenal glands.

Another study, Cobb and Rose (1973), was conducted on a group of tax accountants with comparisons of cholesterol and time-related pressures. Using the measurable norm for cholesterol in the body, the tax accountants showed significant differences as the tax due date approached. The cholesterol level gradually increased as the tax deadline came closer, peaked with the deadline, and gradually decreased to normal after April 15.

A study with monkeys (Brady, 1958) dealt with the bodily effects of being under regulated periods of stress, where responsibility for the safety of another monkey was assumed. One monkey was able to control electrical shocks for both by depressing a bar prior to the regularly scheduled interval. The other monkey also had a bar, but it was non-operative and therefore the "executive monkey" had sole responsibility for controlling shocks. Without warning and without exception, in an approximate six-week period, the "executive monkey" died without prior symptoms of ill health. Autopsies consistently showed perforated ulcers.

These studies are indicative of stress actually inducing functional changes in the body. Law enforcement personnel face constant time and pressure demands, responsibility for the lives of others, and frequent situations calling for use of the adrenal glands. These demands may have potential for physical disability if not handled successfully.

In addition to the physical problems confronting law enforcement officers, there are a number of common emotional problems experienced. Confronting and managing these stressors in a law enforcement career periodically may create emotional problems for individual police officers.

It is the author's experience that underlying several of the common emotional problems are the individual's strong dedication and commitment to the job and what he feels is the invaluable service he and the entire enforcement community provide to society. As a result of this dedication and commitment, the following problems can arise.

Workaholic: Most officers believe very strongly in what they are doing and find it exciting. When these factors are combined with the variety and challenging aspects of police work, they become job addicting. The satisfying feeling of solving crimes and apprehending criminals, eliminating menaces from the community, and preventing crime becomes the sole goal for many officers in these circumstances. Seeing and experiencing the many tragedies that befall fellow human beings can bring about a crusader complex where the officer believes if he continues to work as hard as possible, he will be able to remove at least some of these detrimental societal influences from the community.

Exhaustion syndrome: After years of working extremely hard and, for whatever variety of reasons, receiving little if any recognition, rewards, or advancement from within the law enforcement organization, or from fellow officers, or the citizenry, it is possible for an individual to become "burnt out," cynical and disgusted. Working at a level described in the previous section for minimal compensation, emotionally or monetarily, can cause some officers to go into semi-retirement in their mid-thirties. After experiencing so many set-backs and seeing so many things which are felt to be injustices, the officer's only motivation is sticking it out until time for retirement and the pension money.

The alcoholic: The most socially acceptable way in the United States of relating with other people is in the presence of alcohol. An acceptable manner of commiserating with fellow sufferers is during the consumption of alcoholic beverages. This can become a habit or pattern, not easily broken, and can lead to alcohol being increasingly seen as a substitute for other forms of relieving pressures. While many view alcohol as a shortcut to alleviating the negatives in life, it is a clearly established medical fact that alcohol is a depressant, and continual consumption of these beverages only increases one's depression.

Emotional reactions to traumatic experiences: Police encounter a wide spectrum of situations, and some of these are handled quite routinely; however, there are numerous traumatic experiences which can cause a wide range of emotional reactions from officers. Involvement in events such as killing another human being (explored in detail by Michael Roberts, Ph.D. at San Jose P.D.), being shot at or almost killed, or seeing the aftermath of dead mangled bodies, tortured or sexually abused victims, battered children, etc., takes it toll on the individual officer.

Marital: This area is discussed by Stratton (1975) and covers concerns about the quality of interaction with the spouse, which can often be of short duration, sporadic, and with faulty or poor communication. The partners can grow apart with the non-law enforcement spouse having feelings of unimportance or rejection. The interests of spouse and family appear to them to be low priority, which only reinforces the dissonance already established.

18. POLICE STRESS: CONSIDERATIONS AND SUGGESTIONS

JOHN G. STRATTON

The Police Chief, Vol. XLV, May 1978. Reprinted by permission.

After consideration of law enforcement stress and the physical and emotional problems it creates for officers, it is important to examine potential indicators of stress reactions. Awareness of these early warning signs of stress are important for both the individual officer and supervisors, as quick detection can prevent additional problems.

Reactions to stress should be expected periodically in a law enforcement career; however, when reactions occur, they should be handled rather than ignored. Such avoidance could create additional tensions and stress culminating in more severe and disastrous responses.

Menninger (1963) describes common methods used to cope with stress which are considered normal and can reduce tension and keep the human system operating without malfunction. These regulation devices include self-discipline, laughing, crying, cursing, boasting, overactivity, day dreaming, food, self-medications, and a variety of other like activities.

However, when tensions are not reduced by one of these regulatory devices, stress continues to build. In the first level, the individual is nervous and experiences increased tension; the emotions betray the arousal of aggressive impulses; there is an overabundance of emotionalism; and worry is often accompanied by minor bodily and sexual dysfunction. If the conflicts are resolved, this state can be quickly reversed; however, if ignored, it can deteriorate.

At the second level, the individual experiences growing discomfort, anxiety, and feelings of uselessness; guilts and fears intensify; and there is a steadily increasing inability to perform work or relate with others which may be covered up at great inner cost to the individual, even to the extent that this coverup may be seen as superior performance. The individual often copes by displaying bravado and recklessness, or utilizing defense mechanisms such as blocking or fantasies. The stress agent is not attacked, rather the aggression is diverted to more socially accepted forms of activity such as gambling, reckless driving, physical violence, or becoming overly generous, friendly or enthusiastic, but with frequent mood changes.

At the third level of dysfunction, aggression is no longer inward, but is directed outwardly. There may be violent acts toward animals and a need to destroy "evil" in whatever form evil is perceived by the individual. There will be suspiciousness, hypersensitivity, and overactivity. Responses will be speeded up—too much activity, talking too fast, sleeping too little. Impaired judgment becomes apparent to everyone including the individual.

In the fourth level, controls are no longer effective. This level is characterized by severe blow-ups and temper tantrums, and no longer is any attempt made to live up to expectations. The individual may become manic, depressed, schizophrenic, or paranoid. The facade disintegrates, and suicide may be the result.

Recapping, some of the early warning signs to be aware of and which indicate too much stress are: abrupt change in typical behavorial patterns, rapid mood changes, overly suspicious, excessive use of alcohol, overhostility, extreme defensiveness, use of too many sick days, excessive nervous habits (can't sit still, in perpetual motion), accident prone, taking of unnecessary chances, obsessive about working (overtime, perfectionism), sleep disturbances, digestive disturbances, decrease in work performance (enthusiasm, interest, confidence), depression, use of excessive violence, always blaming others for problems, becoming argumentative, and need to eliminate evil at whatever cost.

Common Management Methods

Law enforcement agencies throughout the country traditionally have dealt with stress in a variety of ways which have been explained by Dr. Michael Roberts, of the San Jose Police Department, at the FBI Academy National Education Institute as follows: ignoring the officer, hiding or transferring the officer, firing the officer, disability retirement, or rehabilitating the officer.

Before explaining the approaches used by supervisory staff in managing their employees, a few points about supervision seem appropriate.

Although officers aspire to supervisory and managerial positions to have more influence on organizational direction and receive increased status and pay, they often ignore the problems in assuming this role. A supervisor is responsible for supervising employees, sometimes including those who were peers prior to the advancement. Managerial and supervisorial assignments are among the most difficult in any organization; however, in many law enforcement organizations, a common belief exists that the essential requirement for an effective supervisor is being a good officer.

While having been a good officer is important, there are additional considerations. Good supervisors are not born with the ability to supervise. Training for new supervisors is important, as they will be expected to perform new functions and duties which can be potentially stressful for them.

There are some basic approaches to use in becoming effective as a supervisor. These include honesty, the ability to be forthright and understanding, but not overlooking deficiencies. The partner system and the stick-togetherness it develops create hazards for law enforcement supervisors. There is a tendency to let things slide by or for a partner or other officers to cover up; and on occasion, this attitude is supported by supervisory staff.

Effectiveness in supervision is a tough, demanding job, often placing the supervisor in ambivalent situations. While deficiencies are recognized, the problematic officer may be a nice guy, perhaps an old buddy, or used to be a good cop. None of the supervisor's alternatives are pleasant, and there are several ways such situations have been traditionally handled. A summarization of the various methods utilized follows.

Ignoring the officer: At almost every station, there tends to be an officer or two who are experiencing problems and are not coping with the demands of the job. Too often, supervisors ignore the obvious difficulties and hope in vain that the problems will correct themselves. This may occasionally happen when the officer is injured or finally retires. The tendency to ignore can be dangerous. The problem officer may become involved in an action which is dangerous or scandalous (i.e., working while intoxicated, involvement in a serious auto accident either while working or off duty, etc.).

If such an incident occurs, the officer can no longer be ignored. His faults, which have never been discussed, will be dredged up to reinforce the fact that the officer is and has been a poor employee. Too often, personnel files are devoid of any mention of deficiencies, while such problems are well known to supervisors and other members of the law enforcement community.

Hiding or transferring the officer: Many times, especially in large organizations, when an officer is performing poorly, there is a tendency to place the problem officer in a less demanding or unimportant function. Smaller agencies cannot hide their problems as easily.

Again, as when the problem is ignored, the officer usually has never had the problem discussed, nor is he told of the specifics behind the transfer other than it is being done for the good of the organization. An officer who at one time may have been performing competently, but who has developed some problem areas, can end up in positions where he may be performing the must rudimentary assignments with the accompanying knowledge that he is seen as incompetent, without ever fully understanding the reason for his transfer or new assignment.

Firing the officer: If either of the first two approaches are utilized, problems will never be confronted and can end with the eventual termination of the officer. Rather than recognizing, discussing, and planning for change to deal with the various difficulties the employee may demonstrate, it is not uncommon for a supervisor to allow the negative behavior to build up and reaffirm itself. Eventually a sufficient case is built regarding the employee's incompetence and he is asked to resign from the organization, or is fired.

Disability retirement: Throughout the country, law enforcement officers are receiving disability retirement as a result of what has been perceived as work-related injuries or illnesses. Some officers, especially those the agency regards as problem employees, have even been encouraged to file for workmen's compensation or disability retirement, even though the loss ranges from $250,000 to $500,000 per officer considering training, replacement costs, and benefits. The local government will have to cover the expense, but the organization does not have to cope with the problems presented by the employee any longer.

Rehabilitating the officer: This approach is highly recommended by the author and agencies who have provided services aimed at rehabilitation of their officers. This approach saves money, and even more important, the humaneness of the approach results in increased productivity and morale.

A large percentage of any law enforcement budget is involved in the expense of training its personnel. Instead of facing consistent losses in this area, if officers experience difficulty, it would appear appropriate to provide various types of services for the troubled employee. The services that can be provided will be dependent on the size of the organization and the various stressors confronting the department employees.

The major ingredients for successfully using this approach entail proper supervisory methods, including honest and open discussions with the employee; providing a variety of services to employees such as those described by Stratton (1977); and an overall organizational attitude that having problems does not make an individual officer sick or incapable of performing the job, but simply acknowledges the fact that police officers are members of the human race. Whatever rehabilitative program is designed, it has to be viewed as a tool to assist individuals, with full knowledge that by aiding the individual the department will also be benefited.

Throughout one's law enforcement career, an officer may see all these methods employed. A tragic example and one which encompasses most of the approaches mentioned is that of Karl Hettinger (Wambaugh, 1973).

This officer was involved in a traumatic incident during which his partner was killed and he luckily escaped. After the incident, Mr. Hettinger was ostracized except by the detectives investigating the homicide. Their major concern, however, was the obtaining of facts with little apparent concern for the officer's well-being. Fellow officers isolated him, and his mistakes were used by training officers in a manner derogatory to Hettinger. The officer's work performance progressively deteriorated to a point where he was assigned less demanding duties ranging from desk jobs to being chauffeur to the chief.

With his physical and emotional well-being continually deteriorating, he filed for a workmen's compensation disability claim which was denied, and he was finally dismissed from the force as a result of petty theft charges against him. Subsequent employment was difficult to secure because of his background, and he eventually found work as a gardener and farmhand.

It is regrettable that at the time of this incident, 1963, few if any rehabilitative services were available to officers. If they had been, it is possible that he could have dealt more effectively with his feelings of guilt, anxiety, responsibility, and the additional emotional pressures he was experiencing. It is even possible that with effective rehabilitative services, the detrimental career experiences described could have been avoided and Mr. Hettinger could have completed his career as a dedicated and competent police officer.

Officer's Stress Reduction Methods

The decision to become a part of the law enforcement profession is reached for a variety of reasons—the profession provides services to the community; it offers a variety of exciting assignments; and job security and financial stability. However, it is rare that an individual entering the profession considers the fact that he is entering a stressful occupation.

Until recently, little training had been given officers in what they could do to reduce the stress they may experience during their police career. There are several methods for stress reduction. Physical exercise is a highly effective stress reducer, although it involves some dedication and physical uncomfortableness. The results to the individual are rewarding in terms of one's physical ability to cope with stress agents.

All types of physical exercises can be valuable; however, aerobic exercises (those that involve the sustained exchange of oxygen) such as running, swimming, bicycling, tennis, etc., are most effective. Anaerobic exercises are good for muscle tone and strength, but provide limited cardiovascular benefit (Cooper, 1970).

Diet is another effective method of providing care for the individual and reducing stress. Officers' diets, because of job demands and shift changes, are often nutritionally deficient. Eating the proper amount and type of food aids health, reduces effects of stress, and enables the officer to perform more effectively.

Other methods of stress reduction would include self-awareness or relaxation techniques (Benson, 1975). Such things as biofeedback, transcendental meditation, and self-hypnosis allow a person to become more relaxed, get a feeling about what is happening with his body, and by this awareness, understand himself more fully. Once a person recognizes some of the dysfunctions and what can be done to alleviate the symptoms, stress reduction techniques can be highly effective.

Each one of these methods involves commitment, time, and also at times extending one's physical limits. If a decision is made to enter a profession which is known to be stressful and places difficult demands on one's bodily system, then a concomitant decision should be made to keep the system in good running order. It would be analogous to racing an old car with an untuned engine in the Indianapolis 500; a few times around the track and a breakdown will occur.

Although some methods require strenuous work, others do not. The major factor in stress reduction requires taking enough time to pay attention to the body's signals and taking care of the symptoms. No agency or organization is able to place a higher value on human life than the individual does himself. If the individual cares enough about himself, there will be an attempt to take care of his system so that it works effectively and handles stress appropriately.

Organizational Approaches to Stress Reduction

Programs and methods can be implemented to assist the members of law enforcement agencies so that the amount of stress experienced throughout one's career is minimal. Top priority should be for administration and management to exhibit genuine concern for their employees, to treat them as human beings, to recognize that law enforcement is a stressful occupation, to acknowledge that an employee having a problem does not make him "sick," and to have realistic expectations of employees, as compared with unrealistic demands which encourage the ongoing presentation of a "superman" image.

Such a humanistic approach with realistic expectations in law enforcement would include the recognition and acknowledgment that law enforcement is a stressful profession and provide programs to assist employees in dealing with stressors encountered.

Programs initiated and developed by Los Angeles County Sheriff Peter J. Pitchess, such as confidential counseling, alcohol rehabilitation, spouses' programs, and the use of various other psychological services for employees would prove of value. Stratton (1976, 1977) has detailed a variety of services which can be made available to employees and their spouses which have proven successful in reducing stress.

Appropriate and comprehensive training is an extremely important component that law enforcement agencies can utilize to reduce stress. Any new, different, or unexpected change produces stress. Throughout an officer's law enforcement career, he will be involved in a number of different assignments. To help reduce the trauma resulting from change, the more exposure the officer is given to the various duties he will have through the use of role playing, practice, and repetitive exercises, the less stress these initially foreign encounters will evoke.

Whatever the goal of the training may be—i.e., basic patrol functions, undercover assignments, hostage negotiations, interviewing rape victims, conducting internal investigations or other assignments—training should also involve such things as an understanding of stress, its effects, and methods of reduction.

Supervisory considerations and effective methods of supervising employees—whether the individual is a first-line supervisor, middle manager, or at the very top levels of administration—is essential. Another necessary function, yet a major stressor in many agencies, is the method and procedures by which internal investigations are conducted. Training in appropriately conducting these delicate investigations, with special emphasis on relating with and treatment of the officer under investigation, would be of benefit.

Training can also be provided concerning law enforcement marital relationships and problems. This training is important for both the officer and the spouse as it is a well-established fact that the more stable one's homelife is, the more effective is the work output and performance. A very effective program for spouses which has helped accomplish these goals was developed by Sheriff Pitchess (Stratton, 1976). The results and successes of this program have also been reported, (Stratton, 1977) and it appears to be very beneficial not only to the spouse but also to the officer. The program enhances marital relationships, diminishes dissonance, and aids spouses in understanding, supporting, and assisting the officers in their careers.

In addition to a humanistic approach to employees, providing specialized services for personnel and spouse, and implementing appropriate training, other successful programs have been implemented by various agencies.

The high correlation between effective exercise and one's health is clearly evident, and agencies have developed unique physical fitness programs for their employees. The Dallas Police Department conducted a study which showed that officers who practiced aerobic exercise used less sick days and fewer were off duty as a result of a disability or injury. Some agencies require certain physical standards for the officer to be able to continue to function in his assignments. The Kansas City Police Department has implemented semiannual physical fitness tests resulting in one to three paid days off for officers who perform at pre-established performance levels.

19. COPING WITH STRESS

MARY JAN HAGEMAN, ROBERT B. KENNEDY, & NORMAN PRICE

The Police Chief, Vol. XLVI, February 1979. Reprinted by permission.

Law enforcement officers have had a number of occupationally related health problems throughout their history. With the use of automobiles and the fast-paced society, more health problems have arisen that could be attributed to the occupation. Authors such as Kroes (1976), Reiser (1976), and Hageman (1978) have tried to categorize the various stressors. In this article, then, we are not so concerned with adding to the already growing list of stressors, but rather with identifying preventive measures that will help one to better manage the stressful moments. In this manner, then, one's health is healthier and one's life might be prolonged.

Physical Conditions

The physical condition of the officer should be a concern for the police administrator and for city officials who fund the operations. Sick leave, training costs for replacement officers, and disability payments are just a few of the more obvious cost factors. Other less obvious spin-offs are accident proneness, higher disciplinary actions, and general ineffectiveness. The general principle is people who are not feeling well do not act well and find it more difficult to be kind and considerate to others.

Stress is a condition of the occupation. Some stressors are controllable and some are not. One fact has been consistent in the earlier literature done by Cruse and Rubin (1972) and Grencik and Snibble (1973). That is, the officer who is in good physical condition will have fewer health-related problems and will be better able to handle the situations that are stressful.

We believe the answer to the problem is adaptability to present situations. For instance, what good are big muscles to a supervisor who sits behind a desk all day when a sudden high-stress situation arises and a heart attack overcomes him? The same events could be illustrated in a patrolman's situation, time and time again. You have little control over your hours and the situations thrown at you, but you do have control over your body and how it functions.

Most physical fitness programs imply muscle strength. In reality, there are three different kinds of physical fitness: (1) endurance, (2) flexibility, and (3) muscular strength.

Endurance should be considered a very important aspect of a physical fitness program. The officer may sit in his car or engage in other activities that require little exertion for long periods of time. He then may suddenly be required to chase a suspect on foot or engage in other activities that place strain on the heart and lungs. This type of activity is hard on the officer who is not in good physical condition.

Many activities are available to build up endurance. Any activity or sport that includes running or walking will help. Some of these activities include swimming, jogging, bicycle riding, golf, tennis, and walking. Jogging is one of the best exercises and one of the easiest to utilize. Yet 10 minutes of jumping rope is comparable to 30 minutes of jogging; plus, one can jump anywhere—even in an office. Walking briskly through a hilly area can provide almost as much exercise as jogging an equal distance. Walking, jumping rope, and jogging are exercises that require little expense compared to many other exercises. The only expense is for proper clothing which should include a good pair of shoes designed for running and a sweatsuit or shorts, depending on weather conditions. Space for these activities can be in a park, on sidewalks, or even up-and-down stairs in the stair-wells. All of these mentioned methods are good for almost all parts of the body. They are particularly good for the lungs as they increase lung capacity. The heart is also strengthened. Most of the muscles in the body are used and strengthened, especially the leg and lower body muscles. While the average heart rate is 70-80 beats per minute, the trained athletic individual's rates are as low as 30-40 per minute. The purpose of endurance exercises is to make the heart beat faster during exercises so that your body will lower the resting heart rate and thereby use less energy when it is not needed.

To test yourself, immediately following your exercising, wait one minute. Then, take your pulse. A good indicator of present level of fitness is the speed with which your pulse drops to normal after exercise. The pulse rate, therefore, should have dropped at least 10 beats. The quicker the heart rate drops after exercise, the better the physical condition.

Flexibility

Exercises to increase *flexibility* can be helpful in preventing lower back problems. They will allow the body to flex more and decrease back problems caused by sudden movements or twisting the body. These exercises are too numerous to attempt to list. Different exercises are necessary for different muscles and are illustrated in many good books.

Patrol officers and staff officers can do much to prevent lower back and neck disorders by following just a few simple rules. Try to reduce the sway or curvature of the spine when standing by consciously keeping the back straight. Stand when possible instead of sitting; however, long periods of standing "at attention" cause severe strain on the lower back. Long periods of standing should be done with one knee bent, preferably on a step or rail to ease the pressure on the lower back. If this cannot be done, one should occasionally get into a squatting position with one knee lower than the other. Using these suggestions will delay fatigue.

When sitting, attempt to have at least one knee higher than the hip and when possible, put feet up with knees bent. Officers in cars have a tendency to ride with the seat so far back that it creates a semi-reclining position which causes swaying of the lower back and the neck. Operate your vehicle with the seat forward enough so as to elevate the knees above the hips and thus cause the lower back to straighten. When dismounting the vehicle, swivel in the seat, and place both feet on the ground, and bend over to get out of the car.

When sleeping, you should avoid lying on your back or on your stomach as this causes swaying of the back and undue bending of the neck with resultant pressure on nerves in the spine. Sleeping should be accomplished by lying on one side with the knees drawn up which facilitates a straight-line effect on the spine. If sleep can only be accomplished on the back, pillows should be placed under the knees to elevate them enough to cause the spine to be flat on the bed.

One of the worst stresses on the back comes when you keep going after you are extremely tired. The back needs rest just as any other part of the body; if you burn the candle at both ends, the body will move from Selye's (1974) reaction stage to the exhaustion stage where, according to Selye, disks collapse and death ensues. The general rule is that proper exercise for strengthening the back is to keep loose flexibility. Constant stress causes tightening of back muscles and results in pain or a tight discomfort. Stretching exercises and sit-ups can help. Stretching exercises loosen up the back and sit-ups tighten the stomach and relieve pressure on the back.

Any back discomfort should not be disregarded as it could be a sign of big problems. When backache or pain in either or both legs or arms persists, contact your physician immediately. If back problems are corrected early, surgery or other drastic measures can be avoided.

If back problems from stress or overexertion (distress) become so serious that surgery is required, one can plan on six weeks to three months recovery time for light duty, and possibly a year to eighteen months for full recovery. Obviously, your back and the care you give it is not a minor thing.

Muscular Strength

Tests used by most police departments that have a physical fitness program are not of a type to accurately reflect an officer's physical ability to perform the necessary tasks related to his job or his physical health. The testing that is done is usually testing of strength or of weight in relation to height.

Muscular strength above normal is not as important to the police officer as the other two areas of endurance and flexibility. If the officer wants to build up muscle strength, weight lifting is one of the best methods. Caution should be used in this type of program as overdevelopment can cause loss of some of the necessary flexibility. This does not mean that muscular strength is not important. Rather *physical fitness to us means adaptability, flexibility, accompanied by reasonable physical strength.*

Physical Fitness Programs

Most departments have some type of physical testing program on a one-time basis for hiring purposes; however, it is not continued past that point. We would urge department heads to pursue a physical fitness program with some sort of incentive to keep officers active physically throughout the ranks, with variations geared toward age and tasks. It is usually assumed that rookie officers stay in shape to perform their duties, but no program is available to assure that officers do so.

Programs for patrol officers should include more physical strength, muscle and back flexibility than staff officers. Staff officers should pursue exercise aimed at strengthening the cardiovascular function-endurance. Exercises such as walking, jogging, bicycling, and swimming are especially good for this purpose, but should be done sensibly and preferably after consulting a physician especially if a long period of nonexercise has been the problem.

The officer starting an exercise program should use caution by entering the program gradually and not overexert. Overexertion can cause a heart attack or other serious illness. It is important to pace oneself so as to gradually build up one's system.

Incentive programs can be offered in the form of a punishment or reward system. Promotions or pay increases could be held up until the officer meets the standards. The officers could be offered a pay incentive for continuing a physical fitness program. No type of incentive system will work unless the officer can be motivated in some way to want to participate in the program. Educating officers and their spouses about pressures and techniques for coping with this distress might be part of the groundwork necessary to accomplish this task of personal motivation.

Another method of obtaining involvement in a physical fitness program is group participation at set times. This type of program works extremely well for recruit training classes since the recruits are all available at the same time without having to disregard other duties, but it can also be adapted for officers after graduation from recruit school. The department, for example, could assemble officers for group programs at the end of a shift and include the work in the "sweat room" as part of their job. Physical exercise is a much better approach to relaxation as opposed to drinking beer after a shift.

Lack of facilities is a problem in most police departments. There is seldom available space or money to set up a gym or exercise room. This problem could be met by furnishing the officers memberships in the YMCA or similar organizations who might even donate the memberships for publicity and good will. Another solution might be to try and obtain donated equipment if the department has available space to set up the equipment.

Any physical fitness program should be flexible enough to be tailored for the individual officer. The three areas it should cover are *endurance, flexibility* and *muscular strength*. The program should be of a type that the officer can utilize the parts of it that fit his particular needs.

In short, any physical fitness program should be designed to *fit the requirements of the police officer's job*. It should not require elaborate and expensive equipment. It should include *testing* to check the officer's physical condition and should offer an *incentive program*.

Tests to determine a police officer's physical ability to perform his job should use basic physiological measurements rather than strength tests. Heart rate and blood pressure tests are a much more accurate measurement of the officer's ability to perform the occasional physical aspects of the job. They can also indicate how one will handle stress. Physical fitness is more than just feeling or looking good—it can also be an insurance policy. An accident, an illness or an operation may fully test the resources of one's body. It is probable that the differences between a state of positive health acquired by daily walking and a state of passive existence (although one is diseased) may mean the difference between living or dying when confronted with a major illness or operation.

Diet

Another important area in which officers can minimize distress is in the area of diet. If an officer's body is likened to a car, it does not make sense to talk only about body repair without talking about the quality of gasoline—the food. Police officers are faced with a raft of "junk food" restaurants on their beats. Their accessibility coupled with the short time allotted for eating makes it easy for officers to grab a doughnut and go on. Leave the "junk food" for the junkies. White-refined sugar and flour products cause the pancreas to produce more insulin to digest the food which, in turn, causes the same bio-chemical responses in the body as a state of fright; i.e., adrenals produce more adrenalin, thyroid produces more thyroxin, heart beat is increased, etc. Alcohol, coffee, tea, cola and chocolate also affect the pancreas in a similar manner. When your body is high on "junk food" and other chemicals, the body is "worn out" and finds it hard to manufacture the needed internal bio-chemical responses to successfully aid you through the on-the-job stress situations.

To reduce stress, we recommend a low stress diet based on three rules:

1. Avoid intrusive foods like white-refined sugar and flour, alcohol, coffee, tea, chocolate, cola;

2. Minimize the factory chemicals by buying natural foods. Many ice cream products contain a form of plastic or clay. Our bodies have only 22 enzymes to digest food. None of the enzymes can handle plastics, hence these undigested particles become stored in the body as waste and clog the system;

3. Reduce the number of different foods per meal. Choose only three different food items per meal, i.e., hamburger, tomato and lettuce. Just as too many people with their demands in one day wear you out, so does having "too many different foods." Your body must consume more energy than necessary in the digestive process, leaving you less energy to function physically. If you run out of energy but still function, you place undue stress on the body.

To accomplish a low stress diet, we suggest several things. First, carry fresh fruits, vegetables, and nuts or seeds with you. Fresh fruit juices, milk, and water are all good substitutes for other more harmful drinks. Try to find a good place to eat on your beat or district that can provide more natural foods to which no chemicals (even sugars) are added. To partially offset the lack of better foods while on duty, the officer can make a special effort to eat better during off-duty hours. A note of caution: As in other drug addictions, when one withdraws from foods to which one is addicted, side effects such as headaches, irritability, and diarrhea, may become more noticable. These side effects are of short duration. Some people, in order to avoid the uncomfortableness of withdrawing from coffee, will continue to drink a cup of coffee in the morning for that "headache." If they would just endure a few days totally without coffee, they will find the headache completely disappears. When you have been riding in your patrol car through traffic, you can become gassed by the carbon monoxide and other pollutants in the air. When the demands are slower, get out of the car and walk briskly, breathing in for one count and exhaling for three counts. This will help clear your head and your cravings for "junk foods."

Conclusion

We have discussed *physical fitness* and *diet:* things you can control to prevent more distress in your lives and to help alleviate the present stress. Both fitness and diet should be included in a program of employee fitness.

How much sick leave can you afford? How much can management afford? Programs need not be expensive or time consuming. Programs should not be punitive. Have a community person come at roll call to talk about the dangers of cigarette smoking. Then *reward* the team or the shift that is able to minimize the number of packs of cigarettes per day.

Award "tough badges" to those who are able to endure the withdrawal symptoms that may include headaches, trembling hands, hunger pains, etc. Anyone can start smoking. It takes a really strong person to stop.

Physical fitness and diet are not the only means to stress reduction. They are, however, the most fundamental. Learning to exercise control over their own bodies will help to make officers healthier and happier. An individual's life may depend upon it.

Concepts to Consider

1. Identify the major stressors found in police work.

2. Describe the four levels of dysfunctional response to stress.

3. Describe the traditional ways that police management has responded to stress.

4. Justify the institution of a physical fitness program as a means of stress reduction.

5. Support the position that diet is an excellent means of reducing stress.

Selected Readings

Burgin, A. Lad, "The Management of Stress in Policing," *The Police Chief*, Vol. XLV, No. 4, April 1978, pp. 53-54.

Postulates that stress management is one mechanism through which police managers can maintain the well-being and performance capacity of a police organization's most valuable resource—its personnel.

Hageman, Mary J. C., "Occupational Stress and Marital Relationships," *Journal of Police Science and Administration*, Vol. 6, No. 4, December 1978, pp. 402-412.

The author presents the results of research that explored the interrole conflict of law officers, specifically the conflict between occupational and marital roles.

Hillgren, James S., Rebekah Bond and Sue Jones, "Primary Stressors in Police Administration and Law Enforcement," *Journal of Police Science and Administration*, Vol. 4, No. 4, December 1976, pp. 445-449.

Identifies many sources of stress that originate from within the organization and its procedures. Points out the similarity between the sources of stress identified by police officers and chief administrators.

Keller, Peter A., "A Psychological View of the Police Officer Paradox," *The Police Chief*, Vol. XLV, No. 4, April 1978, pp. 24-25.

Discusses the multiplicity of demands upon the police and the types of police organizations that have been created to respond to those demands. Considers such factors as stress, organizational structure, and discretion.

Kroes, William H., Bruce L. Margolis, and Joseph J. Hurrell, Jr., "Job Stress in Policemen," *Journal of Police Science and Administration*, Vol. 2, No. 2, June 1974, pp. 145-155.

Through interviews with 100 patrol car officers, this study has identified specific stresses under which the officers work. The most significant center around the officers' sense of professionalism.

Lester, David, "Suicide in Police Officers," *The Police Chief*, Vol. XLV, No. 4, April 1978, p. 17.

Briefly reviews investigations of suicide by police officers and points out the lack of research in this area. Suggests that one reason for limited research is due to a desire to protect the image of policemen.

Reiser, Martin, "Stress, Distress, and Adaptation in Police Work," *The Police Chief*, Vol. XLIII, No. 1, January 1976, pp. 24-27.

Traces stress research with a special emphasis on studies that apply to the police. Describes programs that can be utilized to reduce stress.

Singleton, Gary W. and John Teahan, "Effects of Job-Related Stress on the Physical and Psychological Adjustment of Police Officers," *Journal of Police Science and Administration*, Vol. 6, No. 3, September 1978, pp. 355-361.

The study indicates that police officers who experience increased physical stress on duty appear to have a higher risk for inter-personal difficulties in home life and a heightened sense of anger, suspiciousness, criticism, and social discomforts.

Chapter 9
POLICE PROFESSIONALISM

Introduction

Professionalism has long been an elusive goal of law enforcement. During the last decade considerable attention has been given to this topic, making it possible to say, without equivocation, that many police departments are on the threshold of professionalization.

The capacity and ability to move beyond this threshold is undisputable; however, there must be a concerted effort to build on the present foundation.

The embryo of a profession was conceived by the father of modern police administration, August Vollmer. He developed the first formal training school for police officers at Berkeley, California in 1908, reaching an agreement nine years later with the University of California whereby on-the-job experience could be combined with an academic education. The course included technical subjects along with liberal arts classes, thus leading to the creation, in 1933, of a criminology major. August Vollmer then joined the University staff as a Professor of Police Administration, it should be noted that he subsequently held a similar position at the University of Chicago.

Sparked by the success of Vollmer's efforts, educational institutions in various parts of the nation established programs leading to a major in criminology; but generally speaking, the growth of educational programs for law enforcement has been slow and sporadic.

The President's Crime Commission emphasized the need for advanced education when it stated that, "the quality of police service will not significantly improve until higher educational requirements are established for its personnel. . . ." The complexity of the police task is as great as that of any other profession, and the performance of this task requires more than physical prowess and common sense:

> It is nonsense to state or to assume that the enforcement of the law is so simple that it can be done best by those unencumbered by a study of the liberal arts. The man who goes into our streets in hopes of regulating, directing or controlling human behavior must be armed with more than a gun and the ability to perform mechanical movements in response to a situation. Such men as these engage in the difficult, complex and important business of human behavior. Their intellectual armament—so long restricted to the minimum—must be no less than their physical prowess and protection.[1]

"The need for highly educated personnel was recognized as early as 1931 in the report of the Wickersham Commission. But despite the admonition of that commission to improve low entrance standards, educational requirements remain minimal in most departments."

In 1961, a survey conducted of over three hundred police departments showed that 24 percent of those departments had no minimum educational prerequisite, while less than 1 percent required any level of college preparation.[2]

In one region of the country, the New England States, over 72 percent of the departments surveyed did not even require their applicants to have high school diplomas.[3]

"Although minimum educational requirements have not prevented some persons with higher academic achievement from pursuing careers in law enforcement, these exceptions are few in number. In a survey con-

---

1. Quinn Tamm, "A Change for the Better" in *The Police Chief* (Washington: I.A.C.P., 1962), p. 5.
2. George W. O'Connor, *Survey of Selection Methods* (Washington: I.A.C.P., 1962).
3. Ibid.

ducted of 6,200 officers in 1964, only 30.3 percent had taken one or more college courses and only 7.3 percent possessed a college degree.[4] A 1966 survey of over 5,700 police officers employed by police agencies in the metropolitan area of Detroit revealed that over 75 percent of these officers had not attended college.[5] In the Metropolitan Detroit survey, it was further shown that nearly 13 percent of the officers had not received high school diplomas. In many departments, particularly in New England and Southern States, a majority of the officers are not high school graduates. For example, a survey of one Connecticut department revealed that fifty-three of the eighty-five sworn officers had not completed high school."[6]

The importance of advanced education is also emphasized in Stephen Kennedy's remarks:

> Sworn personnel, who, in various unpredictable situations, are required to make difficult judgments, should possess a sound knowledge of society and human behavior. This can best be attained through advanced education:
>
> A superior officer of any police department should certainly be conversant with the structure of our government and its philosophies. He must be well grounded in sociology, criminology, and human relations in order to understand the ramifications of the problems which confront him daily. He must understand what makes people act as they do and what impact his actions in the performance of duty will have on them.[7]

A Bureau of the Census survey revealed the following about the level of education of the Nation's population:

(1) Of the 127 million people 20 years of age and older, 60 percent are high school graduates;

(2) Of the white collar workers between ages 25-64, 87 percent are high school graduates;

(3) Of the blue collar workers between the ages of 25-64, 49 percent are high school graduates;

(4) Among persons between the ages of 20-29 (prime recruiting ages for

---

4. George W. O'Connor and Nelson A. Watson, *Juvenile Delinquency and Youth Crime: The Police Role* (Washington: I.A.C.P., 1964), p. 79.

5. Michigan State University, Institute for Community Development, *Police Training in the Detroit Metropolitan Region: Recommendations for a Regional Approach* (Detroit: The Metropolitan Fund, 1966), p. 69.

6. *Police and Fire Services of the City of Meriden, Connecticut* (Chicago: Public Administration Service, 1962), p. 121.

7. Statement of Stephen Kennedy, former Commissioner of Police, cited in Franklin M. Kreml, "The Role of Colleges and Universities in Police Management," *The Police Yearbook* (Washington: I.A.C.P., 1966), p. 40.

the police), 80 percent are high school graduates or have attended college;

(5) Among persons between the ages of 20-24 who have completed high school, nearly 45 percent have completed at least 1 year of college.[8]

Additionally, statistics obtained from the Department of Health, Education, and Welfare indicate that the national education picture is not static. During the decade of the 1960s, the proportion of the adult population that completed a high school education rose from 43 percent to 60 percent. During the same period, the proportion of high school graduates who enrolled in college rose from 50.1 percent to 59.8 percent and it is anticipated that it will reach 65 percent by 1979.

These educational statistics clearly indicate that the high school level of education is a questionable standard for the selection of police officers. The high school level of education no longer serves as an index of superior educational achievement; it is common throughout the nation.

The consequences of such a selection standard in an era of increasing educational achievement are discussed in the American Bar Association's draft of *The Urban Police Function*. In this publication, E. Bittner is quoted as saying that the net result of maintaining a high school requirement in a period of rising educational achievement is that police forces are drawn overwhelmingly from those in the third educational and social quartile of the population. Yet many leading police and criminal justice administrators and other government officials have urged that the best human resources be recruited for the police service.[9]

The high school education requirement has prevailed for many years. Initially, it served to identify individuals who possessed a superior level of education and often those with above-average mental ability. However, this is not as true today as it was immediately after World War II. Department of Health, Education, and Welfare statistics show that less than one-half of the 17-year-old population had completed high school in 1946. In 1969, this figure had risen to over 78 percent. Obviously, high school graduation has become a less significant factor in hiring personnel. The police once employed only persons with an above-average education; today they are employing persons with an average level of education that is fast becoming an inferior level.

There are those, however, who argue that while the population has

---

8. U.S. Department of Commerce, Bureau of the Census, *Population Characteristics, Educational Attainment*. Washington, D.C.: Government Printing Office, March, 1971. For more recent educational studies see: U.S. Department of Commerce, *Social Indicators 1976*, Washington, D.C.: Government Printing Office, December 1977.

9. American Bar Association Project on Standards for Criminal Justice. *Standards Relating to the Urban Police Function*, March, 1972.

caught up with and surpassed the police educationally, police work still does not require education beyond high school. If they are referring to the use of police officers to direct traffic, issue parking tickets, conduct permit inspections, perform clerical work, and drive tow trucks, perhaps they are correct. However, in more progressive police agencies such routine tasks are rapidly being turned over to civilian employees, paraprofessionals, and other governmental agencies. Thus, police officers are left with their more essential task which includes social control in a period of increasing social turmoil, preservation of our constitutional guarantees, and exercise of the broadest range of discretion—sometimes involving life and death decisions—of any government service. The need for police officers who are intelligent, articulate, mature, and knowledgable about social and political conditions is apparent.

People with these traits, according to Charles Saunders in *Upgrading the American Police*, are more likely to be found on college and university campuses. Those who possess the requisite personal characteristics are more likely to pursue an advanced level of education, and a college education develops and imparts the requisite level of knowledge. Saunders further comments on the value of a college education:

> The reasons advanced for college education for the police are essentially the same as those used to justify higher education as preparation for any other career. They rest more on faith than on fact. Evidence does not firmly establish the necessity for 4 years of college for entry into any field.... Nevertheless, the worth of a general collegiate education for all youth of intelligence and ambition is unquestioned and the role of the 4-year liberal arts college in providing it is generally accepted as essential.[10]

David Geary, the former chief of police of Ventura, California, instituted a 4-year college degree requirement in 1966, with appreciable benefits: fewer personnel complaints against college-educated police officers, a lower rate of personnel turnover, and an overall reduction of 3 percent in the crime rate.[11]

A 1972 study of the New York City Police, *Police Background Characteristics and Performance*, revealed that men with at least 1 year of college were very good performers and had fewer civilian complaints than average. The men who had college degrees demonstrated even better on-the-job performance; they had low incidence of all types of misconduct—except harassment, on which they were average—and took less sick leave. General speaking, the older, better educated officer received fewer

10. Charles B. Saunders, *Upgrading the American Police* (Washington, D.C.: Brookings Institution, 1970).

11. David Patrick Geary, "College Educated Cops—Three Years Later," *Police Chief*, August, 1970.

civilian complaints than the younger, less educated officer.[12]

These findings were similar to the results of the 1968 Chicago study, *Psychological Assessment of Patrolman Qualifications in Relation to Field Performance*, which revealed that the highest rated group of tenured officers were those with significantly higher levels of education.[13]

Raymond Witte, former director of the evening division of Loyola University of New Orleans, in *Police Chief Magazine* reported on an experiment conducted in an anonymous police agency. Two similar patrol divisions were involved, one staffed with college-educated police officers, the other with officers with less education. The 6-month study revealed higher morale among the college-educated officers, less time off in the experimental division, and quicker response time.[14]

Reports in the *Journal of Criminal Law, Criminology, and Police Science* have indicated that college-educated police officers are not only significantly less authoritarian than noncollege-educated police officers, but also less authoritarian than college graduates in other fields.[15]

The National Advisory Commission on Criminal Justice Standards and Goals in 1973 stated that to insure the selection of personnel with the qualifications to perform police duties properly, every police agency should establish the following entry-level educational requirements:

(1) Every police agency should require immediately, as a condition of initial employment, the completion of at least 1 year of education (30 semester units) at an accredited college or university. Otherwise qualified police applicants who do not satisfy this condition, but who have earned a high school diploma or its equivalent, should be employed under a contract requiring completion of the educational requirement within 3 years of initial employment.

(2) Every police agency should, no later than 1975, require as a condition of initial employment the completion of at least 2 years of education (60 semester units) at an accredited college or university.

(3) Every police agency should, no later than 1978, require as a condition of initial employment the completion of at least 3 years of education (90 semester units) at an accredited college or university.

(4) Every police agency should, no later than 1982, require as a condi-

---

12. Bernard Cohen and Jan M. Chaihen, *Police Background Characteristics and Performance: Summary* (New York: Rand Institute), May, 1972.

13. Melany E. Baehr, and others. *Psychological Assessment of Patrolman Qualifications in Relation to Field Performance* (Washington, D.C.: Government Printing Office), November, 1968.

14. Raymond P. Witte, "The Dumb Cop," *Police Chief*, January, 1969.

15. Alexander Smith, and others. "Authoritarianism in Police College Students and Non-Police College Students," *Journal of Criminal Law, Criminology and Police Science*, Vol. 59, No. 3 (September, 1968).

tion of initial employment the completion of at least 4 years of education (120 semester units or a baccalaureate degree) at an accredited college or university.[16]

"Important as education and an appropriate climate are to the establishment of a profession there are a number of additional considerations which must be met. The United States Bureau of the Census has established the following prerequisites: 'a professional worker is (a) one who performs advisory, administrative or research work which is based upon the established principles of a profession or science, and which requires scientific or technical training equivalent to that represented by graduation from a college or university of recognized standing, or (b) one who performs work which is based upon science or art, and which work requires for its performance an acquaintance with the established facts, or principles, or methods gained through academic study or through extensive practical experience, one or both'."

Amplification of this definition was provided by J. A. Greening who listed the following elements of a profession:

(1) An organized body of knowledge, constantly augmented and refined, with special techniques based thereon.

(2) Facilities for formal training in this body of knowledge and procedure.

(3) Recognized qualification for membership in, and identification with, the profession.

(4) An organization which includes a substantial number of the members qualified to practice the profession and to exercise an influence on the maintenance of professional *standards.*

(5) A code of ethics which, in general, defines the relations of the members of the profession to the public and to other practitioners within the group and normally recognizes an *obligation* to render services on other than *exclusively economic considerations.*

Professionalization is accomplished through:

(1) Prescribed course of study, standardized and geared to one another in high schools, colleges, and universities.

(2) Application of prescribed methods in practice teaching, reading, briefing, etc.

(3) Post-graduate courses, prescribed and administered if a specialized field is selected.

(4) Internship for application of theory to practice for the purpose of developing skill.

(5) Acknowledgment and acceptance of self-imposed ethical stan-

---

16. National Advisory Commission on Criminal Justice Standards and Goals, *Police* (Washington: U.S. Government Printing Office, January 23, 1973), pp. 369-371.

dards of professional practice and personal conduct.

(6) Examination to determine fitness to practice and enter the profession.

(7) Continuous study and research for improvement and advancement of professional techniques and their application within the profession.[17]

The definition of a profession and the method of attaining that status provides a yardstick for measuring the present position of the police in terms of a standard of excellence. Outstandingly evident are a number of criteria that must be accomplished, including:

(1) Mandatory educational standards.

(2) Lateral transfer.

(3) Transferability of retirement credits.

(4) Ethical standards.

(5) Career development program.

(6) Certification of eligible professionals.

(7) Specialized literature.

(8) Continuous research.

*

The process of professionalism is in its incipience, and its attainment will only be possible if the police respond to the tasks at hand with zeal and determination. There are numerous stumbling-blocks that must be overcome; the three articles selected for this chapter discuss some of the changes that will have to occur before law enforcement can achieve professional status.

---

17. J. A. Greening, "Report of the Committee on Professionalization of Police Service," *Yearbook of the I.A.C.P.* 1938-39, p. 20, cited in V. A. Leonard and H. W. More, *Police Organization and Management, Third Edition* (Brooklyn: The Foundation Press, Inc., 1978, pp. 658-659.

20. POLICE PROFESSIONALISM: A NEW LOOK AT AN OLD TOPIC

RICHARD V. MECUM

The Police Chief, Vol. XLVI, August 1979. Reprinted by permission.

The ways man has endeavored to protect himself and his property is a truly interesting and fascinating story. Traces are to be found in every organized society of some system of rules for the maintenance of peace and order. In the days of the Pharaohs, as in modern times, a group of men were needed to carry out the laws of society.[1]

In 1829, Sir Robert Peel, then prime minister of England, introduced into Parliament a bill providing for the organization of the professional police force, later to become known as the famed Scotland Yard. This was the first real attempt to professionalize police. American police departments today can trace their origins back to the ideas of Sir Robert Peel.

The view of police work has changed very little since the 1800s. An early student of police administration wrote,

> It is certainly not necessary and some have even maintained that it is not desirable that police patrolmen be men of large intellectual ability... (It is) extremely unlikely that, for the present at least, any considerable number of men who have enjoyed even a secondary education will turn to the police business... The most important asset of the ideal policeman is unquestionably his physical constitution and condition.[2]

While this idea was expressed several years ago, it is still shared by many citizens as well as policemen today.

Despite the belief of some, the police service has changed, and by its very nature, is continuing to change. There is a nationwide awareness today that the police officer of the 1970s is concerned with problems significantly different from those of his predecessor. But, to date, efforts to improve significantly local law enforcement agencies have been met with frustration. Only a few departments can point to any real breakthrough in this effort.

Change in police work has been made with the idea of improving the

---

1. V. A. Leonard, *The Police of the 20th Century* (Brooklyn: The Foundation Press, Inc. 1964), p. 1.
2. Leonhaul Felix Fuld, *Police Administration* (G. P. Putnam's Sons, 1909), pp. 90-91.

overall efficiency of the police, which would lead to the professionalization of police. But what is professionalism? How have other occupations acquired the social recognition of being "professional"? Are efforts to professionalize police going in the right direction? It is not intended to try and cover the many obstacles in the path toward the professionalization of police in this one short paper. It is, however, intended to discuss the elements of a profession, a map, a guide toward the desired outcome. Just how did medicine and law and the other professions of our society become professions? Can we relate these thoughts to the police occupation?

. . . .

A task or a job does not suddenly become a profession. In tracing the history of several professions, definite patterns can be established. Certain professional elements generally precede other professional elements. As a child must learn to crawl before walking and be capable of walking before running, jobs must also pass certain criteria before being considered a profession. As a result it becomes possible to determine a time sequence to the elements of a profession.

Time/Element Sequence

The contrast between planned and accidental entry into job a is depicted in *Figure 1*. As a job progresses and acquires the various elements of professionalism, the number of accidental entrants into the job decreases. The ultimate takes place at the Time/Element Sequence (TES) #7. It is at this point when all entry into the job is planned. An example of this is the

Figure 1—Time/Element Sequence and Linear Progression of the Task Development Towards a Profession

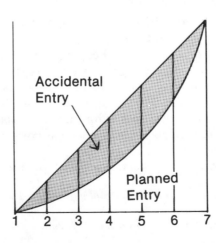

person entering dentistry. An individual desiring to become a dentist must first successfully complete a four-year college program involving biology and chemistry courses while maintaining a grade point of at least 3.5 out of a possible 4.0. The competition is becoming much stiffer as many of the prospective dentists have completed their undergraduate studies with a 4.0, or nearly a 4.0 average. A four-year course of study in dentistry must also be completed and with the emphasis still on good grades and application procedures. After all the study and work involved in successfully completing eight years of school, the individual must now pass a state licensing examination and once successful, often he must go into debt to purchase the equipment necessary to perform in his occupation. It is indeed unlikely for an individual today to enter dentistry by accident. Can the same be said for police work?

Time/Element Sequence #1—The task need recognition stage. As shown in *Figure 1* TES #1 is the beginning of a job. The job begins to take shape as people realize the need for someone to actively perform various duties. The total job concept is far from being understood at this point; however, the basic job idealogy begins here. Law enforcement history reflects this, for as society began to regulate itself through laws, it became evident that the laws were of little value without enforcement. While societies have always had some kind of law, the key to establishing predictability within society is the enforcement of those laws. Thus, we can find law enforcement officers as early as 1947 B.C. enforcing the laws established by the Code of Hammurabi.

Time/Element Sequence #2—The definition of expected behavior stage #1. Though society realized the need for enforcement of their laws, little was known of the actual tasks involved in such a job. Because of the lack of a format, the first person to take a new job made that job for himself. It was up to these early experimenters to define the tasks and training needs. The lack of training facilities for a new job brings about the implementation of on-the-job-training and apprenticeship programs.

Training through apprenticeship and testing at the time of admittance to full membership were characteristic of the guild system. In the Middle Ages, surgeons and apothecaries, no more and no less than other vocations organized in this way, were thus trained and tested.[3] As the apprenticeship process continues, the beginnings of a small cadre of semi-skilled persons develops. With the advancement of knowledge and the raising of standards, the content of the courses of theoretical training will greatly increase.[4] Nowadays, apprenticeship is confined to practical instruction;

3. A. M. Carr-Sanders and P. A. Wilson *The Professions* (Oxford at the Clarendon Press, 1933), p. 307.

4. Ibid., p. 375.

and if there are no institutions in which the pupil can learn the theory, he must do so by private study.[5] Thus, apprenticeship is steadily losing ground before the universities and other training institutions.

Time/Element Sequence #3—The definition of expected behavior #2. Persons on the job during this time are beginning to develop and collect a common body of knowledge. They are determining the nature of the job, and the job elements are beginning to be understood. Information about the job begins to be collected and perhaps a job manual is prepared. *Figure 1* indicates the number of persons entering the job on a planned basis is on the increase while accidental entry decreases.

Time/Element Sequence #4—The plan of study stage. The incumbents of the job are beginning to develop a "plan of study" to prepare future job entries as well as those already on the job. This is accomplished through guidance manuals, seminars, local newsletters, or simply an exchange of information between two persons doing the job. Education begins to play an important role as police training schools and police academies are developed to reach various new and improved methods of job techniques. Training for the job begins to become formalized as it is introduced into the public education system.

The advancement of a combination of education and training results in society viewing the job more closely. As the appeal of the job increases, there is an increase of planned entry into the job's labor force. Federal and large metropolitan police organizations, for several years now, have experienced large numbers of applicants for each police position available. At the same time, the smaller agencies are having difficulties in filling job vacancies with competent applicants. To say that education and training are the only reasons for the discrepancies between the larger and the smaller agencies would be in error; however, education and training are found to be direct components of professionalism.

Time/Element Sequence #5—The restriction stage. As a result of society's increased recognition of the job, the quality of recruits is established as a primary concern. Usually an organization or association is formed, and the organization or association does the restricting. In 1852, lawyers began restricting entry into their ranks with the Council of Legal Education, requiring that individuals pass examinations held by that body before being called before the bar and accepted to practice law. In recent years, several of the state's legislatures have enacted laws to provide for police training councils. These councils are generally responsible for restricting access of applicants into the police area, studying the duties and performances required in police work, and advancing law enforcement toward a more professional stature.

---

5. Ibid., p. 317.

During this time/element sequence, the job makes an impact on colleges and universities. There are several interesting comparisons which can be drawn to illustrate the close tie that exists between education and the professions. The most commonly identified professions of medicine and law require extensive education.

While some may disagree with defining a mortician or a barber as a professional, both require licensing by the state and both require more education than most police officers must have. In some states, barbers are required to attend a barber college for one full year, pass the state examination, and go through a two-year period of apprenticeship. In order to be qualified to embalm the dead, the mortician must have the equivalent of an associate's degree, one year of a professional mortuary school, and serve one year in resident training before he may apply for the state board examination.

Education is an integral part of gaining the status of "professionalism," and if the police are to become professional, they must accept the requirements of some formal, higher education as a minimum standard for their occupation.

Time/Element Sequence #6—The control stage. Problems begin to develop as people who are not prepared for the job try to enter the field anyway. Thus, the restricting becomes more intense. A form of licensing is required of persons desiring to enter the job. The control is exerted by the state along with an association. There is also a noticeable increase in the public's requirement of accreditation or licensing of the person(s) entering the job.

Time/Element Sequence #7—The code of ethics stage. Thus far a system has been described which is designed to exclude altogether from the professions those who fail to pass certain preliminary tests. Such tests must inevitably be somewhat formal in character and take into consideration intellectual attainments rather than competence and integrity under conditions of actual responsibility. However, the quality of the service rendered is of the deepest concern to the client. He places his health and his fortune in the hands of his professional advisors, and he entrusts them with confidences of an intimate and personal kind. He is interested, therefore, not only in the technical, but also in what may be called the moral quality of the service.[6]

Enforcing Professionalism

It is unnecessary to study the charter or memorandum of every association, since they are very much alike. The more important unregistered

---

6. A. M. Carr-Sanders and P. A. Wilson, *The Professions* (Oxford at the Clarendon Press, 1933), p. 394.

professions have chosen the more important registered professions as their model, and have set out to penalize moral offenses, and not so much technical inefficiency. Chemists and druggists are examples of professions where people can be released from their positions for violations of technical procedures. The civil servants, such as police, are liable to be dismissed at any time on any ground, and are subject to maintain a standard technical and moral competence. While observance of moral standards is of the utmost importance at present in police work, emphasis on the technical aspects in the police field appears to be on the increase. In the near future, we may find police officers being released from their job for the lack of proper technical efficiency as well as for the lack of proper moral conduct.

In 1957 the International Association of Chiefs of Police adopted a Code of Ethics for police. The Code is designed to provide police with a guide for patterning their professional behavior; however, in most professions there is the power to exclude from their ranks those who fail to conform to certain standards of conduct. While individual police departments may enforce their own departmental rules and regulations, these criteria cannot be brought to bear upon another police agency that does not have or does not enforce its own rules and regulations. Within the recognized professions such as medicine, dentistry, and law, an organization or board has been formed and given the authority to enforce the standards as set forth within their code of ethics. Punishment for performance considered contrary to the ideals set forth in their code of ethics is also decided upon by the organization or board.

A statewide police organization designed to represent all police in the state concerning the enforcement of a police code of ethics would require formulation by the state's legislature. This concept is not intended to punish a police officer twice for the same incorrect conduct. The strongest action the state organization could take would be to suspend or cancel a peace officer's state certification. Such action would prohibit an officer from performing police duties within that state for a period of time determined by the organization.

The seven stages of professionalism discussed above have taken a job from its conceptual beginning to a highly skilled and recognized profession. Time/element sequence #7 is not the end of the pursuit of professionalism. The professions are continuing to increase the requirements on individuals desiring to enter their professional ranks. More selective course requirements in college along with higher grades are evident.

Compensation

Generally, when the topic of professionalism for police is discussed by the peace officers themselves, money is also discussed simultaneously. The peace officer sometimes feels he should be compensated for his professional endeavors simultaneously with his professional actions; however, this has not been the case with the recognized professions of today. The increased compensation occurs after the attainment of the desired professional goals and public recognition of the professional advancements.

An example of this can be seen when comparing urban and rural police agencies. The large urban police departments, such as Los Angeles, Chicago, Philadelphia, and New York, have for a number of years supported and provided for police training and police training facilities for their peace officers. During this same period of time, the police agencies of rural America were receiving little if any police training. The urban communities are now beginning to recognize the professional accomplishments made by their police organizations and are compensating them accordingly. At the same time, the rural communities do not view their peace officers as being anything close to professional. They feel it takes very little skill to be a police officer, and the police are compensated accordingly.

For compensation of police to be increased to a professional level, the police must be considered totally as professionals. When the professional status of doctors is discussed, all the doctors in the country are considered with little or no thought given as to their location. A doctor in a rural area is as much a professional as the doctor in an urban setting. States providing law enforcement officers with equal accessibility to training, large and small agencies alike, are encouraging professionalized qualities of training throughout the state.

Several law enforcement agencies in the United States have demonstrated an advancement in their professional accomplishments and have obtained time/element sequence #6 while other agencies remain at time/element sequences #3 and #4. The opportunities for peace officer professionalization have increased considerably over the past few years. A greater attendance of law enforcement training is more prevalent now than at any other time in law enforcement history. The problems faced by law enforcement officers today are extremely complex and go beyond the skills required of his predecessor. It would appear, from all indications that today's law enforcement officer is on the verge of turning his job into a true profession.

21. OVERCOMING OBSTACLES TO PROFESSIONALISM

CARL F. LUTZ

The Police Chief, Vol. XXXV, September 1968. Reprinted by permission.

Much has been written in recent years concerning the vital need to improve local law enforcement, increase the compensation of police officers, and professionalize the police service. The President's Crime Commission reports have sharpened the focus on the need and have detailed the requirements for meeting it. This article summarizes the needs and the objectives, describes some of the obstacles to meeting the objectives, and suggests practical means whereby the obstacles can be minimized and immediate progress can be made toward major improvements in the police service.

The Changing Police Job

The police service has changed and is changing in its very nature. There is now a nationwide awareness that the police officer is concerned with problems radically different from those which concerned his predecessor.

Increased concern with the civil rights of all citizens, including criminals, has resulted in the need for each police officer to be highly trained in the legal authorities under which he operates and to be highly skilled in scientific detection. In the words of a veteran Manhattan detective, the newly defined rights of suspects "of necessity, make us resort to the sciences."

The requirements and complexities of the police function also increase as our social complex changes—that is, as we become increasingly conscious of poverty, mental illness, unemployment, racial problems, and other social ills. The police department is often the only governmental agency available twenty-four hours a day, seven days a week, to which people can turn for help in family disputes, handling problems with landlords and neighbors, resolving difficulties with youths, and mediating disputes among racial and special interest groups. In many respects and in rapidly increasing numbers of instances, the patrolman of today is assuming a dynamic role that in earlier times was played by the family patriarch or ward boss. Cast in this role, the police officer is increasingly expected to exercise independent judgment, discretion, sociological and psychological skills in coping with some of the most complex social problems of our times.

TIME magazine has commented that while all this may produce better policemen, it also will require far higher pay than many communities have yet faced up to. The need exists, in this period, for a very high level of skillful performance on the part of law enforcement personnel in an area fraught with social unrest and legal technicalities—for the manner in which many of these problems are ultimately resolved depends in large measure upon the degree of public confidence and respect earned by the individual patrolman in the initial action he takes. The demands on every police officer to meet this test are severe.

Nationally recognized law enforcement agencies state that the results of recent self-security by the police service and the implementation of the findings are gaining momentum throughout the country. One of the major results has been the trend toward more diversified police organization in which an increasing number of auxiliary functions are being performed by individuals less well-trained than police officers have to be, and in which the police officer is emerging as a professional law enforcer, equipped with a thorough knowledge of criminal and civil law and its intricate processes, skilled in scientific detection, and trained in human relations.

In the recent past, truly professional law enforcement positions were found only in federal agencies and a few in state and some large city governments. In these times the most serious and wide-spread law enforcement problems exist at local levels. The increase in crime on the streets has made it necessary for all local governments to face up to many more new and serious problems of law enforcement than they have ever before encountered. Local police, even in small suburban and rural towns, have suddenly found themselves confronted with extremely difficult problems in the areas of civil rights, interpretation of constitutional rights of the individual, protest demonstrations, and the growing philosophy of civil disobedience and resistance to law and order.

Recent acts of violence and arson by mobs and individuals have created a national emergency. Hence there is a sudden realization by most local law enforcement agencies that they must now strive for standards of employment and performance at least as high as those in the federal professional law enforcement agencies.

The local police officer is part of the judicial system which includes many professional positions in the courts, the prosecutors' office, the probation departments and in the penal institutions. Almost all of these positions have higher professional requirements than those of law enforcement officers. However, the local police officer has the closest and most sensitive relationships with the community. He has responsibilities that none of the other people in the judicial system are directly involved with—the *maintenance* of law and order, the *prevention* of crime, and the *courteous* and *helpful* treatment of all the many non-criminal citizens with which he has frequent contact. An increasing consciousness of the role of the police officer in dealing with and protecting the ordinary citizen, and gaining his respect, is a significant element of the changing police job.

What Kind of Man for Police Work?

The changing nature of the police job requires a major swing from "brawn" to "brain." The complexities and the broad scope of law enforcement activities today make it extremely difficult for a person without a high school education to be an effective law enforcement officer. Recent experience has shown that the greater amount of higher education that a police officer has, the greater the possibility that he will carry out his duties successfully. In part, this is because the greater his educational attainment, the more likely it is that he will have the social and other skills necessary to communicate effectively with persons of various cultural, economic and ethnic backgrounds. Following are pertinent excerpts from *Police Compensation*, a research study for the President's Commission on Crime and Criminal Justice by William F. Danielson, Director of Personnel, City of Berkeley, California.

> The educational standard for law enforcement of less than high school will seriously affect the quality of police recruits who will be attracted to the position. There is a kind of "Gresham's Law" which operates in recruitment standards. The recruiting agency tends to attract in greatest quantity the persons who barely meet the minimum standards for the position. Persons whose educational attainment exceeds the minimum standards for a position will not often apply for a position which requires lesser standards of education. If there is no educational requirement to enter the police department such as in the case in a number of eastern cities and states, the attraction of the police job for the high school graduate or the young man with college education is much less than if a high school minimum is required. . . .
>
> The police officer should have the mental capacity to learn a wide variety of subjects quickly and correctly. He must continue his learning and training throughout his active police career. He must have the ability and the desire to adapt his thinking to technological and sociological changes which affect his law enforcement work. . . .

The effectiveness of a police officer today more than ever before, because of the changing nature of police work, requires that he be held in high respect by the community. Therefore, his integrity must be of the highest order. The acceptance of petty gifts or bribes and special favors, once more or less accepted as part of the compensation of the grossly underpaid policeman of yesteryear, is no longer acceptable in today's society. Even where it may be condoned or not considered a criminal act, whether it be looked at with humor or scorn, it reduces the effectiveness of the police officer by reducing the respect of the community. This adversely affects the cooperative spirit of the citizenry, which is so necessary to effective law enforcement.

What Does It Take to Recruit This Man?

A reasonable starting salary is the most important, but certainly not the only requirement for the effective recruitment of the right kind of man for the changing police job. The "going rate" for the average high school graduate in the community is the absolute minimum that must be provided. In determining that going rate, it must be taken into account that in a period of relatively full employment the high school graduate has worked for a few years after graduation before he achieves the minimum age of eligibility for police service. If a better than average man is to be obtained, it must be recognized that he will have progressed in salary by perhaps as much as 15 percent since he first went to work. It also must be taken into account that the young man who has had a year in college would be worth, and might well expect, at least 5 percent more than one who had not. Each additional year of college study that might be desired would require correspondingly higher starting salaries. If, as recommended by Mr. Danielson, applicants with intelligence among the upper 25 percent are desired, the starting rate must be even higher to attract them.

If scientific selection procedures, which are of extreme importance, are effective, sufficient applicants must be obtained to allow for rejections resulting from character reference, criminal record checks and psychiatric examinations, as well as other tests of competence. Mr. Forbes McCann, a recognized specialist in recruitment and selection, suggests a rule he calls the "tenfer" rule—ten applicants for each vacancy you expect to fill with a highly qualified person. In order to have enough applicants, another 5 percent had best be added to the entrance rate as previously determined.

Of course fringe benefits and working conditions are important, too. However, most police benefit packages are already from 30 to 40 percent of salary, including liberal pension privileges, and the police work week is almost universally down to 40 hours, frequently with premium pay for overtime work.

Of next importance is career opportunity. If the young police applicant is not smart enough to look at his long range opportunity for salary advancement and promotion in a police career, he is not smart enough to be on the force. If he finds that after a few years of modest salary advancement as a patrolman he might have to wait for years more to gain a promotion, primarily on the basis of seniority, and that even if he eventually makes chief, the salary structure is so compressed that such high responsibility is inadequately recognized, he is bound to be disinterested in the job. If he calculates anticipated career earnings over thirty years of police service and finds there is likelihood that it may be thirty times the annual maximum salary of a patrolman, or at best a sergeant, and compares this to what his total earnings might be in other occupations, he will certainly look elsewhere in spite of good starting salary.

Regardless of the salary in higher ranks, if the applicant feels that there is no program to help him develop and qualify for those ranks, other than by gaining long years of service, he will also be disinterested, particularly if he is one of the bright young men that the police force needs to ultimately fill the commanding officer positions of tomorrow. The customary road to command must be changed.

Lastly, men of the type needed by our police service today will hardly be attracted by yesterday's typical recruiting method—examination announcements posted on the city hall bulletin board. An energetic, indirect and direct recruiting program will be required.

Indirect recruiting—the general promotion of the police service as a rewarding career, of course, requires that it be made so. The image of the average municipal police department can and must be significantly improved. Corruption, well on the road to elimination in most of our cities, must be completely eradicated, and the people must be convinced that it is. Added emphasis must be given to internal investigation by the establishment of strong intelligence units reporting directly to the chief or deputy chief. The police department must clean its own house. This means not only ferreting out the few bad apples that are found in every barrel, but taking a modern scientific management approach to improvement of its organization, administration, equipment, and enforcement and detection techniques. Much useful help in this regard can be obtained from the International Association of Chiefs of Police, from some of the universities, and from private consulting firms which have specialized in local government operations.

In the direct recruiting effort, recourse must be taken to all modern techniques of positive recruitment with which most public personnel directors are now familiar. In this effort, a new attention should be directed to minority groups, not only because an integrated police force has proven to be a more effective force, particularly in the area of civil disturbances, but because here is a source of well educated and intelligent candidates for the police job that has been overlooked before. There is no need for lowering of standards in the hope that this will increase the employment of persons from underprivileged minority groups. Mr. Danielson, in the paper previously referred to, closes an interesting section on the recruitment of minority group persons for law enforcement positions with the following paragraph:

> The causes of racial justice, equal employment, and law enforcement are not well served by proposals which would lower the necessary standards for entrance into police work. Neither are these causes well served if unnecessary standards are imposed for entrance into police work (such as restrictive residence requirements). If young minority group men are to be recruited into law enforcement, there is no substitute for having a salary and compensation for police which is highly competitive, for requiring unnecessary standards to enter the field of law enforcement, and to use recruiting methods which will reach all sections of the community.

What Does It Take to Keep Him on the Force?

Some of the things already described which will attract good people to the police service will also keep them in it, particularly a good career development program which consciously plans the careers of young policemen with intelligence and high potential. Maintaining and improving a good image of the police department will also help. The provision of a good retirement plan, already available to most police officers, will naturally reduce turnover. However, the most important single element is probably the opportunity for development and promotion. In many police departments, the organization is such that as few as one in four patrolmen has an opportunity for promotion.

The typical police department has a low promotional ratio for one or both of the following reasons. First, there are usually too few ranks in the organization structure—only one broad class of Patrolman, then Sergeant, Lieutenant and/or Captain, and Chief. Within these broad classes or ranks there are substantial differences in individual position values which normally would result in two or more distinct levels of compensation among the positions included in the class. This is particularly true in the typical rank of patrolman.

The other common deficiency is an inadequate number of supervisory positions resulting in spans of control that are too broad. A precinct shift commander, often a lieutenant, or even a sergeant in the smaller cities, may have a large number of men scattered over a fairly broad geographical section of the city. Even fifteen or twenty men on scattered beats afford a situation where supervision can at best be extremely periodical and limited. In contrast, a fire company, consisting of from three to five men, always has a fire lieutenant or fire captain directly supervising the company.

These deficiencies in many police organizations reduce the effectiveness of the department through inadequate supervision, minimize incentive, and, of course, result in limited opportunity for promotion from the rank and file.

Last but not least, the intelligent young policeman with potential must be given the guidance and incentive, through the effective execution of a career development program, to develop to his maximum level of competence. This requires that he be afforded opportunity to gain additional education at minimum cost to himself, both in the form of adequate in-service training programs and through the facilities of outside educational institutions. Once having completed his recruit training, a police officer has practically no opportunity for educational development on the job. If he is to be expected to develop to his fullest potential on his own time for the benefit of the department (as well as his own), the minimum incentive that can be supplied must be the payment by the employer of the costs of the training. In addition, there must be tangible reward for educational accomplishment; for example, eligibility for more rapid promotion, extra in-grade salary increments, or cash bonuses.

Obstacles to Progress

To date efforts to significantly improve local law enforcement agencies through the upgrading and professionalization of their personnel have been fraught with frustrations and externally imposed limitations. Only a very few departments can point to any real breakthrough in this effort. There are several obstacles to progress to be discussed here.

There is an inherent rigidity in many civil service laws and regulations which inhibits or even prohibits the exercise of some of the generally accepted practices of modern personnel management. The old concept of equality in treatment of civil service personnel fails to recognize that people are not equal in educational background, intelligence or other personal attributes, and absolutely equal treatment only encourages mediocrity in the public service.

To name a few examples of inflexibility in civil service regulations which are impediments to progress:

(1) The requirement for promotional examinations in any case where there is a higher maximum rate of pay provided for the classification, and requiring slow progress through every successive rank or pay grade.

(2) Provision of heavy weight to seniority on promotional examinations with insufficient or no consideration to past performance or potential.

(3) Rigid and overly restrictive height, weight and residency requirements.

(4) Prevention of rotation of assignments, sometimes even at the same pay level, without reclassification action.

(5) Prohibition of entrance into the police service at any level other than the lowest uniformed rank.

(6) The rule of one on promotional examinations, whereby a promotion might be made on the basis of a written test score highest by one tenth of a percentage point, without regard to other factors.

(7) Stiff tenure and disciplinary requirements which make it almost impossible to remove "dead wood."

Further, there are signs of increasing intervention of state legislatures in local affairs through the passage of certain laws detrimental to progress in the improvement and professionalization of the police service. Although several laws have been passed which assure better working conditions and better starting salaries in the police service they tend to hamstring local authorities or impose costs which the local governments are ill prepared to immediately assume. Most serious are the attempts being made to have legislation which would lock the pay of policemen with the pay of firemen without any regard to the differences in the kind of work involved and particularly to the changing nature of the police job. Although these latter attempts have met with little success to date, there is an ever present danger.

A more indirect blocking of improvement in police pay has been accomplished by some legislatures through the passage of laws which arbitrarily and drastically limit fire service hours without regard to the fact that a fire duty week of fifty-six hours provides a much more advantageous working arrangement than the eight-hour shift, forty-hour week of the typical police department. These laws have burdened municipalities with substantial increases in fire department costs which have naturally left less money available for improvement in police pay....

Again referring to Mr. Danielson's study—because of the disastrous impact on police compensation of the organized campaign of fire-fighters for so-called "parity pay" and for substantially reduced fire duty hours, he has seen fit to document in a remarkably complete and factual way the ramifications and details of this campaign as it has been waged in many parts of the country. An attempt will be made only to summarize the problem here.

The firemen have done much to improve their lot in the last couple of decades, and their lot needed improvement. Traditionally the firefighter has been paid the same as the patrolman, and understandably the average firefighter looks at any increase in patrolmen's pay above his own as indicating a "downgrading" of the fire service with resultant loss of prestige. It doesn't do any good to try to explain to him that an upgrading of an entirely dissimilar service does not represent a downgrading of an entirely dissimilar service dos not represent a downgrading of his service. The unfortunate fact that must be faced is that the organized firefighters are bound to use all of their strength and resources, which are considerable, with the public and the politicians to preserve parity not only to increase their pay but as a matter of pride and prestige. In doing this they will continue to oppose in any way they can any move to improve police pay unless fire pay is concurrently and equally improved.

In commenting on this obstacle to progress in police compensation improvement, Mr. Danielson says in part as follows:

> When salary improvements are proposed for municipal police, however, the demands of firemen's groups are that firemen *must* receive identical salaries.
>
> Acquiescence to demands of firemen's groups undoubtedly has resulted in holding down the salary level of many local law enforcement agencies. To the degree that they caused police salaries to be kept low below the point where qualified men can be recruited and retained as policemen, the demands of firemen's groups have adversely affected the maintenance of law and order in American cities.

The campaign of the firefighters will intensify as the trend towards higher police pay increases. Of course, crusades are important to unionism and this is one in which a great deal of emotionalism is involved. It is highly unlikely that there will be any lessening of this strong opposition to significant improvement of police pay. On the other hand, there is some hope for compromise in the situation—not compromise for compromise's sake but a well justified compromise based on certain facts and conditions.

Representatives of the fire service themselves have often said "stop complaining about the lack of opportunity for promotion in the police department as compared to the fire department and create more opportunities for promotion for police officers." Also, the use of scientific evaluation methods on police assignments indicates that there are some assignments for patrolmen which, if properly isolated, classified and evaluated separately, would not justify higher pay and may not justify pay as high as that of the basic entrance rank of firefighter. this will be discussed further in a later section of this article.

Limitations on funds can also be a formidable obstacle. Obviously it relates directly to the preceding one in that available funds are seriously depleted if any increase in police salaries has to be duplicated in the fire service. However, there is a natural reluctance on the part of municipal government to grant extraordinary increases to any particular occupational group. All employee organizations and all municipal employees always exert maximum pressure on governmental bodies to cut up the pie on an across-the-board basis as evenly as possible. One cannot expect to convince easily the rank and file employee or his union representatives that a particular occupation has changed so much more than others as to justify salary adjustments significantly above those provided to other occupations. And yet there are many clear indications that can be brought to the attention of all employees, and the taxpayer as well, that if better police services are required, they must be paid for. The simple facts concerning police turnover and unfilled vacancies, as compared to those in other municipal occupations, present a very convincing picture. It has been estimated that two-thirds of the police departments in the United States are below authorized strength. In contrast, most of the cities which have published turnover figures by department indicate that the department with the lowest rate of turnover is the fire department.

Although the tie-in of fire pay with police pay reduces the availability of funds where they are most needed, it must be recognized that, to a lesser extent, across-the-board increases within the police department without regard to the complexity and difficulty of the respective jobs concerned also represents improper utilization of available funds.

A common problem found in the public service, whenever there is reason to substantially upgrade and increase the pay of an occupation, concerns those incumbents who do not meet newly established higher requirements of education and mental ability, but who are present and will be present until retirement due to the typical provisions for tenure. These incumbents should be protected because most of them have rendered long and faithful service, and it is no fault of theirs that qualifications were lower at the time they entered the force.

Nevertheless, the argument is often used by city councils, city administrators, and taxpayers organizations that you can't raise the pay grade by an significant amount because you will be overpaying too many people at the taxpayer's expense. This has encouraged the proponents of the slow "leap-frogging" approach to police department upgrading—a small percentage increase in salaries this year, accompanied by a tightening of the selection procedure; another small increase next year, accompanied by a small increase in the educational requirements, etc. Hopefully, by the time salaries get where they should be and are accompanied by substantially higher entrance requirements, most of the "old hands" will have been retired. Although this approach makes a lot of good political and realistic sense, the requirements of the situation regarding law enforcement today makes this snail's pace unacceptable.

It is a well known principle of job classification and compensation that if a job comprises various tasks at different levels of skill, the pay should be set in recognition of the highest skill required to be exercised by the incumbent. It is appropriate, for example, to pay a clerk at the going rate for stenographic skills even though the job may require shorthand only 10 percent of the time, and the rest of the time is spent on simple filing and other clerical tasks.

In the typical police department there are ranks or classifications that comprise a wide variety of tasks and skills, some of which require high qualifications and other which are more simple and routine. In departments with only a few broad classes or ranks, this situation is found to be extreme. A patrolman classification usually comprises widely different ranks such as directing traffic at a street corner, riding a three-wheel motorcycle to tag illegally parked cars, patrolling in a one-man police car, investigating accidents, and even, in a few departments, performing plainclothes detective work. In many cases certain officers are regularly and permanently assigned to these respective tasks which differ substantially in qualification requirements, complexity, hazard, and the degree of skill required. To make matters worse, these tasks are often assigned on the basis of choice by those with seniority, which frequently results in the most experienced officer performing the lesser tasks.

Yet, in following the principle of paying for the highest skills, all patrolmen must be paid at the level appropriate to the assignment of the highest value. This is expensive and wasteful of funds. It also encourages mediocrity since no incentive is provided for the officer with unusual ability to strive for the more complex and highly skilled assignments. Those who are given such assignments are inclined to resent the fact that others with lesser tasks are paid the same and, therefore, may not perform as well as they otherwise might.

One kind of "lack of room at the top" has been described under the subject of promotional opportunities. Here we are concerned with the unrealistic ceilings imposed on salaries of the commanding officers of most municipal police departments. Even where the patrolman's pay has reached a reasonable level, there is often failure on the part of city councils to adequately recognize the responsibility and heavy burdens that rest with the executive officials. This is a common problem, not only in the police department, but in other departments as well.

Many cities have a history of salary compression brought about by yielding to union pressures at the bottom and retaining an unreasonable ceiling on executive salaries at the top. There is no worse violation of the principles of sound salary administration than that of failing to recognize the unusual burdens and high responsibilities of government executives at the highest levels. Carried to an extreme, this compression can eliminate all incentives for the better people to aspire to the top position.

The incongruity of this obstacle lies in the fact that, with the relatively small number of executive positions involved, the total cost of providing reasonable salaries to executive positions is insignificant compared to the steady succession of periodical across-the-board dollar and the percentage increases granted to the mass of the employees. Often such increases are limited when extended to executive positions.

Unbelievable as it may seem, one state legislature recently adopted pay plan revisions that provided an increase of 20 percent in the rates of the lower half of the pay schedule and 10 percent in the upper half. Another legislature is now considering a bill which would provide 15 percent for the lower third, 10 percent for the middle third and 5 percent for the executive and other higher positions. This bill is being seriously considered because, as one might expect, it was proposed by and introduced for the State Employees' Association, whose membership naturally comprises a high majority of employees in the lower more populous classifications.

Last, but by no means least, is the obstacle presented by the labor market situation in most of our cities today. The very kind of well educated, young men required in the law enforcement agencies are those being sought after by industrial and commercial employers. Law enforcement agencies are engaged in heavy competition for this kind of manpower. It has been estimated one and a half million young men are of the proper age and have the intelligence, educational background and physical ability for service in local police agencies. About fifty thousand of this one and a half million will be required by local law enforcement agencies this year. The competition for the group comprises far flung industrial and commercial organizations as well as our armed forces. The growth of police departments, now rapidly accelerating due to the increase in population and crime rates, is occurring at a time when the labor market is tightening—and this presents a very difficult obstacle indeed.

In view of certain changes in the organization of police work, however, advantage can be taken of some sectors of the labor market that are not tight as described in the following excerpts from a U.S. Civil Service Commission bulletin:

> In spite of the reduced over-all level of unemployment there remains a number of groups where unemployment is high and where, consequently, prospects for recruitment are quite good. . .
>
> *Young workers, in the 16 to 21 age group.* This group including many with limited education, has had an unemployment rate nearly three times the average for all workers. While some of the men in this age bracket will now go into the armed services, the group will remain one of the larger pools of available manpower. . . .

In the above reference to the young workers, sixteen to twenty-one years of age, the police cadet program or the establishment of lower level

police classifications as discussed later in this article, affords the opportunity to tap this source for the police departments. Before these young
men get involved in other careers, the department can skim off some of
the cream for ultimate development as professional police officers.

Position Management the Best

The concept of position management, suitably adapted, offers the best
hope of overcoming some of the major obstacles to progress in the improvement of local law enforcement and the professionalization of the
police service. Before dealing more specifically with solutions that are
possible through the application of position management, the principles
and techniques involved should be reviewed.

Position management is an important management system that enables
the manager to effectively utilize and control the manpower resource. If it
were to be described by a single phrase, the best words are "organization
analysis to the position level." Position management is the responsibility
of the line managers. The technical work involved is best accomplished
through the cooperative efforts of the organization or "O & M" analysts
and the personnel staff.

The objective of the position management system is: to develop and establish a position structure that provides optimum balance between needs
for accomplishing the mission of the organization, economy and efficiency, sound utilization of skills, attraction and retention of competent personnel, motivation of employees, and employee development.

In order to accomplish the objectives of position management, a detailed analysis of the individual positions of the organization is undertaken. In too many organizations, employees in critically short occupations and the more skilled employees (often synonymous) are spending
disproportionate amounts of time on tasks that either do not utilize their
specialized training and talents at all or do so only to a minimal degree. In
order to achieve utilization of such people, position analysis may result in
the restructuring or "redesign" of individual jobs as follows:

(1) The "shred-out" of non-professional tasks, so that a smaller number
of college trained employees can do the same volume of highly skilled
work.
(2) Establishment of new lower level, nonprofessional positions to take
over the simpler tasks removed from the professional positions.
(3) Stripping of the simple, unskilled tasks from technical, office, and
blue collar jobs so that a smaller number of employees can do the skilled
work in these areas.
(4) Establishment of helper, assistant, and junior clerical jobs to take
over the tasks removed from the more highly skilled office and blue collar jobs.

In this process of organization analysis at the position level, several considerations must be kept in mind. Briefly enumerated, these are:

(1) The first and fundamental consideration is whether or not the position should be allowed to continue at all. Where duties and tasks can be taken over by others, or no significant contribution to the mission is being made, the position should be abolished.

(2) Workload forecasts must be developed and considered in order to determine the number and type of positions needed.

(3) Work methods must be understood and consideration given to their improvement in the interest of efficiency.

(4) The relationships among positions must be understood and consideration given to changing them to more effectively accomplish the mission.

(5) The effectiveness of personnel management must be considered and improved if necessary to achieve effective position management.

(6) The characteristics of the labor market will often influence the design of positions; consideration must be given to the shortage or abundance of different kinds of employees needed for alternative position designs.

(7) Pressures from organized employee groups and political pressures must be considered as an obstacle to the design of certain kinds of positions which might otherwise be theoretically advantageous.

(8) The psychological needs of employees should be considered; positions should be designed with thought to the morale and job satisfaction of the incumbents.

Applying the concept of position management to the police department would undoubtedly result in beneficial changes in the structure and the composition of the individual positions themselves. The most revoluntionary result of position redesign would be the "shredding-out" of the simpler, more routine, and less hazardous tasks from the basic ranks or broad classes in the typical police classification structure.

Some of the "shred-out" positions of lesser value will become "civilian" classifications—clerical, technical or blue collar jobs. They would include such classifications as records clerk, armament repairman, storekeeper, precinct desk clerk (assistant to a desk sergeant), automotive maintenance foreman, etc.

After separation of the "civilian" assignments, position redesign at the patrolman level would result in something similar to that proposed by the President's Crime Commission, i.e., a three-way breakout to a *Community Services Officer*, a *Police Officer*, and a *Police Agent*.

The community services officer was suggested as a uniformed but unarmed, young and not necessarily high school trained officer who would be used primarily for improving communications between the people and the police, particularly in slum communities, and in working with under-privileged juveniles. The police officer would be quite like a patrolman in most departments except that he would be relieved of responsibilities which could be performed by community services officers, and he would not have the educational background nor have reached the level of development required of the police agent. The police agent was envisioned as the "professional police officer" of tomorrow, better educated, better trained, highly intelligent, and possessed of scientific and social skills.

Among the tasks normally performed by uniformed personnel, certain assignments certainly can be identified and classified at several levels below that of the new "professional police officer." There are many routine, simple duties and tasks performed by some patrolmen, not those of a "community service" nature, that could be incorporated in lower police classifications. For example, the detective bureau could undoubtedly utilize sub-professionals of lesser qualifications to perform some of the routine digging in libraries, newspaper morgues, and public records that one hears the "Sergeant Fridays" complain about as the bane of the detective's existence. Other simpler police tasks now often performed by a "patrolman" include street intersection traffic control, supervision of school crossing guards, fingerprinting, parking violation and other routine and less hazardous patrol, serving as public building guards, and aides or chauffeurs to commanding officers.

It has already been demonstrated in at least one comprehensive position analysis study of the police assignments normally performed below the lowest supervisory rank of sergeant that as many as five levels of police work may be identified:

(1) A "cadet" or trainee.

(2) A "police services officer" to perform the simplest police tasks.

(3) A Police Officer I to perform the simpler and less hazardous tasks requiring arms and power of arrest.

(4) A Police Officer II, requiring higher intelligence and some college training for the more complex assignments presently included in the typical patrolman rank.

(5) The Police Officer III, requiring substantial college education and in-service training and performing the scientific detection and most complex and sensitive investigation work—a super-detective, if you will.

Among the supervisory and command ranks, the result of position analysis could well be the creation of additional levels or ranks such as *corporal, major,* and *lieutenant colonel,* to augment and improve supervision and decrease the spans of control now often too broad.

The net result of effective position management in the police department should bring about several significant benefits and go a long way toward reduction or elimination of some of the obstacles described earlier in this article.

The "shred-out" of the lesser skilled, simpler, and safer tasks from the broad scope of the typical patrolman classification would result in the establishment of more civilian positions and one or more uniformed police classifications properly evaluated at or below the level of firefighter. This would provide "parity" or "parity plus" for the firefighter classification and should remove the obstacle of militant opposition by the International Association of Firefighters.

The establishment of higher level professional police classifications with higher qualification requirements at both entrance and promotional levels, and additional supervisory positions where appropriate, would at once accomplish the following: (1) provide attractive salaries for college-trained men without overpaying those presently on the force who do not have the higher qualifications and who are not performing the work of highest value; (2) encourage in-service personnel to higher educational and performance achievement in order to qualify for higher pay; (3) provide improved promotional opportunities for all police personnel; (4) hold down the cost of salary improvements by selective establishment of higher salary ranges only for those assignments which justify the same and, incidentally, eliminate the bad economics of paying people at a rate appropriate to the highest skills exercised, while much of their time on the job is spent on simpler and less valuable tasks; and (5) reduce the proportions of higher-educated personnel required by the police department in a tight labor market situation. In regard to the latter, some of the lower police classifications could be filled from the pool of labor that is available in certain categories as described previously in the discussion of the labor market.

The ultimate in professionalization of the police service will require the cooperation of our educational institutions. Some have already established police science programs at the junior college level. A graduate of such study must be afforded opportunity to enter the police service at a level above the lowest patrolman rank. Such a curriculum would ideally by an officer training program similar to the ROTC which has worked so well in augmenting the officer corps in the armed forces.

Other Efforts for Other Obstacles

Position management alone will not do the whole job. A continuing campaign will be required by public officials and police administrators to fight the passage of bad laws and to liberalize civil service regulations. There is no panacea for success in this area. However, education is the key. City councils, civil service commissioners, legislators, and the public generally must be made fully aware of the facts on the need for improvements and the right ways for bringing about such improvements.

The best position management system will not achieve the improvements of which it is capable unless sound, modern personnel management, including an effective career development program, provides the basis for paying higher salaries to those specific jobs and people that justly deserve higher pay. And it must be part of the educational campaign to convince legislative bodies and the taxpayers that paying executive salaries commensurate with the responsibilities involved represents a small cost, proportionally, and is the only way to provide adequate incentive for executives to shoulder the responsibilities and exert their maximum efforts toward achieving effective service to the public.

Conclusion

In conclusion it appears that a concentrated effort by police administrators, the personnel staff, and the organization analysts, can change the prospect of a long, slow evolution in improving local law enforcement and in the professionalization of the police service into an immediate *administrative revolution,* in spite of the formidable obstacles that appear to be in the way at first glance. The extensive research and new ideas developed by the President's Crime Commission, backed up by an imposing body of work by a long list of consultants and advisors and aided by the techniques of position management, provide a large stepping stone for substantive progress.

Concepts to Consider

1. Support the statement that a college education should be a prerequisite to entry into the police service.

2. Identify the characteristics of a profession.

3. Describe the techniques that can be utilized in a career development program.

4. Justify the elimination of civil service protection of the police.

5. Justify the need for "parity pay" for police officers and firefighters.

6. Describe the objectives of position management.

Selected Readings

Bell, Daniel J., "The Police-Personnel Upgrading for Professionalism," *The Police Chief*, Vol. XLV, No. 1, January 1978, pp. 32-33.

The author stresses that without the implementation of a new personnel management perspective and civil service police application, police officers as productive employees will be extinct.

Dearing, Don R., "The ABC's of Professionalism," *The Police Chief*, Vol. 39, No. 7, July, 1972, pp. 24-26.

The key elements of a professional are identified by the author. In addition, he emphasizes three qualities—courage, optimism, and pride—that define police professionalism.

Grossman, Jack H. and William Kohnke, "Police Professionalism: An Attitudinal Approach," *The Police Chief*, Vol. XLIII, No. 11, November 1976, pp. 46-48.

The authors describe the need for the inculcation of professional attitudes within the daily work styles of law enforcement. Stresses that professionalism is reflective of positive human behavior patterns.

Gross, Solomon, "Higher Education and Police: Is There a Need for a Closer Look?," *Journal of Police Science and Administration*, Vol. 1, No. 4, December 1973, pp. 477-483.

This study reviews the growth of higher education for police and the placement of its graduates. Noting the limited information in these areas the author suggests a survey supplemented by interviews of colleges, graduates and police departments.

Hanley, David M., "Police Professionalism: A View from the Middle," *The Police Chief*, Vol. XLIII, No. 11, November 1976, pp. 50-52.

Postulates that police professionalism has three sides: traditional, nouveau professional, and middle man. Supports the position that it may be better educating policemen rather than recruiting educated people.

Kelly, Clarence M., "Professional Status," *Law and Order*, Vol. 22, No. 3, March 1974, pp. 11-13.

The author postulates that excellence in training is becoming standard, and excellence in training, added to imagination in training, is a major step toward achieving professional status.

Miller, Jon and Lincoln Fry, "Measuring Professionalism in Law Enforcement," *Criminology*, Vol. 14, No. 3, November 1976, pp. 401-413.

Describes an organizational survey of three law enforcement agencies utilizing a five-dimension scale of professionalism.

O'Rourke, William J., "Should All Policemen be College Trained?," *The Police Chief*, Vol. 38, No. 12, December 1971, pp. 36-38. This article identifies eight specific refutations of the usual arguments against college training for law enforcement officers.

Sandman, Henry J., "Partners for an Improved Community: Police and University," *The Police Chief*, Vol. XL, No. 4, April 1973, pp. 42-44.

The author describes a consortium between the police and the university in Cincinnati, Ohio. Three areas of involvement are utilization of university expertise, development of solutions to law enforcement problems and a continuous dialogue between the police and the university.

Staufenberger, Richard A., "The Professionalization of Police: Efforts and Obstacles," *Public Administration Review*, Vol. 37, No. 6, November—December 1977, pp. 678-685.

Reviews the progress toward professionalization of the police. Points out some negative attributes of present police systems, such as promotional systems, the lack of mobility among officers, limited career opportunities, and an unhealthy pessimism regarding research and change.

Stinchcomb, James D., "It's Time for the Police to Take a Professional Stand," *The Police Chief*, Vol. XXXVII, No. 2, February 1970, pp. 37-40.

An emphasis upon the critical importance of establishing formal requirements between the law enforcement community and higher education.

Sullivan, Robert C. and Kevin O'Brien, "For All the Work That is to be Done," *The Police Chief*, Vol. XXXVII, No. 5, May 1970, pp. 40-45.

Changes in scientific criminal investigation are pointed out, while emphasizing the professional status of the director of the laboratory, the first line supervisor, and subordinates.

Weirman, Charles L., "Cops Should Get Tickets Too!" *The Police Chief*, Vol. XXXIX, No. 7, July 1972, pp. 46-55.

The author proposes that state law enforcement officers training councils or similar bodies should have their powers structured so they can be the licensing agency for all police officers within a state.

Index